Scripting (Im)migration

Also from the Editor

Theatre and (Im)migration: New Essays on Canadian Theatre Vol. 10

Scripting (Im)migration
New Canadian Plays

Edited by Yana Meerzon

Playwrights Canada Press
Toronto

LIBRARY AND ARCHIVES CANADA CATALOGUING IN PUBLICATION
Title: Scripting (im)migration : new Canadian plays / edited by Yana Meerzon.
Other titles: Scripting migration
Names: Meerzon, Yana, editor.
Description: First edition.
Identifiers: Canadiana 20190105577 | ISBN 9780369100009 (softcover)
Subjects: LCSH: Immigrants' writings, Canadian. | LCSH: Immigrants—Canada—Drama.
| LCSH: Refugees—
    Canada—Drama. | CSH: Immigrants' writings, Canadian (English) | CSH: Canadian
drama (English)
Classification: LCC PS8309.I49 S27 2019 | DDC C812/.6080352691—dc23

Playwrights Canada Press acknowledges that we operate on land, which, for thousands of years, has been the traditional territories of the Mississaugas of the Credit First Nation, Huron-Wendat, Anishinaabe, Métis, and Haudenosaunee peoples. Today, this meeting place is still home to many Indigenous people from across Turtle Island and we are grateful to have the opportunity to work and play here.

We acknowledge the financial support of the Canada Council for the Arts—which last year invested $153 million to bring the arts to Canadians throughout the country—the Ontario Arts Council (OAC), Ontario Creates, and the Government of Canada for our publishing activities.

Canada Council Conseil des arts
for the Arts   du Canada

ONTARIO ARTS COUNCIL
CONSEIL DES ARTS DE L'ONTARIO
an Ontario government agency
un organisme du gouvernement de l'Ontario

ONTARIO | ONTARIO
CREATES | CRÉATIF

Contents

Scripting (Im)migrant Canada: Monologues, Dialogues, Conversations

by Yana Meerzon

The anthology *Scripting (Im)migration: New Canadian Plays* is a companion volume to the scholarly essay collection *Theatre and (Im)migration: New Essays on Canadian Theatre*. It features six new play scripts that wrestle with the issues of (im)migration, zooming in on forgotten moments of Canadian history and on contemporary landscapes of urban Canada, in which many migrants and refugee subjects settle. Collectively, these plays cast a broad look at the problems of (non)verbal communication, memory, identity, integration, and nostalgia that (im)migration prompts. Individually, each script offers a different experiment with language(s), characters, and structures of drama; every play chosen for this publication exemplifies a new and particular performative method to speak to the journey of migration as experienced by its fictional and real-life subjects. Each script, in other words, proposes a unique take on what constitutes a dramatic composition today and how the process of playwriting can unfold. It also challenges the idea of a pure dramatic genre that each playwright opts to adapt when it comes to representing migration and its consequences on stage.

In his recent book, *Performing Statelessness in Europe,* S.E. Wilmer describes a broad spectrum of dramatic genres and performative styles that mark today's theatre work dedicated to and made by artists (im)migrants. His examples include contemporary adaptations of Greek theatre, fictional stories about asylum seeking, documentary- and verbatim-based productions about and often with refugees on stage, and, similar to Brecht's *Lehrstücke* plays, stories that bring awareness about the hardships of migration and thus instigate spectators' empathy (51–55). Wilmer also reminds us that in constructing a refugee on stage, one must remember the complexity of this figure. A refugee is often someone who has endured suffering (55) and can be of high moral stature (56); at the same time, this character is not completely faultless (56). What Wilmer seems to propose is that the plays featuring the crisis of migration and its stateless citizens develop an idiom for a new tragic character, mirroring a stylistic shift in dramatic canon that had previously taken place in Arthur Miller's masterpiece *Death of a Salesman* (1949). Miller's salesman of the late 1940s was a tragic hero whose flaws and ordeals were caused by the commodification of people in modern capitalism. The character of migrant, I argue after Wilmer, has recently gained significance similar to Willy Loman.

The present anthology exemplifies these changes in the dramatic canon. These changes and tendencies include the move toward a tragic status for the migrant character, mirroring Willy Loman, and experiments with different strands of immigrant theatre and dramaturgy as outlined in the previous paragraphs. The selected scripts also reveal two leading vectors of artistic exploration in Canadian plays and productions that focus on the issues of migration. These vectors unfold simultaneously, despite moving in opposite directions.

One vector points at the process of creating the *mythopoetics of migration,* or "'making myth' out of migration" on stage (Cox 10). On one hand, this process refers to "an accumulation of visions of foreignness that have collided in the globalized, bureaucratized present" (10); on the other, it elevates modern-day stories of war and flight to the dimensions of myth and tragedy. Dramaturgically, making myth out of migration can capitalize on the leading elements of classical tragedy, with the playwrights relying upon tragic characters, themes, plots structures, and elevated language of expression. Unlike classic tragedy, however, today's dramas of migration tend to feature ordinary people in the roles of tragic heroes and their nemeses.

The other vector in the dramaturgy of migration points at a variety of plays that engage with questions of truth and authenticity. This vector mobilizes devices of documentary, verbatim, and testimonial theatre. Often based on refugees' testimonials, interviews, and even their personal presence on stage, these performative events aspire to raise migrants—ordinary people—to the status of tragic heroes. This way, and although somewhat paradoxically, these documentary play scripts also add to making the *mythopoetics of migration.*

The plays collected in this volume exhibit these two tendencies. Politically, they actively participate in discussing the pros and cons of Canadian multiculturalism and staging imaginary nationhood. Dramaturgically, they use tropes of tragedy and poetry, memory and testimony, but also structures of comedy and musical, dramatic skit and devised performance to tell multidimensional and multifaceted stories of immigration and Canada. Often language—both verbal and physical—serves as the major terrain for experimentation, and as the vehicle for artistic resistance within these plays.

Each of the chosen plays is prefaced by an extensive dialogue between its author(s), other artists, and scholars. These conversations focus on the questions of dramatic craft and of (im)migration as it is depicted, imagined, and constructed in the chosen scripts and/or experienced by their authors. The dialogues echo the themes and topics touched upon in the volume of scholarly essays. The geographies and experiences these plays discuss are different, but the artistic and ethical quests they identify resonate with each other.

The volume opens with the play *The Aeneid*, written by Olivier Kemeid in 2007 and translated by Maureen Labonté for its 2016 staging at the Stratford Festival, directed by Keira Loughran. A retake on Virgil's mythic and classic tale of searching for a new home, this *Aeneid* is reimagined as an urgent refugee story. In its desire to elevate the modern-day story of war and flight to mythological dimensions, *The Aeneid* also attempts to humanize the *object of human waste* (Bauman) to which migrants and refugees are often reduced by the cruelty of the flight and by the impersonality of the state apparatus. As Kemeid re-casts the myth and its characters into the drama "about humanity, our errors, and suffering," he turns his play into a philosophical proposition on the urgency of the global migration. This global urgency finds direct echoing in the political, economic, and cultural climate of today's Canada as a potential host state for refugees and asylum seekers. Retelling Virgil's poem anew, Kemeid wishes to bring the story of the elsewhere home. His *Aeneid* concretizes historical events and movements of global migration through the workings of individual gazes and the experiences of its characters.

The 2014 *Settling Africville*, by George Elliott Clarke, grapples with a similar dilemma. Dedicated to the African American refugees of the War of 1812 who settled in Nova Scotia, *Settling Africville* presents an example of an activist theatre work that "*un-*covers and *re-*writes the past to assert a perspective of history in opposition to the official metanarrative." This work is another example of the *mythopoetics of migration,* as it proposes an alternative narrative to the official history of Canada as it was experienced by its Africadian (African Nova Scotian) subjects and imagined by one of their most prominent artistic voices. Written in rhythmic prose that resembles verse, *Settling Africville* exemplifies what Clarke identifies as a theatre of "ideas in action; ideologies or theologies or principles or ideals in conflict. Whether we wish them to do so or not, characters—even if a mix of virtues/vices—end up embodying particular drives/passions/interests. [. . .] the more conflicted the character is, the better is the play."

The Tashme Project: The Living Archives, by Julie Tamiko Manning and Matt Miwa, presents another example of how a monumental history can be contextualized through the stories of ordinary people and turned into a powerful dramatic narrative. A documentary-style play, *The Tashme Project* carefully pieces together the experiences of Japanese Canadians who were incarcerated in internment camps in the 1940s. It insists on offering this historical memory as a living object that continues to make a profound effect upon the experiences and feelings of the third- and even fourth-generation Canadians who do not possess any direct access to this history. In their dialogue with the artists, the scholars Matthew Chin and Izumi Sakamoto examine "the impetus for *The Tashme Project* as a quest for personal, family, and community history. Manning and Miwa touch on the challenges of bringing these histories forward when the violence in which these histories were forged often works against transparent and direct means of knowledge transfer."

Foreign Tongue: The Musical, by Lola Xenos, changes the tone of this collection. This play capitalizes on Brechtian devices of alienation, irony, and humor to speak of the hardships of cultural and economic integration that await an immigrant subject upon their arrival in the new land. Inspired by the medical condition foreign accent syndrome, which refers to stroke survivors who wake up speaking their native language with a foreign accent, *Foreign Tongue* tells a story of Kathy Woodrough from Peterborough, Ontario, who falls victim to this condition. As Kathy wakes up in a Toronto hospital speaking English with a heavy East European—possibly Russian—accent, her life turns into a series of unfortunate and humorous events. Kathy's encounters reveal the underbelly of the multicultural Toronto with its ESL classes and populations, and provide multiple points of identification for its diverse audiences. These multiple identifications encourage empathy through recognition. On one hand, Kathy's journey reflects a fear of becoming the other—a fear familiar to many spectators of Lola Xenos's work. On the other hand, it makes the other—the immigrant—familiar. It also demonstrates that it is in this tension between the stranger and the familiar where the truth of the immigrant story lies.

The two scripts that close this volume—*My Name Is Dakhel Faraj* by Nada Humsi and *"In Sundry Languages"* by Toronto Laboratory Theatre—present examples of cutting-edge dramatic research in theatrical multilingualism. They aspire to enhance debates on using multilingual paradigms in dramatic writing, both as a type of multilingualism "from above," "linked to economic privilege, free mobility, and commodity exchange; and as the multilingualism 'from below,' associated with 'minor' languages, non-marketability, and invisibility" (Karpinski 154).

Written, directed, and produced for the IMPACT15 Theatre Festival, and based on interviews with Dakhel Ali Faraj Al-Bahrani, *My Name Is Dakhel Faraj* is the true story of a refugee of the Iraq war. In this performance, the leading character, Dakhel Faraj, is played by three actors speaking in three languages: Arabic, English, and American Sign Language. This choice, as Humsi explains, was dictated by her wish for "as many people as possible to understand how cruel it is to conduct a war on other people: to destroy their homeland, kill their children, and send them as disabled refugees around the world. I wanted this message to be heard but also seen across any physical barriers."

The experimental project *"In Sundry Languages"* continues this search to cross linguistic and physical boundaries on stage. It exemplifies the effect of *multilingualism from below* (Karpinski 154) and offers a view of today's Canada as a common space of post-multiculturalism, emerging within the complex movements of global travelling. Designed by a group of mono- and multilingual performers, working in their dominant, non-dominant, and unfamiliar languages, *"In Sundry Languages"* depicts (im)probable encounters between Canadian multicultural and multilingual subjects. In its techniques of theatrical non-translation, it aims to challenge an assumption that although theatrical multilingualism includes experiments with the formal patterns of theatre speech, it remains closed to creating poetic utterances and metaphors (Hauptfleisch 74–75). An experiment in a multilingual theatre of non-verisimilitude, it relies on somatic and affective aspects of verbal communication, and on our experience of language as a sensory, embodied, and auditory construct close to music.

In his introductory notes to the publication of *Kim's Convenience,* by Ins Choi, Albert Schultz, the artistic director of Toronto's Soulpepper Theatre Company at that time, suggested that this work about Canada and immigration has arrived to the artistic scene of multicultural Toronto "both an artistic triumph and a major cultural event" (5). In its specificity, "the play's universality is sprung," and so it "becomes *our* story about *our* family in *our* community" (4). Indeed, immigration makes Canada's history and to that extent it is shared and is *ours*. However, as this anthology demonstrates, it is not just one story of travelling and immigration that makes Canada one family or one community. The multiplicity and the simultaneity of many stories of migration depicted in these six scripts point to the multidimensionality of Canadian experiences. The difference of specificity is the key to our Canadian multitude.

Similarly to the scholarly essay collection, this companion volume aims to "take the temperature" of our collective historical moment. The method it uses is artistic, not analytical, as collectively through their creative search and linguistic experiment the six plays chosen for this book appeal to readers' cultural memories and personal experiences of travelling, using laughter and tears to create moments of affect, sympathy, and identification. Drawing on affective feelings and the personal experiences of readers and audiences, each of the six scripts not only describes and examines our current moment but collectively aspires to indicate directions of where we might head tomorrow.

Working on this anthology has been a true pleasure and pure excitement. However, its conceptualization would not ever have come to fruition without the enthusiasm of the artists who have agreed to publish their plays in this book and the scholars who helped conducting, transcribing, and editing the conversations and play texts. I am forever grateful to Olivier Kemeid, George Elliott Clarke, Julie Tamiko Manning, Matt Miwa, Cynthia Ashperger, Nada Humsi, and Toronto Laboratory Theatre, who entrusted their scripts to me and decided to go ahead with this publication, as well as for the time and effort each artist spent preparing their work for publication. My special thank you goes to Maureen Labonté, Keira Loughran, Diana Manole, Izumi Sakamoto, Matthew Chin, and Shelley Liebembuk, who not only conducted interviews and worked on their technicalities but also helped the artists through the tedious process of editing scripts, sometime in many languages. Without this work, many scripts would not have been available for readers. My special thanks goes to Roberta Barker, Annie Gibson, and Blake Sproule, who accepted this project and provided enormous help in editing these multilingual and multi-genre-based texts and interviews, polishing and finessing them. It is with high hopes for the scripts and conversations in this volume to enter the dramatic and performative repertoire of Canadian theatre practice and serve as essential source material for class syllabi on theatre and immigration that I entrust this book into the hands of readers.

Works Cited

Bauman, Zygmunt. "Symptoms in Search of an Object and a Name." *The Great Regression*, edited by Heinrich Geiselberger, Polity, 2017, pp. 13–25.

Cox, Emma. *Theatre and Migration*. Palgrave MacMillan, 2014.

Hauptfleisch, Temple. "Citytalk, Theatretalk: Dialect, Dialogue and Multilingual Theatre in South Africa." *English in Africa*, vol. 16, no. 1, 1989, pp. 71–91.

Karpinski, Eva C. "Can Multilingualism Be a Radical Force in Contemporary Canadian Theatre? Exploring the Option of Non-Translation." *Theatre Research in Canada / Recherches théâtrales au Canada*, vol. 38, no. 2, 2017, pp. 153–67.

Schultz, Albert. Foreword. *Kim's Convenience*, by Ins Choi, House of Anansi, 2012, pp. 3–5.

Wilmer, Steve. *Performing Statelessness in Europe*. Palgrave MacMillan, 2018.

The Aeneid

Inspired by Virgil's *The Aeneid*

by Olivier Kemeid,
translated by Maureen Labonté

For Charles Kemeid
the Aeneas of our family.

Acknowledgements

I would like to thank the Stratford Festival for commissioning this translation. I believe that *The Aeneid* is an important play, a play for our times, and I am so very grateful to everyone there for the premiere production in English—the amazing cast, creative and production team, and administrative staff.

A special thank you to Artistic Director Anthony Cimolino, for his belief in the play. Thank you as well to Director Keira Loughran. There's no doubt in my mind that her passion, drive, and determination helped make it happen.

My gratitude as well to the many actors who read various drafts of the translation with such skill, dedication, and generosity.

And an enormous thank you to Bob White, dramaturg extraordinaire! It was so great to work with you again, Bob.

And finally, thank you to Olivier Kemeid for writing such a beautiful and inspiring play.

—Maureen Labonté

L'Énéide was first produced by produced by Productions des Trois Tristes Tigres at L'Éspace Libre in Montréal on November 29, 2007, with the following creative team:

Olivier Aubin: Coreobus, Robert, the Compatriot, Achmaenides, Tagger, the General, Old Farmer
Marie-Josée Bastien: Bereo, Hotel Manager, the Sibyl, Allecto
Simon Boudreault: Hector, Anchises, the Scavenger, Clan Leader
Eugénie Gaillard: Creusa, Lucy, Immigration officer, the Old Woman, Lavinia
Geoffrey Gaquère: Achates
Johanne Haberlin: Pyrgo, Helen, Elissa
Emmanuel Schwartz: Aeneas

Director: Olivier Kemeid
Assistant Director and Stage Manager: Stéphanie Capistran-Lalonde
Set and Prop Design: Jasmine Catudal
Costume Design: Romain Fabre
Lighting Design: Étienne Boucher
Music and Soundscape: Philippe Brault, assisted by Liu-Kong Ha
Technical Director: Anne Plamondon

This play was written during a writing residency at the Centre des écritures du spectacle (CNES), La Chartreuse, Villeneuve lez Avignon, in 2007. This was made possible by a grant from the Conseil des arts et lettres du Québec. The play was also given a workshop at the Centre des auteurs dramatiques (CEAD) in 2007.

This translation of *The Aeneid* was commissioned by the Stratford Festival under the artistic direction of Antoni Cimolino. It premiered at the Studio Theatre in Stratford, Ontario, on August 19, 2016, with the following creative team:

Gareth Potter: Aeneas
Monice Peter: Creusa
Malakai Magassouba: Ascanius
Michael Spencer-Davis: Anchises
Saamer Usmani: Achates
Mike Nadajewski: Hector, Robert
Andrew Robinson: Coroebus, Graffiti Artist
Bahareh Yaraghi: Pyrgo, Lavinia
Karen Robinson: Berol, Immigration Officer, the Sibyl, Allecto
Lanise Antoine Shelly: Lucy, Helen, Elissa
Tiffany Claire Martin: Hotel Manager, the Old Woman
Rodrigo Beilfuss: Fellow Countryman
Josue Laboucane: Achmaenides, Old Farmer
E.B. Smith: the Scavenger, Allecto's Son

Director: Keira Loughran
Designer: Joanna Yu
Lighting Designer: Itai Erdal
Sound Designer: Debashis Sinha
Dramaturg: Bob White
Singing Coach: Suba Sankaran
Movement Coach: Tedi Tafel
Assistant Director: Jessica Carmichael
Stage Manager: Melissa Rood

Characters
(In Order of Appearance)

Part 1: Fire

Aeneas: a man forced to flee from his country
Creusa: his wife
Ascanius: his young son
Anchises: Aeneas's father
Achates: Aeneas's best friend
Hector: narrator and seer
Coroebus: a friend of Aeneas who chooses to stay and fight
Pyrgo: a countrywoman who flees with Aeneas and his family
Beroe: another countrywoman who also flees with them

Part 2: Water

Robert: a tourist staying at an island resort
Lucy: his girlfriend
Hotel Manager: manages the resort and will have to deal with the refugees
Fellow Countryman: has fled like Aeneas and found refuge on another island
Helen: his wife
Achmaenides: rescued from drowning by Aeneas; one of the enemy; blind

Part 3: Earth

Elissa: a woman seeking refugee status
Immigration Officer: a government official
The Scavenger: runs a squat in town; ruthless
Graffiti Artist: paints scenes from the capture of Aeneas's homeland

Part 4: Underworld

The Old Woman: guards access to the Sibyl and the Underworld
The Sibyl: will guide Aeneas and Achates to the Underworld

Part 5: Blood

Allecto: strong-willed woman who has been living for a year in the refugee
camp where Aeneas and company end up; resents the new arrivals
Her Son: the leader of their band of refugees in the camp
Lavinia: the camp nurse
Old Farmer: gives Aeneas land in what will become his new home

Setting

The play takes place in multiple locations as Aeneas flees from his homeland,
which is under siege, with his family and best friend. We follow him on his
quest for safety and a new home.

Time

The present.

Ibant obscure sola sub nocte per umbram
Indistinct amid the shadows they walked through the lonely night

—*The Aeneid*, Song VI

I—Fire

Scene One

A city.
A crowded discotheque.

Hector, a homeless man, rushes in.

HECTOR: Get out!
Leave run fast go now!

That's what I told them but they didn't believe me
I even waved my arms making signs for them to get out in case some of them
   didn't understand me
But it's always like that right?
Either you say nothing and then they say: How come you didn't say anything?
Or you say something and they tell you to shut up
Anyway I told them they should listen to me

The whole thing started with a column of black smoke *fschhhhwww* that bil-
   lowed up into the sky *fuuuuuuu*
There right there
Then a second column even blacker than the first—*fschhhhhh*
Then a third bigger higher
And a fourth
Then a whole neighbourhood both banks of the river and before long the
   entire city

They don't believe me

Men women children old people run through the smoke-filled air of the now-
  deserted streets howling like animals
The ones crying are the victims
The ones shouting are the attackers
But you can't recognize anyone because everyone's covered in a thick coat of ash

They laugh at me

Like this:

He spreads earth all over his face.

Like the condemned of the Earth like helpless men in a fiery furnace
And on every street buildings blazing spitting fire
Some of you throw yourselves off your balconies to escape the flames and crash
  in a heap of cracking bones at the feet of innocent passersby
A cracking that will echo in your heads until the day you die
Others stand in silence and watch their pasts being devoured by the flames
Family photos the painting mother gave you and the little wooden horse grand-
  dad carved
The dogs howl at the moon but the moon can't see them because it's hidden
  behind a thick veil of anguish and pain
The howling of the dogs can't cover the looting the rapes and the murders

Hey youhooo hey

You have to leave here right away you have to leave now

It's useless
I don't know why I'm telling them to
It's useless totally useless

Scene Two

An apartment.

AENEAS: The necklace go wake up our son where's the necklace don't take anything else with you just the necklace that's all

She runs around looking for the necklace but doesn't find it.

CREUSA: I can't find it

AENEAS: Keep looking

That's when I lose it I start yelling and the yell releases a heavy cloying smell into the air
It smells like flowers like a funeral wreath

I'VE TOLD YOU A HUNDRED TIMES A HUNDRED TIMES PUT IT IN A SAFE PLACE

I grab the phone—no dial tone

The phone's not working
What are you doing with that?

CREUSA: The photos just the photos that's all I'm taking
What's happening who are these people what do they want with us what have we done they're burning the whole city

We won't get out of here alive

AENEAS: I don't know
Go get Ascanius and come on

CREUSA: You saw them right?

AENEAS: Yes now find the necklace please

The airport we've got to get to the airport

CREUSA: And?
What do they look like?

AENEAS: I don't know try the second drawer of the cabinet in the living room
Like us they look like us
they're from here

Burning rags are thrown into the room and land at their feet.

CREUSA: Water I'll go get some water

AENEAS: No no don't

CREUSA: What are you doing let go of me I said let go

AENEAS: Don't
Leave them let them burn
As long as our house is in flames they won't come in they'll think we're dead
When the flames start licking at our feet that's when we'll leave
Maybe they'll be gone by then
Do what I say
Our house will burn but we'll live
We will live

Scene Three

A street. Hector is watching the people as they flee.

HECTOR: The city is being swallowed in the roar of the flames
A city as old as the world becomes a raging funeral pyre in the dark night
You laughed at me at the homeless guy brain-addled with dementia
Gather your loved ones I said and now what are you doing
HA! YOU DIDN'T BELIEVE ME
WILD CRAZY
DANCING LIKE THERE'S NO TOMORROW
SO NOW BURN
My city is going up in smoke they're burning the country of my childhood the
    garden of my ancestors
My mother's orange tree in flames
Those of us who want to live
Have to leave must leave

Aeneas runs by with Creusa. Coroebus catches up with him.

COROEBUS: Aeneas I looked everywhere for you
In the smoking ruins of your house on the few terraces that are still intact in
   lanes black with soot
Come with me I have an old rifle that's itching to be used again
There are twenty of us now there'll be one hundred later
We have to defend ourselves I refuse to fall without taking a thousand down
   with me
Come be quick there isn't much time you too Creusa and even the little guy we
   have to teach him how to handle a gun so that when we fall he'll be able to
   avenge us
The time for fighting has begun
You know this reminds me of the stories my grandfather used to tell me
I remember what was most beautiful about those stories
It was dying in battle

AENEAS: Coroebus I don't want to fight I've never asked anything of anyone
I have a family it comes first before my country
I must get them to safety then I'll see

COROEBUS: Safety what safety forget safety there isn't any and there won't be
   for a very long time
You have to fight for your wife and your child
You aren't going to save them by running away like a coward

AENEAS: I won't save them by fighting either

COROEBUS: If you leave you'll live the rest of your life in shame

AENEAS: I prefer to live in shame than die proud

CREUSA: What do you want to do with that old rifle of yours, Coroebus
You're one man alone, there are thousands of them
They'll run you down and even if you manage to push them back they'll return
Their sons will seek revenge and your sons' sons will be forced to take up arms
Our land has been spoiled defiled
Nothing will ever grow here again

COROEBUS: Our land is defiled because you're abandoning it
I spit in the faces of those who don't deserve to be counted as one of us

That's what I said to them
And then I left

AENEAS: I watch as Coroebus disappears into the distance
Above his head a small flame burns bright
The spirit of resistance
I wish I didn't have a wife or a son and the only thing on the horizon was the battle
Creusa grabs hold of me and begs me to keep running but I don't want to lose sight of
Coroebus
That's when she asks the impossible of me

(to Creusa) I'll never have to
Nothing is going to happen to you

CREUSA: Swear

AENEAS: I can't
Not if they hurt you not if they touch you

CREUSA: I want you to swear right now here in front of me

AENEAS: And so I swear I'll never try to avenge her no matter what happens and we continue on our mad escape

Scene Four

A seniors' retirement home.

ANCHISES: No
That's what I told him it's a definite unequivocal no but he's persistent like his father

Go away
Why did you come here?
Are you crazy Aeneas?
Leave get out while there's still time

AENEAS: I've come to get you

ANCHISES: Have you taken a good look at me?
Do you think I have the strength to leave with you?
If the gods had really wanted me to go on living

They wouldn't have allowed my city to collapse
Leave with your wife and son
Leave quickly I beg you no I order you
I've already got one foot in the grave
I've been dragging myself along for too many years already

AENEAS: I won't leave you here

ANCHISES: Creusa
Reason with your husband
I'm too old to live in exile

CREUSA: Your son won't leave without you
You know that

ANCHISES: Listen to me
Flee!
Don't worry about me
I'm too old too weak and I'm not a rich man
The only thing they can take from me is my grave

AENEAS: You don't have the right to do this to me
To me or to our family

ANCHISES: Don't tell me what I have the right to do or not do
Even if I don't come with you I'm still your father
I'm not abandoning you Aeneas
I'm not going with you but I'm not abandoning you

AENEAS: All right

He takes his son from Creusa and goes and leaves him outside on the doorstep.

CREUSA: Aeneas!
Aeneas!

She rushes to get her son. Aeneas holds her back.

AENEAS: Choose old man
Choose between your grandson and your home

ANCHISES: WHAT ARE YOU DOING!
GO GET ASCANIUS BRING HIM IN HERE RIGHT AWAY GO GET HIM!

CREUSA: Aeneas don't do this
Aeneas

AENEAS: Hurry up Dad my son may already have been taken

ANCHISES: We're all going to perish because of you

AENEAS: Together we have to stay together that's all I want

A bomb goes off. They all hit the ground.

I can't hear anything anymore I'm alive but I can't hear a thing
As the dust settles I see Creusa protecting our son
The two of them are alive
My father on his knees
Alive
Destruction all around us stone split from stone foundations ripped out of
  the earth
Hell has opened up and swallowed the entire city in its raging maw

ANCHISES: We're alive
Heaven has given you a sign, Aeneas
it's fate

AENEAS: FATE DON'T TALK TO ME ABOUT FATE NOT NOW
MY HOUSE IS IN FLAMES THEY'VE SET FIRE TO MY CITY I HAVE TO LEAVE MY
  COUNTRY AND YOU TALK TO ME ABOUT FATE
All I have all I've managed to save is a necklace a necklace Dad what am I sup-
  posed to do with it what are we going to live on can you tell me that

ANCHISES: Our ancestors left the mountains on foot to come here to the sea
They crossed burning deserts and valleys scorched with misery
But they succeeded
Some of them perished but others made it all the way here my son
They succeeded

AENEAS: I don't want to do that
That's
That's not my life

ANCHISES: You have to do it

AENEAS: I won't be able to do it alone

ANCHISES: The road will be a long one I won't have the strength to keep up
with you

AENEAS: You won't have to walk I'll carry you
And I'm not going to wait around for another sign from the heavens to convince you

He bends down. Reluctantly, Anchises climbs on to his back.

Creusa give me our son I want you to be able to run as fast as possible

CREUSA: Don't ever do that again
Never abandon him again

AENEAS: I promise
Walk behind me stay very close
We're heading for the port now
It's our only chance

Here I am
Aeneas
My ancestor on my back and my future in my arms
I run between walls of fire looking for the shore
Only yesterday I was dancing today I'm running
And I know now in this moment
That I'll never be back
That I'll run and keep on running forever

Scene Five

The port.

ANCHISES: The desperate are huddled all around us
An enormous crowd of men women children gathered to go into exile
A nation of people in pain
All they have with them is a few belongings and their courage
Ready to leave the shores of a country that is no longer theirs

AENEAS: The fire devours everything its fiery fury rolls high up into the sky all
   the way to the stars
We're alive
Uprooted from our homes our lives
But alive

ACHATES: Old Anchises was the one I spotted first his head stood out above a
   sea of bodies
And then I saw Aeneas under him

AENEAS: Achates!
Achates!

ACHATES: I take my dear friend in my arms
He is all I have left

Where's Creusa?

AENEAS: Behind me she's coming

ACHATES: I don't see her

AENEAS: She's coming

I know she's coming I put my father down I hand my son to Achates
I turn around
I turn around
And you're not there

Stay here with my son and my father

ACHATES: And he disappears into the darkness looking for his wife
In smoke-filled streets on the doorsteps of empty houses
In the darkness of smoldering churches in every possible place
One name echoes desperately
Creusa

CREUSA: Don't fall
You don't have the time to bury me and what's the use anyway
It was meant to be I wasn't supposed to leave our city
I'm bound to these shores there's nothing you can do about it
Don't fall
You'll find someone else in another country another land

Don't fall
I'm the one who won't see our son grow up
I'm the one who won't know the long road of exile
Don't fall
If I hadn't trusted you to carry our son you would be alone now
You have to keep going he needs you
Watch over him and I will keep an eye on both of you from here
I love you Aeneas I love you and I'm waiting for you

ACHATES: And so he put his arms around her three times
But three times his arms closed over nothing
Death is emptiness a gaping hole an abyss dug out of the walls of our existence
An emptiness that can never be filled

II—Water

Scene One

Along the shore. Not too far from the city.
In a small boat.

The next morning.

ACHATES: Far off in the distance at the end of our boat's foamy wake
The day is struggling to break over the smoking ruins of our city
We try to understand what has just happened but
There are no answers

Behind us what's left of our butchered past
Ahead of us the unknown an endless blue
Around me
Aeneas locked inside walls of pain his son his father and two women I don't know
We let ourselves drift
Then we run aground

PYRGO: I'm stopping I'm not going any farther

ACHATES: Are you going to stay on this island?

PYRGO: No I'm going back where I came from
Back to the place I never should have left

ACHATES: It doesn't exist anymore forget about it

PYRGO: I want to see it with my own eyes

ACHATES: They'll kill you before you even have a chance

PYRGO: What can they do to me they've won
Their victory is right there in front of them covered in flames
They can put me in chains but I prefer to be a prisoner in my own land than
      dead in a foreign one

ACHATES: A prisoner you think you'll be taken prisoner?
They didn't take Aeneas's wife prisoner or all the others I saw burned alive

PYRGO: And what if some of our people are back there fighting?
They might need us

ACHATES: What's your name?

PYRGO: Pyrgo and I want to be with my people

ACHATES: All right now you listen to me Pyrgo
All that's left of your house is ashes all that's left of your family is you
Don't think of anything else but that
Don't hope for anything else
When you're finally safe that's when you can mourn them not before
Not before

Pyrgo points at the other refugee, Bereo. She's just pulled a plant out of the earth.

What's that?

BEREO: I don't know
There's some kind of black liquid pouring from the roots

PYRGO: BLOOD

ACHATES: What are you doing why are you pulling up that plant

BEREO: To make a fire of course I can't stop shivering it's so cold!

PYRGO: Blood there's blood pouring from it

BEREO: Calm her down

PYRGO: There are bodies buried in the ground

BEREO: What?

PYRGO: When black blood pours from plant roots like that
It's because the trees and the plants are feeding on dead bodies

BEREO: I don't believe you those are old wives' tales

She continues to pull up the plants.

PYRGO: Don't do that stop DON'T DO THAT
PUT THAT DOWN PUT IT DOWN RIGHT AWAY

ACHATES: She pulls up a third a fourth a fifth plant the black liquid pours out
all around her
All over her all over her hands

Bereo smears the liquid all over her face.

PYRGO: We have to leave
A lot of people have been killed here
And it may not be over there might be more killings

*Achates joins Bereo and so do the others, all except Pyrgo. They start pulling up
all the plants. And then they smear the liquid all over themselves.
We hear deep groans rise from the depths of the earth.*

Scene Two

*A beach.
On a different island. Time has passed.*

ROBERT: You know I've been thinking
we should do this more often

LUCY: Hmmm

ROBERT: Take a holiday
How great is this eh I mean stop for a minute and look at that horizon
The sea is so blue look at the sun isn't this great
And we deserve it we do you know we really do
We worked hard enough for it we sweated and slaved to be here and let me tell
you I don't feel guilty not one bit
But you have to make the most of moments like this appreciate just how special
they are
Maybe that's why they're so beautiful

LUCY: Hmmm

ROBERT: We have to do this more often Lucy

LUCY: Mnhhh

ROBERT: What's hard isn't the money people think it's the money but the money's nothing well not nothing but what I mean is well you understand what I'm getting at right

Money even when you've got some or you're barely making ends meet of course there are people who don't have any at all and that's awful I don't mean

Okay take for example people who have just a little bit set aside

Have you seen the prices of these all-inclusive package deals right now?

Look around you see all sorts of people in this type of hotel and that's fantastic

That's democracy Lucy even the poor can afford to come to the beach these days that's pretty remarkable if you think about it

So no what's hard isn't the money

What's hard Lucy is the time

First and foremost you've got to find the time

Where when how big questions

But then you actually have to take the time

Where to take it when to take it

And finally hardest of all

What to do with it when you have it

Do you realize some people will spend their entire lives trying to answer a question like that?

Time

It's all a question of time when you get right down to it

LUCY: Hmmmh

ROBERT: We've got to do this more often honey I mean come to the islands

LUCY: *(never raising her eyes from her magazine)* This isn't "the islands"

ROBERT: What do you mean this isn't "the islands"?

LUCY: Here this this isn't the islands

ROBERT: Okay then what is this if it's not "the islands"?

LUCY: "An" island

ROBERT: Oh and what would "the islands" be then?

LUCY: The islands dammit!!
In the Caribbean look I don't know

In exasperation, Lucy has looked up from her magazine.

ROBERT: Oh right okay well then maybe you can tell me what other islands are
supposed to be called if you can't call them "the islands" even if they are islands

LUCY: You use their name, Robert

ROBERT: Okay the islands or not this is a fucking great place
Right, baby?

Pause.

The South?
Can I call this the South or is that name taken too?

LUCY: Call it whatever you want I don't care
It's getting too hot for me and I don't feel like swimming I don't know what to do

ROBERT: That's it
Complain
Some people have to go to work in the snow or the pouring rain and you're
complaining it's too hot
We're never satisfied that's another problem
I'd even go so far as to say it's the main problem today in our—

Pause.

LUCY: Now what's wrong?

ROBERT: Was there a show planned for today I don't know there are people over
there with strange makeup and—
Oh my god

The refugees are crawling along the beach.
Lucy screams.
One of the refugees holds out his hand, asking for something to drink.

I think he's thirsty Lucy give him something to drink

Lucy automatically hands him her cocktail.

I'll oh my god what should we do oh there's even a baby we have to—
Help I'll call for help no don't call for help you don't want me to

In a kind of pidgin English.

Me go get help . . . me get doctor . . . no—
Here here take my towel yes you're cold Lucy give him your towel—

LUCY: I'll call the people at the hotel they'll be able to—
No you don't want me to
Me call office . . . hotel—
No they don't want me to—

ROBERT: Lucy, go get some water in the bar

LUCY: Right water
You must be thirsty eh
We water . . . for you . . . get
You thirsty . . . glug glug glug?

She mimes drinking.

ACHATE: We speak the same language as you madam

LUCY: Oh you do fantastic oh very good right I—
Water

To Robert, before she runs off toward the hotel.

Be careful okay

ROBERT: You got here in a boat I mean a rowboat
You
You fled your country?
I
That must be terrible
I

He's very moved.

I'm sorry

ACHATES: Tell me where we can find something to eat

ROBERT: To eat yes
There's the buffet which starts—
Well actually not right away they open in an hour and a half but maybe they'd
    make an exception for you
The buffet is quite good there are even—
I'm so sorry

Scene Three

The hotel.

MANAGER: Could you tell me what you're doing here?
OH MY GOD OH MY GOD don't come near me I but who are you?
No please please could you leave that—
Could you ask him to put down that roast chicken right away?
Excuse me but you don't have the right to come in here this is a private hotel
You have to understand this buffet brunch is for the patrons of the hotel
Don't touch me do NOT touch me

George we have a problem here

Listen to me I'm going to have to make a call please put those hors d'oeuvres
    back on the table please
I'm going to have to call don't TOUCH me I'm really very sorry but I must ask
    you to leave immediately

George call security right away the police too maybe even the army George can
    you hear me?

You must leave the premises immediately do you understand immediately
You . . . go . . . (gestures) now . . . partir bye-bye
Oh my god no no please don't hurt me yes yes eat help yourselves yes take any-
    thing you want just please don't AAAAAH
Who are you I haven't done anything

ANCHISES: Forgive us please
We haven't eaten for days

MANAGER: Fine but you do realize that this is a hotel I mean I understand it must be very difficult but we're not some kind of humanitarian organization we don't get funding to give out food to refugees you understand you're refugees right not beggars
I mean you weren't poor before
You had to flee your country right?
But what's that on your faces—
Could you tell your friend not to eat all the brochettes I—
There are professionals who look after people in need like you it's not too far from here I can call them they'll take good care of you you'll see they're very kind and used to this kind of thing
The woman in charge has even worked in Africa—

ACHATES: Where's the closest city?

MANAGER: City?
Ah right why ah oh not too far could you ask him not to stare at me like that umm so you umm you came by boat I mean boat people oh my god I'm sorry this wasn't part of my training I don't know what to do I can't find the right words all of this is beyond me you know oh he's a very beautiful child he looks a lot like you

PYRGO: He's not my son

MANAGER: Oh okay I hope you're not trafficking children are you I mean no I just said that I didn't mean anything by it but look let me call the police I'll be right back—

ACHATES: No no calls no police a boat that's all we want

MANAGER: A boat ha ha ha a boat why?
Oh my god DON'T HURT ME I'M BEGGING YOU PLEASE

ACHATES: Listen to me you're going to shut up for a minute and you're going to listen
We need a boat food for a few days water and gas
After that we'll leave you alone

MANAGER: But I don't have we don't have I can't I really can't it's impossible oh my god

ACHATES: There's a boat tied up down at the dock

MANAGER: But it belongs to a guest it's not the hotel's

ACHATES: All right
Go get the guest

MANAGER: Yes okay right away

ACHATES: With me

MANAGER: I'd prefer to go alone you know the guest in question might be a little thrown by you by your—

ACHATES: With me and no calling George understood?

Scene Four

A luxury motorboat.
They're cutting through the water at breakneck speed.
Loud music blasting.
A bottle of champagne.

Scene Five

Under a tarp or tent.
Yet another island.
The man and his wife, Helen, have been on this island alone since the city was set on fire. They come from the same city as Aeneas. The man hasn't spoken to anyone for weeks.

FELLOW COUNTRYMAN: I've heard a camp's been set up just the other side of the border
I don't know how long it would take you to get there by boat a few days that's for sure
On foot I don't even want to think about it
Be very careful they arrived by sea you know and some of them are still prowling around out there they're everywhere
Last I heard the capital's calm that's the news that's what they're saying I'm not so sure and then you have to ask yourself what they mean by calm
So if you want to know what I think for what it's worth you shouldn't stay around here there's nothing to hope for not anymore

I knew it I could feel it I said to my wife I've got a really bad feeling she laughed okay I'll admit I say that even when things are going good because well to be fair there were days when things were okay I'm not saying life was easy I've never been rich but well we've always had enough to eat

I've got nothing to offer you I'm sorry but you'll find something to eat in the camp that's for sure the problem is how to hold on until then I'd give you something to tide you over if I had it but I don't that's the problem

We'll have to get used to it eh because from now on it's going to be the norm but well we're not the first it's happened before that's what I tell myself

My own father used to get an orange a single orange for Christmas and he'd cry for joy today an orange is nothing well it was nothing before all this but now I guess we're going to have to get back to what's really important

You're going to have to find some food for the little guy eh I don't know who his mother is and I don't want to come across like someone who doesn't know how to mind his own business but he doesn't look good

So there you have it back to basics from now on real values are what count the small things a single orange will make us as happy as as well whatever we liked before

Tell the old man to lie down here the ground isn't as rocky

My wife's gone to get water we'll have to boil it and wait for it to cool down but of course you'll be able to have some

What's wrong with him he doesn't look good

ACHATES: He lost his wife

FELLOW COUNTRYMAN: I'm sorry to hear that

A woman arrives running. She makes straight for Ascanius and grabs him out of Aeneas's arms.

HELEN: Oh my god thank you thank you thank you

FELLOW COUNTRYMAN: Euh
Helen

HELEN: I knew it I knew it I told you and you wouldn't believe me

FELLOW COUNTRYMAN: Helen please

HELEN: Look at him he hasn't suffered no scars no wounds nothing as beautiful as the day he was born oh my god

FELLOW COUNTRYMAN: Helen that's enough give the child back to them

HELEN: I told you we should wait I believed I believed it more than anything
I knew it deep down inside me I could feel it
You can feel those kinds of things
I'm not superstitious or even religious well no more than the next person
But there's this I don't know what to call it this link this bond that ties us together
    something beyond time and space
If he had been killed I would've felt it here
Deep in my gut in what was once his home
Those kinds of things don't lie
Men can't understand don't understand
But that's over now and you'll have to kill me first if you want to take him back
D'YOU HEAR KILL ME

AENEAS: Madam
That child
Is mine

HELEN: If you're the one who found him
Thank you
If you're here to take him from me
Leave

AENEAS: I'm not here to take him from you
You're the one who just grabbed him from me

HELEN: I did
And I'm ready to strangle him with my own hands rather than give him back
    to you
I won't lose him a second time

AENEAS: The boy you're looking at his name is Ascanius
His mother's name was Creusa

HELEN: Ascanius isn't his name and Creusa isn't mine
I'm keeping him
Back away you have no idea who you're talking to

FELLOW COUNTRYMAN: I'm sorry really very sorry at some point she'll come out
    of it she'll be herself again and you'll see she'll give him back to you

AENEAS: What you're holding in your arms
Is all I have left he's everything
Everything they couldn't take from me
We share the same sorrow the same pain madam

HELEN: Don't talk to me about pain don't try to share anything with me I have
nothing to give you
What I had to go through waiting even prisoners on death row don't have to
suffer through something like that—

Aeneas takes a step toward her.
She threatens to strangle the child.

AENEAS: You wouldn't

FELLOW COUNTRYMAN: Unfortunately she would yes she isn't all there anymore
you know
Oh my I didn't want it to come to this
Okay wait a minute wait leave her alone for a minute and—

AENEAS: That woman doesn't leave here with my child
Not while I'm alive she doesn't

FELLOW COUNTRYMAN: Let me handle this
I promise I'll give your child back to you
Trust me

AENEAS: I don't know you you can't ask me to trust you your wife is trying to
steal my son

FELLOW COUNTRYMAN: Please
You know she won't harm him just the opposite
She'll feed him give him a mother's love one night only one night
Your son definitely needs it and at dawn I'll bring him back to you
Believe me
I won't make you go through the suffering that's been inflicted on me

AENEAS: I see real pain in his eyes I see it I recognize it
This man will bring my son back to me
I can sleep
He walks away bent double weighed down by hopelessness

Night.
Everyone is lying down.

ACHATES: Aeneas
Aeneas are you asleep?

AENEAS: No

ACHATES: Where are we going, Aeneas?

AENEAS: I don't know

ACHATES: We have to stop somewhere we're all exhausted

AENEAS: I know

ACHATES: Why don't we go to the refugee camp?

AENEAS: Because I don't want to live in a camp

ACHATES: It's more like you don't want to live at all
Not anymore

AENEAS: That's ridiculous
Go to sleep instead of saying the first stupid thing that comes into your head

ACHATES: It's not stupid and you know it
Aeneas, every morning since that night when our world changed every morning
for just a few seconds before I open my eyes I tell myself the nightmare is over
I think I can hear my aunt calling me to come and eat she tells me you phoned
and want me to meet you at the cafe you know the one where the waitress has
bleached blond hair and this really casual sassy kind of walk her sandals go
flopflopflop when she walks I used to tell myself she was born to live with me
under a palm tree somewhere
So one day I finally decide to talk to her and another waiter a guy with a beard I'd
never seen before appears out of nowhere behind the counter and he kisses my
waitress and the whole time he keeps looking at me with this smile on his face
and you know what I burst out laughing I couldn't stop you either remember?
Then suddenly I open my eyes and the nightmare starts again or maybe it never
stopped
There's no aunt no cafe no waitress with bleached blond hair no crazy laughter
only the total dislocation of our world our shattered lives this strangeness and
hostility that won't go away

They reach out and take each others hand. For comfort.

Their Countryman enters. He speaks softly.
He's carrying the child in his arms.

FELLOW COUNTRYMAN: It's time for you to go
My wife is still sleeping when she wakes up it would be better if you weren't here
   it's going to be terrible
Well I'm used to it but it's still going to be terrible really terrible
So go go I'm sorry and don't make too much noise okay?
Oh if my wife wasn't in such bad shape I think I'd come with you there's nothing
   for me here but she wants to stay
And wait she still believes I don't know I don't want to—
I'll cry when I see my son's body that's what I tell myself

AENEAS: Thank you for what you've done
I'm very grateful

FELLOW COUNTRYMAN: Protect your son
Love him cherish him and don't raise him in hatred or resentment
Don't give our enemies names
He should know what we went through yes but he mustn't want to return
Find him a country that will welcome him a smiling country a sure one a
   solid one
And those of us who are barely alive we'll live like shadows somewhere in his
   memory without haunting him
No we won't haunt him like vulgar vengeful ghosts
You know
The day he owns land his own land has a wife from that country a job a roof
   over his head his first born in his arms
That day he'll truly be of that new country
That's the day we will have won this war
And the gods will be forced to bow before this truth

Scene Six

They continue on their journey.
On the bridge of the motorboat they stole.

AENEAS: We take up our journey
fleeing as mad winds toss about in the skies above us

ACHATES: The grey sea is swollen the far-off shores invisible and soon we are
swallowed by the fog
What is heading our way doesn't look good

AENEAS: Fear grips us and eats away at what is left of our humanity
Then we hear a long plaintive wailing

ACHATES: Who cried out like that?
Be brave this isn't the time to cry and lament

ANCHISES: It didn't come from the boat

AENEAS: Another cry cuts through the air
Shattering the low-hanging clouds
Man or beast no one could tell

ACHATES: Stay on course do not let yourselves be distracted

PYRGO: What is it it's gotten closer we have to get away from it quick

ACHATES: Be quiet Pyrgo you're going to make the others panic

AENEAS: The cry was heard again it ripped through the fog
One thing was clear
The creature was dying

ANCHISES: Achates
If it's a man we have to help him

ACHATES: I don't know what it is and I don't want to know
Let's keep going

ANCHISES: We could throw out a rope with a life buoy
If he grabs it that means this man was meant to live

ACHATES: And if it's not a man?

ANCHISES: Ah but if it is one and we don't save him
Then we are the beasts

They throw out the life line.
They wait.

PYRGO: That's not a man we're hearing it's a sea monster it will pull us down
  into the ocean's depths
Quick we have to let go of the rope untie it before the beast grabs it quickly now

ANCHISES: Don't
Don't touch that rope

PYRGO: Shut up old man you're mad didn't you hear that wail no man can cry
  out like that
leave me alone leave me alone

The rope goes taut.

There look we're done for oh my god oh my god

ACHATES: Aeneas help me here
Let's settle this once and for all

They pull on the rope.
And drag a man up into the boat.
Everyone freezes.

IT'S ONE OF THEM IT'S ONE OF THEM LOOK AT HIM HE'S ONE OF THEM
YOU'RE GOING TO PAY YOU'RE GOING TO PAY FOR ALL THE OTHERS
YOU SON OF A BITCH YOU BASTARD LET ME AT HIM I'LL KILL HIM WITH MY
  BARE HANDS

BEREO: THROW HIM BACK IN HE WANTED TO BURN US WELL WE'LL DROWN HIM

AENEAS: Wait stop
I want to know what he's doing here

BEREO: What he's doing here?
I'll tell you what he's doing here
He's looking for us following us and now he's going to round up the others
Help me throw him overboard

AENEAS: Don't Bereo

ACHMAENIDES: Thank you thank you

AENEAS: Don't thank us
We saved you because we didn't know who you were

ACHMAENIDES: I understand thank you thank you so so much

ACHATES: What do you understand?
There's nothing to understand
What do you understand look at me I said look at me

ACHMAENIDES: I am looking at you but I don't see you

ACHATES: I'll open your eyes for you with a knife you will see

ACHMAENIDES: Your knife will be useless
I'm blind
My name is Achmaenides
I'm one of those you hate so much
I went along with them on their mission
I waged war against you
But I don't want to die by drowning
If I have to die I'd like it to be at the hands of a human being

I kneel here before you and beg you to kill me

AENEAS: Speak first
What are you doing here how many of you are there how many cities like ours
    have you captured?

ACHMAENIDES: I'm alone they're far away now
There are tens of thousands of them and it's no longer cities that are falling into
    their hands but whole countries
Your people are trying to flee as best they can but they're often caught
And subjected to the worst kinds of torture
I was blinded in the battle and since then I'm of no use to anyone
My people kept me with them for a while in one of their boats
But then they threw me into the sea like you throw away a dead fish

ACHATES: You're of no use to us either

ACHMAENIDES: Wait wait

I

I can take you to a safe place they don't know about

I can do that for you I'll take you there and from there you'll be able to make it
    to the border really easily

If you describe the horizon to me I'll be able to navigate

Achates is about to throw him into the water. Anchises stops him.

ANCHISES: Blind as you are

You cannot see our faces ravaged by fatigue and hardship

You cannot see the bodies of our people heaped in common graves

Or the ashes of my city scattered on winds of fury

You were meant to be here

Otherwise you'd be dead

drowned

The gods have sent you to us

And the storm that's about to hit is proof of that

The gods have decided to put us to the test one more time

Scene Seven

A storm.
*They are all silent. Achmaenides, his headband pulled down over his eyes, is
at the helm of the boat.*
The wind howls.

AENEAS: The darkest of nights falls on the emptiness that surrounds us

We feel the cold to the very marrow of our bones

The grey waters swell the storm clouds gather

And then the watery plain all around us starts to heave

The wind mixes sky with land

It blows so hard and lifts the waves so high they seem to lick the stars

In the fathomless depths dormant expanses of water now rise to the surface

Mountains of seawater keep us hanging on the crest of every wave

And then we fall into chasms so deep we catch a glimpse of the ocean's bottom

Where the sand is alive boiling with fury

I hear the cries of my people mixed with the hammering of the motor the crack-
    ing of the hull

Everything makes us aware of the presence of death
And when the tumult of the sea throws us onto invisible rocks
We believe we've arrived in hell's deepest cauldron.
Thrown out of the boat we try to keep our heads above water
My son is in my arms I can see no one else
I look for my father I look for Achates I call their names yelling into the star-
  less night
All I hear is the wind howling and Ascanius screaming in my arms as he gets
  hit by the waves
As long as he's screaming I know he's alive
Scream son
Scream I want to keep hearing you
I drift all night
I drift for the rest of my life

III—Earth

Scene One

A few weeks later.
An office. In a city.

IMMIGRATION OFFICER: No
No
No
Tell her I'm not in the office today yes I'm not here
What do you mean she saw me okay then tell her I'm busy that I'm busy
Yes even immigration officers can be busy sometimes
Very funny
I don't know
Do your job
Well if you think mine's any easier—
Listen I'm not interested so stop complaining
I don't feel like listening to your tale of woe
Yes that's what I said
Oh don't try that you know that little break in your voice
Doesn't work with me
Well too bad
What?
What are you doing no don't do that I'm warning you don't let her come in here
don't let her—

Elissa enters. Pause. The Immigration Officer pulls herself together and puts on
her professional demeanor.

I'm sorry Elissa
You're going to have to be patient

ELISSA: Patient? Before being patient I have to eat

IMMIGRATION OFFICER: Well yes of course I know I know but I can't provide you with a work permit as long as your status hasn't been officialized you have to understand my position here Elissa—

ELISSA: I left my country because it was a matter of survival it seems to me that should be reason enough for me to be given the status of refugee

IMMIGRATION OFFICER: You *left* your country you weren't *thrown out* it's not the same thing

ELISSA: I left it before I was thrown out

IMMIGRATION OFFICER: Had it been the other way around we wouldn't be here

ELISSA: Had it been the other way around I wouldn't be here because I'd be dead

IMMIGRATION OFFICER: That's what they'll try to establish by studying your file
Of course I believe you Elissa but I don't have the power to give you refugee status try to understand my position

ELISSA: Expulsion doesn't exist in my country
Either you leave or they kill you
So I don't see how expulsion can be established

IMMIGRATION OFFICER: For political reasons

ELISSA: The reasons are always political

IMMIGRATION OFFICER: They have to study your request Elissa
Not just anyone is eligible for refugee status

ELISSA: What am I supposed to do in the meantime?

IMMIGRATION OFFICER: You stay in the transition centre you wait for your request for asylum to be officially registered
Once the official registration has gone through then you'll receive an acknowledgement of receipt

ELISSA: A what?

IMMIGRATION OFFICER: An acknowledgement of receipt

ELISSA: And what does an acknowledgement of receipt do for me?

IMMIGRATION OFFICER: It's a document that proves you're waiting for a ruling on your status

ELISSA: Can I work with an acknowledgement of receipt?

IMMIGRATION OFFICER: No

ELISSA: Can I leave the country with an acknowledgement of receipt?

IMMIGRATION OFFICER: No

ELISSA: SO WHAT CAN I DO WITH AN ACKNOWLEDGEMENT OF RECEIPT?

IMMIGRATION OFFICER: Please calm down
The document is your guarantee you won't be deported

ELISSA: Deported?
I'm not officially in your country yet
How can I be deported?

IMMIGRATION OFFICER: You can be deported because you're an illegal and because the authorities in this country fight illegality wherever and whenever possible

ELISSA: I'm an illegal

IMMIGRATION OFFICER: Exactly

ELISSA: I could be deported at any time

IMMIGRATION OFFICER: At any time

ELISSA: Unless you give me a document that states I'm waiting for an acknowledgement of receipt which proves I'm waiting for a ruling on a request for asylum which in turn will attest to the fact that I'm waiting to be accepted into your country

IMMIGRATION OFFICER: No
I can't issue you with that kind of document
I could at one time
Last year I was able to issue a temporary document that preceded the acknowledgement of receipt but the police authorities no longer recognize that kind of document

It didn't have a great deal of legal value anyway because it hadn't been ratified by all the countries that signed the international agreement

Pause.

ELISSA: A signature a single signature by you and I'm a free woman

IMMIGRATION OFFICER: There's nothing I can do for you please believe me

ELISSA: The ink in your fountain pen is worth more than the blood in my veins

She stands up. Threatening. The Immigration Officer pulls back.

I'm not going back to the transition centre

IMMIGRATION OFFICER: You don't have a choice
What are you going to do if you don't go back?

ELISSA: I don't know go into town find a place to sleep find a—

IMMIGRATION OFFICER: If the police stop you outside the perimeter of the transition centre there's nothing I can do to help you

ELISSA: For all the help you're giving me now

IMMIGRATION OFFICER: I need confirmation that you're returning to the transition centre
Otherwise I'll have to alert the local authorities

ELISSA: All right
I confirm that I'm returning to the transition centre
I also confirm that I'm eager to return in fact I can hardly wait to get back there because we're so well treated. The rooms are lovely the meals are delicious and the staff is so welcoming you should drop by for a visit you won't have any trouble finding the place just follow the sound of people crying
Crying for joy of course madam

IMMIGRATION OFFICER: You're discouraged I understand that it's only natural but listen
If you really want refugee status in this country that's the price you have to pay and I do realize it's a large one
Otherwise you can always go back to your country
The situation there has calmed down considerably you know
And we've been informed that order is slowly being restored

ELISSA: Order!
That's precisely why I fled madam I didn't want to live under that kind of order
Oh you do your job well
I know that your goal your only goal for that matter
Is to discourage us completely discourage us from staying here in your country
I have to tell you something
It's impossible you'll never succeed
Hardship and desperation are like a wind that will never stop filling our sails
Put up your barriers install your iron bars build your walls
Patrol the seas scour the deserts as much as you want
We will continue to arrive
Wave after wave of us
We will wash up on your white beaches and you will never be able to stop the flood

Because you can't stop the sea with your arms

Scene Two

A squat.
Later the same day.
Two men.

THE SCAVENGER: When they realized we'd escaped from the camp they came after us
Like a pack of dogs
Fangs bared drool dripping
We wanted to make it to the mountains as quickly as we could
Ohhh we walked and walked ohhhhh I can't even begin to tell you how many kilometres
We walked for days and days we even walked at night
Until we came to a small abandoned house
And there well I don't know if it was a shepherd or someone else
Someone we never saw I don't know but if I ever run into the guy ohhhhh

He pulls his thumb across his throat, making the appropriate sound.

He tipped off the police
They showed up herded us into trucks and dropped us in the middle of the desert yeah the desert

So we'd die out there like cattle
Sand that's all there was sand as far as the eye could see
The tracks saved us
Their tire tracks Ha! The idiots forgot about their tire tracks
So we followed the tracks back to the city
And I found this abandoned building it's become my little kingdom

> *Elissa enters.*
> *He lets out a wolf whistle.*

Evening ma'am
Welcome to my domain to my lands

> *He stands up. Walks over to her.*
> *She steps back from him.*
> *She notices the other man.*

ELISSA: Hello

> *The other man says nothing.*

THE SCAVENGER: Hahaha you won't get much out of him
He's been here a few days now and he hasn't said a word not a single word noth-
  ing nada zip
A madman if you ask me a madman with a poor little baby *(cackles)* hihihihi

ELISSA: How many are living here?

THE SCAVENGER: Depends on the day
You left the camp eh
Tst tst that's not nice shouldn't do that

ELISSA: Can I put my things down over there?

THE SCAVENGER: No

ELISSA: Okay
Tell me where then

THE SCAVENGER: That depends on your budget

ELISSA: My budget?

THE SCAVENGER: You bet this may not be a palace but it's got a roof and you've
  got to pay for that missy pay for it oh yeah gotta pay for everything in this world

ELISSA: I've got nothing

THE SCAVENGER: Oooooooh
We've all got something and if we don't we gotta get some

ELISSA: I'll take this corner here and tomorrow you can tell me how much it'll
cost me and then we'll see

THE SCAVENGER: Mnnnnnh okay by me

If you want curtains for a little privacy just let me know I sell them
Partitions too but they cost more yep a lot more

ELISSA: Is there a place to wash up?
Obviously not

THE SCAVENGER: Obviously
No toilets no baths no running water and I highly recommend you not use the
public toilets the police watch them very closely
If you don't want to be returned to the camp or dumped in the middle of the
desert you'll have to be very careful
Okay I'm going to bed tomorrow I'm getting up early I'm doing the grocery
shopping hihihihi
Oh yeah up at the crack of dawn every morning
That's when I do the shopping
Gotta go to market and do the shopping
That means we scavenge for tomatoes and eggplant that's thrown out right
Sometimes we find loose change and other times people give us some
Then we can buy rice
Yeah we get by
Barely
But we get by
Like a pack of dogs

ELISSA: Okay
Good night

The Scavenger doesn't leave.

Is there something else?

THE SCAVENGER: I don't know you don't need anything?

ELISSA: No thank you see you in the morning

THE SCAVENGER: Can't be easy for a woman alone eh I mean on her own like you are

Wouldn't you like to be more comfortable
I've got a mattress if you like

ELISSA: I have no money I told you

THE SCAVENGER: I didn't say it would cost you money

ELISSA: I'm fine here where I am

THE SCAVENGER: You wouldn't like to be more comfortable
Warmer for example

ELISSA: No thank you

THE SCAVENGER: Come on fuck relax life is hard enough what harm is there in
a little human comfort?
It'd do you good

ELISSA: Let me go to sleep now

THE SCAVENGER: Hey who the hell do you think you are you land in here you
have nothing to offer you take over a corner of the room like you owned the
place and you turn up your nose at me
Come on get over here fuck

He moves closer to Elissa. She pushes him away. He tries to force her. She fights back.
Aeneas stand up.
He grabs the Scavenger and immobilizes him.

You're not going to hit me you're not goin' to hit a brother are ya?
You can't do that

Aeneas lets him go. The Scavenger pulls a knife and tries to stab Aeneas.
They fight. The knife connects with flesh. Two bodies fall to the floor.
And then we see Aeneas kneeling beside the Scavenger's body. His hands are
covered in blood.

Scene Three

Months have gone by.

A city lane.
Night.
Sounds of the city.
A Graffiti Artist is working on a painting, a mural.
Achates watches him.

ACHATES: On the black sweaty walls of a narrow back lane
The painting of a city in flames
My city

Look here
My people running hair dishevelled terror on their faces
And there the looting of the old movie house there the bloodbath in the market
   place and over there the destruction of that building on Providence Boulevard
Here Creusa's body defenceless and alone
There they are
Marching triumphant over our dead bodies
And us
In tears fleeing in a small boat

How do you know all this how can you possibly know all this?

GRAFFITI ARTIST: I don't know anything I paint that's all

ACHATES: You saw them tell me did you see them?

GRAFFITI ARTIST: Leave me alone I haven't done anything

ACHATES: Tell me where they are

GRAFFITI ARTIST: Who are you talking about look I don't know

ACHATES: There on the boat
That man there with the child
I'm looking for him tell me where he is

GRAFFITI ARTIST: I have no idea I don't even know who he is

He hands Achates his can of spray paint.

This is what decides not me

And he runs away.
Achates turns the can toward the wall and sprays.
Aeneas and Elissa appear, laying in each others' arms.

Scene Four

An apartment.

ELISSA: Someone's at the door

AENEAS: So go answer

ELISSA: You go lazy-bones
You haven't been outside in three days

AENEAS: I'm not moving

ELISSA: Don't start

AENEAS: Go answer

ELISSA: I'm warning you if you don't get the door the evening's taking a turn
for the worse

AENEAS: Pffffff

Halfheartedly, he drags himself to the door.
He sees Achates.
Freezes.

ELISSA: Who is it
Aeneas
Who's at the door

Achates grabs Aeneas in his arms.

ACHATES: I've been looking for you for months

Aeneas pulls himself away.

AENEAS: Elissa
This is Achates

ACHATES: His best friend

His brother

He must've spoken to you about me

ELISSA: Aah yeah yes
Yes

ACHATES: Is Ascanius with you?

AENEAS: Yes
He's sleeping

ACHATES: And your father?

AENEAS: Drowned in the storm
I found his body at dawn on the shore

ACHATES: I'm so sorry Aeneas

AENEAS: I'll go get us something to drink

ELISSA: You stay I'll go

   Elissa leaves.

ACHATES: What's happened to you since the storm

AENEAS: I don't know
I
I've forgotten a lot of things and I don't know if I want to remember them
But you
Talk to me about you

ACHATES: I managed to make it to shore
More dead than alive
Some men helped me
I was alone
I wandered through town
Looking for you
And here I am

Aeneas not everything's lost
Bereo and Pyrgo are alive I found them

AENEAS: Thank heavens
The storm only took my father

ACHATES: They're waiting for us they're ready to keep moving
We can't stay here Aeneas the situation is impossible

AENEAS: Not for me

ACHATES: What do you mean not for you?

AENEAS: I'm fine here with Elissa

ACHATES: Who is this woman is she from here?

AENEAS: No

ACHATES: But she's not from home either

AENEAS: She has a temporary residency permit
She has a job a place to live and we manage to eat every day

ACHATES: But what about you?
What do you do stay here and—

AENEAS: I've been resting that's what I've been doing Achates and after what I've
    been through I think I'm entitled to a few hundred years of rest

ACHATES: Are you telling me you've stayed here lying on that sofa while I was
    out there looking for you walking the streets of this city begging for bones
    like a dog?
Are you telling me you're being fed while our people are fighting for a crust of
    bread?

AENEAS: I didn't ask you to come looking for me
I'm not stopping anyone from living the way I do
What? I should be miserable because my people are living in hardship?

ACHATES: And what about me did you know whether I was alive or not?
Did you worry about me?
Are you even happy to see me Aeneas?

Listen to me I've come to get you
I need you we need you our journey doesn't stop here
There's nothing in this city for us
We have to leave

AENEAS: Achates
I'm exhausted
I don't want to do anything anymore
I don't want to get up in the morning I don't want to go out or walk I don't even
    want to fight anymore
I don't know whether I should stay here
But this is where I washed up
Now you're talking to me about our journey what do you want me to do about it?
Was my journey about seeing my city burn?
Losing my wife?
Holding my father's dead body in my arms?

I'm alone Achates alone with a child
There's a woman here I love and who loves Ascanius
The three of us are happy together
We don't have a lot but we have everything we need
And you want me to take to the sea again to continue on our journey

No my friend
I want to lie there because when I stood up the gods turned on me

ACHATES: And your people?
Out there two women from home are waiting for us
You led us you saved us you can't drop us now like this

AENEAS: Led you?
Saved you?
What are you talking about?
I ran and jumped in a boat the gods did the rest

You go
Guide them carry the torch
I'm tired I've done my share

ACHATES: And what about your son?
Do you really believe he'll be happy here?
An immigrant he'll be an immigrant all his life they'll never accept him as one
    of theirs

AENEAS: Wherever he goes he'll be an immigrant

ACHATES: Not if we find him land

AENEAS: There's no more land Achates
It's all been given out
The only land that's left is in the desert or underwater at the bottom of the ocean
What do you want us to do?
Steal land by drenching it with the blood of the conquered?
Become the same as those who chased us from our home?
I don't want to do that

ACHATES: You've become a coward
Soft and cowardly

AENEAS: I refuse to fight yes
And I'm in love

ACHATES: You're under a spell I can't believe it

AENEAS: Whatever
I'm happy
I've never been so happy

ACHATES: You're tarnishing Creusa's memory

Aeneas grabs him by the throat.

AENEAS: Never say that again
Never

Elissa comes back in.
Aeneas lets Achates go. Achates leaves.

Scene Five

A window.

Aeneas stands there, alone.

AENEAS: The days go by and I stay glued here waiting by the door hoping Achates
   will return
But he doesn't
The days go by and I disappear
I lose myself more and more in the flow of time
The man who once survived every storm
Has never been closer to drowning

Creusa's ghost appears.

Not again
Have you come back to haunt me again please go away
GO AWAY CREUSA

CREUSA: I'll stop when you leave here

AENEAS: I'm not leaving I'm never leaving again
For once in my life
I'm trying to live entirely in the present

CREUSA: The present
You don't have a present anymore they took it away from you
The one you're trying to build for yourself is false

AENEAS: Creusa I battle with images of the past every single day of my life
My house burning
My father drowning in the sea
Achates insulting me and running away from me
And images of you
The wife I couldn't bury

CREUSA: You will carry your past in you forever
But you also have an enormous duty to your future
Memories

And hope
You're nothing more than a hyphen
A little hyphen
Between the two
You have to accept that

AENEAS: My life was taken away from me

CREUSA: Let it go
Don't try to get it back
Don't try to go back to what you were before

Your old life is lying beside me in my grave
You have to give yourself a new one
You have a chance to
And you have our son

AENEAS: I don't know where I'm supposed to go

CREUSA: Your father will tell you

AENEAS: My father!
He died in my arms
I'm alone now your ghost is all I have left of my past life

CREUSA: The dead never stop talking to us
And you were able to bury him
Those who have been buried can provide answers to the living

   Creusa disappears.
   Then, without making a sound, Aeneas goes and picks up Ascanius.
   He stops and looks around for a long moment.
   And then gets ready to leave.

ELISSA: Can I ask where you're going?

Aeneas

AENEAS: I'm sorry

ELISSA: Don't

You were going to leave without saying anything

AENEAS: I'm sorry I know I'm the basest of men but
If I stay here I'll only lead both of us to our deaths

ELISSA: If you leave the only one who'll die will be me

AENEAS: I'm not asking you to understand
I'm not even asking you to accept what I'm doing
I wanted to leave without your knowing because there's nothing to say

ELISSA: Look at me
Look at me and tell me that everything we've said to each other everything we
   promised one another won't make you stay
Tell me that
Nothing will stop you from going?
Is it land you're looking for Aeneas or are you running away from me?
Answer me

My love I beg you not to do this if you have any pity for me any pity for us don't
   do this
If you leave what'll become of me what can I hope for from life what will be
   left for me?
You leave me with nothing not even a child who has your eyes and who'd remind
   me of you

AENEAS: I will remember you
As long as there is breath in my body
But there's my father who died so I could find us land
And my son and the promise I made which ties me to his future
It's not that I want to leave you Elissa
It's that I have to
It's my duty

ELISSA: YOUR DUTY
I DON'T CARE ABOUT YOUR DUTY
Your desire is gone and you don't love me anymore you've never loved me
If you loved me you wouldn't leave me

I took you in when you had nothing
I offered you a roof over your head I fed you and I gave you my body
I pulled you back from sure death and now you're pushing me toward it

Go I won't stop you
Go look for your paltry plot of land
But I'll pray that you encounter raging storms on your way
I'll pray you die in agony and call my name until your last breath
And I'll know you're dead when at last your cries reach me in the Underworld

*In the distance, Achates climbs on board a train and reaches out his hand to
Aeneas. Pyrgo and Bereo are with him.*

ACHATES: Aeneas!
Quick the train's pulling out

Aeneas comes running.

Hand Ascanius to me

ELISSA: Forget what I just said
Stay one night one more night
I beg you one last night and then I'll let you leave

Aeneas hands his son up to Achates.

Aeneas
Take me take me with you

Aeneas reaches his arm up toward Achates. Looks one last time at Elissa.

A dead woman is begging you
Please

The train leaves.

Aeneas
My love my final flame
I'm standing here
Burning for you

I WANT TO DESTROY YOU
YOU YOUR SON THE SONS OF YOUR SONS AND THEN THROW MYSELF ON THE FIRE
It's the only thing left for me to do

I know you you're doing this for your son
Your son!
If I'd known you would leave me because of him I'd have torn him to pieces
    with my own hands
I curse you Aeneas
I want you to die before your time I want you to die unburied
I want men to take up arms one day come to your new city set it on fire and
    cover you in ashes again

I wasn't meant to be happy
My life is disappearing on the wind
And I am descending
Under the ground

    The train enters a tunnel. Darkness.
    The earth rumbles and quakes.

IV—Underground

Scene One

The catacombs. A row of skulls.
Aeneas and Achates. Bereo and Pyrgo follow behind them.

OLD WOMAN: This way
Ignore those things *(the skulls)* they won't hurt you
Welcome to the catacombs

She chuckles.

Not many people know about this place
No not many

ACHATES: And you're sure this will take us to the woman we're looking for?

OLD WOMAN: Oh her the Sibyl as you call her hihihi

Chuckles.

The one who gets the dead to talk oh yes hihihi
But be careful the Sibyl is a woman with a lot of charm oh yes ohhh like me
A few years back
Come on follow me be careful this is a real labyrinth
Walk in front yes
Good
Stop Mr. Aeneas
You have to
Pay me now

AENEAS: When we get to this Sibyl woman

OLD WOMAN: No now

AENEAS: Half now the rest later

OLD WOMAN: No
I'm risking my life too
Trafficking immigrants

Chuckles.

We're talking ten fifteen years maybe
And at my age prison hard labour
Oh no not for me

She slaps Achate's hand as he reaches out to touch one of the skulls.

Don't touch

ACHATES: You just said they won't hurt us

OLD WOMAN: That's not a reason to touch them

ACHATES: I'm not afraid of the dead

OLD WOMAN: You should be

ACHATES: It's the living who scare me

Achates picks up one of the skulls. The Old Woman lets out a scream.

OLD WOMAN: A curse!
A curse on you
And on all of us!

Achates throws the skull over to Aeneas who catches it.
They play a deadly game with the skull.

Scene Two

The sewers.
The two women have fallen even farther behind.

BEREO: Aeneas!
We followed him in a boat on foot in a train
We washed up on shore with him landed on every island in the sea wandered
   around every port
Now here we are tromping through shit in this sewer
And we still haven't reached our destination
How many days how many months have gone by and I still don't have a life well
   nothing you could call a life
And you Pyrgo look at you!
I feel sorry for you
You've gone back to being a nanny that's all you're good for apparently
And to think he was being kept by his princess while we were hitting rock bottom
We're still hitting it

PYRGO: What do you want us to do where do you want us to go?

BEREO: Here or somewhere else what's the difference?
Who's gonna stop me from staying here if I want to?

PYRGO: The smell

BEREO: Let him take care of the kid let him try to get along without us
Let's leave right now
I've got the water and you've got the food
We could manage on our own with that

PYRGO: Stop Bereo you're crazy

BEREO: Leave me alone!
I've given enough
That man is bringing us bad luck
Look what happened to his wife to his father and now to us
Why are we roaming around in these sewers?
To find a woman who can make the dead speak!
The dead don't care about us or about Aeneas
What are they supposed to say to him?

They watch him walking and they think
That man's crazy let's drop him
And so we're abandoned by the dead and by the gods
I'm telling you some time or other Aeneas made a very serious mistake and since
    then he's been paying for it
The problem is we're paying along with him
Come on
What are you doing?

PYRGO: I promised I'd take care of the child

BEREO: You sound like a slave

PYRGO: And you sound like a woman who's off her rocker

BEREO: I said come on

PYRGO: If we leave the sewers the police will pick us up right away

BEREO: So?

PYRGO: They'll dump us in the desert

BEREO: So what?

PYRGO: We'll die that's what

BEREO: I just told you I've got the water

PYRGO: Bravo
That'll keep us alive for two days

BEREO: That's enough time for us to find a road out

PYRGO: It's also enough time for us to die on the way

BEREO: Do you really believe Aeneas will find us somewhere we can live
    peacefully?

Answer me

PYRGO: I don't know

BEREO: I want you to answer me

PYRGO: You want to know the truth there's not much I believe in anymore

BEREO: So what have you got to lose by coming with me?

PYRGO: The respect of my family and friends
That's all I've got left

Bereo runs at Pyrgo and grabs her bag with the food.

What are you doing?
Let go of me
Let go of me
Don't hurt the child

Bereo now has Pyrgo's bag.
The two women stare at each other.

BEREO: I'm really sorry, Pyrgo
You didn't give me a choice

She exits running.
Aeneas and Achates enter and rush over to Pyrgo.

ACHATES: We heard shouting what happened?

PYRGO: Bereo's left
With her bag and mine

ACHATES: What do you mean "left"?

PYRGO: She's abandoning us

ACHATES: She can't we have to catch her

AENEAS: Forget it
Let her go

ACHATES: We didn't travel together over land and sea to split up now
We have to convince her to come back

PYRGO: I
I tried to stop her I swear but she wouldn't listen she said she didn't trust you
   anymore Aeneas
I kept saying she should stay but—

AENEAS: I understand her your faith in me has been shaken I know that
I abandoned you Bereo and Achates
But I won't let you down ever again I'll be here to help you
Once my father tells us where to go
I'll lead you to a safe place I promise

The Old Woman enters, out of breath.

OLD WOMAN: You've got to get out of here you have to leave it's not good to stay here

PYRGO: You go I'll try to catch up with Bereo

To Aeneas.

Here take Ascanius that's safest

ACHATES: But Pyrgo
Wait
Wait
How will we find each other again?

PYRGO: We'll figure out how
A storm couldn't separate us
Trust in fate Achates

ACHATES: She leaves and I don't lift a finger to stop her
I lose the two women left in my life who were from my country
Why? To go talk to a dead man
There are days when I'm sorry I didn't burn with my city
And there are days when I wonder whether I burned with it but haven't noticed

Scene Three

A brothel.

THE SIBYL: If you're here for the girls
No problem I've got one for every taste
If it's for something else you've come to the wrong place

AENEAS: It is for something else and I know this is the right place

THE SIBYL: What do you want exactly?

ACHATES: You know perfectly well what we want
so give it to us

THE SIBYL: Whoa calm down my young friend
You're not the boss around here
First of all I don't know what the two of you are talking about
And second I don't give I sell
Big difference

I asked you what you want exactly

AENEAS: Answers

THE SIBYL: And you believe you'll get them with what I've got

AENEAS: Yes

THE SIBYL: Don't make me laugh

ACHATES: We've been told that if you use it a person can talk to the dead

THE SIBYL: Tell your friend to keep his voice down

AENEAS: Sorry
Can you help us yes or no?

THE SIBYL: That depends on you

ACHATES: Ah!
So you do have something

THE SIBYL: I didn't say that
I've got girls that's for sure
And they'll give you any answer you want

AENEAS: I didn't come here for one of your girls
What do you want in exchange?

THE SIBYL: Hey how about that now you're asking my question
What do I want?
I don't know what have you got to offer?
Not your kid I hope

AENEAS: Not much

THE SIBYL: That's too bad
Really too bad

ACHATES: Aeneas let's go
She can't do anything for us

THE SIBYL: Your friend
Maybe he could be of use to me

ACHATES: I'm not for sale

THE SIBYL: Oh aren't we a good little boy!
Handsome too

AENEAS: Of use to you in what way

THE SIBYL: I don't know maybe he could distract me
I bet under all that toughness he's a real pussycat

ACHATES: A pussycat?
I don't feel like being nice to anyone least of all you

THE SIBYL: You haven't seen what I can do yet

ACHATES: Oh I have an idea—

THE SIBYL: Do you?

Give me one night and I'll give you what you want

ACHATES: Let's get out of here Aeneas she's laughing at us

AENEAS: Wait
How do I know that what you've got is what I really want?

THE SIBYL: How can anyone know what they really want?

AENEAS: I do
I want to see my father

THE SIBYL: And your father's dead

AENEAS: Yes

THE SIBYL: Okay
I might have something for you
But you have to pay first

AENEAS: Achates

ACHATES: Aeneas

AENEAS: Achates

ACHATES: Out of the question

AENEAS: Achates it's the only way

ACHATES: I don't see how your father can help us Aeneas

AENEAS: He'll tell us where to go

ACHATES: Look I'm leaving I'm not staying here another second

AENEAS: Only one night

ACHATES: The answer's no

The Sibyl bursts out laughing.

Shut up
Or I'll shove that laugh of yours right down your throat

THE SIBYL: Come on
It'll take your mind off things after everything you've been through

AENEAS: She's got a point Achates

The Sibyl forces Achates to follow her.

ACHATES: There's no reason to believe we'll meet your father!
Even less that he'll tell us where we should go!

THE SIBYL: Never underestimate the dead
But come have some fun with the living instead

Scene Four

A little later.

The Sibyl places a pill on her tongue and then she kisses both Aeneas and Achates.
The descent into hell begins.

THE SIBYL: Now listen to me carefully
In a few moments you'll descend to a place where few men have ever been
Even fewer have ever returned
Be very careful
The black of night hides human beings
but it excites animals and beasts

AENEAS: I can't bring my son where I'm going

THE SIBYL: I'll keep him with me
Don't worry
This place is safer than where you're going

She leaves with Ascanius.

The howling of dogs under an uncertain moon.
A silhouette with the head of a bull crosses the stage.
A three-headed watchdog howls.
A dark shape throws a cake to the creature. The howling stops immediately.

AENEAS: Achaemenides
You survived the storm!

ACHAEMENIDES: No and neither did you if you're here

ACHATES: What do you mean by "here"?

ACHAEMENIDES: The world of shadows
Of slumber
Of sleep-giving night

AENEAS: I'm alive and Achates here is as well
Stop your boat we're coming on board

ACHAEMENIDES: No living person can come onto this boat

AENEAS: I'm not going to give you the pleasure of dying so you can ferry me across in your boat
I've come to speak to my father and not even a dead man can stop me

He gets in the boat. Achates hesitates.

ACHATES: I really don't like this place Aeneas

AENEAS: You'll have to get used to it
There's a pretty good chance we'll end up here one day

ACHATES: I hope that day is a long way off

Achaemenides looks at Achates and bursts out laughing, which annoys Achates.

ACHAEMENIDES: Whether you're alive and faking it or really dead
You're not welcome in my boat

They move quickly through the dark waters of the river.
We hear babies crying.

ACHATES: What's that?

ACHAEMENIDES: The souls of newborn babes dead before they ever knew the sweetness of living
Next to them the Fields of the Innocent where the grief-ridden souls of the falsely accused wander aimlessly

Pause. Terrified, Achates and Aeneas stare at the shores.
Then, a woman appears.

AENEAS: ELISSA!

ACHAEMENIDES: If you leave this boat I won't let you back in

Achates holds on to Aeneas, stopping him from getting out.

AENEAS: Elissa
What is she doing there?
Where are we stop the boat
I said stop the boat

ACHAEMENIDES: Impossible
We've arrived at the Fields of Mourning
This is where you find those who took their own lives
An act which goes against the world's sense of order
But that doesn't matter to someone who has decided to kill themselves

Elissa disappears.
The boat continues on its way. Aeneas remains silent, kneeling in the boat.

This is only the beginning of the suffering
Can you hear the wailing that's coming from the road over there?
Those are war heroes who once shouted victory and who are now lamenting
    their defeat

ACHATES: Aeneas!
I see Coroebus
COROEBUS!

ACHAEMENIDES: He can't hear you look at him carefully
His body is mutilated his ears have been ripped off
And where his nostrils should be there's a gaping wound

ACHATES: Shut up
Be quiet

ACHAEMENIDES: Even here your friend Coroebus continues to fight
Even here they tear each other apart
Because that's the way heroes are

Look up ahead
The river divides in two
The way to the right leads to the abyss
That's where you'll find those who hated their brothers mistreated their fathers
    and betrayed the confidence others placed in them
Misers adulterers and worst of all
Those who while promising peace led their people into unjust wars
The worst punishments are reserved for these corrupt souls
There's the man who sold his country for gold subjecting it to the rule of a
    dictator
The man who soiled his daughter's bed
And countless others
There aren't enough punishments for all the crimes that exist

To the left the landscape is much more pleasant
Fields basking in a soft warm light

ACHATES: Light?
Here?

AENEAS: Turn left then
The man I'm looking for will be there

ACHAEMENIDES: That's what everyone believes that's what everyone hopes
But—

ACHATES: We said go left

ACHAEMENIDES: As you wish

The darkness lightens.
We hear singing in the distance.

Here are the happy dead
They used their intelligence to make life better
Their art in order to advance civilization
They left something productive behind remembering that others would follow
   after them

Aeneas sees his father.

ANCHISES: You've come at last
I can see your face and hear your voice again
I've counted the days since I left you
I knew you'd find your way here

Aeneas gets out of the boat before Achates can stop him.
He tries to take Anchises in his arms but holds emptiness.

AENEAS: Father I don't know if everything I see is real
But I do know one thing
I don't want to fall again because if I do I won't be able to get up
Now tell me where I have to go
And what I must do

ANCHISES: Listen well my son
You must learn the ways of the world if you want to continue on your journey
From here
We can at last see the order of things

Firstly Aeneas
Look at the sky and the continents
Then at the vast watery expanses
The shining orb of the moon
The radiant fire of the sun
It is the fire of the sun that gave birth to man and to beasts
All living things contain the vigour and energy of fire
A celestial imprint
But quickly matter takes hold of us and weighs us down
Fear and desire
Sadness and joy
And that is how life slows us down here on Earth
There are times when we become prisoners of the shadows and can no longer
    feel the breath of Heaven
And then the fateful day of eternal night
Life leaves our bodies
Souls heavy with sorrow drag their filth to some infernal place
Souls light with joy let the winds carry them this way and that
All of them end up burning because fire purifies everything
Virtue and vice
And the long trail of time takes us back to our beginnings
Where we wait for the day when we will return to Earth once more

Look at the souls you see here
There are many among them who have never committed a single crime
But despite that they are weighed down by sorrow
They are exiles
In search of a new land

Jews from Russia looking for their New Odessa
Algerians
Bengalis walking toward India
Cypriots
Vietnamese fleeing Hanoi and Saigon
Khmers

Hazaras from Afghanistan
Guatemalans
Indians
Miskits from Nicaragua
Native people of Mozambique
Namibians fleeing Lubango
Kurds from Iraq
Somalis trying to make it to Ethiopia and Ethiopians fleeing their own country
Rohingyas from Burma in the marshes of Bangladesh
Liberians in Sierra Leone
Tutsis and Hutus their blood mixed
Tadjiks Ossetians Kosovars
People from Mali drowned in the Strait of Gibraltar
Mexicans shot down in Tijuana
The mutilated of Angola
Sudanese fleeing to Kenya
Congolese from Goma
Palestinians from Gaza
Iraqis Azeris Colombians Sri Lankans Georgians Haitians Dominicans Togolese
    Central Africans Chinese Indonesians Syrians

And at the end of this long line of wanderers you and our people

All of you carry the rich seeds of your civilizations within you
You have the power to found nations
Or destroy them

Aeneas my son
Your search will be over soon
You will find the land you're looking for when you've laid down your hatred at
    the foot of a barbed wire fence
Don't forget to establish rules for peace
Respect those who have been repressed
Disarm the conquerors
Marry a woman from the new country
A woman who has settled the land before you
A woman you will love and cherish
Mix your blood with hers
Don't wait for war to do it for you

Then a New World will be born
It will be our world Aeneas
And let this new world be beautiful

AENEAS: I'm not sure I'll be able to take up the journey again Father

ANCHISES: You won't have to walk Aeneas
I'll carry you

> *Aeneas wants to take him in his arms, but his arms remain empty and wrap themselves around his own body.*
> *The darkness grows thicker.*

ACHATES: Achaemenides
I can't see Aeneas anymore
I CAN'T SEE HIM

ACHAEMENIDES: He shouldn't have left the boat
Now it's too late
He won't be able to come back

ACHATES: AENEAS
AENEAS?

ACHAEMENIDES: Bid your friend farewell
We must keep going

> *Achates jumps out of the boat and goes looking for Aeneas.*
> *He disappears into the darkness as well.*

V—Blood

Scene One

A refugee camp.

Outside a makeshift shelter.

ALLECTO: Aw look at them don't they just break your heart
The new refugees
Bent over double eyes glassy so pale
More dead than alive
Now they'll be cared for in the infirmary bags of rice will be dropped from air-
    planes for them and they'll be given the best shelters in the camp
And what about me what about Allecto?
I left my country with my sons and daughters
I lost my husband dead back there in our native land
They tell me to wait they tell me to be patient
They tell me others have suffered too
What do I care about their suffering!
Why should I be expected to carry their exile on my shoulders?
I've been in this camp a year now and I'm still not allowed to cross the border
I only want one thing only one
To leave this cursed country

Her son, who is the leader of their band of refugees, comes and sits on a chair and lights up a cigarette.

And you all you do is sit there calmly smoking a cigarette

SON: Yep

ALLECTO: I don't know if you've heard there's a rumour they're going to be
staying here a long time

SON: Oh yeah?
That's too bad

ALLECTO: They're already stealing our food
In a few days they'll be taking the roofs from over our heads
And what'll it be after that?
Your sisters?

SON: Calm down
We were here first and we'll make that very clear to them believe me

ALLECTO: Don't forget they've got the nurse on their side
She's the one who convinced the authorities they should stay
Get your men together and follow me let's go talk to them right away
They're not going to tell us what to do not in this camp

SON: Whoa I told you to calm down Mom

ALLECTO: You know what's going to happen if we don't do something
The media will show up
Then the whole world will know
After that we'll have our hands tied
We won't be able to do a thing

SON: I don't need you interfering
War and peace are a man's business
Back to your pots and pans woman

Allecto pulls her son's cigarette out of his mouth and throws it on the ground.

ALLECTO: Don't talk to your mother like that
Peace is very much my business and
I'll wage war if I chose to
And right now
I choose to

SON: Mom!
I want war with them as much as you do
I've already gathered my men I didn't wait for you to come see me about it

ALLECTO: Okay then what's the plan?

SON: For now I've forbidden anyone to go talk to them
We're figuring out our strategy

ALLECTO: A strategy for?

SON: A strategy for how to get rid of them

ALLECTO: Oh right
And what exactly is this strategy of yours?
Tell me
What will get them to leave here?

SON: Fear
Fear's the only thing that makes people run

ALLECTO: And if they're not afraid?

SON: They've fled their country
They've felt fear once and believe me they'll feel it again

ALLECTO: All right and how are you going to get your men geared up to fight?

SON: Alcohol

ALLECTO: Alcohol
What?
You're going to get them drunk that's it—

SON: They're bored they're already looking for a fight so I won't have to do much

ALLECTO: It's going to take more than that

   Pause.

Okay listen it's simple I'll tell one of your sisters to say she was raped

SON: Don't get the girls mixed up in this
And anyway it could put ideas in their heads

ALLECTO: We'll go and explain how we see things before they have the time to
   get ideas of their own

SON: I don't like it when you get worked up like this

ALLECTO: Am I going to have to whack you?
You're getting on my nerves and that's reminding me of your father and
Well that gets on my nerves even more

Suddenly sad.

He would've made them run for their lives
He would've gone and talked to them right away
He was a man oh yes a real man

SON: Okay okay don't start
I'll chase them from the camp
If only to shut you up

Scene Two

The infirmary of the refugee camp.
Aeneas and Achates with Ascanius.

LAVINIA: Here we are it's not much but you can't expect five-star accommoda-
tion in a refugee camp right so your arm please I have to do another blood
test sorry by the way my name is Lavinia I'm the camp nurse and I
Where are you from exactly
You don't have to tell me most of the refugees here prefer not to and I under-
stand completely
Are you feeling okay?
I mean better of course because well no I suppose you no it's not possible
Poisoning is serious you know I don't want to say because it's not up to me but
well that kind of drug can cause death
You were lucky we got there on time
You kept repeating a name over and over when we found you
Creusa I think it was
It's pretty
Good everything is back to normal I mean your blood pressure
So listen if you ever need well I'd be happy to—

AENEAS: How long are we going to stay in this camp?

LAVINIA: How long oh well that's ah I—
I'm not the one who can—

A long time

Pause. Lavinia gets ready to leave.

Don't stay here

AENEAS: Pardon?

LAVINIA: There's no guarantee of safety
Leave here as soon as you can

She leaves.

AENEAS: Bereo and Pyrgo

ACHATES: Nowhere to be found
I looked everywhere

Aeneas I've been made to feel we're not welcome here
Even the nurse is advising us to leave
I don't understand what are we waiting for

AENEAS: Describe the border to me

ACHATES: It's at the north end of the camp
Watchtowers every one hundred metres
A double set of chainlink fences
The first to stop people from getting out of here
The second to stop people from getting in there
Between the two
A no-man's land
Barbed wire
On top of each fence

AENEAS: This is where we're going over to the other side

ACHATES: The other side we've just been there I'm not sure I want to repeat the
experience

AENEAS: I'm talking about the border Achates

ACHATES: I know you are
Do I have to remind you the place is crawling with soldiers?
And they're under orders to shoot anyone who comes near the fences

Pause.

Did you see your father were you able to talk to him?
What did he say?

AENEAS: He told me our search would soon be over
And we'd find our new home

We can't pull this off alone
But there are men and women here who are ready to fight with us to get across
    the border
I know we can win them over
We have to Achates

Scene Three

The refugee camp.
A gathering of the clan faction.

ALLECTO: They attacked my daughter
We shouldn't be subjected to these kinds of outrages just because we don't have
    a country anymore
As long as I'm alive
No man will come and soil one of mine one of ours and not be punished for it
You saw them
They occupied our allotments received health care grabbed food right out of
    our hands and now they're raping our women
What next?
Will we have to sit by and watch these criminals cross the border before we do?
We've been waiting in this mud-infested camp a whole year now
And still no papers no legal status nothing
These newcomers aren't the only ones who have suffered
We were here first
We're already packed in here like animals
The authorities think there's room for all of us
We know there isn't room in this camp for even one more person
We have to fight tonight fight for a home we don't even own
My son will head the attack
And if they don't want to understand

Well then
Blood will flow

Scene Four

A shelter in the camp.

ACHATES: Here they come there's a lot of them more of them than us

AENEAS: Get ready grab whatever you can to use as a weapon
Shovels sticks picks

LAVINIA: They won't dare attack if I stay with you

AENEAS: I'm not sure that will stop them
Go home miss

ACHATES: Aeneas
We won't be able to hold out against them

AENEAS: We have to Achates
We are so close to our goal
It's just the other side of those fences
Nothing will make me turn back

ACHATES: I don't feel good about this

AENEAS: There's land right over there calling us

Burning rags.

ACHATES: What's that?

Aeneas tries to put them out.

AENEAS: Help me
What are you waiting for?
Help me!

ACHATES: It's starting all over again
The same flames the same burning skies the same screams in a moonless night

Leave them
Let them burn

AENEAS: Achates
Achates come on

ACHATES: Don't
Let it burn let everything burn let everything be consumed in one huge bonfire
   so we can join our families at long last
We were the cowards who ran who left who didn't fight who gave in and fled
So that we wouldn't have to kneel to them we crawled away and now look we're
   going to die here in this filth

AENEAS: Achates
This time we won't let them burn our houses
This time we won't run away

SON: Hey Florence Nightingale!
You should go home 'cause things are going to really heat up here

LAVINIA: I'll go home when your men have calmed down

SON: I can't control them you know that
Leave now or I won't be able to help you

LAVINIA: I'm staying

SON: I'm sorry to hear that
I really am

   To Aeneas.

You their leader?
Okay listen to me
I'll give you one last chance
You gather your people and you leave right away
Go wherever you want but don't come back to this camp
We won't tell the authorities you've got my word
That should give you time to get far enough away so you won't be recaptured

AENEAS: No
No one's leaving
We're staying

SON: I'm looking up at the stars and I'm thinking they're not aligned in your
  favour
Stranger
Think carefully about what you're going to do

AENEAS: No fate hangs over us
No supernatural being
No god
We are mortal
But so are you
We have a life a heart and lots of tears
So do you
Okay let's fight

SON: You'll find the land you're looking for
At the end of my arm

  Aeneas lets out a war cry.
  Charges toward the camp.
  The battle. Body to body. Silhouettes in the half-light.
  Then: a splash of blood across a canvas.
  A woman screams.
  Everything stops.

  Allecto kneels beside her son's body.

ALLECTO: This isn't you, my son
This isn't you leaving me here all alone
This isn't you dying in an unknown country
This isn't you lying here before me breathing your last
And this isn't me I'm not your mother
I'm not washing your wounds I'm not closing your eyes for the last time
If it isn't you where are you in what far-off corner of this Earth should I look for
  you where is your body where are your torn limbs
Is this all that's left of you?
Is this all is this what I crossed land and sea for?
STRIKE ME DOWN
YOU UP THERE
SINCE YOU HATE ME SO MUCH KILL ME HERE NOW

Scene Five

The camp.
Outside.

Time has passed.

AENEAS: We've decided to go tonight
There'll be more than a hundred of us
They're going to shoot but a few of us should make it through
And I'll be one of them

LAVINIA: And if you're not?

AENEAS: At least I'll have tried everything

LAVINIA: I can't let you do this

AENEAS: I know you won't notify the authorities

LAVINIA: And once you're over there?

AENEAS: I'll be safe they won't kill me
It's against the law to shoot people on sight over there

LAVINIA: And what about your child?
How are you going to get across with him?

AENEAS: I'm not taking him with me

LAVINIA: I don't understand

AENEAS: I'm entrusting you with what is most precious to me in the whole world
I know you won't betray me

LAVINIA: I can't don't do this to me don't—

AENEAS: If I don't make it to the other side
Tell him that he came from a far-off country from which he was banished by
   his own people
Tell him that his mother died in the flames of our city
That his grandfather drowned
And that his father died searching for a new country for his son

Pause.

LAVINIA: I can't make you change your mind

AENEAS: No

LAVINIA: Don't leave me alone with him

AENEAS: I promise you I won't

Achates enters.

ACHATES: Aeneas
It's time

AENEAS: Good
I'm ready

ACHATES: So am I
And I'm not afraid
We come from a dead city
And we're going to found a new empire a truly universal empire
The empire of the displaced the defeated the fugitive the runaway the immigrant
The diaspora of wanderers and exiles
The empire of those who have something broken inside them
The largest empire in the world
So dying isn't such a great tragedy

Scene Six

OLD FARMER: And that night they rushed the fences
There must have been about a hundred of them
Some of them had ladders
Others shovels for digging
The ones who were better prepared wore gloves so they wouldn't rip their hands
  on the barbed wire

Two men were the first to make it to the border
They dug at the earth with their nails
It was a mad scramble
Refugees running every which way

The siren went off the spotlights snapped on
The two men succeeded in crossing under the first fence
They started digging again
Bullets were whistling round them in the bloody night

Then one of them said
"You go first"
The other refused but his friend pushed him into the hole
A guard yelled
"Don't move or I'll shoot"
The one who was still between the two fences said
"I'm two steps away from El Dorado nothing can stop me"
So the guard fired
And the one who had spoken about El Dorado was shot

At the second fence.

AENEAS: ACHATES!
Come on come on give me your hand I'll help you

ACHATES: Go join your son Aeneas
Or all of this was to no avail
Go
Go

AENEAS: Achates my friend my brother
Speak to me please
Achates

OLD FARMER: And he lay down gently
His grave in a country with no name

Kneeling on the other side of the fence, Aeneas takes Achates's hand.

AENEAS: Your lips embrace land that isn't yours
Your mother won't come here to bury you
You'll be left to the wild birds
You'll be carried off in the raging waters of the sea hungry fish will lick your
  wounds

He raises his fists and looks up at the heavens.

We don't count because we aren't kings!
But I know that this land wasn't worthy to receive a man like you Achates

Scene Seven

Months have passed.
A piece of land.

OLD FARMER: It's a piece of land
Close to the river
The land stretches toward the sunset on the far side of the pine trees at the top
    of those hills
If you're willing to give me a hand harvesting the wheat
And if your intentions are honorable
You could settle on it

You've got blood on your hands

AENEAS: Yes but don't be afraid
I left all my hatred at the foot of a barbed wire fence

All I ask for is peace
That's what all of us ask for
We've seen enough death
We've crossed enough lands emptied by exile
We don't want to cover these plains with our bodies

OLD FARMER: Are there many of you?

AENEAS: Probably millions
But today there's only me Aeneas
My son
And a woman

OLD FARMER: Welcome Aeneas
Welcome to your land
Welcome home

Aeneas puts down his bag.

The end.

A Dialogue Between Olivier Kemeid and Yana Meerzon

YANA MEERZON: *The Aeneid* opens this collection of recent plays written in Canada that focus on the topic of immigration. In choosing these texts, I was looking for plays experimental in their approaches to language and dramaturgy. Olivier, your work was inspired by the tale of Virgil—it is not a translation but rather an adaptation. Here we're publishing it in English, translated by Maureen Labonté, as it was staged at the Stratford Festival in 2016. So my first question is very simple: Why Virgil? And why today?

OLIVIER KEMEID: I came across Virgil when reading *The Divine Comedy* of Dante. I was fascinated by that story and returned to it several times. I was specifically interested in the figure of Dante's Guide, who takes us through the circles of Hell. I was seriously troubled by the recent events in the Middle East and saw lots of connections between Virgil's poem and what happened there. I also saw many similarities between the story of my grandfather, who ran from Egypt, and Virgil's tale. It is of course not the same story, but I thought there were many overlaps. I saw the faces of my father's family in Virgil's characters. In its portrayal of the exilic voyage, Virgil's tale reminded me not only of the story of my father's family; I saw in it a universal story of exile. The cultures of Ancient Greece and Rome are very significant for me, I feel very close to them. Working on this poem also gave me a chance to touch other foundational texts of the Western world, such as Homer's *Odyssey* and *Iliad*, as I saw in them many echoes between the story of Aeneas and other exilic characters.

The play was written in 2007; I was then a playwright-resident in the Chartreuse de Villeneuve lez Avignon. In the fall of 2007, I started rehearsals with the actors here in Montréal. We started working on this play when the first part had been already written. While rehearsing here, I was writing the second part—it was very intense time for me. We were young, very enthusiastic, and we worked together in a very good creative spirit and conditions. We were in Espace Libre—a theatre that seats about 150 people—but we were very motivated and we believed in the project. We did not plan a huge production that would travel across Canada. At that point, we simply enjoyed working on it. But after the opening night, the text started to travel on its own, not only in Canada but also in Europe. In fact, since 2007, the play is constantly getting new staging, one or two different productions per year and across the world. Many people think that I wrote this play because of the current refugee crisis, because of Syria, but this is not true at all. Immigrants and refugees have existed for many years, since way before this crisis, but it becomes really fascinating to see how a play like this can differently reflect the historical time it was written in and the historical time it gets produced.

MEERZON: The very first production of this text was done by your company Trois Tristes Tigres in 2007 in French. How did the play find its way into English?

KEMEID: The CEAD (Centre des auteurs dramatiques) commissioned Judith Miller of the French Department at NYU to do the English translation. This version had many public readings in New York, and was used by Zach Fraser for his production at Talisman Theatre, presented at La Chapelle in Montréal. The Stratford team, including Bob White (the company's dramaturg) and Keira Loughran (the play's future director), read the text and recommended a new translation, more suitable for the Canadian context and less literary in its approach. We needed a text close to the stage, to the needs of the actors.

To translate for theatre is very difficult. It is not just a literary text we're dealing with, it is a text to be played by actors. So when you're translating for theatre, you have two objectives: to translate the text itself and to translate it for future staging, for the actors and for the director. To translate a text based in the music of the French language, in its orality, into English, for Anglophone actors who are not used to such style, is very difficult too. I was very enthusiastic when I learned that Maureen Labonté was chosen as the new translator. We have known each other for many years, since my time in theatre school, and I knew Maureen as one of the best translators in Canada.

MEERZON: I think I know what you are talking about. I have encountered a similar problem when I worked on co-translating Nikolai Gogol's comedy *Marriage* into English. The text needs to be speakable for the actors, so we had to seek special ways to move the music of Gogol's text into English, to seek its rhythmical equivalents in a new language. So I do see translation for theatre as a process of (en)acting the text, in which both the translator and the writer are involved. I would even call it "a form of embodiment," when a translator builds this type of visceral relationship with the original work and tries to move this sensation into a new language. Your text is very poetic, very rhythmic. What were your sources of inspiration or influence? How did you decide to work in this genre and style?

KEMEID: For me, Virgil was interesting because of the epic quality of his text. On one hand, it is a magnificent, epic story, with many layers and time periods of action. On the other hand, it is not realistic; it has this sense of everyday life but it is not like that at all. It was very important for me to show that the characters are relatable, everyday people, not kings or queens, but because of the circumstances they are forced to make extraordinary decisions and act heroically. For me, in general, realistic theatre is not very interesting; I prefer poetry and poetic forms, so Virgil was a natural choice for me. I like to engage, to play with this literary style and form; to give a character a long speech, a moment of solitude, a philosophical monologue, not to make him address the audience in some very concrete manner but rather speak to them in more abstract terms. I like this type of writing, it changes the tone of your voice. It was also a special pleasure to navigate the world of Virgil. Because it is an epic poem, I had to find new forms to recreate it in today's theatre.

In theatre, our main goal is a production—putting the text on stage, not the book. When the Stratford team worked on its staging, sometimes the text required cuts and adjustments. I was open for these changes, as I do similar cuts to my other texts as well. Sometimes your text sounds and looks good on the page, but then you come into rehearsal and the actor starts working with it, and the text doesn't do well; sometimes it is a matter of speaking, of pronunciation or stage time, so you must cut. Usually I am open for such cuts, but sometimes it becomes too much. Sometimes, when other people stage this play, it becomes too political, too close to what is happening to the refugees, but I think it is an error. I believe poetry and all those surrealist moments in the play help us realize that this is a work of art, not a political manifesto. The play is about humanity, about our errors and suffering, and is not an instrument of political fighting. For me, a playwright is more like a conductor of an orchestra or a composer of an opera, listening to the music and noises of the world and bringing them into the text. When I was writing *The Aeneid*, I was thinking of Purcell's famous opera *Dido and Aeneas*. In fact, I liked writing this text while listening to the recording of that opera.

MEERZON: Speaking of influences and intertextual references in your text, Olivier, I have a question concerning the ending of the play. Virgil's poem served, to a certain extent, as an ideological underpinning to the making of the Roman empire. Its ending is, however, unclear, but in your version it is not so. When your Aeneas reaches the new land, he is greeted by an old man who welcomes him into a new home. In response, Aeneas says: "Probably millions / But today there's only me Aeneas / My son / And a woman." I am curious to the meaning of this sentence, provided if we read it in line with Virgil's own text. What I mean is: Are you trying to suggest, in this line and image, that the exiles, the immigrants, the barbarians who are coming today will be the founders of this new empire tomorrow, a new world order to come, that we might not even know or imagine?

KEMEID: It is not a simple question. The original text was not finished; it was co-opted by Augustus for his own needs. There is this very good book, *The Death of Virgil* by the Austrian author Hermann Broch. It describes the last hours of Virgil's life, when he had to make his decision to burn his *Aeneid*, and his need to reconcile with his destiny. Broch started writing the book before the war, in 1938, during the Anschluss, when German troops were marching through Vienna. He was afraid that his book might be co-opted by the Nazis; the idea of political co-option is always present when we touch this story. I'm not interested in creating political controversy. For me, the story of Canada is not the story of an empire, really; it is not like the US, with Canadian peace missions posted outside the country and the government making an effort of accepting as many refugees as we can, on our own territory. The second question has to do with the Métis people and how they are accepted in Canada. This is very close to me, as my father is Egyptian and my mother is "une Québécoise de souche," and I myself am the product of this mix, so there my story gets included into in Aeneas's narrative. As children of immigrants, we must think about this story. It is not just about our parents; it is more about us, the children, who will be building the country together. The story is very symptomatic for my family. My parents met in 1967 at the Montréal Expo, in the German pavilion. It was very courageous of my mother to start dating someone from the Middle East; so the story of the child in *The Aeneid* becomes my story, my personal attachment to this narrative.

MEERZON: I hear in your response an interesting proposition that has to do with rethinking what today's Québec is or might be as imagined and constructed by the children of immigrants, by the second and the third generations Québécois. Can you comment on this idea?

KEMEID: It is interesting to think about this question within theatre practice, not politics. In English Canada, there is this practice of colour-blind casting, and it was fully implemented when the play was produced at Stratford. In Québec, it is not like that yet, specifically on the mainstream stages. There is a tendency to cast diverse actors, but we are truly late. What really touched me is that when Keira was casting "diverse" actors at Stratford, it was not done because of her political agenda or because she wanted to make a statement. The actors were cast because they were fitting the roles, because they were good performers, not because of the colour of their skin. I really liked this approach—diversity was not something exceptional, it was normal. In Québec, it is still different; it still takes that political gesture, that serious political decision to cast someone different. There are of course cultural and historical reasons why it is like this, but a play like *The Aeneid* allows such experiment. This would be my response to your question about mythmaking and imagining a new Québec.

MEERZON: I believe for Keira Loughran, the director of the production at Stratford, this play was a chance to talk about Canada and its history of immigration. Were you involved in making those decisions?

KEMEID: For me, it was important to give space to the director. We were there if she had any questions, but in fact it was interesting for me to stay away from the process. We were happy to consult on some cuts in the text, but didn't really discuss casting or other ideas Keira would have. I really liked the fact that Keira took a personal route to this story. I truly believe the director must be emotionally involved, not just intellectually, with their material. It was also evident that all actors involved in that staging were personally involved in this story.

But we introduced some cuts, they were necessary. For example, there are some passages in the text that have very French references, like the speech of General Charles de Gaulle or the issues of colonialism. They don't have the same resonance in English Canada. The play is not set in Québec or any other historically recognizable space. It has this sense of a Mediterranean culture and landscape, but nothing too specific. When we staged the play in Montréal these references were also somewhat lost on our audiences, specifically younger people who don't really know the history of France of that period, or the history of Québec for that matter.

Producing *The Aeneid* in different contexts I realized that the text is very much open for interpretation. When I presented it in France, there were no questions about this text coming from Québec, no cultural misunderstandings. It is really becoming a universal project. Once, there was an audience member from the Congo who told me that I wrote a truly Congolese story, about his family. In fact, it was Valentin Mitendo, a well-known figure of the Congolese theatre (RDC, Congo-Kinshasa), himself a national deputee who was one of the African experts on the CITF (La Commission internationale du théâtre francophone). For him, *The Aeneid* was the play that described exactly the situation in the Congo, and he wanted to produce it in Kinshasa with the support of the National Assembly of the Democratic Republic of the Congo, for the fiftieth anniversary of the country. I even received a tribute from our House of Common Chambers in Ottawa, proud that a Canadian play would celebrate the fiftieth anniversary of the Congo . . . Ironically, it was a sovereigntist deputee (from the Bloc Québécois) who was at the origin of the tribute . . . But finally, unfortunately, the Congolese project hasn't been realized, because—of course—of political turmoil.

But the challenge of moving this text into English has to do with different theatrical traditions of performing in French and English. In French, it is in the tradition of the neo-classical theatre, with our admiration for the structure of a phrase, a long tirade, poetry in general, and so on. In English, it is all about precision and clarity of dramatic action; at this level, translating is very difficult and contextual. For this, I had to work on clarification of certain images and ideas, certain sentences and phrases.

MEERZON: I think, during the rehearsal process, Keira was looking for a new theatrical equivalent of the poetry of your text, Olivier. Did you see it coming through in the production?

KEMEID: Yes, indeed. Keira found a new physicality in this text. She was successful in discovering this atemporal, acultural language of physical movement on stage, to go away from the particulars of any historical referents. I really liked this approach. This theatrical language really met my language of dramatic writing; it became this space of inspiration and collaboration, and it also allowed her to speak about some contemporary issues—questions of identity and history. In my own staging, I did not have time to really think about how to translate the words on the page into actions or movements on the stage. I was directing this text as I was writing it, so often movements would replace words and the other way around. I really appreciated this flow of movements in Keira's work, because mine was a little static as I did not really have time to work on the physical image of the text. I became the "writer in space" (l'écrivain de plateau), as I needed my actors to be grounded in space, I needed to see them moving across the stage to give them their dialogue. Seeing this text produced at Stratford was very special for me. It was very exciting to hear people asking whether this text was written in English. To receive such praise from the Stratford audience is a gift both for the writer and for the translator.

A Dialogue Between Keira
Loughran and Yana Meerzon

YANA MEERZON: Keira, we are discussing your staging of Olivier Kemeid's play *The Aeneid* at the Stratford Festival in 2016, in the context of the text's publication in English. My first question has to do with the history of this staging: Why Virgil and why in 2016?

KEIRA LOUGHRAN: I read Olivier's text in 2008, and I was drawn to it because of his language and the play's premise: Olivier's decision to recast the classic hero, the founder of Rome, as a refugee of today's world. It was very exciting to see that it was possible to re-examine this old story, so it would speak to the thousands of Aeneases of today's world. I thought it would be very exciting to put this world on stage. In 2013, Antoni Cimolino, in his first year as Artistic Director at Stratford, started an initiative called the Laboratory, as the company's nexus of experimentation and creation, and asked me to be its Associate Producer. His idea was to develop productions that could match the size and scope of the world of Shakespeare, but that would reflect a more contemporary practice and diverse world present in Canada today. I immediately thought of Olivier's play. As a director, I was interested in how you create this world on stage; how these thousands, whom Aeneas represents, who continue to be present and marginalized, could still make history. I went to Montréal to discuss the project with Olivier, and he confirmed my responses and impulses to his text. We started doing workshops with a small group of six or seven actors. My immediate impulse was to use the principles of ensemble storytelling and physical theatre. We used the divisions of Fire, Water, Earth, and Blood that exist in the text to develop a physical vocabulary for the production; we worked with contact improvisation to find interdependency between images, words, and movement to develop the basis for the group narrative. Later I introduced basic principles of Carnatic music (the music of Southern India) to continue the non-textual storytelling exploration. I liked this non-Western sound and tone on stage, how it underlined Olivier's poetic text.

Bob White, the company's dramaturg, recommended we commission a new translation. We asked Maureen Labonté, who had taught Olivier at the National Theatre School in Montréal, to take on this task, and the work entered a new stage. Maureen's translation was very practical and good for actors. It was perhaps less poetic than the original text, but it provided the actors with a very solid foundation for action and gave us the sense of well-rounded characters.

I went to Montréal to work with Olivier and Maureen. We looked into the text's structure and other dramaturgical questions. Olivier talked a lot about his family, how the story of his grandfather became the background of the play. We discovered that the two of us had many things in common: both of us are third-generation Canadians, assimilated but still different because we look "ethnic." Both of us are optimistic and passionate about Canada as a plural society, about its future. Both of us see compassion as a foundational value.

MEERZON: When I watched your production, my major discovery was its ending. I always thought that Olivier had imagined an open ending. But in your interpretation, it acquired a new meaning. It became quite affirmative, with the old man welcoming Aeneas into his home, onto his land.

LOUGHRAN: I always saw the ending as optimistic, as it has some potential for the future. I thought it was a story of Olivier's grandfather with the French farmer giving the land away. But I did not want the play to be set in that time. I wanted it to be in a contemporary Canada, so if we were going to talk about welcoming people to their land, I wanted to make sure it was an Indigenous character making that choice. Being generous in that way. The actor who played the old farmer, Josue Laboucane, is actually Métis. I spoke to him about my idea, even though I did not want to make it too obvious. I wanted him to be comfortable with my vision and to be actively involved in creating this character, including input on his costume. Josue drew on his own family history and gave us suggestions for some designs. If you noticed, his shoes were very special: a beaded leather vamp that would go overtop of boots that some Métis men would wear to work in the fields. So, although the text did not change that much in terms of words, the production did subtly carry that interpretation.

The last line has a symbolic meaning and we tried to show it in the production. The Old Farmer asks, "Are there many of you?" and Aeneas responds "Probably millions/But today there's only me Aeneas/My son/And a woman." But Aeneas never gives us the name of this woman or the child, so we played with the blocking to reflect this ending. At first, our final tableau presented an image of a happy family; but then we changed it to isolate just Aeneas and his son. The Old Farmer and Lavinia are there, too, but they are not necessarily one family. What we know is that this woman was given a chance to escape the camp together with Aeneas and she helped him to carry the child, but they are not necessarily a couple. At the same time, we wanted to show that Aeneas recognizes how much she has done for him and that he appreciates her.

The play portrays female characters in interesting ways. We had many discussions about this during the rehearsal process. Many of these women die or fall victim to some horrible circumstance, but I don't think Olivier wanted them to be weak. For me, their fate was determined by war, as much as the war determined the fate of Aeneas. To me, these women were integral to the story, to Aeneas's journey; they were there to make sure this journey would continue. That is why I wanted the ending to be more ambiguous, to give Aeneas and us some space for contemplation.

MEERZON: Did you introduce any other changes into the original text? Did you ask Olivier to rework anything for the production?

LOUGHRAN: We did not ask Olivier to do any major changes in the script, but we did allow ourselves to ask for edits to the existing work, and we introduced some shifts in the production, specifically connected to the character of Aeneas's son, Ascanius.

I wanted Ascanius to be a little older, not a baby, and to be present on stage, watching the whole journey. I wanted him to carry the weight of story, to show how important it is to keep its memory alive, to tell new generations about the past and not shield them from the truth, to remind them that they also carry these stories within them. To me it was vital to show that children must know the complexity of their own families' migration, and that they need to tell these stories to their kids and to as many people as possible. So in our production, we cast a young boy in the role of Ascanius, as a witness to the story. He joined Aeneas at the end, when he is arriving in Canada. Both Olivier and I have children now, they are of similar age, so we saw *The Aeneid* in a new light, as parents. I know that Olivier really appreciated this new take on his text.

In terms of the production, we cut and trimmed some lines here and there, but not much. In terms of the translation, I noticed that Maureen would change the line endings. In the original, Olivier did not use much punctuation, only the line endings. Sometimes in English, she would change that, she would join the lines. Sometimes all the words would be there but she would change where that stop might be, which was quite effective. It was very important for me to have a translator who knows Québécois theatre, who understands where its drive comes from, how it is different from the English-Canadian stage. I like Québécois theatre, it is often more visceral than English. It allows actors to embody their work differently; to go away from the psychological realism that often dominates English stages. Working with this text allowed me to draw on my own training in physical theatre, and to experiment with it. I liked this fusion of a text rooted in the French language and Québécois theatre, as well as my own interest in movement—all this representing what Canada is about, its mix of cultures.

MEERZON: This is very close to me, too, I can easily see how the poetry of this text can invite this sort of visceral response, your desire to respond to it with movement. I can also see how the actors who are trained in seeking psychological motivations for the actions of their characters might feel uncertain about the play. How did you approach such situations?

LOUGHRAN: Yes, the situations these characters are in are so extreme that "realistic" motivations or reactions are very difficult, I think. We are just too privileged. The best we can do is not judge these characters but commit to their actions—both those who flee and the authorities—based on something we can more easily relate to or understand moment to moment. I wish I could say that I would behave better than the hotel manager in this play if a group of refugees appeared on *my* doorstep. But in reality, in that kind of extremity, I don't know if I would, so I cannot judge her. This is the sort of ambiguity that this play wants us to delve into. Some of these characters are prompted to real violence. We don't know why they do it; we don't know whether they are always this violent or if their circumstances have isolated them to that extreme action.

MEERZON: This play builds on the traditions of great tragedy. Would you agree that it makes us look into the essentials of human existence, that it takes the story beyond the particulars, and that's why I think we're drawn to it?

LOUGHRAN: The text invites you to think about the humanity of each of those characters. There is this long list of refugees that Olivier puts into the text. It shows us that migration is everywhere and is not a very new phenomenon; it makes you think of what is truly human in the history of humankind.

MEERZON: I want now to ask you a question about your casting choices. You cast Gareth Potter in the role of Aeneas. This choice created some controversy, but I think it was an interesting idea specifically in the context of Stratford and its audiences. Aeneas is not your typical tragic hero driven by his own will to make great deeds. He is neither a great warrior nor a king. He is a soldier who happened to be there, who is forced by circumstance to take on the role of leader. He is an anti-hero this way. Can you talk more about your choice?

LOUGHRAN: I'm glad you picked up on this because indeed my decision was somewhat controversial, but casting Gareth Potter in this part was a true blessing. The way he conducted himself in rehearsals and the way he engaged with the material, he was truly fearless when launching into the most ambiguous and dark spaces of the character.

When we approached the casting issue, we really wanted this cast to be as diverse as possible. Gareth joined us in the very first workshops, and he was my Aeneas from the get-go. Gareth is from Montréal; he is bilingual and he knows Québécois theatre inside and out. He also knows devised theatre and physical work that I wanted to incorporate into this show. He has been working at Stratford for several seasons, and hence is familiar with its audiences. Also, he happened to be a new dad, so there were many aspects of Aeneas's character that he could tap into and investigate. But of course, casting Gareth—a white, blond guy—as Aeneas, I knew that it might be taken as some sort of statement. But I also knew that he would be my anchor and deliver the part the way I saw it.

MEERZON: What was the reaction of your "typical" Stratford audience to this play?

LOUGHRAN: The response from the Stratford audience was amazing—the show moved them; it made them think about what it means to be a migrant or a refugee, even though our lead actor happened to be a white male. But I do understand why some critics or spectators felt uncomfortable about this choice.

I often think about the difference between art and activism. I believe all art is political, but that good art embraces ambiguity, and by doing so provokes people to take action and form an opinion. The ambiguity challenges them to do something in their own world, and this becomes an avenue for activism.

I am very happy this text reached the Stratford audience, but I was worried about all those scholars of antiquity who would find our production too divergent from Virgil's text. My goal was to stay loyal to the story that Olivier was telling, not the original by Virgil, but I knew what expectations a typical Stratford spectator might have. It was a relief to see these academics slowly falling under the spell of our production and wanting to come back to it, to see it one or more times. I understand that many of them took this play as our response to the crisis in Syria and so found it very topical, but I also think they were taken by our artistic work.

MEERZON: You mentioned earlier that *The Aeneid* is a very Canadian play because it proposes a vision of Canada as a nation embracing diversity, beyond the ideological implications carried by the word "multiculturalism." Does it mean that this play and your production of it invite us to revisit the ideas of nation, nationhood, and nationalism in Canada today?

LOUGHRAN: Yes, exactly, it was Olivier's idea at the time and it became mine as well. I'm directing a play, *The Komagata Maru Incident* by Sharon Pollock, for Stratford's 2017 season. It is set in Vancouver in 1914, and I also set it in 1914 but with a very diverse cast. It seems that we don't know our own history: in 1914, Vancouver was very diverse, my family was already there, but the city was incredibly ghettoized and racist. But we don't know that. At school, we learn the story of white Canada, so for me it is important to reinstate this other story as a part of Canada's historical narrative. The effects of internalized racism are very present in today's Canada, and we see it both in Olivier's play and in this one. By telling these stories, I hope we can help people better understand the impact of these experiences: what it means to be marginalized if you are new to the country and trying to become a part of this nation. It is important to remind our audiences that everybody in this country comes from somewhere else, apart from Indigenous people, who have suffered even more than immigrants from the impact of colonization. If we are to continue living together, we must decide what determines nationhood, what truly makes Canada a special place. *The Aeneid*, in my opinion, was exactly the play to allow us to raise these questions about Canada and its future.

Settling Africville

by George Elliott Clarke
(with print dramaturg Diana Manole)

For Geraldine Elizabeth Clarke
(1939–2000)
&
William Lloyd Clarke
(1935–2005)

Two Believers, Both African Baptists

Settling Africville was commissioned by the Africville Heritage Trust and was produced by Juanita Peters and Marty Williams for the Alderney Landing Theatre in Dartmouth, Nova Scotia, in September 2014 with the following creative team:

Naomi-Joy Blackhall: Bailey/Calypso/Postill
Jacob Sampson: Preston/Tar Mouth/Dude
Drew O'Hara: Howe/Styron
John O'Keefe: Haliburton/Dalhousie/Drunk

Director: Juanita Peters
Design: Susan Macdonald
Costume Design: Andrea Ritchie
Sound Design: Greg Simm

A Note on the Text

Africadian English boasts elemental ornaments. It is a speech too plain to be poetic, but yet cannot be prose. In sensibility, it is nearer to *Beowulf* than Chaucer, but edges toward the biblical between the twain.

The plot echoes history, but executes ecstatic liberties in chronology. Save for Styron, the characters exist in history: Howe and Haliburton were friends; Howe used to debate Preston; and Haliburton's racist tale, "The Black Brother" (1840), likely targets Preston.

As for the settling of Africville, Nova Scotia, the play is credible: the "African" settlement began as soon as there were free Negroes wishing to reside near waged jobs in downtown Halifax, the colonial capital. It was a sensible location for them to settle, for it even offered marine access to the central market. Thus, a trickle of Planter-era Blacks (1750s) and a dash of Black Loyalists (1783–92) and a smattering of Jamaican Maroons (1796–1800) would have lived at the north end of Campbell Road (now Barrington Street) on the shores of Bedford Basin. But we do know that the War of 1812 brought to Halifax a flood of Black Refugees, many of whom either "founded" Africville, or if deposited elsewhere, migrated soon to the site of the best work—and, when necessary, begging—opportunities, namely, Halifax/Africville. By 1828, Joseph Howe was writing about black women selling strawberries by Bedford Basin (the Africville site). By 1849, Campbell Road Baptist Church was erected as a result of the apostolic efforts of Rev. Richard Preston (who landed in Nova Scotia in 1816) and his construction of the African Baptist Association of Nova Scotia (established in 1853). At this point, Africville is still "Campbell Road," and its church is not yet "Seaview." But there is a black community there, and its members are slowly being perceived and dubbed as a little Africa, supposedly alien, yet stubbornly rooted. As they remain.

George Elliott Clarke
Harvard University
November 2013

The splendour of beauty is lasting.
—John La Rose

He disports himself amid his northern snows fashioning his own brand of Christianity.
—Luís Vaz de Camões

Players

Black

(Father) Richard Preston: "Apostle to the African Race"
Louisa Bailey: poetess
Mary Postill: "runaway"
Dude: ignoramus
Tar Mouth: servant to Haliburton

White

Bull Styron (also "Dr. Bull Styron")
Ninth Earl of Dalhousie: Governor of Nova Scotia
Drunk ("Sam Slick," or Haliburton)
Thomas Chandler Haliburton: judge and author
Joseph Howe: journalist and printer

Act I

Scene One

A slave market in rural Virginia. 1815. Louisa Bailey, twenty, is to be sold on an auction block by her master, Bull Styron, thirty. She is black, beautiful, tough, and witty; a gag covers her mouth. He is white, half in love with her, but an ice-hearted capitalist, too. As he speaks, he fondles Bailey, who winces and flinches, but cannot do more for her hands are—literally—tied. Nor can she offer verbal protest, for she is gagged. She is an ironic version of the Goddess of Justice.

STYRON: Stead of breakin soil,
Bleedin-heart Baptists just break wind.
They whine bout pickaninnies split from mammies,
Bout lil suckers ripped off black dames' tits,
But that's just business!
Why don't Northern snivellers weep and whine
Over all the natchal-bo'n dead,
Them stillborn babes tossed out as trash?

I, Bull Styron, of Tidewater, Virginia, Dixie,
Hear the banshee howls of black bitches
Watchin their brats sold off,
And I do feel bad. Promise!
But business be business,
And slave sales yield cold, gold coin.

That's real truth this War of 1812,
When Britain patrols, controls, our Yankee coast,
And I can't get no new slaves
Save those I get off the old slaves:
My pleasure is to plunger some dark gal's snatch,
So I hatch homemade, gold-skin profit . . .

(A woman is one-third posture, one-third perfume,
and one-third paint.)

Eh, Louisa Bailey?
Whaddya think of that?
Cat got your tongue?
Your puss might get my tongue!

Sure! Slave trade scuttles babe from mom—
And wife from husband—
But folks' roots are always scraggly:
Blood don't run straight.
Bloodlines are unruly, all tangled up.

Yes, a buyer splits mama from child,
But gold always outshines blood.

And it demands expertise to breed niggers—
To turn a black man's wife into a white man's whore—
Or let black bulls stun and stud her—
And still avoid pricey defects in limbs
That devalue the Rape-bred pup . . .

> *Styron forces Bailey to bend over. He lifts her dress and runs his bullwhip*
> *between her thighs. She is shocked erect by his violation. He chuckles while she*
> *screams through her gag. Styron slaps her and wags a finger to counsel silence.*
> *He removes the gag.*

Aye, Louisa B., I've a taste for skirt.
I like the caramel milk skin
And to gulp dark meat
And slurp sloppy juice.

BAILEY: You have a wife—milky as can be!
Why bother us black maids
Who you view and use like "beasts"?

STYRON: You, Louisa Bailey, be resilient, difficult.
Maybe cos you magine yourself a poetess.
Ha! God damn who ever gave you the alphabet!

And ya choose to love a slave boy
Defiant as an axe striking a redwood:
Preston!

BAILEY: No! I love a man,
A strong, dark man,
Strong and dark like iron.

He is hot-blooded when he dreams of me,
But cold-blooded when he "goddamns" you.

STYRON: I'll break his granite words,
All his bumf.

I'll crack whips to bloody his black ass.
Til he drops heavily, heaving,
As clunky as a put-down animal.

His won't be minor hurts either.
He'll feel a lust for defecation,
Piss salt and vinegar . . .

No room for a slave preacher on a proper plantation—
And no room neither for black poetess cogitation!

BAILEY: You best attend Preston's preachin plus my poems!
To excuse your inexcusable self from Hell!

Preston arrives, brandishing a bullwhip. He's dark, handsome, twenty. There's a yellow glow about his head: hint of a halo.

PRESTON: As my Lord and Saviour Jesus Christ saw fit to whip
Moneychangers out his Father's temples,
So I'll make you, Bull Styron, as jumpy
As a cathedral on Easter.

BAILEY: Flee, Richard, flee!
Forget about me!

PRESTON: No! I demand *our* liberty!

STYRON: Boy, nigger, you gonna die, Preston!

Styron brandishes his whip. Two whips lash out in opposite directions: a duel. But
Preston gets the better of Styron, whipping the white man's whip out his hand.

Dare you take one more breath near me!
Your flesh will be dirtier than it is,
Once you're chopped up and fed to pigs.

PRESTON: All of us pulled from the womb
Get soon or late shovelled into dirt.
We're loved at the start and mourned at the end.
But the body isn't loveable—
Especially yours.
I won't hesitate to lash your flesh!

STYRON: You're not a Christian, but a hot-head criminal—
Spawn of a shitty pappy and a big-titty mammy!

PRESTON: You dare wash my mama with your filthy mouth?

Preston whips Styron, and he flees. Preston frees Louisa's hands. They kiss.

BAILEY: Richard, you must flee!
Bull Styron won't rest til you're a grainy corpse,
Seething with maggots.

His anger will bottom out at whipping
And top out at hanging.

Dogs bark in the distance, but the noise approaches, closer and closer. The lovers
regard each other with alarm.

PRESTON: I hate leaving you to such a hateful man!
Rather, I'd have us both look invisible here
By mutually darkening a different shore.
A place where readin, writin be legal.

BAILEY: You run east, I'll take the west:
Confusin darn dogs is best.

PRESTON: What if Bull Styron—"BS"—captures you?

BAILEY: I don't fear his bullshit!

He's an ape. I'm an angel;
And you're my Adam.

Bull bother me, he'll bother no one again:
I'll hammer a nail in his skull—
Like did that good lady in the Good Book,
Doin in a bad man.

Sounds of gunshots and barking.

PRESTON: Let's try for the British boats offshore!
Ferry us to Liberty!

BAILEY: As a couple, we're crippled. You go, solo:
I'll follow, today, tomorrow, day after tomorrow.
Go!

They kiss, vamoose, zigzagging as opposites. Gunshots and barks close in.

Scene Two

A Halifax dock. A slave sales podium. Beside it, a gallows. Bailey stands amid barrels, casks, nets, and wooden boxes. Peripheral paraphernalia. Part of a ship's rigging and deck is near. The year is 1817. Bailey is liberated, but seeking Preston.

BAILEY: Look at this goddamn bric-a-brac—
Evil clutter used to sell off black folk.
This city of Halifax
Is a real hell—in fact.
If only I could set this whole waterfront on fire!

Bailey produces and lights a lamp.

But if I burnt down this tear-jerking port,
They'd catch me, hang me:
I'd lose my Richard for good.

I trust he got away slick and clean
From Bull—"Bullshit"—Styron,
Massa as stingy as a ghost.

I did get away,
And I guess Richard reached Halifax here,
But where he be now,
Only God doth know.

Does Richard miss his Lousia Bailey—
His right flighty gal, his poetess,
Up from Chesapeake Bay?

True: I take zero shit.

Styron thought I be his "ginger blessin,"
His "lollygaggin sweetness"!
Wished to tump me in his bed
And pump me big with child.

But I hid a secret penknife, necessary
To gash him a flood of cuts, if necessary.

(Prefer a pen to write,
But a penknife to keep the right to write!)

Backra, the light-footed jackal, creep,
Try to make me accept his dirt.
Took my blade and stuck him good.
Quick had I a greasy dress,
And had to up and run,
His blood slippin off me like I was leaky.

(Oh God, did he die?
Dear God, I hope so!)

When I run, I ran.
Skedaddled to the shore
And paddled to a British brig.

We came to floating upon sail-shaded crests,
A rumpus of water, the salty utility,
Our throats burning with a sun-lit thirst.

Landed in Nova Scotia last May
Mid weight of guano and slick of slime.

Nova Scotia still got a bunch of slavers—
Scarlet eyes and scarlet lies—
All as edgy as a baby,
For they can't keep hold their slaves,
Cos we blacks steal away
With clockwork proficiency.

Bailey mounts the slave sale podium.

Still, th'Atlantic is the swallower of tears—
So it must be saltier now—
All them Africans drowned dead,
But first bawling, sobbing, weeping,
Pourin salt tears into salt water:
Lavish murk.

Fog rolls in, obscuring even Bailey's lamp. Preston materializes. He's dressed as a preacher.

PRESTON: I hear a woman's voice.
Sounds an awful lot like Louisa's—
My Louisa, poetess.
But I can't see a thing in this fog.
Haven't seen her in two years—
Not since 1815.
Did she get away?
Did she scape?
I think of her every second—
With every heartbeat and breath.
How I long for her still!

The fog dissipates, carrying Preston offstage in tandem.

BAILEY: Yep, I'm talkin bout slavery:
Can't help it:
It's how blacks reached America, ain't it?

Packed off from Africa,
Stacked atop each other like kindling,
Stored side by side like cutlery,
And whored about.

Blacks were locked down all over America:
The Dutch/French/Spanish/British works.

Then, forty years back, Yankees shot lead
At the Royal Majesty's men,
Loosed cascades of blood and tears . . .
Their white butts wailed for freedom.

Not that I weep for the Brits!
Or pray for the Yanks:
Some are routed, some are uprooted,
But all are en route to Hell.

Look it! Washington, a king minus a crown,
Was an inhuman monarch,
Odious as the crowned heads of Europe.

Now, this War of 1812 is pungent legions,
Ale, ailments, and lesions.
But I can't say I give a damn who beats whom
So long as we black folk can breathe free.

Now, some of us wept to leave America—
This War of 1812 and all such bother—
But we ain't got no choice in it—
Just like long-gone slaves had no choice.

See? To beat down Uncle Samuel,
John Bull grab us and ship us up north
To this here "Nova Scarcity."

Brits call us "refugees,"
And once I thought the word named our colour—
Like we're fudge—
Brown, black, sweet, nurturing fudge.
But now I know "*refugee*" means
Someone who's flyin to safety.

I got a mouth and mind
And a mind to speak my mouth.

So, lemme tell ya bout "Nova Scarcity":
Make that "Scar City."

A white Drunk shambles onstage and accosts Bailey.

DRUNK: Whodya think y'are, you molasses lass,
You tarbaby tart, you wench?
Sure got a lotta lip.
Maybe you got a hot tail, too?

Bailey swings her lamp to light up the man. She steps back, pulls out her penknife.

BAILEY: Better hotfoot it, mister man!
I'll stick this knife up your ass:
Give you a red-hot tail!

DRUNK: Tarnation! Can't see why Gov Dalhousie
Let niggers land here and take lands here.
Landsakes! Ya's ornery, lazy, and talk bout God
Like He's your Pal.

BAILEY: Humph! You folks stole Red folks' land!

Now get out my face 'fore ya find my blade
All erectile in your rectum!

Bailey waves the penknife and the Drunk staggers off.

Union Jack don't mean jack to me.
George III be a third-class king.

So we blacks got to Nova Scarcity as scruffy flotsam;
Were beached on pebbles, shells, seaweed,
Hissing with surf,
Falling silent where sand begins.

We came ashore to bitter, white winds:
We thought that snow was sugar!

Worse were our welcomers—
As bad-tempered as an execution—
Just like that drunk Jack Tar.

It's a bumpy existence here.
Just touch and go.
No gross of food to top a pot.

Humph! No time for tears.
Folks have to burn twigs for heat,
Dig holes for poop.
Get a scanty fire goin,
Ply pitch to keep out rain.

Otherwise, we gotta eat hard ruins,
Erect headstones stead of huts:
But that's one way to put down roots!

Up yonder Beechville
Or out back Preston—
A settlement where Maroons once were
And where my man might be—
People give the earth civic prickings—
To interpose potatoes mid pesky flowers.

(But Love is oblivious to weeds.)

Geez, I miss Richard, my Preston, right hard.
Befo we got split by splittin from Styron,
My man took a whip to bullshitter's ass
Like King Jesus did the moneychangers.
Richard had to run while he could.
I had to run after, later.
I pray one day to give him
A wife's happy, weeping answer,
"Yes, yes, yes, yes, yes, yes, yes . . . "

Mr. Richard Preston, my man,
Got a silver tongue in a golden mouth.
How I pray, good God, to taste it!

If I ever see my man again, I'll ask,
"Where was you
When you wasn't
Where you was?"

  The Drunk reels back.

DRUNK: I'll be your sweet man, girly;
You just be my hot chocolate!

Bailey swings her lamp menacingly.

BAILEY: Come closer, sir, so I can scald you
With this lamp oil:
Then you'll be "hot milk"!

Drunk goes away again.

Some folks say they love Nova Scotia.
I say they lie—big time.

This is the kind of place where, when you land,
Ya gotta say,
"Someone drank up all the wine
And ate up all the salt ham,
And left us neither dram nor morsel."

Halifax is a flea on the bitch that's Britain:
It roars like a lion, but it's really a kitten.
No, Britain's a bitch—all flea-bitten.
Her sailors curse when they think they're spittin.

Hmmm!
I'm gettin back into a poetess mood!

Lord Dalhousie, forty, portly, top-hatted and jackbooted, arrives. We hear his
horse whinny and his carriage creak to a stop. He doffs his top hat to Bailey.
She curtsies. He steps into her lamplight.

Lord—Governor—Dalhousie!
Why I merit this pleasure?

DALHOUSIE: At ease, Louisa, gal, I just need to question you
About you people, you Blackie Yanks.

BAILEY: We're not "you people"!

DALHOUSIE: You people remain a cogent problem.
Your complaints are like brackish coffee.
Every other settler fits in, but not your type.
It's as if you're in a fog.

BAILEY: Pardon me, but our funds are fog:
That's the core collapse, the chief crisis, right there!
Give us tools, seed, wood, letters,
And fog will turn into silver coins.

DALHOUSIE: Well, you Negroes make quarrelsome farmers.

BAILEY: It's hard to farm where the topsoil's stone.

DALHOUSIE: The Negro is a nettlesome fisherman.

BAILEY: It's hard to fish where the water's weeds.

DALHOUSIE: You Negroes are really just "loveable children."

BAILEY: Our masters are damn child molesters.

DALHOUSIE: Why must you always spit insolent talk?

BAILEY: Blacks sweat and bleed to build Nova Scotia.
We're gold nuggets, but you treat us like dirt.

DALHOUSIE: Just read what Thomas Chandler Haliburton says bout
You Black Refugees.

BAILEY: I don't credit his mouth as bein any cleaner
Than a nun's anus.

DALHOUSIE: No, Louisa! Girlie, you blackies must learn
Some us white gentry know you inside out.

BAILEY: Haliburton, who loves to champion slavery,
Should be horsewhipped and bullwhipped,
Then see his kids sold off to serve blacks folks for life,
While blood limps down his face.

DALHOUSIE: Haliburton's writin satire, funny stuff.
Don't take him seriously!

BAILEY: Really? The man's comedy hits us as pointed
And hard as spikes.

DALHOUSIE: If ya don't like what he gotta say,
You people ought to be raisin grape vines
Outta snow clusters and clumps.
Or cut down remnant pine trees
Outta each April-green niche,
So you got heat and light come winter.

BAILEY: One rotten pen is Haliburton.
I should take my penknife to him!
He's a purple-face, redneck pain in the ass—

DALHOUSIE: Louisa Bailey, you go way too far!

BAILEY: Crucial is clarity.
Nothing's so crucial as clarity.

Dalhousie tries to kiss Bailey. She squirms free.

DALHOUSIE: To be happy, you need wine's purple sleep.
Step into my coach and try a swig.

BAILEY: And couch in your coach?
Uh uh, I'm foresworn.

DALHOUSIE: To a ghost. This man, Preston, who's likely
Returned to what he knows best: lassitude.

BAILEY: No, no, he's as active as a woman—
We who give birth, nurse, nurture,
And give mates pleasure and children comfort.
We tend bed, bath, cradle, and table.
And Mr. Preston, he tends God's word!

DALHOUSIE: If you loved me, you'd be as free as a bird!

BAILEY: If I loved you, I'd be absurd.
Sir!

Dalhousie retreats. His carriage departs.

Scene Three

*Preston is in Preston. A sign should read "North Preston." A church is visible
behind him. A black Jesus Christ looms in the stained glass window.*

PRESTON: My faith warns, "Sinner's death is forever."
Gotta have redemption,
Or you ain't got nothin;
Gotta have the Cross,
If you wanna have the Crown.
But ya gotta have Liberty,
If you wanna have Love.

That's why I rowed myself to British boats
Off the Virginny coast.
I had to "borrow"—*ahem*—a boat,
Then row, row, row,
Away from Sorrow . . .

My ol massa, I call him "Antichrist."
Mr. Styron was monumental drunkenness—
He'd waste no alcohol, but use it for milk—
And all his thoughts were burps and grunts.
Had a face like pain,
And his salty, assaultin eyes
Saw black gals as ceaseless molasses,
He could slosh and seesaw and spread
Cross his sheets white as bread.

I pray my Louisa Bailey escaped
His capacious rapacity,
His rapacious capacity!

Where's my Louisa now?
If you see her, tell her that I, Richard Preston,
Outta Virginia, too,
Love, love, love her still.

When she blushes, I see rose petals aflame;
And then her scent is milk, and my feelins hot.

But children are the fruit of Purity.
(Slavery is a desert of such fruit.)

I come ashore here to "Nova Scarcity."

Studyin on bein a minister—
Baptist—
Coloured Baptist—
To preach the Gospel frank,
My speech too sassy, pungent, for bleached pulpits.
But I say I follow Christ—
And God the Father—
For namin things as things is.

What brings out Believers
Is when they hear
Forked-tongues bein called forked-tongues,
Cutthroats bein called cutthroats,
Masters bein called torturers,
Overseers bein called rapists.

My words are treasonous
Wherever slaves can read
Or hear.

Our patois injures schoolmarms' blackboards
And hurts reporters' spelling.
But that's cuz a black tongue
Is too honest for whitey's ears.

And Louisa—poetess—got that same Virtue!

We were both slaves way too long—
Labourin to make white men rich,
Labourin in someone else's vineyard.

Had to get away
Come that War of 1812,
When Yankee and John Bull got to shootin
Or cuttin each other . . .

So, the contest twixt "Man o' War"
And "Manifest Destiny"
Freed me to slip away
And home to this homely redoubt.

Where might I see my love—
Lovely Louisa?
Here? So I pray.

Yet, "Nova Scarcity" got the substance
Of a shark-chewed-up gull;
Here rats squeak like seagulls
And seagulls squeal like rats.
Every summer feels like a steady winter—
With flowers of frost.
All our land grants be mosquito farms, really,
Just swamps and stones.
Even if a crop appears,
Mice bite it off at the roots.

The Drunk reappears.

DRUNK: You black blankety-blanks got liver lips
And rubbery, hubbub tongues.
Just shut up—and drink up—
As King Georgie commands!

PRESTON: Halifax liketh to amuse itself with hangings—
Why don't you "hang out"—hang yourself—
Where Africville is growin?

Or come to church and hang out with Christ?

DRUNK: Why should I go where you black people go?
That's hell!

PRESTON: I hear Halifax is ideal for suicide:
Just jump off a wharf and start to breathe.

The Drunk shambles off.

Over on Bedford Basin,
At the crooked narrows,
That crooked strait,
There's Negro Point,
Where dozens of freed Negroes now camp,
Preferring to tramp or hike downtown
For odd jobs
Than try to rear roses out of shale.

I trust in God!
The Creation proves He's no lunatic architect,
But got plans for us,
Even if conclusions seem elusive.

Funny thing: When I landed here,
A year and a half back,
I had no place to go.
But I told folks my surname;
They directed me out here to this spot—
Of desolation plus beautifying—
Where the settlers call their rudimentary gardens
And huts,
My family name, "Preston."
Coincidence? No: Miracle!
I went knockin on crude, flimsy doors,
Boards and nails hardly able to block a breeze,
And no one could spare a room.
I thought I'd bed down under the stars,
Under a pine,
Beside a fire warring with wind,
When I come to the last house in the last of the light.
Rattled the door as my fist thudded.
Old, grey woman came and shone a lamp.
She looked at me, said she, too, had no room.
A tear started as I started away.
Then she said, "Wait!"
She fingered the starry scar on my cheek:
Asked, "You know Bull Styron and what he like?"
I told about Tidewater and my sold-off mama,
And we both fell to our knees, weeping,

For we knew, instantly, that she was my mom
And I was her son.

If God can bring me to my mother,
Then He can bring Louisa to me.

> *Now the Drunk staggers back, to clutch onto Preston. He's a paleface Tar Baby.*

DRUNK: If you're not ever drunk, preacher,
You're too soon dead.

PRESTON: Rather have the golden sunrise and sunset
Than a golden ale!
That's the devil's brew,
Pull ya straight down to Hell!

DRUNK: Preacher, gold got spendin power.
Ale's got elbow-bendin power!

Rain paddles us,
Sun straddles us,
For extra nothing.

Just spoiled people
Need a steeple
To point right from wrong.

PRESTON: Don't you make Halifax
A true Hell-in-fact?

DRUNK: The violent confederacy is a wife
And kiddies—
Odours soured of coal and onions;
A butter knife used as a sword.

PRESTON: You think drink solves everything?

DRUNK: Hate to say it,
But truth is truth:
Drink dissolves practically everything.

Try it! Don't deny it.

> *The Drunk saunters off.*

Scene Four

Bailey stands outside the Nova Scotia Legislature Palladian-style building. She speaks through a primitive bullhorn before a sign that reads, "Africa for the Africans!"

BAILEY: When will Slavery—
Crime Against Humanity—end?

When will we receive Reparations—
Compensation—
In millions of pesetas, pesos, pounds, guilders, francs, and bucks—
To repay Europe's theft of Africa's labour?

When will White Rapists of Black Women
And White Thieves of Black Children be shot down
Where they stand
Or hanged from the closest tree?

When will Oppression and Imperialism end?

VOICE: Shut up! You're a loudmouth!
Trust the British Crown!

BAILEY: I can't! Only a fool could!

George III is white Death in a scarlet robe
With blood-purpled lips.
His Empire's a sunrise to sundown plantation.
And his bastard brat America's no better!

VOICE: You black wench! You preach sedition!
Careful! I'll summon the soldiery!

BAILEY: I call on my Black Brothers, Black Sisters:
Remember Phillis Wheatley's bony letters
And Crispus Attucks's great faith,
How they defended all Liberty
In bleating winds
While flames squirted, squirmed, from cannon.

Both drove off fleas, but welcomed flies.
They knew a slave hosts fleas,
But a dead fighter hosts flies.

If we be more than kind beggars,
We must cast off hurts,
And craft ourselves rough delights,
Hacking crops into the earth
(This tundra is more dirt than snow),
And raise shelters from crude foundations—
Prayers, songs, dreams,
Before we be, finally, as inconspicuous as grass.

DUDE: Yo, woman! Where you man?
Ya talk too much—too much shit!
Rile up whitey so he fire our asses.
We hard up for jobs, land, and cash as is!
Why ya beggin more trouble?

"Africa for Africans?" Shit!
Ain't nothin in Africa, specially for Africans!

BAILEY: You talk like you brainwashed!
Like you're a Zombie, brother!

DUDE: Quit actin like a mutant schoolmarm!
You should be married—and mute!

　　Dude shakes his fist at Bailey. She sticks her bullhorn in his face.

BAILEY: Even if I was mute, I'd not be dumb—
Not like you!

DUDE: If you weren't a woman, I'd hit ya!

BAILEY: If you were a man, you'd join me!
Your type of spineless Negro is exactly our problem.
I want a black man with backbone, brain, and Bible wit.

DUDE: All ya do is bitch and bow-wow!
Bow-wow like a bitch!

BAILEY: Better that than bow to my knees,
Bendin my backside to some white boy.

DUDE: I's gonna come up upside your head and clip ya!

VOICE: Go on up there, boy, and clip that wench!
She makin all ya niggers look bad!
And ya wonder why we whites don't respect yas!
Black gals got the balls black boys wish they had!

Bailey brandishes her penknife.

BAILEY: While you're clippin my head, I'll be slicin your dickhead,
Then writin my name in your blood.

Dude harrumphs away.

Scene Five

Dalhousie is in his Halifax study. His maid, Mary Postill, joins him at the end. She is his concubine. Dalhousie struts before a giant globe emblazoned with the word "BRITISH": it girds the world. He also parades before a giant world map: The word "BRITISH" spans the wall-size sheet.

DALHOUSIE: Preston's voice rolls rivery with rhythm.
So un-Scottish a New Scottish man:
He cometh to Nova Scotia
To speak back to Nova Scotians;
To make history,
And not to study it!

But his watery itinerary—
Escape and voyage to these shores—
Is an experiment in mischief,
If he plumb won't understand
Immigration is class warfare:
It's violence against the already settled,
Who must be uprooted and robbed
To make way for the new settlers;
Or th'already settled must oppress

Th'incoming settlers,
Render em slaves, servants, serfs.

Check the Original People here
In what they called "Megumaage,"
In a city they called Chebucto:
The Mi'kmaw—or Indians—prove perishable
And are already mainly obediently dead,
And our scientists intrigue to dig up their graves
And raid their tents,
Send th'artifacts to the British Museum.
And we take their land,
By treaty synonymous with theft,
And we scalp em if they protest,
Axing out their brains if they sob too much.

Now, Preston runs a considerable congregation
Of coloured people.
But we whites won't let his black pioneers muck up
Our cemeteries' white bones.

As His Majesty's Governor of Nova Scotia,
I, th'Earl of Dalhousie,
Propose we tame Negroes by culture—
Agriculture, silviculture, pisciculture . . .

I'll have em eat cold, sparklin snow,
Gnaw no grits or greens,
Chew no bread or beans,
No hunk of beef,
No good helpin of pork,
If they won't break backs
Diggin up gypsum
Or pitchin turds on fields.

Why should the Government of Nova Scotia
Toss the blacks bread in the streets?

If the Black Refugees won't take
The work we have to give,
Let em starve
Til crows chow down on their bony hides.

Th'outcrops they do work
Yield dust and thistles,
Inedible mosquitoes, inevitable maggots.
So, the blacks fail to set roots in slime.

But still they breed broods of brats—
Squalls of girls, storms of boys.

But our State can show its might
And smack em with shackles,
Shellac em with swords.

Preston and his ilk think they're as clever as fungi,
As surreptitious as mushrooms,
To cling to this land where they've no roots.
But their presence is only tolerated.

Gold demands harsh government.
(Statecraft is a brand of witchcraft.)

A governor—like me—must be like Confucius:
Put stock in potatoes (not poetry);
Balance books even if bellies get upset.
(Anyway, stomach cramps make for dinky coffins.)

Too, I know sailors and slaves make slippery citizens—
Unruly as air-strangled cod—
But I remind robbers and rebels and ruffians
That the noose is an itchy necklace,
And the gallows sits next the auction block
Smack dab on the Halifax docks.

(Sometimes, a black steps off the auction block one day
And climbeth the gallows steps the next.)

And I suspect that, just like the Loyalist blacks,
The Refugees will petition to slip to Sierra Leone—
That mountain range that pierces clouds and soaks up rain—
To people that shore,
Emerald as Madeira,
Where the ocean arrives as an austere sparkle—
Like furrows and furrows of diamonds . . .

Mary Postill enters. She bears a drink tray. Dalhousie embraces her meaning-fully as he takes the drink.

POSTILL: Guvner, I got Madeerra for ya. Heard ya menchun it.

DALHOUSIE: Merry, merry Mary, you're my dearie, dairy dear:
You suck my "ice cream"; I lap up your "milk."

POSTILL: Suh?

DALHOUSIE: I mean, you pleasure me unto a froth!
I churn your bowl to get good broth.

POSTILL: I know you like to lick my bowels . . .
But I don't tell no soul, Guvner!

DALHOUSIE: That's a good maid!
The way we sleep, there's never sloth.
If I'm a flame, then you're a moth.

But, tell me, Mary Postill, how you see that black priest!
Preston!

POSTILL: I make my livin with ya, Lord Dal:
I make no excuses for Dicky Preston,
Who makes too much noise
And too little sense.

Dalhousie drains his drink and sets the glass back on the tray. He slaps Postill's derriere.

DALHOUSIE: Right you are! Now, freshen my glass.

Postill curtsies and exits.

Ah, Richard Preston!
That showman is disappointing:
He proves the poor are poor
At economics
And even poorer
At finances.

The dollar sign is a serpent in a gilded cage.
That's a fact.
But these folks just get fangs in their butts:
They're stupid about work and wealth.

If Preston's Black Refugees
Don't wanna go about as naked and bony
As cockroaches—
All hard shell and sour guts;
If they want to breakfast on tidbits and lunch on full plates;
Let em work for whatever wage we'll pay.

Moreover, I'm sick of the bedlam in Parliament,
The shrieks and curses in the House of Commons,
The unparliamentary boos and catcalls in London
Because Whitehall fantasizes
Nova Scotia can accommodate the black scum
And sewage of the War of 1812.

Postill returns with a fresh glass of Madeira.

Mary, you're a commendable slut—
A nice, flexible urchin.

POSTILL: Haps I'm still a virgin.

DALHOUSIE: *(laughing)* You're uncertain?

POSTILL: No one's called a doctor to see.

DALHOUSIE: *(laughing)* Your discourse proves my point:
Your type is natural comical.

A blackamoor can make white rum,
But still he's worth less than a keg of white rum.

POSTILL: And a black nigger can piss out white rum!

DALHOUSIE: And his horse piss quite negates the original sugar.

Come, Mary! Help off my boots!
Be my sweet, sable bootblack.

Mary grunts with the effort.

Everywhere I peep round Halifax,
I see so many blackened characters,
That all our English sugar
Is almost displaced by pepper.
The Refugees are a flock of scorpions—
A murder of crows—
Clamourin for food, wood, and good
Shelter that's not helter skelter . . .
But our money supply isn't endless,
And our goodwill's already run out.

POSTILL: But I please ya, guvner, don't I?

DALHOUSIE: You're a masterful mistress, Mary,
With hair like Medusa's,
Not full of serpents, but currents—
Black lightning come to life.

He pats her head and then pours her some wine.

POSTILL: Bread and wine make a feast,
But bread is best at breakfast,
While wine's good for toast
And roast
Anytime.

DALHOUSIE: Now I'm sated in belly, but not in bowels,
And want voluptuous kisses
And thy Negress's pink nautilus.

POSTILL: You want to be pointedly naughty—
Make jolly my honeypot? Eh?

DALHOUSIE: I want us to be as festive as a beehive:

Come, fall, sprawl, now, crooked—
So you can be unstayed, unhooked,
And no intolerable blushing!

I want to graze skin as divine as pollen,
And smell all your little scents,
In our jocular wrangling.

POSTILL: Bull-like suh, ya bust china in our tangling!

*Dalhousie leans Mary down on the chaise longue, then extinguishes the candles
and lamp. Sound of tussling and then of breaking china and glass.*

DALHOUSIE: Mary, there's only one way for you to pay
For this broken china and smashed glass!
Only one way!

Scene Six

*Preston is on the Halifax docks, ready to weigh anchor for London. We hear the
ack-ack of crows; the squall of seagulls. Sails bluff, rigging creaks.*

PRESTON: I cross an ocean that's gold and blue—
Not the Atlantic, but the Ethiopian Ocean.

Waves spout, spurt.
Liquid, salty stuff floods twixt continents.

Ship quakes over shaking fathoms—
Foam and froth that's ceaseless pearls.

I go to London
Where fog is so thick,
Air's water and water's air.

England's an island of grass that's also real blades—
Steel blades—
And lead shot and iron cannon—
Arsenal of an Empire.

(Empires arrive—thrive—on battlefields.
But, battle by battle,
Little by little,
They parade finally into the poorhouse,
With rusted weapons and bloody bandages,
And kings tumbled down in their armour.)

I cross crinkly waves—
The sea's meringue—
To discover London,
Its tottering aroma of rot—
Like Rome, falling.

I go to be ordained;
To win election—
Appointment as Baptist minister—
From the West London Baptist Association,
So I can stare down the phony, white Baptists of New Scotland.

I want to succeed in erecting the Coloured Baptist Church.
I want every history of religion to include Nova Scotia.
I want every study of theology to mention
The Coloured Baptists of Nova Scotia.

Success is a mountain top;
Defeat is a desert!

I'll return to this salty climate,
Meaningful warmth—
To again seek my Louisa.

I've heard of a black woman who yells out her lungs
Detesting Colonialism, Imperialism, Enslavement.
Sounds like her!
Smart, sweet poetess!

When I return, I'll find her:
I'm a-gonna build churches for God—
And for her, mortal, earthy goddess!

Preston boards a vessel. His coat whips in the wind.

Scene Seven

Fat gut, cherry-faced, Haliburton struts about his parlour in top hat and tails. Writing papers are scattered about. He toasts a portrait of George III. Next, he picks up a painting of Preston, studies it, and puts it in his fireplace among the logs.

HALIBURTON: I think that Preston's as loud
As a big liar:
That persnickety nigger speweth much hogwash.
No: He speweth bullshit from a horses's ass!

He swaggers, acts like he speaks for God,
As if he can dare say,
"Thunder is talkin,
Y'all better listen."

His voice is a crow, pickin at carrion.
He tongue-lashes English.

(Niggers swallow vowels
And vomit consonants.)

When th'Africans berth on our shores,
I see decay's birth.

Bluntly ugly, their history's immature:

If they're not cutlery butlers and chambermaids,
They're cutthroat butchers and chamberpots.

And I don't trust the big nigger bulls, anyhow:
I fear their ten-foot poles stickin my five-foot wife—
Her thighs like cotton pincers,
Her throat—a crucible of snow,
Her bottom like a lily stem . . .

Problem is—
Ethiopes love their undulant copulation
More than they love Christ.

Enter an elderly servant, shuffling, bearing a tray with a drink. Haliburton takes it.

Remind me, Tar Mouth, how you reckon your age?

TAR MOUTH: Bout seventy times folks must've throw "Happy Birthday" down my ears.

HALIBURTON: You come up to Nova Scotia with my granddaddy,
Carried in his carriage like his best rocking chair.
When I was a boy, you used to scare me,
Makin your rubbery face look like the Bogeyman's.

TAR MOUTH: It was just fun, boss.
You was quite a rascally boy, a scalawag.

HALIBURTON: You're my kind of nigger, Tar Mouth.
You give service—like it's love.
You were born to love me, it's clear.

TAR MOUTH: Yessum, Judge Haliburton.
I've liked you heaps lots
Ever since you sucked dry ma wife's teats.
God rest her blessèd soul.

HALIBURTON: Your mammy-wife had sweet milk, so they say.
Each teat was full of sweetness.
Like brown sugar.

TAR MOUTH: Shame, she never got to suckle our young'uns.
All sold off.

HALIBURTON: But that's a nigger's lot, eh?

TAR MOUTH: Yes, boss; that happen to a lot of niggers.

HALIBURTON: But you've done well.
Imagine: you serve a judge of the Nova Scotia Circuit Court!

TAR MOUTH: Yessum, Judge Haliburton:
Got a front-row seat to all the hangins!

HALIBURTON: You sure do, Tar Mouth.
Rustle me up nother Scotch!

TAR MOUTH: Yes, boss. But remind me how I got this name?

HALIBURTON: You tend to speak a bit slow, Tar Mouth.
Your tongue moves lazy, as do your lips.
And your feet!

Tar Mouth shuffles out.

I need to write about Preston and Tar Mouth:
Two different Moorish specimens.

Now, I see the Refugees as a horde of Negroes,
Infestin Nova Scotia,
Nestin in caves—
Just like the Nigger Loyalists,
With their boisterous, obnoxious,
Barbarous spirituals,
Okaying a sermon's hootin service
So curiously silly,
All that incomprehensible chatter.

No Negro be any good for Nova Scotia
Than a spavined horse is for a farmer.

When I look at this lot of ex-slaves,
I see a lot of filthy slaves still.

The so-called Refugees display
Unmitigated laziness,
But blame our colonial authorities for their shitty crops.
To me, the fault ain't their bush-and-boulder properties
But their desire to be back in Dixie,
Where our white brethren go way too easy
On these soft-headed critters,
Lettin em eat watermelon, fried chicken, roast pork, the works!

They should be treated as raw, dark materials
To be exploited as white men see fit.

Now, Tar Mouth is a mighty good manservant:
Perfect role for a nigger.
But that rabble-rousin damsel,
Louisa Bailey,

Happy am I to have her in my bailiwick!
She might be cold-blooded as a viper,
Crafty as a serpent in logic,
But I think she's as graceful
As a falling leaf;
She looks leather-brown, leather-soft.
And unlike too many white ladies,
She's no turnip of a woman,
Rotund and squat.

Rather, she's a champion scorpion—
Lean and copper—
With a likely sting in her rear,
If camouflaged in satin garnishes.

Beautiful, pitiful, spiteful, painful,
Like all women—
All false face and endless surface—
I'll make her a nude, crude Christian,
Happy to experience
Rhythmic pricking—
Fresh giggles
And serpentine quivers.

So the bedroom looms best for face-to-face,
Toe-to-toe, back-to-back, hand-to-hand tussles!

(I remember Governor Wentworth:
He loved his wife,
But he liked women.)

I'm glad I've hired Louisa as a maid,
Though she's not servile,
And refuses to smile,
And I catch her pretending to write—
Like the best poetesses white.

> *Tar Mouth returns with a drink. Haliburton takes it, downs it at once, and dismisses his servant.*

Anyway, I see nothing wrong with slavery.
To be a slavemaster is to enjoy life!

He is Byronic Hamlet, sardonic Caesar,
And if he accepts to enact the inevitable peccadillo,
To approach a dark lady,
He cometh unto her as hard as a tower,
So that the dissembling whore
Is soon a disassembled creature,
Shown to be a nasty, tasty, pasty tart,
Who lies as she laughs.
(*Truth* is just folly to the blacks.)
What woman is not a hellish woe
With a heavenly face?

So, happy am I to have Louisa in my employ.
Thus, I duplicate governors, judges, lords.

He rings a bell.

A harem scent amid maremma—
Ochterloney studs his seraglio
Where grass gives way to mud.
But Wentworth kept his Maroon women
Where grass gives way to dirt—
Preston, north and east.

Bailey enters. Haliburton adjusts his peacock-shaded, paisley-design silken robes.

BAILEY: You called me, Judge Haliburton?

HALIBURTON: A mermaid in a desert is a mirage,
By definition, eh?
So you should understand
How your unexpected beauty
Begs unprecedented adoration.

Nor do I think you a vindictive girl,
Though I'm a fountainhead of gifts.
Thus, do not serve me unless you're truly willing to serve.

BAILEY: Sir, I detect words suspiciously painful:
To speak plainly,
Ya wanna "muckahigh" with some "molasses"?

HALIBURTON: Well, my attentions would uplift you.

BAILEY: By lifting up my skirts?

HALIBURTON: I want to do right by you, girlie!

BAILEY: And what about your wife?

HALIBURTON: I'm the lord, she's the lady, you're the serf.
Whatever mischief you and I perpetrate
Means zilch for my family.

BAILEY: Slavery means washtub abortion,
Kitchen-sink abortion,
Backyard abortion.
The bellies of female slaves
Hate to belch forth baby slaves.
No family for em.

You should look to your wife.

After all, a man's breath is flimsy:
Hubbies do perish in bedroom whimsy.

HALIBURTON: How dare you preach to me!
Can't you listen?!!

BAILEY: Can you be silent?

I know what acid you draft
To illustrate black folks as comic monsters.
You cast us in humiliating slanders
So that we who read and hear
Must feel only despicable Scotians.

HALIBURTON: Louisa, listen: ink can be soap—
To scour away lies and polish the truth
So it glistens, spic and span.
I make truth as elegant as undiluted ink
Is black.

BAILEY: Yeah, you're a carpenter of ink—
And guilty of crafting cranky cartoons—
To render us Ethiopes as dupes and dopes.

HALIBURTON: My portraits are no betrayal.
I'm as unquestionable as a tombstone.

BAILEY: Writing is difficult
When honesty is difficult.

HALIBURTON: Ink is the pen's dream:

A fine line of verse
Waves off the preceding lines.

Read me well enough,
And you'll see I read well.

BAILEY: Sorry: I don't confuse
Vomit and poems.

HALIBURTON: Why do you oppose me so much?
I prefer simply a Scottish-infatuated New Scotland.

BAILEY: I'm a bell chiming, "I am."
You're the silence tolling, "Thou art not."

HALIBURTON: I'll ask you now to hold your tongue.
After all, a woman's belly can contain a baby,
But her mouth can't ever contain a word.

BAILEY: Why should I be silent?
Your filth adds heaps to Nova Scotia's dirt.

HALIBURTON: I'm simply tryin to warn ya niggers:
An empty head prefaces
Empty hands and an empty belly.

You're all cunning enough to wheedle and whine,
But not to build good wood houses
Warmed by good wood fires.

BAILEY: We all know more about hard work than you ever will.

Haliburton offers Bailey a drink. She spurns the glass.

HALIBURTON: Alcohol is consolation, solution:
It dissolves pain in sweetness
That dizzies the mind.

Look it: it's not your fault and it ain't mine
That you're scamps who live off scraps—
Just like goddamn savages.

God made you as you are
And we white folks must love and lead you, anyway.

But the problem is, by being here,
You extend the boundaries of Africa,
So that we white Nova Scotians
End up with Africans and little Africas—
All about us.
It's like we got chunks of coal
Tattering all our snow.

BAILEY: I gotta struggle against this world you designed
And endorse.

HALIBURTON: Come off it, Louisa!
Even you Negroes prefer an Africa
Peopled by albinos and mulattoes!

BAILEY: With all due respect, sir,
If feces tumbles out whenever you speak,
It's your brains, being flushed.

HALIBURTON: Really? No. You know I speak fact:
No black buck's any good for a wench like you!
If you were a toad, he'd make a fine toadstool;
If you were a corpse, he'd make a fine grave.
But I look at you and see a fresh maiden's breast.
There's no reason for you to protest—
If you employ God-given Reason.

Haliburton retrieves the portrait of Preston from the fireplace. He holds it up.

BAILEY: Preston! Richard!

HALIBURTON: I thought you'd recognize this "Christian brother,"
This nigger!
Well, he's just a silk preacher yearnin for a cushy church.

BAILEY: No, that man is definitely "holier than thou!"

HALIBURTON: Oh, Louisa, you're sweet on the varmint?
Figures!

BAILEY: Where is he? Where is he?

HALIBURTON: Don't you know it's better to drink wine with a friend and a lover
Than have friends and lovers pour wine on your grave?

Well, too bad if you don't see what's best for you!

Preston's off to seduce London to name him a Baptist.

Don't be surprised if he comes back
With a white abolitionist slut
And a brown Frankenstein-creature pup.

BAILEY: So what? What is love but trust?
I do leave, quit, your service.
Adieu, adieu,
I remove to Africville.

HALIBURTON: Africville? Africville?
How dare you plot an Africa-ville!

BAILEY: It's no plan; it's a fact:
A dollop of geography—
A wallop of geometry—
And we Africans have seaside homes
To call our own:
With Royal say-so, too!

HALIBURTON: Damn fool!
I wouldn't be so sure bout that.

He tries to grab at Bailey again, but she hustles for the door.

You know, you're better off as my maid
Than as a woman with an invisible man.

BAILEY: Haliburton, you're visibly a no-good man.
I can't see you as any decent judge.
Why, as soon as you see a Negro, you call for a jail cell!

She tears free her apron, throws it down. Down falls her handy penknife.

HALIBURTON: *(spluttering)* You're carrying a concealed weapon!

BAILEY: Better that than concealed vice and secret dirt!

Bailey snatches up her penknife and exits.

Scene Eight

Preston is at sea. He climbs rigging and looks toward probable shore.

PRESTON: How can we ever be respectable as a people,
Interpose Heaven between our oppressors and ourselves,
Unless we have our own church?

That's why I ride this wobbly wash,
The sea's inconsequential furrows,
So I can return ex-England a divine,
Ransom my people from white Baptists
Who despise us so despicably,
Just because we black Baptists
Don't like Christ's delirious words
To be spoken so frigidly.

The pale Christian services
Follow a cheap, inferior recipe,
As if making eyes water
Instead of making wine.

Their pastors are Sisyphus at Golgotha:
They heave and heave to roll the stone away
From Christ's should-be-useful tomb,
Only to watch it roll back again

As their congregation falls
Into a drowsy mood
And then blissfully into sleep.

But the Coloured Baptists want a lavish blend—
Glorious violin, gaudy piano,
Drumming that's an alchemical additive,
Plus sorrowful voices as heartbreaking as whips.

Following the notes of the tuneful papers,
We stomp our feet—
Romp so much in each seat,
The visceral pews threaten to buckle.

For us, churchgoing means cheerful business!

So we need the avid clanging
Of church bells in every hamlet,
Houses showing rangy streaks of paint,
Precarious scaffolding uplifting churches.

We want curry and mulligatawny.
We want mackerel, which is good,
Not rum, which is not.

(Better fish soup with partridge feathers
Than to stagger about,
Unhealthily intoxicated.)

We gotta snack loudly on sardines,
Smacking our lips!

We want household lanes, uneven as clouds,
But gussied up with rose petals.

We gotta march into the weathered forest,
Carve out walls, ceilings, and floors,
To be as established as stone—
Like those granite behemoths
That crouch and bunch up at Peggy's Cove.

And I will warn my brethren and sistren,
Beware politicians' fish-lipped mouths!
Their shark mouths, piranha mouths, barracuda mouths,
That bite down as they talk:
Their words stream into us as so much venom.

So we Africadians must establish one town
Immediately off th'Atlantic,
But near to the white bosses,
Their copper-penny payrolls.

I'll have a church downtown and one out there
On Campbell Road.

It will be, they both will be, an African Baptist Church—
If I know my ABCs!
Two African Baptist churches,
Both overlooking the sea.

And I'll find Louisa and bring her to both.
Solemnize our marriage in both.
That's my oath!

Scene Nine

Bailey is at Africville. A sign tells us it is "Campbell Road." Bedford Basin shimmers in the background.

BAILEY: Geez, I'm so glad to get away from that scalawag,
"Helluva-burden"!
If only Preston were back—
Alone, ready to wed.
I'd be even happier to be here
In this "Lil Africa"
On Campbell Road.

Greyed folks say when David George,
O' South Carolina,
Preached in Nova Scotia,

After Washington's revolution,
He got along so far as to set up a church
With a piano in it,
Before a pale mob,
Angry he planned to baptize a white lady,
Broke up the meetin house,
Set all ablaze,
So what was left of the piano
Gave out smoky music, burnt melodies.
What some of us now call "Blues."

(I think that piano still tears up, sobs—
Smoke snarled in its lungs.)

Just last June, I saw a Coloured bride drowned
By her white wedding gown.
Perched on the river edge in Truro,
Kissing subtly with her beau.
The tide rose up quick as it does off Fundy,
Lapping at her train
So that it got so sodden, it was leaden.
And so, backward was she pulled—
Lulled—
Into the surge.
Her beau grappled after her,
But he was impotent gainst the impudent tide.
The dress was so heavy,
It was a cast-iron coffin,
And dragged the bride
To the bottom of the flood.

Too many us freed slaves
Are like that new bride:
So not used to our new state,
We make missteps,
Misjudgments,
That prove our doom.

But here's this space yonder Halifax—
All mushrooms, burrs, dandelions, yes,

And blueberries, blackberries, raspberries,
Plus omnipresent rhubarb, mint, and strawberries:
An "Africa for us Africadians!"
As some of us say.

Here we gotta be as thrifty as breath itself.
Gotta knock together hovels, four-square shacks.
Begin with sticks,
Then graduate to bricks!

It don't matter whether we're low down
Or highfalutin:
We just need to settle *here*—
Along the Haligonian haunches,
Flanking Bedford Basin.

A hundred huts by the seaside,
A painted job on each one:
That's Shangri-La.

This village atop toothy water
Gnawing a beach,
Hinging upon a frill-fringed sea,
Is our prototype of black liberty.

See Campbell Road, "Africville":
The place is beautiful
Because black is beautiful.

Our massed faces—
Black versus snow—
Are beautiful.

Our massed faces
Among sunflowers
Are beautiful.

Our stubborn huddle against
North Atlantic waves—
Is beautiful.

Miller, Carvery, Dixon, Black, etc.,
We are beautiful precisely where we are.

After we set down glasses of ale
And glasses of rum,
We need to think about stained glass:
A church. Our own.
Because we desire irresistible flowers.

For now, there's the slop of brooks,
Slapping through soil bare or green;
There's the soggy, germinating muck.

We already have seafood—
A watery banquet:
The splash of a paddle
Only attracts the mackerel.

We just gotta add copper pot cookery—
Choreography of flame and fire—
To swell up bellies
And never let wine and beer abate.

Oh, I pray I see my darling Richard again,
So we enjoy the stink of sex so much,
It becomes a perfume,
If not soulful food,
And we multiply, multiply.

Whether any but Preston find me beautiful,
I can't care—
So long he return soon and safe from London.

Sound of a horse-drawn carriage. The Earl of Dalhousie dismounts.

DALHOUSIE: Louisa Bailey, you terrorize the legislature
With your bullhorn bullshit, "Africa for the Africans!"
And you disgrace the monarch,
Suggesting Slavery and Empire are wrong.

Slavery is legal—
And Empire brings civilization.

I wish all you sooty gals would follow the example
Of my servant, Mary Postill.

BAILEY: Guvner Dalhousie, you mean your slave.

DALHOUSIE: She's my indentured servant.
You should be the wise wench she is
And be happy to serve your superiors.

BAILEY: I'd be happier if y'all paid superior wages.

DALHOUSIE: Miss Bailey, most of you coloureds
Are glad to have rags on your backs,
Oatmeal in your mouths.

BAILEY: Guvnor Dalhousie, I ain't no horse.

DALHOUSIE: Excuse me, Miss Bailey, but you're no white lady either.

BAILEY: Sir, nor am I a dressed-up, puffed-up ass,
Mistakin my buttocks for my brain.

I aim to write.
I want ink on my fingers
And a new poem on every page.

DALHOUSIE: Ha! That's a load of cow crap!
Your inky colour suits you to be my page
Or Judge Haliburton's page.
But you'll never ink up a page—
And surely not in any university—
Except as a criminal record
Or as an obituary.

Good day, madam!

> *He turns stiffly to return to his carriage. Bailey is outraged. She can hardly curtsy.*

BAILEY: *(whispering)* Go to hell, damn you!

> *Sound of carriage retreating.*

We need now noisy poetry—
Ramshackle carpentry,
Not good-lookin headstones,
But a clear foundation—
A cleared foundation—
To raise the subject
Me, myself, and I doth raise:

Africville.

And I want Preston:

Africville plus Preston!

   She pulls out a page of poetry (by the real Louisa Bailey) and reads:

Here are my thoughts of Heaven:
"And you poor sinners, though last not least,
Come bow before the mercy seat;
And pour out there your sad complaints,
For God can turn all into saints."

Act II

Scene One

Joseph Howe—"The Tribune of Nova Scotia"—is in his newspaper office. He is at work on an edition of The Nova Scotian. *He is thirty. The year is 1820.*

HOWE: Haliburton's a gent, but wheezes shit—
Turds straight from a horse's mouth.
He's got giddy words;
Looks roly-poly:
He oughta be as happy
As an oinkin pig.
But whenever he discusses the Negro,
Gets he so apoplectic
He just about vomits vinegar.

Sometimes I suspect and/or think
Haliburton suspects
His mama loved too much a slave
With visceral desire
That now tarnishes his blood
Or tints the family name.
I can't conceive another credible cause
For his behaviour:
He's as venomous as an *albino* tarantula.

So Haliburton's prose leaks melancholy ink.
I publish him; there's a market;
I applaud some of his braying.
Still, he's tough to stomach.
His hatred of the blacks drives straight to the gut.

But I feel differently bout Ethiopes!
I adore those "dusky Pomonas"
Raining berries down my throat,
Every time I ramble by Bedford Basin,
At Campbell Road.
O! They're a bevy of bold hussies—
Beauties who can't be turned down or overlooked!

I kiss em, when they allow,
And I discover honey mouths.

O! I bet a dark-skinned lady
Makes her husband as thin as a stick . . .

And I like to see sable maidens straddling oxen;
I like to see the dames who can despoil a man
Delicately, intricately,
Crumbling his bones,
Humbling down his spine.

Clearly, I like indigo women, swarthy women,
Gold women, even white women . . .

I'll wed a white woman,
Get us a blond son,
Then I'll sport with a Negress.

Yes! I'd like to rescue all those uncommon beauties
From commonplace marriages,
And bid us welcome uncommon—if unrecognized—children!

Why, Nova Scotia should be as homogeneous
As a rainbow!

Enter Mary Postill with a tray of drinks.

Ah, Mary Postill, how goes it with you?
How are ye now that the law set you slave, but free?
I pray you stop and drink our health.

Postill sets down the tray. She and Howe toast each other and drink.

POSTILL: Well, sir, well.
You know I skedaddled from Dalhousie
Who claimed he bought me for a gross of potatoes,
But he had no bill of sale for the deal—
Not that I'd ever agreed to be bought and sold!
I'd had too much of slavery in the Boston States.
And, pound for pound, I got as much common sense
As any scholar at that new Dalhousie University.
I was too sweet to Dalhousie:
He thought me his dull slave.
I had news for the buster!
I up and left, soon as he pulled his pants right down.

HOWE: But he came after you, pursued you,
Sued you into court.
Acted like he was panting,
Or romantic . . .

POSTILL: There he was, the Guvner, still after me,
A simple maid, but no simpleton.
All his pals—a trio—sat on the court,
And by deciding I *might* belong to him,
Decided—in truth—I was free,
For none could prove I was his slave.

HOWE: I was there as journalist, and seeing how
Judges were doubtful and Dalhousie in doubt,
I stepped forward to ask you to be my apprentice—
Not slave, never a slave, at least not ever for me.

Postill pours them both a fresh drink.

POSTILL: I'll drink to that!

HOWE: What say you of Preston?

POSTILL: Preston the preacher or Preston the place?

HOWE: The preacher.

POSTILL: I've heard him less than I should;
Heard more bout him than you would.
He questions why we blacks gotta live
In huts and holes or stranded in swamps.

HOWE: He speaks like an icy volcano:
Frosty when silent, hot when coaxed!

When he starts condemning slavery,
I gotta be fearful of his statistics,
For then his *truth* resembles
A herd of bullets.

POSTILL: No one should discount Dicky Preston.

She drinks, and then she exits. Howe studies her leave.

HOWE: Oh, I say she has a poetic subtlety.
Perhaps a question of perfume?
Her beauty is obvious—
Yes, even from behind.
She pours out honey
Simply when she speaks.
Marshalls caresses and kisses, does she,
Like a Venus of the hearth.
And wherever she moves,
I scent the most gaudy scents.

Scene Two

Preston is at a podium on a Halifax stage. Behind him, a sign reads, "Slavery Abolition Society of Nova Scotia." He is now garbed effectively as a preacher. Applause often interrupts his speech.

PRESTON: Names shadow us:
Names we do not choose.
How'd I become "Preston"
If not after the man who bought my daddy?

VOICE: Christian names are slave names!
And the joke is,
The so-called Christians are no-good Christians.

PRESTON: I pray to see the South torn to pieces!
I pray it becomes a land
Of desolate spirituals and unanswered prayers.

Let slavemasters loll among ashes
While their streets and sewers gush blood,
So Dixie faces its gurgling defeat.

Slavery ploughs up roots.
But so does Abolition!

VOICE: Preach, master, preach!
Preach, goddamnit!

PRESTON: We blacks demand liberation:
To boss, not sob!

Our people must waft
Aromas of soil—
Implant Coloured Christian colonies
All bout Nova Scotia.

VOICE: Can I get an "Amen"?
This be the Revolution Africadian!

PRESTON: Truro can be more than
The simple sourness of a salt marsh;
The black waterways of Yarmouth
Allow for fishing, much fishing;
At Windsor or Three Mile Plains,
Mosquitoes and dragonflies dart up
From hill-high hay.
Campbell Road, Alpha and Omega, of Halifax,
Is a fringe of foam where sea bends to rock
At Negro Point.
These places bellow out to us, "Home!"

If we blacks establish our own cottages
And homespin industries,
We gain plump pears, luscious, Annapolis apples,
August-smitten hay, golden-yellow orchards:
We'll get all we need for painstaking eating,
Satisfactory and fulfilling eating.
We won't always sweat, raise weeds,
That we watch mice gnaw down to dust.

A Drunk intrudes; he means to disrupt all.

DRUNK: Quit yer pickanniny hollerin!
Ya don't wanna set up no houses,
Ya just wanna sit up in taverns
And tee-hee and pour rum in tea.
Black folks? Shit!

PRESTON: Well, sir, you're as cocky as a stinking corpse!

DRUNK: Your lungs storm, but all I hear is a church organ—
A lot of braying and wheezing.
Look at yas!
Ya been here a decade,
But a small rainfall will splinter your huts.
Yas've made a world of shoddy.

You're peasants still,
And a peasant is just a slave.
Your lot ain't improved no ways.
But you're still black anyhow:
That's the permanent blot!

PRESTON: You're so uncouth and unlettered,
You should be unconscious!

DRUNK: All of yas've done badly;
None of yas've done well.
All of yas are ne'er-do-wells.

PRESTON: And you seem effortlessly evil,
A grubby image, indecorous dirt . . .

DRUNK: Yeah, I ain't all boisterous with religion,
But nor am I a cardboard priest—
Meticulously and as mellifluously as black as a crow . . .

Bailey approaches the podium. Preston gives a start: he hasn't seen her in six years.

BAILEY: I know this man's accented squint,
His awkward lope like that of a scaredy cat.
This destructor is no other than Judge Haliburton
In the guise of his mouthpiece, the cartoon Yankee,
Sam Slick.

Squire Haliburton's all tricked out
As his confederate derelict,
Slick,
And that's why we smell an acerbic scent . . .

Now, Slick removes his white-makeup mask. Yes, he is Haliburton.

See! He's got a clamped-on face!
Some alabaster artifice.

PRESTON: What purpose breeds this blunt fraud?

HALIBURTON: Preston, I say you're a compound of blarney and bullshit,
Sugar miscegenated with soot.
To hear you pretend to preach or lecture
Is to meet true fraud as slippery and tricky as black ice.

You're either high-grade pork
Or low-quality pork.
Can't decide.

BAILEY: If I were vulgar, I'd say
Your tongue articulates
What your ass evacuates.

HALIBURTON: You must be lame, Preston!
Lettin this skirt lob dry turds on your behalf?
Cripes!

Preston motions Bailey to silence, but she runs to him. They hug and kiss.

PRESTON: But, sir, why are we—two Christians—
Fighting each other?
What's the point of all this fussin
And tussling?

HALIBURTON: Don't you dare confuse your wild people with mine!
While you were diggin shit-holes
We were raising cathedrals.

We had Latin
Before you discovered the latrine.

My folks are diamonds;
Yours are coal.

PRESTON: Diamonds mustn't forget they're basically coal.

BAILEY: Never mind that!
Their cathedrals got built on our backs!

HALIBURTON: You're both practically mud!
I can't believe Christians come steeped in mud.

PRESTON: Mud isn't dirt; it's a different kind of clean—
The fertile stuff that makes a field green.

HALIBURTON: Washing your faces
Must be like washing a gutter.

BAILEY: Least we got faces to wash.
Your face is your ass.

PRESTON: Let's all calm down here.

HALIBURTON: Yeah, sir, tell your bitch, "Shut up!"
Quell that queynte!
She's a seditious, lil slut—
Makin speeches gainst the king!

BAILEY: Richard, my darlingest man,
You took a whip to Bull Styron!
You took a boat to England to get your divinity!
You ain't one to be calm!

And I know this theatrical fool,
His bone-dry speech,
His dry as dust face.

Just to look at him is to see shit
Dribble down the back of his throat.

HALIBURTON: Preston, I salute you on your choice of tramp!
She's a brawny trollop, this one:
Got a voice of lava, eh?
Right suitable for you,
Her unscrupulous consort.

PRESTON: She's my fiancée! You cur!

Bailey produces her penknife and flashes it. Preston is shocked, but grapples with Haliburton. Instead, Haliburton jumps from the stage and takes to his heels. Bailey throws a book at Haliburton. Offstage, he yelps, "Ouch!"

Scene Three

Bailey and Preston hold each other tight in a church.

PRESTON: Oh, I've prayed nightly, daily,
For just this exquisite miracle.
Now, let's feast.

BAILEY: The British sent almost all us to Nova Scotia.
I kept hearing about you, but when first
I thought I'd meet you here again,
Off you went to England.
I don't blame you:
It's good you have Baptist papers
To back your attack on Haliburton's papers.

PRESTON: Haliburton's a rat as plump as a dump.

BAILEY: Excuse me for saying these words in church, but
His paunch pisses; his mouth shits.

PRESTON: We shouldn't badmouth. He isn't all dirty, I wager.

BAILEY: Shit is unsanitary, but he loves it.
He must:
He scrawls crap that crawls with maggots.

PRESTON: He's as loud as a drum and just as hollow.

BAILEY: Haliburton suits this country of grass
That's also snow, or sleaze-greasy streets.

Landing here,
We who descend from Adam and Eve
Descended into a frigid hell.

PRESTON: Naw, it's not that bad. Not really.

BAILEY: It's always cold peas and cold potatoes,
And never grapes and never wine.

PRESTON: We shouldn't have the wine!

BAILEY: Why not? It makes folks feel fine.

Anyway, in summer, we see worm-infested clover;
In winter, we eat cheese that's wormy.

We can't show Nova Scotia the tyranny of the plough
Because rocks are too numerous
And swamps too deep.

Our fields are rough as winter stubble.

Why must we breakfast on thorns
And lunch on mushrooms?

PRESTON: We are progressing; we're raising churches,
Children, and homes, if not castles.

BAILEY: Deft enemies hate our deafening pleas:
They delay; they dilly and dally;
And leave us hungry and homeless and naked,
And so, black men who worked iron filigree—
Elegant, hand-wrought iron filigree—
Now just tack down tarpaper to seal our shacks.

In the meantime, witness moonshine-brilliant monkeyshines—
Legislators gone ape:
They molest our Coloured women—
Cuddle old ladies and diddle young ones.

PRESTON: My darling, we need an ally, a friend:
I think it be ol' Joe Howe,
Whose newspaper congrats us
More than it condemns.

Maybe he'll even publish your poetry.

They kiss.

Scene Four

Preston and Bailey visit the offices of The Nova Scotian. *They await an audience with Howe. Mary Postill has just left the antechamber.*

BAILEY: Mary Postill, who we just saw?
Well, she's well known
For being known well
By Dalhousie—
And by Haliburton—
And by Howe.

PRESTON: I know we shouldn't gossip,
But corrosion is hypnotizing.

BAILEY: That gal will make love atop any man
To make some money "under the table."

PRESTON: My love, we really shouldn't gossip.

BAILEY: Gossip is more accurate than lies.
And a lot more fun.
Sides, I'm not sayin anything false:

PRESTON: Shouldn't we try to transform or translate "gossip"
Into "Gospel"?

BAILEY: Here comes that master of words—
Editor Joseph Howe.

Howe enters.

HOWE: If one is Preston and the other Bailey,
I expect you want marriage—without fail!

BAILEY: That's right, sir—and better articles in the press.

HOWE: And maybe the poems of a certain poetess?

Bailey can't hide her delight at these words, but maintains her serious poise.

Good people, you're both as high profile as volcanoes.
I can help your interests.
Perhaps you, Reverend Preston, will sit
For an interview bout your London voyage . . .

PRESTON: Before that, I prevail upon you, Mr. Howe,
To expose Judge Haliburton's hokum, bunkum.
For dull folks believe his slander and libel,
And injure and impede the Negro . . .

BAILEY: His words are as cutting
As a steak-knife abortion.

HOWE: Haliburton means well.
I class him as friend—
As I also am to you.

BAILEY: Strange how some "friends"
Always have less power than enemies!

PRESTON: What Sam Slick sets down in black and white
Is as contradictory as a zebra's stripes.

BAILEY: Howe, how can you befriend bullshit?
Haliburton's just a rat in a judge's robe.

HOWE: No, he is a Privy Council wit—
As deadpan as any civil servant—
But . . .

BAILEY: You can't say what I can say:
Haliburton's a withered, pudgy body,
A graveyard mouth and gravedigger eyes!

PRESTON: As Miss Bailey alleges,
Haliburton seems a pious sewer—
As low-down as a rat hole—
And peeps bout in others' guises,
Playing off as a slithering drunkard,
Higgledy-piggledy,
But that jig—that gig—is up:
None is fooled by his foolishness now.

BAILEY: Good news is,
He got a bit battered about
Once his Sam Slick mask slipped off.

So, Editor Howe, will you now expose
Judge "How-ya-burnin" as the varmint he be?

HOWE: Doncha want Marriage more than Vengeance?

PRESTON: We want Fairness, Justice, Equality.

Howe checks his timepiece.

HOWE: I'd better get started on the newspaper headline:
Judge Haliburton will stand exposed by deadline.

Howe exits.

PRESTON: Remember: We want Justice!

BAILEY: Get "How-ya-burnin" into the courtroom,
And then we'll get us into the bedroom,
After we jump the broom!

Bailey and Preston hug and kiss.

Scene Five

Haliburton is in his study. He nurses a bruised neck. He is packing briefcases and suitcases. He is all in a tizzy.

HALIBURTON: Sambos scoff at chores
And cheat for chocolate.

A bunch of heathens,
They fail always to ponder sufficiency.
Thus, their treasure chests are mudholes
And their flowers gather mildew.

As for Preston and his bitch,
I feel a leaden pain
Each time I face their lead-dark faces.

Civilized Christians gotta understand:

If ya don't catch a nigger by the toe
And then cut off his head,
He'll have a white lady on his say-so,
And splay her in his bed—

Unto the most impatient swelling
Of her belly.

Let Joe Howe editorialize
All his grotty, True Grit lies.

I, this true Tory—
Scribe the real history—
In inky handwriting,
Indelible as lightning.

The blacks are a king-killing spawn!
Recall Toussaint Louverture in Haiti
And Nat Turner in Virginia.
To sing or kill? Both games, to blacks, are equally fine.
That's why their crimes keep my quill in ink.

But they got a buddy
In my ex-buddy, Howe.

That sweet-talkin strutter with a puffy belly
And the government Cabinet form a cabal,
Then a cabaret,
Or a liquor cabinet.

But so it always is:
Liars lead us to the future.

In their mouths is rum;
In our ears is rumour.

They pretend to befriend the niggers,
But break their word easy as they break wind.
They're a pack of white-lie liars.

And I can't believe they let that Abolitionist scum
Run me out the auditorium
Like some obscene, obnoxious cockroach,
Then swat at me like an annoying mosquito,
And riot bad enough to strike my skull with a book.
Well, I'll not squabble more with this rabble!
I'll sidestep these sideswipes,
Traverse the Atlantic and take up a seat
In the British House of Commons,
To complain A-to-Z therein
About Abolitionists and Zealots
(Or maybe I should call em,
"Aborigines" and "zebras.")

Farewell, then, to nigger-settled Nova Scotia!
I sail to London, the Empire,
To win authorial respect
Where White Might makes Right.
To be a Member of Parliament
And utter wistful mutters—
Putting niggers in their low-down places,

While I act a lord,
And get paid—
By the word—
For all the evil I've said.

Haliburton swallows some alcohol. Tar Mouth enters.

TAR MOUTH: Boss, I got your bags all packed.
Now, I'll pack mine.

HALIBURTON: No, no. Y'aint comin with me:
Got plenty niggers in London already.
I'll just engage a man over there.

TAR MOUTH: But I give your family generations of service!
My gone wife fed all her milk to you.

HALIBURTON: You've been repaid, Tar Mouth:
You got to serve a judge—
Not a shit-kickin farmer.

TAR MOUTH: But I'm old now, who'll care for me?

HALIBURTON: If I were you, I'd call on your "Black Brother,"
That cultivated, Coloured Christian, Preston.
See what he'll do for you.

Oh, you can finish what's left of the Scotch.
So long!

*Haliburton exits. Tar Mouth picks up the Scotch bottle. Pours out what's left:
a drop.*

Scene Six

Bailey and Preston are in "Africville." They stand beside the Seaview Church,
under construction. Bedford Basin is in the distance. Bailey wears a wedding
dress. Preston is in his preacher clothes. He lays down a broom before his bride.

BAILEY: Now Noon wants one
To work alone:
But Night wants two,
For sleep's a duo.

PRESTON: In you, I see a copper rapture
Only true love can capture.
That Egyptian-Ethiopian bliss
Of King Solomon and his princess.

BAILEY: Why do you love me?

PRESTON: Because I love Truth—
And all you say and do is truth.

BAILEY: But I speak so uncouth!

PRESTON: No! Your beauty is your bravery—
Your courage. Not just your comeliness.

BAILEY: Sir, you made me love you
When you cracked whip at Styron;
And I loved you more,
When you spat back at Haliburton.

PRESTON: (I read lately that he's gone
To London,
Scurrying and hurrying abroad
With a cockroach slither.)

BAILEY: I marry you:
For better sweet
Or bittersweet.
I marry you,
My sweet, sweet, sweet.

In your style, there's no step dance;
In your thought, there's no limp ink.
You disregard wordy "Romance,"
Don't give a damn what others think.

Many whites confuse the Dead Sea
And the Sea of Galilee.
They got a sinister, left-hand, slit-eye bible.
But you got God's Word that brooks no rival.

PRESTON: Let all us buy up all Africville's proxy lands
Set up homes, gardens with moxy,
And exalt in weddings—and babies.

BAILEY: And finally now I can write my poems—
Gazing out over Africville homes!

Bailey casts down her penknife and shows off her pen.

Now I can replace my "sword" with a pen.
I need no knife, now I can use my learnin.

I say to you, my husband,
A wife's sweetest words,
"Yes, yes, yes, yes, yes, yes, yes!"

PRESTON: Sweetheart Louisa:
First love is always cursed
By the second lover.
But my first love is both you
And Africville.

BAILEY: So long it's taken us
To find freedom
None take from us:
Jubilee's now come.

Someone get a fiddle!
Someone bang a drum!
Let no one diddle:
We have overcome!

Time to now build
Home-sweet Africville!

The lovers kiss. And they jump together over the broom. They are joyous, but soon they face alarm: Bull Styron arrives, huffing and puffing, waving a piece of paper.

STYRON: Sorry to bust up your happy matrimony,
But you're still my slaves say the courts of Virginny.

PRESTON: Bull Styron, you're in British North America:
There's no force here for law from Virginia.

STYRON: Well, I'm draggin yas back t'Amurka, anyway.

BAILEY: Help! Africvillers, help! Help us!
Calling all Africvillers, come and help us!
Whitey here's tryin to take us back to slavery!

Bailey drops her pen and picks up her penknife and points it at Styron. Styron looks about worriedly. We see projections or cardboard cutouts, throngs of Africvillers converging on the scene. They are serious, even if they sing. There is a quiet menace in their determination to defend their liberty and their neighbours.

STYRON: Preston! Bailey! Call off these people!
You're supposed to be Christians!
Don't let em hurt me!
Okay, okay, you have your freedom!

PRESTON: Yes, Bull Styron, we have our liberty—
We were born free—
In the eyes of God.

BAILEY: And we live free
Where slaveholders ain't allowed:
Right here in Africville.

STYRON: To hell with yas then!

BAILEY & PRESTON: No, you go back to Hell:
We're in Heaven, here in Africville.

They embrace. Styron flees. Africvillers—as images—look on with approval.

Postscript

The Scene

The year is 1962. A married couple, also named Bailey and Preston, are sitting at a table, sipping tea in their Africville home. There is a harbour-view, partly obstructed by sunflowers in the garden. We hear sounds of children playing outdoors, the horn of a freight train passing through, and the chime of the church bell.

BAILEY: It's so nice to have a nice home—
Then, woodsmoke is like cream;
Fire is as good as rum.

PRESTON: You know us Baptists don't drink or dance.

BAILEY: My scripture is poetry, honey.
My church is pleasure.
I'm not a perfect Baptist,
But I am a perfect dancer!

PRESTON: And you're an excellent wife!
Louisa, I do feel blessed.

BAILEY: And I'm glad to live here.

I'd hate to live in downtown Halifax:
Folks pay high rent to live in cockroach boxes.

PRESTON: Yet, city folks complain we're too country—
With horses, pigs, chickens, and a fishery
Right in our backyard.

Not to mention the rats.

BAILEY: The City of Halifax brought us the rats:
Those are South End rats, not Africville rats.
They're the byproduct of the Halifax dump—
That auxiliary wreckage of dirty citizens—
Who show us poisonous contempt
By littering our doorsteps
With their garbage and their rats.

PRESTON: Strange thing: The city gets taxes off us,
But won't give us water or sewer.

BAILEY: No, Richard: They give us their sewer pipes!
Twice I boil water before I cook us anything.

But I like our Liberty here.
Every meal—with mackerel and home fries—
Is like a traditional feast.

Look at our tables here in Africville:
Every inimitable table
Yields a never-withering feast.

That's why citified Coloureds are so jealous:
We've got our own culture here.
We don't humbly ask white folks' permission—
To have Duke Ellington come in and play a waltz;
To have Joe Louis quit the segregated Lord Nelson
And come out and stay here
And shadowbox with the boys.

> *There is a knock at the door. They answer. Dr. Bull Styron, Ph.D., strides in, doffing his hat.*

STYRON: Sorry to bother you good folks on this sunny day,
But I'm just here this afternoon
To ask questions about conditions in Africville
So that I can make appropriate recommendations
To Halifax Council about your futures in a modern,
Twentieth-century city.

Here's my card:
Dr. Bull Styron, Ph.D., Sociologist,
From Dalhousie University.

PRESTON: Styron, you say?
That's a coincidence.
My great-grandfather, bless his soul,
Passed down a story in our family
About his escape
From some Bull Styron in Virginia.
That your lineage?

STYRON: Could be.
But slavery is history.
I'm here to talk about your today.

BAILEY: Before we're gone tomorrow?

PRESTON: Where we are, is our historical escape.

STYRON: No landscape is an escape.
That's delusional living.
Instead, landscape can be landscaped—
Improved.

BAILEY: Oh, so you've come to cart away the dump,
Fix up rundown houses,
And give us sewer pipes
And water pipes
Our taxes have already bought us
Many, many times over?

STYRON: Well, we will see.

PRESTON: Who directed you here?

STYRON: I'm hired by the city manager,
Tommy Chandler Haliburton.

BAILEY: Isn't he required reading for racists,
The guys and gals who wear white sheets
Stained yellow with piss,
Brown with shit,
And red with blood?

STYRON: No, that's his great-grandfather.
Died in London, 1861, and a Tory.

Look it: I look at Africville and I see the dump,
And no proper civic services.
Your flowers here are weeds.

BAILEY: Oh, to you, roses are weeds.
You must live in Heaven.

PRESTON: Tell the city to provide what we're paying for.

STYRON: Why should they?
How can you have luxuries beside a dump?

BAILEY: But we already have luxuries:
Waterfront baptism, backyard boating, sunrise services,
Communal childcare, fresh fish:
All free, all available to African citizens.

STYRON: All that may be so,
But Africville isn't Harlem,
That truly great slum.

PRESTON: And Halifax isn't New York,
That truly great city.

BAILEY: But Halifax does have a great dump.
And the world's best-fed rats:
All that South End champagne and caviar!

STYRON: You people can't stop the future.
Everywhere, progress is progressing:
Even in Vietnam!
There, we're clearing jungle
With fire and bullets and pavement.

BAILEY: So, is that your plan for us?
Clear us out with fire and bullets?
Try a down-home version of a Nazi solution?

STYRON: Nothing so bad. This is Canada!

PRESTON: And who you callin "you people," Doc Bull?

BAILEY: And what about the people?

STYRON: There'll be Relocation, Reconciliation, Rehabilitation.

PRESTON: Only criminals need rehabilitation.
And I see only one crook here.

BAILEY: The remedy and the rehab
Is for Dr. "Bullshit" Styron here to relocate himself
Off our premises.

Styron exits in a huff. Preston and Bailey embrace. Sound of a church chime.

Curtain. Suddenly, a black man, a black woman, and a white man emerge from behind the curtain. They speak into phones, oblivious to each other.

COMPANY: Yeah, just landed in Halifax. Lookin for Africville. Heard a lot about it. People say it's gone. Can't be. Everyone keeps mentionin it. Something about *Justice! Liberty! Faith!*

A Dialogue Between George Elliott Clarke and Diana Manole

After a history of more than 100 years, the African Nova Scotian community of Africville, located on the northern shore of Halifax Harbour was destroyed to make way for industrial development [. . .] Between 1964 and 1970, residents were removed with many families being placed in public housing projects. Homes were demolished and the church bulldozed in the middle of the night.
—Africville Museum, "About the Museum"

DIANA MANOLE: The existence and destruction of Africville has been kept silent for decades, while its former residents have been asking for compensation. In 2010, after a long fight, a settlement was finally reached with the city of Halifax, which included 2.5 acres of land to serve for the reconstruction of the church, $3 million toward the construction costs, and a formal public apology by Mayor Peter Kelly ("About the Museum"). In 2013, the Africville Heritage Trust commissioned you to write a play about Africville, as a fundraiser for the Africville Museum. *Settling Africville* (2014) has proven a relevant example of an activist work that *un*-covers and *re*-writes the past to assert a perspective of history in opposition to the official metanarrative. You're one of the most revered Canadian poets and, yet, you've consistently come back to playwriting. What does theatre "give" you that other genres . . . maybe don't?

GEORGE ELLIOTT CLARKE: Theatre is ideas in action; ideologies or theologies or principles or ideals in conflict. Whether we wish them to do so or not, characters—even if a mix of virtues/vices—end up embodying particular drives/passions/interests. Of course, the more conflicted the character is, the better the play: the priest who lusts for a harlot while venerating the Virgin; the communist who hoards gold while plotting the overthrow of a tsar/czar. These are all potentially intriguing characters to see depicted as flesh-and-blood on stage.

I've been privileged to see all my plays and operas staged, although, I have to say, none has become a standard offering or revival, regardless of their initial success. One theatre company decided against doing *Beatrice Chancy* because it believed there aren't enough "Shakespearean"-calibre (black) actors about (which is flattering, I suppose, in a way, but is also shattering if true); another has rejected *Trudeau: Long March, Shining Path* just because there's no room in its schedule for it. My response to that has to be a Trudeauvian shrug!

MANOLE: And one would had thought this play were a *prime* [ministerial] choice today. The loss is theirs, but, sadly, also of the audiences!

CLARKE: Yes, I'm disappointed by the lack of "pick up" of my properties, and I am left to wonder whether it's just a reflection of the obscurity of my interests or the dauntingness of my verse. Yet, I've just written and published a new play, *The Merchant of Venice (Retried)*, which is a Shakespeare rewrite, and I'm hoping that a Toronto composer will create an operatic version. And then we'll see (and hear) what sort of reception it achieves.

MANOLE: Great news about an opera on your *Merchant of Venice*! Fingers crossed. Your plays and opera libretti include a large range of topics, which transcend historical, geographical, and cultural borders. How did you feel when you were asked to write a play about Africville?

CLARKE: Whatever my failings as a writer, I remain—I am—the best-known Africadian (African Nova Scotian) author, with a strong track record of being able to write lyrically and pungently, poignantly and raucously, about Africadian subjects and the folks themselves—in plays, novels, essays, screenplays, and poetry, of course. So, the decision to recruit me to write a play about the Africville Relocation (or Tragedy) was, perhaps, a natural one. They could have reached out to George Boyd, whose *Consecrated Ground* (1999) is already a fine treatment—for the stage—of the Africville saga. Similarly, Lawrence Hill's novel, *The Book of Negroes*, and the TV series (screenplay) were award-winning, smash hits. He would also have been a logical choice for penning a new play about Africville. However, I do have the advantage—like Boyd—of being a Haligonian. Thus, I grew up with—but not in—Africville, and its destruction and the dispersal of its former citizens to the slum properties of North End, downtown Halifax was a common reference point of my childhood, but also of elders, parents, mentors, teachers, artists, and activists.

MANOLE: Did you ever visit Africville before it was destroyed?

CLARKE: I have no conscious memory of Africville itself. Although I was seven before it was basically destroyed (by 1967), my father walked me up to the demolished site only in 1970, when it was rubble. It was by reading Clairmont and Magill's sociological classic, *Africville: The Life and Death of a Canadian Black Community* (1974), that my anger over the relocation was stoked. So, I was ten when I first viewed Africville's remnants—right beside the rat-infested rubbish of the then-still-active Halifax garbage dump; nineteen when I first began to protest the destruction of the community. (See a CBC TV series, *Contact,* circa 1979, hosted by Rita Shelton Deverell.) I was twenty-three when I first read and reviewed *Africville,* and I included a couple of poems about the community in my first book, *Saltwater Spirituals and Deeper Blues* (1983). It has always loomed large in my politico-cultural consciousness, as it has for most Africadians: Africville symbolizes the power of the State to rearrange and erase marginalized (ethnic) communities via Machiavellian propaganda of welfare-do-goodism and the Stalinist bulldozers of urban planning.

MANOLE: Set in 1965, *Consecrated Ground* is "a fictionalized account of this catastrophe" (Boyd 7), the demolishing of Africville. In your comments on the play, you support Boyd's perspective: "The only good produced by the disappearance of Africville was the appearance of a conscious black nationalism . . . In this regard, *Consecrated Ground* is the heir of fierce, vengeful, and epic activism" (Clarke). Nevertheless, you have chosen to do the opposite: re-enact the settling, not the destruction of Africville in your own play.

CLARKE: My desire was to remind audiences that the formation of Africville was a statement of anti-slavery and anti-racist Black political action as much as its destruction was the culmination of anti-Black racism and white supremacist whitewashing of a history of aforesaid racism. I thought it was important to show that powerful members of the white settler colonial State apparatus opposed the presence of Black people in Nova Scotia and, in particular, in Africville, right next door to Halifax. I wanted audiences to see that the settling of Africville was a political act—answered seven generations later by its allegedly economic-motivated destruction. In other words, the early 1960s debate over "what to do about Africville" had its origins in the War of 1812-era decision, of mainly ex-slaves, to respond to their socioeconomic marginalization by establishing a black community, distinct from, but still within, the city of Halifax.

MANOLE: Your erudition in African Canadian history is well known. Yet, in the note that precedes the play, you make it clear that *Settling Africville* "echoes history, but takes liberties." What kind of "liberties" did you take?

CLARKE: I took major liberties with "lifelines." So, I present the historical writer Thomas Chandler Haliburton as an established personage much earlier than he was in actual history. Similarly, it was important for me to have the historical figure of Richard Preston, a pioneering Black minister, available for debates with Haliburton, Lord Dalhousie (the founder of Dalhousie University), and Joseph Howe (a progressive reformist, friendly to Blacks), regardless of whether their bios all line up so dutifully. Louisa Bailey was also a real person—the first poetess of Africadia—who lived at the turn of the last century, in the Victorian era, and who has a couple of poems included in McKerrow's *A Brief History of the Coloured Baptists of Nova Scotia 1783–1895* (1976). But I present her as being born substantially earlier than she was in history, and I also present her as a Virginian slave, which was also not her birth condition. I also sought to speak back to the maligning of the Black Refugees (1812–15) as a lazy, illiterate lot who deserved oppression and starvation. I needed to remind folks that today's "Negrophobia" is rooted in attitudes that grew up during mass Negro slavery that was practiced throughout colonial North, Central, and South America.

MANOLE: This kind of perspective toward the Black Refugees has been disseminated even by more recent works. In *The Blacks in Canada: A History* (1997), Robin Winks describes them as "a disorganized, pathetic, and intimidated body who seemed unable to recover from their previous condition of servitude [. . . who] unwittingly fanned the sparks of a more conscious, more organized, white racism than Nova Scotia had known, just as the last vestiges of slavery were passing" (114). In contrast, *Settling Africville* reclaims them as Canadian settlers in their own right. Does this reassessment have a historical foundation?

CLARKE: Yes, the historical foundation is supported by at least two sources. Joseph Howe—a printer, newspaper editor, champion of press liberty, and a future premier and lieutenant governor of Nova Scotia—wrote in his *Western Rambles* (1828) about "dusky Pomonas" hurling strawberries and raspberries down his throat all around Bedford Basin (which is where Africville was situated). There is an erotic charge to Howe's writing up of Black women as fertility goddesses. In his much later *A Brief History of the Colored Baptists of Nova Scotia*, Peter E. McKerrow, a native of Antigua, tells us that what was then called "Campbell Road Settlement," boasted schoolkids (if not a school) and a church (if not quite enough Christians). It is pretty easy to surmise from these sources that Africville was an agricultural, seaside village where residents supplemented (cheap) wages from day labour and/or maid service in Halifax by raising some vegetables and berries, keeping some livestock and poultry, and fishing from their properties. The existence of a church by 1849 says that residents felt that they were there to stay.

MANOLE: In the production's Prologue, Louisa Bailey enters the stage carrying a book ironically entitled *Black Refugee History: For Beginners*, from which she reads about the arrival of over 2,000 later-called "Black Refugees" from the US and the foundation of Africville by "100 brave women, children, and men/[Who] Stayed—strayed—within the Halifax City limits." In my view then, *Settling Africville* does not attempt "a post-colonial RE-writing of national history, i.e. uncovering events that were intentionally omitted and / or completely erased, but rather a diachronic and intentionally anachronistic (in other words, post-modern) re-reading of said documented facts from a contemporary and, in fact, very Canadian perspective" (Manole). Despite your fictional interventions in the documented timeline, did you intend to *re-settle* Africville in our culture and history?

CLARKE: The play's title says it all; and it's meant to be read in a double-tongued sense. *Settling Africville* is partly about Black settlers deciding to make a home there; but it is also about white power brokers trying to settle "The Negro Question" by getting rid of Black settlers in Nova Scotia, especially in Africville. But the title also refers to the unsettled pain and agony of the Africville Relocation survivors and their need for a financial and political set-tlement for their loss. At the same time, some continue to "settle Africville" by either "squatting" on the site or by trying to dispense with it utterly. The title is meant to refer to this polyphonic and polysemous history. But the play also suggests, I hope, that Africville resists "settlement" as a resolvable issue, though I believe that re-settlement of the property by Africville descendants is the way forward—by going backward (physically, not politically).

MANOLE: According to Yana Meerzon, the editor of this anthology, this project's main focus is on the dramatic representation of immigration and displacement. Does your play address this subject?

CLARKE: The play engages this politics of spatial location, relocation, and dislo-cation by clarifying—specifying—that the movement of Black people into (and settling upon) Canada has always been a political act, in terms of flouting white supremacist racism, which, when it cannot deport Blacks, does its best to ignore or erase our presence. *Settling Africville* insists that it was (and is) heroic for folks of Black African admixture or identity to seek to build homes, neighbourhoods, and/or communities, and/or to hold and own land collectively (as opposed to renting individual, and isolated units or residing in public housing), in a nation whose elites conceive of its being—racially—truly—"The Great White North."

MANOLE: How would you describe the movement of the Black population to Canada in the general framework of the country's immigration policies?

CLARKE: The movement has been a double-negative consistently. What I mean is, Blacks have come to Canada to escape slavery in the United States, white-supremacist/imperialist colonialism in the Caribbean, and racism elsewhere; however, there was slavery in colonial Canada—along with white supremacist/ imperialist colonialism and anti-Black (Negrophobic) racism. So, Black people have also fled Canada—or been deported. This "double-negative" exists also in the sense that the first Blacks to "migrate" to Canada were imported as slaves in colonial Nouvelle-France and British North America, a situation that lasted centuries, from 1608 to 1834 (when Great Britain abolished slavery in British North America). The next major influxes into colonial Canada—1760, 1783, 1812–15, 1848, and the Underground Railroad era (1831–61)—were also, for the most part, involuntary, i.e., forced—either via transportation by slave masters (1760 and 1783) or forced removal from Jamaica (the Maroons—1796), or exodus from the slaveholding United States (1783, 1812–15, 1848, 1831–61). Yet, at the same time that tens of thousands arrived in colonial Canada, there were spasms of out-migration, either slaves escaping colonial Canadian enslavement by decamping for free American states (in New England, Ohio, and Michigan) or free Blacks (in Nova Scotia) being re-settled by the British in Sierra Leone (1792 and 1800) or Trinidad (1821). After the US Civil War concluded, tens of thousands of Underground Railroad and/or fugitive Slave Law (1851) refugees abandoned the generally unwelcoming colonies of Canada West (Ontario) and Canada East (Québec) and returned to the United States. Black settlers from California were welcomed to British Columbia in 1848. These folks sought to escape the anti-Black racism in their homeland (even though the state is named, ironically, for a Black woman). BC accepted them, though, as a bulwark against American annexation efforts. A half-century later, hundreds of African Americans, to escape Ku Klux Klan violence in the post-Reconstruction South and in Oklahoma, accepted the Dominion of Canada's offer of "free land" in the latter days of Queen Victoria's reign, and migrated to northern Saskatchewan (the Battlefords) and Alberta (Amber Valley) to become homesteaders. However, Negrophobia in the brand new provinces of Alberta and Saskatchewan, circa

1905, led the Laurier national premiership to begin to restrict Black immigration into Canada, via orders-in-council that were not expunged until 1955. During this period, too, some Blacks were deported to the US, while some West Indian Blacks were accepted as railway porters, sailors, or university students. As of 1955, Blacks were again allowed to enter Canada—from the Caribbean—but only as students (men) or domestic workers (women), in a plan that was racist, sexist, and classist. (Three oppressions in a single policy: how very, efficiently, Canadian!) To conclude with a single sentence: the history of Black migration to Canada has been as much a matter of unsettling and deportation and exodus as it has been one of voluntary, wilful, Black-popular efforts to actually settle, belong, and become *Canadian*.

MANOLE: Thank you for this informative history review! Like your other dramatic works, however, *Settling Africville* somewhat distances itself from facts with many lines, and especially with speeches having a lyrical diction. How does poetry inform your playwriting?

CLARKE: In all my earlier plays, I embraced degrees of obvious artifice, to accent "poeticality"—or the fact that one was not witnessing anything truly natural. I liked the approaches of Brecht and García Lorca, who in different (maybe even opposite) ways insisted upon the theatricality of setting and speech, the surrealism of folkish or criminal principals, and/or the hyperrealism of stage events and personae. Maybe I decided this time to root everything in everyday speech so that it could be more readily comprehensible by all and so do a better job of overturning the historical maligning of Africville and the treatment of its people as malignant.

MANOLE: And yet, this everyday speech, as you call it, has a remarkable poetic dimension in this play.

CLARKE: I chose to write the lines of *Settling Africville* as "orature"—oral-oriented poetry—not wanting to write anything difficult to say. I wanted the lines to sound utterly natural and close to how Africadians talk/speak. I wanted the language to "flow" and seem completely unforced. I did sound aloud every line—many times—before committing them to paper. I should also say that I came to the writing of *Settling Africville* while also writing the dramatic monologues that compose *Canticles I* (two volumes, MMXVI and MMXVII). In both cases, I'm trying to let characters "speak for themselves"—without censorship.

MANOLE: What are the most relevant differences between writing lines for the characters in your poetry, especially in *Canticles*, and, respectively, in a play?

CLARKE: The major difference is that I seldom allow the play's characters to wander off into erudite tangents; yet, the poems' personae are able to "speak" for oodles of pages, which is not a luxury permitted to the play's characters. The speakers in *Canticles I* are almost all limited to a particular circumstance; each refers to a specific moment. But the characters in *Settling Africville* develop from one crisis (or context) to the next. They are consistent in their views, but they are called upon to react to different personages and events. In this sense, they are more dynamic than the speakers in *Canticles I.*

MANOLE: Your "Note on the Text" that precedes the play mentions: "Africadian English boasts elemental ornaments. It is a speech too plain to be poetic, but yet cannot be prose." The language of *Settling Africville* is so rich and vehement that even Haliburton, as a character, states that Richard Preston "tongue-lashes English." How much of it is your own poetic syntax and how much is African Canadian English?

CLARKE: I'd like to think that the lingo of *Settling Africville* is pretty much Africadian English, which does not tend to be as "free" as African-American Vernacular English, but is defiantly—definitely—more posh than Standard (Nova Scotian) English. My own "natural" way of speaking English is to produce a fairly sophisticated diction, but with a very "loose" grammatical structure. I use a similar style in my first novel, *George & Rue* (2005), where I describe it as "Blackened English" as opposed to "Black English." I think the best comparison is with the scripts produced for the *Studio Black* CBC TV series, presented by Picture Plant of Lunenburg, Nova Scotia. Newfoundland-born Bill MacGillivray, who is European/Caucasian Canadian, drafts scripts based on Black Nova Scotian folklore; these are then voiced by Africadian actors under the direction of Africadian directors. The result is exactly what I aim for in *Whylah Falls* (1990), *George & Rue*, *The Motorcyclist* (2016), and *Settling Africville*: the crafty artistry and/or Blackened English of Africadian English.

MANOLE: In *Black Skin, White Masks*, Frantz Fanon argues that to speak means "to be in a position to use a certain syntax, to grasp the morphology of this or that language, but it means above all to assume a culture, to support the weight of civilization" (18). Is this the reason why Bull Styron, the slave owner from Virginia, is so angry with his slave, Louisa Bailey, for her ability to write poetry?

CLARKE: Well, literacy was a definite technology in the struggle to end slavery. A literate slave could weaponize—so to speak—the US Declaration of Independence ("all men are equal") or the Holy Bible ("call no man lord") or various verses from the Anglo American poetic canon (John Greenleaf Whittier or Longfellow or Shelley or Blake or Milton or others). So, for Styron to have a literate slave on his property (as his property) is to have a possible female Spartacus in his midst—someone who could rally other slaves to escape, to sabotage crops, to kill livestock, to commit infanticide, to torch the master's edifices, to cut the throats of all the white folks. Many slave rebellions were led, in fact, by literate slaves (such as Nat Turner). In many slave states, slaves were forbidden knowledge of letters and they and their teachers could be executed if said knowledge was discovered or divulged.

MANOLE: Our collaboration has started with my dramaturgical—i.e., surgical— assistance on *Settling Africville* and continued with editing several other projects.

CLARKE: Diana, I again thank you for your editing "surgery" on *Settling Africville, Gold, Canticles I (MMXVI)*, and *The Motorcyclist*. I was happy to savour your insights and assistance on these projects, just as I was also glad to receive some very helpful ideas and edits from Paul Zemokhol—my long-time editor-friend—and several other folks. From as far back as *Whylah Falls*, I have been circumspect about my talents enough to welcome the input of others—and to offer other writers my ideas (such as yourself, for example). Far from being ashamed for my outreach to "primary readers," I have been—and feel—proud to be humble enough to accept their suggestions and improvements.

MANOLE: When you look back, was there a difference between my insight as the print dramaturg/editor on *Settling Africville* and that as the editor of the other books, especially when receiving insight from the same person in three genres? In my notes, for instance, there are several suggestions to shorten, or rather condense, some longer lines/monologues. The *poet* might had been enraged by such suggestions. How did the *playwright* feel about this?

CLARKE: As a Pound-influenced poet, I have a predilection—I hope—to be succinct; to favour the condensed and that which is to the point. I did strive for that notion of precision, which means eschewing any cliché or prolixity. To me, a striving for simplicity and concreteness is the point of all four works we named—regardless of genre. However, character development was vital, of course, to the novel and to the play, if not so much the poetry in *Gold*. As an editor of the play, you also had some great ideas regarding increasing the number of characters and adding an opening scene of a slave auction. (Merci encore!) Then, Juanita Peters, in actually staging the play, had to make decisions (given limits of funds and the actual theatre) on how to present it most effectively. There's no question in my mind that *Settling Africville* benefitted from both of your ideas/interpretations.

MANOLE: The opening night audience of the show directed by Juanita Peters was extremely enthusiastic. What were your own first impressions?

CLARKE: It was impressive to me that a cross-section of "Scotians"—including the then-Lieutenant Governor—found the play to be relevant to "now" events (in 2014) and yet were also open to the "history lesson" that the play relates. I was also astonished by the spontaneous audience reactions to some repartee and events. I was gratified thoroughly by the mass response, which was worshipful (of the play and its characters/actors).

MANOLE: Lesley Dunn, the executive director (2012–16) of the Dartmouth Learning Network, forwarded to me the reflections of the then-students in the Adult Learning Program who saw the 2014 production of *Settling Africville*. Mike Boutilier, for example, exclaimed "What an eye opener. I could not believe that is how it was," while Terry Wilson noted "It is a part of Nova Scotia history, which I didn't know before," and Meleesa Clarke concluded "At the end I cried; it did get to my heart on a lot of things" (qtd. in Dunn). The play clearly succeeded in reaching the Nova Scotian audiences as both a history lesson and an empowering piece of theatre. What would you like to tell the future readers of *Settling Africville*?

CLARKE: Stage it! Fearlessly! Passionately! Relentlessly!

Works Cited

"About the Museum." *Africville Museum*, https://africvillemuseum.org /the-story/.

Boyd, George. *Consecrated Ground*. Talonbooks, 2011.

Clarke, George Elliott. "Quotes of Note." *Internet Archive*, 4 Jul. 2017, https://web.archive.org/web/20170704110357/http://talonbooks.com/authors /george-boyd.

Dunn, Lesley. "Level 2 Adult Learning Program Settling Africville Reflections." Personal email to Diana Manole, Dartmouth Learning Network, 5 May 2015.

Fanon, Frantz. *Black Skin, White Masks*. Grove, 1967.

Manole, Diana. "The Elephant in the (Green) Room: Imperialism Revisited in George Elliott Clarke's *Settling Africville* and Sang Kim's *A Dream Called Laundry*." Remembering and / or Forgetting? Staging History, Memory, and Exile in Canadian Theatre, Canadian Association for Theatre Research (CATR), Ottawa, 1 Jun. 2015.

Winks, Robin. *The Blacks in Canada: A History*. 1971. 2nd ed., McGill-Queen's UP, 1997.

The Tashme Project:
The Living Archives

by Julie Tamiko Manning and Matt Miwa

We would like to dedicate *The Tashme Project: The Living Archives* as a love letter back to our Japanese Canadian family and community.

Acknowledgements

We wish to thank the Miwa, Taira, and Takeda families for their support and encouragement; the sixty-plus Nikkei interviewees from across Canada for their invaluable participation—especially the Nisei and Sansei, whose stories are woven throughout this play, for sharing their memories and strength. We are forever touched by: Jean Fujimoto, Molly Morita, Jane Uesugi, Kunio Takeda, Sumire (Vi) Uchiyama-Frye, Richard Takeda, Terry Yasunaka, May Yasunaka, Harold Miwa, Yasuko (Alice) Aihoshi, Dave Sakamoto, Shigemi (Sed) Mitobe, Midori (Dori) Mitobe, Teiko Takeda, Ty Mariyama, Kay Suzuki, Ryuko (Pat) Ikeda, Tad Suzuki, George Ikeda, Kazie Burke, Shoji Nishihata, Ko Kadonaga, and Helen Tamiko Manning.

Thank you for teaching us about resilience, love, and community.

We would like to thank Arashi Daiko for the use of their recording of "Sanya" in the 2015 production at the MAI and Emma Tibaldo of Playwrights' Workshop Montréal for her support from the beginning.

The Tashme Project: The Living Archives is a verbatim play that has been edited from one hundred-plus hours of interviews with Nikkei* across Canada. It has been performed in staged readings across the country since 2011. Workshop productions were mounted in 2014 as part of the Undercurrents Theatre Festival in Ottawa, Ontario, and in 2016 as part of Soulpepper Theatre's Tiger Bamboo Asian Performance Festival. *The Tashme Project*'s first full production was presented in May 2015 at the MAI (Montréal, arts interculturels) and produced by Tashme Productions in association with Playwrights' Workshop Montréal.

The script for *The Tashme Project: The Living Archives* was created and developed in collaboration with Playwrights' Workshop Montréal. Additional development support has been provided by the Powell Street Festival Society, the MAI (Montréal, arts interculturels), and Soulpepper's Tiger Bamboo Festival.

The Tashme Project has received financial support from the Cole Foundation, the Canada Council for the Arts, the Conseil des arts et des lettres du Québec, the Conseil des arts de Montréal, the Ontario Arts Council, Fu-GEN Theatre (TCR), the Ottawa Japanese Community Association & Community Centre, Montréal Shokokai, and the National Association of Japanese Canadians.

---

* *Nikkei*: Members of the Japanese diaspora.

The production at the MAI (Montréal, arts interculturels) in May 2015 featured the following creative team:

Julie Tamiko Manning: Performer
Matt Miwa: Performer

Director: Mieko Ouchi
Video Design: George Allister and Patrick Andrew Boivin
Sound Design: Patrick Andrew Boivin
Technical Direction: Tristynn Duheme
Production Assistance: Isabel Quintero Faia
Set and Costume Design: James Lavoie
Assistant Set and Costume Design: Laurence Mongeau
Lighting Design: David Perreault Ninacs
Stage Management: Merissa Tordjman

The 2018/19 Canadian tour to Centaur Theatre, Factory Theatre, Firehall Arts Centre, and the Prismatic Arts Festival featured the following creative team:

Julie Tamiko Manning: Performer
Matt Miwa: Performer

Director: Mike Payette
Video Design: George Allister
Sound Design: Patrick Andrew Boivin
Technical Direction: Tristynn Duheme
Stage Management: Isabel Quintero Faia
Movement Dramaturgy: Rebecca Harper
Set and Costume Design: James Lavoie
Assistant Set and Costume Design: Laurence Mongeau
Lighting Design: David Perreault Ninacs
Head LX: Jon Cleveland

Prologue

A wooden table with two wooden chairs. Julie and Matt sit at the table, contemplating a closed briefcase that once belonged to Julie's grandfather. Each waits for the other to begin. Finally, Matt moves to open the briefcase, startling Julie. He opens the briefcase and pulls out an origami crane. Despite a show of reluctance from Julie, Matt unfolds the crane and reads its contents aloud.

MATT: "Notice to Enemy Alien. Vancouver, BC. March 16, 1942.

"To Torao Takeeda."

JULIE: Takeda

MATT: "Japanese Registration Number 07441.

"The government instructs me to advise you that you must present yourself on the 17 March, 1942, nine AM at the Royal Canadian Mounted Police Barracks at 33 and Heather Street, Vancouver. Failure to comply with this order will, on the instruction of the government, result in the issuing of an order for your internment."

JULIE: By the time I was old enough to want to know what that meant, Grandpa was already gone . . . as were most of the Issei.* My grandpa and I didn't share much. He was born in Japan. I was born in Canada. He spoke Japanese. I spoke English. He was a reticent old man. I was a chatty little girl. He wrote haiku. I wrote down the lyrics to Duran Duran. But I was his blood, and our blood was thicker than anything. My uncle said that after Grandpa died, my grandma's purpose was gone. She turned his desk into a shrine. Hotokesan. I dunno. I guess it's a Buddhist or Shinto thing. It held memories of him: his ashes, his photos, freshly made green tea, a bowl of rice, flowers from his garden, his haiku, mandarins. Offerings of the things that he loved. The things she loved about him.

Grandma died a few years later.

---

* *Issei*: First-generation Japanese; those who immigrated.

Julie carefully folds the document and places it back in the briefcase.

MATT: What are you doing?

JULIE: Putting it back.

MATT: Why?

JULIE: Because . . . No one wants to talk about it.

MATT: Your family kept that letter for a reason.

Beat.
The phone call.

Oh, hi, Grandpa, it's Matt . . . Grandpa, what camp were you in? . . . Ya, internment camp . . . Tashme?! Well, I met a friend who's half-Japanese, yes like me, and her family was in Tashme . . . Her name is Julie . . . last name? Ah, Manning . . .

(to Julie) What's your family name again?

JULIE: Takeda

MATT: Takeeda

JULIE: Takeda.

MATT: *(to Grandpa on the phone)* Takeda . . . Yeah, they were in Tashme, funny, eh? You might remember them? Well . . . that's why I'm calling . . . Doing a play. I met her doing a play . . . this year, yeah.

Well yeah! In fact, we both were wondering if we could come talk to you about that . . . about Tashme . . . Well, we just wanna know what it was like to live there every day, what you did . . . and we'll have to record what you say . . . Well, so that we don't have to remember everything. Okay, do you still know anyone else who was in your camp? Oh, well, can you ask them if they would like to talk to us, too? Okay, but if you're bowling on Tuesday then we can come another day . . . Okay, I'll call you later. Okay, bye.

Matt hands the document back to Julie. She folds it in two and places it back in the briefcase then closes the briefcase.

JULIE: So, he said yes?

MATT: First, he said the Nisei* were too young, so it was no good talking to them, and if we wanted to know about internment . . . we really should've talked to the Issei.

JULIE: You know who the Issei are, right?

MATT: Yeah, first generation.

JULIE: Ya. Your great-grandparents, my grandparents. And they're . . . gone. They never would have talked about it anyway. We didn't even speak the same language! So, who does he want us to talk to? The Nisei are the only ones left who lived through the internment.

Why do they keep saying that they don't remember anything when I know that they do?

> *Shift.*
> *A Nikkei kitchen.*
> *Julie transitions into Alice. Alice gets photo albums and sets them on the table.*

MATT: So . . . this was Julie's grandpa's briefcase, we've been looking through it and we thought we might show you . . .

> *She gets a jubako† filled with onigiri,‡ sembei,§ and mandarins, which she sets out on the table.*

Oh, you didn't have to go through all this trouble . . . So my grandpa says that you've known him since Tashme . . . Let me help you . . .

> *Matt gets a Japanese teapot and teacups, sets them on the table.*

We just have a couple of questions . . . They're easy questions, eh? You answer however you want . . . You could even just tell us your name.

---

*   *Nisei*: Second-generation Japanese.

†   *Jubako*: Traditional lacquered serving dish. It usually has multiple layers that stack.

‡   *Onigiri*: Rice ball. A favourite Japanese snack made of seasoned rice and often filled with various treats.

§   *Sembei*: Rice-cracker snack.

Chapter One / Pre-War Vancouver

ALICE: Do you want my, um, do you want my name right now? I mean, cuz you don't mean my child, uh, former name— Well. It's Alice.

She turns to the audience.

But my Japanese name is Yasuko. My dad had a tailor shop. Right on Main Street. My dad's store was on Main Street, but we lived in a house in Grandview. GrandVIEW, not Granville. GrandVIEW. Now, let's see . . . what else did you wanna know?

Matt becomes Molly and Alice becomes Julie.
A lumber mill.

MOLLY: Molly, yes . . . Uh where . . . ?

JULIE: Where did you grow up?

MOLLY: Oh! Ah, I was born in Fraser Mills, BC. That's outside of New Westminster, Sapperton. It was a lumber mill, very well known at that time. A lumber mill, the logs would come down the Fraser River and it would go up and they would strip it, they made lumber. And so we would play on the lumber piles like Tarzan, you know, we would swing on it and then we would leap into the grass, and "youppie!" and that was our playground and ah, it was a good life because at Fraser Mills maybe we had eight families . . . that's all. That's all.

Uh, we would not take rice balls to school or anything like that because we were the odd ones. We ate sandwiches, sandwiches! We did not dare do rice balls, because, because they would always say, you know, you know, "What are you Eating!" Yeah. But at school, there was one kid that picked on me a lot, I hated him, I hated him, he, he picked on me and nobody stuck up for me because I was Japanese, but I would tell him no, you know. I wouldn't do what he said, but he was not a good guy and I often think what happened to him. I bet he was a meanie or he was a robber, he was that kind of a person, yeah. I didn't think he would become a good person. Yeah, yeah.

Shift. Present.
Molly becomes Matt.

MATT: A lot of Japanese Canadians that we've talked to now, coming from my dad's generation—the post-war generation—often speak about growing up not wanting to be Japanese, or thinking of themselves as not. When I asked my cousin what she saw herself as, she yelled: "WHITE!" But she's full Japanese . . . looking.

But she is also, we're also Japanese in ways we have always felt . . . feel, but can't . . . it's always hard to say. Until I . . . I didn't know how to look into our past—or the hard facts of being Japanese Canadian. These things have always been kept out of sight, and out of mind. Then I met you.

Shift. Vancouver Island.
Julie becomes Jean.

So, Jean, where did you grow up?

JEAN: In Chemainus, there was three sections that the Japanese lived in. One was called Chinatown, because most of the Chinese lived there, but there was maybe thirteen Japanese family in that town. They called it town. And then next to us was Okada Camp. Which, the reason why they named it that was because there was about, how many . . . three . . . or four Okada family, living in this— But anyways, that's why they called it Okada Camp. But then, the other section the Japanese lived in was called Karahara Camp. Because there was so many Karahara family, you know what I mean? You know, the uncles, and then they get married and there was, what, about four Karahara family.

Everything was done at the Japanese school or at the church. If you wanted to go to church, you just went to whatever church you want to. Which is not Japanese, it was you know— Congregation was Canadians and— So . . . it was mixed. Mother sent us—she didn't care which church we really went to because she needed to clean the house and she had to get all the kids out, right? So, Sunday morning, she'd tell us older ones, "Okay you all go to church, I don't care what church you go to." She didn't tell us to go to play. She told us, "You have to go to church." So, you know, we went, and then, that's why we went to, ah, United Church, because they gave the most stars and little books and what not.

MATT: You tried all your churches out.

JEAN: Yeah! Mom, you know, at least she had a little bit of peace while we were away.

Shift. A fishing village.

Jean becomes Julie and Matt becomes Kunio.

KUNIO: I got into trouble once. I must have been about nine or ten, I guess. I used to go fishing quite often, and the Japanese ships used to come into the docks in Port Alberni and I befriended one of the people in the ship. He showed me all around the ship and he said that he's going to come to visit our house after. And instead he went to somebody else's place, and I went with him and I asked him if he was going to come. He says yeah. But I think it was past midnight. Finally, he told me I better go home because it's too late now. When I got to my home there was a whole line of people with lights, flashlights and that. And they were all out looking for me. My parents thought I was drowned because I went fishing that day. And boy, my dad was mad. I got the whipping of my life. I never even realized time though, I just thought the guy was going to come, and I just wanted to take him home and show him to my parents. And the branch that I used for fishing—my dad, he took that and whacked, whacked the hell out of me. I'll never forget that.

Shift. Present.
Kunio becomes Matt

JULIE: I've never heard my uncle speak about my grandpa that way. It makes sense though. He was an intimidating man—Grandpa.

He used to have this chair in the living room, and if anyone was sitting in it when he came into the room—boy, you'd move fast to get out of it before he got there or else . . .

The whistle of a kettle boiling.

When you heat water for green tea, you should never let it get to the boiling point or it will burn the leaves and the tea will become bitter.

Julie pours tea

Shift. A living room in Toronto.
Matt becomes Dave.

DAVE: Just when I was starting kindergarten, over here, in Canada, I was taken back to Japan with my mother, and we were only supposed to be there for two months. But we stayed there for two years. My mother had infection in her, ahh, legs, from hop picking. You know, the hops, for making beer. She got infection from that and didn't matter how long she tried to get it fixed, couldn't fix it, so my father sent her back to Japan. Took two years. From five years old until seven years—going onto eight! And that's when I started Grade 1. When I was eight years old, when I came back to Canada. I didn't know a single word of English. Two words: "mamma, papa." That's the only two English words that I knew when I came back! Even from before the war, okay, because, the family, our family, was sooo poor, we used to just live in a shack. When I say a shack, I mean we had a roof over our head, yes, but I mean, how many buckets did we have to have, you know, in the room. To catch all the rain. And then the first year in Grade 1, I failed. Because I didn't know anything. I couldn't pass. And every single day when I get to a certain corner of the street, you see—one head there, one head there, and one head there. All waiting to GET me. And I would run like hell to get to the school.

JULIE: Were they white kids? Hakujin?*

DAVE: Noooooo. Everyone was blackhead like me. I was always a loner. It's not that you prefer to be alone. It was almost—that's why even today—I should've been up here, I'm down here. I'm trying to catch up but I can't. Was too tough. That's why I said to Mom, I said, before you people came, I was, you know, I don't want to go through all this garbage anymore, because I've gone through too much. I don't wanna bring up all that memory that I'm trying to, you know, put it back right, but now it's all coming back and it kinda chokes me up.

Shift. A seniors' home in Burnaby. Photos.
Julie becomes Jane. She sets the teacup down for Dave. Dave becomes Matt

JANE: I was a rebel, I hear, when I was very, very young.

But I changed. I changed when my mother passed away. And my sister passed away, just around the same time. Oh, I just couldn't take it. I just couldn't take it. I just felt I was all alone that I was very cautious after that. Up till then I was so carefree—I didn't have a care in the world. This was when I was in Mayo. You wouldn't know about that. I was eleven at that time when my sister passed away. It was a train accident. My sister was twenty-four. She had four children by that time. We couldn't tell our mother, she was in the hospital, so when they visited, they always, they took the band, you know, Jap'nese used to wear a band—

MATT: The mourning band. A black band.

---

* *Hakujin*: Japanese word for white people.

JANE: —they took it off. But we had to tell my mother when she came home, because my sister's children were with us. And then a little later my mother passed away. She was forty-two. But that was a bad time. It's just as well you don't know, because it was a very sad time at that time. But anyway, life goes on.

Matt pours tea and offers it to Jane. Jane offers Matt a crane.
Shift. Present
Jane becomes Julie

JULIE: Did you notice that during the interview, Jane kept looking at the pictures of her family on the wall behind me?

MATT: No, I was just listening.

Matt opens crane.

JULIE: Are we being responsible, stirring up so many memories and then just leaving?

MATT: They're passing on something vital, and no, we are not there afterward, but we're not . . . I don't think we're doing anything wrong. I am shocked by all the things we would never have known, what they never asked us to remember. She told us. It was a gift. I can picture my own mom in her story. And the consequences, we couldn't know them before we asked, but then again, what they are asking of us through all this: Who are we to them?

Matt reads the unfolded crane/document.

"Notice to all Japanese persons and persons of Japanese racial origin. Monday, February 2, 1942.

"No person of the Japanese race shall go out of his usual place of residence, upon the streets or otherwise during the hours between sunset and sunrise."

JULIE: We should call.

Shift. An attack. The sound of an overhead bomber zooming by is heard, followed by the release of a missile and a huge Explosion!
Julie becomes Molly. Matt becomes Kunio

MOLLY: I remember it was in the weekend and the, listening to the radio and hear Japan had bombed Pearl Harbor . . . Japan, how could they come this way, you know, how far, it was far, neh,* Japan to come to bomb Pearl Harbor. We didn't even know where Pearl Harbor was until that day. At that time, when the war came, you could not believe it was the Japanese, you know, because you didn't think Japanese would come over and start a war, neh, in America. Never. Never.

Shift. Under curfew.
Molly becomes Teiko. She joins Kunio.

KUNIO: I remember in Port Alberni, they built a, a—I think it was about six feet high—fence, all around the whole community—

TEIKO: —so that they can't get out.

KUNIO: —and they had a gate at the end of the road like, uh, you know each end, there was only one road going in and out and at the end of the community, they had a gate, they close it at nighttime and then open it up again in the morning.

TEIKO: This was after the war started.

KUNIO: Ya.

TEIKO: Ya. In Vancouver it was like that, right in the city of Vancouver. After nine o'clock the Japanese weren't allowed on the street—

KUNIO: —blackout, eh? After the blackout / you're not supposed to leave your house, you had to stay in your house.

TEIKO: —the Jap'nese. The Chinese people could, but not us.

KUNIO: But I think after about a week or so everybody started getting brave, started taking their flashlight and going sneaking around us to visit. We couldn't get out of the gate but we can, you know, we wanted to go see friends, eh, so— you're not supposed to leave the house, not after dark.

TEIKO: Ya. After nine.

KUNIO: Even if you're gated, ya, you're not supposed to / leave.

TEIKO: Oh we weren't gated or anything, but I remember me and my cousin said, we said, "Let's try it and see what happens." So we stayed out after nine o'clock and the police car came 'round and shone a HUGE light on our face . . . we got scared . . . we ran in the house. We just wanted to try it to see what happened!!!

---

* *Neh*: Japanese slang for "eh."

Chapter Two / Evacuation

Shift. At the doorway.
Kunio becomes Ty and Teiko becomes Molly.

TY: They came to the house, the Mounties did, and asked for Ji-chan,* and they just took him away! And we didn't even know where he went!

MOLLY: I just know Papa was gone, and one day we would be together, but I didn't know when. We didn't know where he was. You just took it as "She said" that "he will come back." Didn't think it was strange. At that time there was so much upheaval, you just didn't think, you just—whatever was told to you, you know? Yeah, and so Mama had to do all the gathering of what we could take. We had the Japanese, uh . . .

TY: Kori

MOLLY: Kori, yeah, straw, straw—soft basket—has a top and a bottom.

TY: You were able to bring that?

MOLLY: Hai, we tied it up!

TY: Oh, we couldn't bring that, we were just allowed ah, one clothes bag and one suitcase, that's all we were allowed to take out.

MOLLY: No, no, we had the kori, and then we had a suitcase each—

TY: Ya?

MOLLY: Ya, suitcase each.

It was sad because Mama, all our mothers had to do this gathering up what we're going to take, and then it was sort of like a garage sale, we would put things we can't take outside, and then the people would come and they would put twenty-five cents or whatever, and my sister Toyo said, "No, I can't do it." But I would stand there and I said, "No you can't, you have to pay a little bit more," you know, and I was young then but I wasn't going to let them have everything free. That

---

* *Ji-chan:* Japanese word for grandfather. Here, Ty is actually referring to her father, Matt's great-grandfather.

was hard. Dishes and just, you know, big display things, and here they would just, just, not even offer a dollar. We did have one friend, a friend of a friend said—

TY: "We will keep your things."

MOLLY: —so we trusted—we shipped, you know packed it and put it over there at their house, but that was all gone, I mean they didn't keep for us, it was gone. Yeah so. It's a case of you just . . . lost it, neh—

TY: Yeah.

MOLLY: It would be beautiful Japanese old vases that you see in these collector things, beautiful things and dishes that . . . were beautiful. But you couldn't take them with you, and it was more clothing you took. Kimono? Those kind of things, you know, you didn't know where to give it—you just put it outside because you couldn't pack it, no.

TY: Those were luxury, neh.

MOLLY: You didn't do kimono or anything that you had for odori.* No, no, those were luxury, they were not necessity, and this was necessity time. It was sad because the mothers at that time—

TY: They were young mothers, eh?

MOLLY: —and here they had to just gather up things that they could take, and no pots and pans, no kitchens knives, nothing like that. So, we all had to start over again, didn't we?

TY: Hardship all around, you know—

MOLLY: But it's wonderful in the way that everybody looked after each other, cuz in our way, families with little children, you would look after the little children, for mommy, you know, for the mom. I always think that the mothers had it so hard.

Ty becomes Matt. He slowly moves toward Molly.

One lady had a mental breakdown on the train, because her husband was taken away, her son was taken away, she was all alone. And she had a mental breakdown. She accused everybody and there was no one to help her, and we had to live with this for, I think, two to three days on the train. Yelling. We didn't know

---

* *Odori*: Traditional Japanese folk dancing.

what to do. The mothers all had little ones to look after and here she is walking around, ranting away, but she was so—she just lost it because her husband was taken away, her son was taken away, and she's all alone.

That was hard. Ya. So that was a lesson for me, to see something could go wrong, mentally.

Matt puts his hand on Molly's back, surprising her. She gives Matt a crane.
Shift. Present.
Matt opens the crane and Molly becomes Julie.

MATT: *(reading document)* "Notice to all Male Enemy Aliens of the ages of eighteen to forty-five years inclusive: the Government instructs me to advise you that you must leave the protected area by the 17 of March, 1942. That is to say, the area of British Columbia, including all Islands, and one hundred miles east of the coast."

JULIE: Not only were the men taken away, but the women and children had two days to pack up their homes to leave. Kay remembers that day well because it was her tenth birthday. Ten. No matter how resilient a ten-year-old is . . . they're still TEN.

Shift. A bonfire.
Matt becomes Kay.

KAY: I remember something about Deep Bay, the day before we moved. I remember all our toys and everything had to be burnt. There was a huge bonfire and we burnt everything, and I know that I really wanted a teddy bear for Christmas and I got a calico horse—no, it was a Pluto, I think—but anyway, Pluto got burnt and I remember that, you know. There was nobody to send it to. Our parents burned it because they couldn't take it. But I'm sure we weren't the only ones doing it. The funny thing is, when we had to leave Deep Bay, we were on the island at the time, we had to go into these, ah, Hastings Park, and then get relocated. And I remember, our neighbour was German and I was only ten, but I remember thinking, how come we have to leave and he doesn't have to leave? You know. It just sort of struck me even then.

Beat.

The only time I've ever seen my mother cry was when dad and my eldest brother were sent to the road camps. And then I've never seen her cry since and never before that day. But that day, she thought she was never going to see them again. So it was just, ya, one and only.

Shift. Present.
Kay becomes Matt.

JULIE: My family has ONE heirloom that is shared between nine children. Eight now. They pass it around so that every eight years it hangs on a wall in my parents' living room.

Years ago, my ex and I drove from Nanaimo to Tofino on Vancouver Island. To get to Tofino, you have to drive through Port Alberni. We stopped there for lunch. And even though he knew that we were stopping in Port Alberni for more than just lunch, I pretended like it was just lunch.

Port Alberni was where my family lived before they were branded enemy aliens and removed from the coast, where Grandpa was separated from Grandma and their four children for a road camp somewhere in the BC Interior. It was where they had to leave so many things behind, the things that would never become our heirlooms, the things that would never have any stories attached to them. Stopping in Port Alberni for lunch was the closest I was ever going to get to any of that. And it made me angry. So angry I couldn't think straight. So angry I couldn't speak. So I just stood at the edge of the water, staring into nothing. But in my head, I was smashing the whole town. Setting the water on fire. Bursting into neighbourhood houses with my guns blazing and taking it all back.

MATT: And then what happened?

JULIE: We just got back into the car in silence and left . . .

MATT: They've let go, I think. Or, I don't know . . . but they've not passed it on to me, because I've never felt that loss. My grandparents' home was always an easy place and, in my mind, growing up I knew that they came from the coast, through Hastings Park, internment to Toronto, but *stuff*, or things that were lost was never part of that story. So how do you feel that . . . how do you have that connection to what was lost?

JULIE: . . .

Chapter Three / Hastings Park

Shift. Sounds of an amusement park.
Matt grabs Julie's hand and leads her laughing through the park. They stop at
the sight of a fence.
Matt becomes Harold.

HAROLD: Okay, when the war broke out, okay? Right away we became enemy—in Canada we were enemy aliens, 'kay? Now to keep track of where all the Japanese people were, all the people living outside of Vancouver: Ucluelet, Cumberland, or Victoria, they're all over the place; they couldn't keep track of where they were, so it was easy for them to round them all up and bring them to Vancouver, but they had to put them somewhere so they put them in Hastings Park. You with me so far?

Julie becomes Jane.

Hastings Park was like a CNE Exhibition, right? They still have one every summer—they call theirs PNE: Pacific National Exhibition. And they have it in August, like same as Toronto, CNE.

They used to call it Happy Land, you know, they had all the rides an' all the games and everything? When we first went into Hastings Park, they forgot to put the fence up, so we're all out there on the rides and everything else, but it only lasted for a couple days then they all, they put the frost fence—barbwire fence up so we couldn't use it anymore.

JANE: I went to Victoria for a while to work as a domestic. I was thirteen. We got into very nice families, then I think about a few years later my sister musta phoned and said, "We have to go to, ah, Hastings Park." She felt the family should be together. I remember when we left there to evacuate, Mrs. Proctor, she was a very nice woman, she says, "You know, fear makes people do strange things." You know because of this war, ah, people panic—I guess this is what she meant. Yeah, "We do strange things."

I certainly knew when we went to Hastings Park that we were different. You know, you see people looking at you as you're lined up, lined up for supper or something. In Hastings Park, there's sort of a fence with wire. Well, they would go to the racetracks and they would sort of look down and I thought, gee whiz, I sure KNEW I was different at that time. I mean, you know, there was no barriers between Japanese and other nationalities back in Mayo, but when it came to Hastings Park there, well, they would look at us like this, I felt like something in a zoo. We were quite young but, but I didn't like it at all.

Harold becomes Teiko.

TEIKO: It smelled like a barn for sure, and supposedly it was washed, but I guess it still smells. You know, like, you had these little quarters with curtains hanging and that was your place to live, but they all had bunk beds, so the children all slept on the bunk beds so if you go on the top you can see. Like, everybody. You know what I mean? You could see everyone sleeping. Then you get up in the morning you start to see all the heads start to pop up. And I remember the bathroom, eh? Just like the horses when they drink from—it was one long thing, eh? It was like a trough, I remember that. A trough with a partition but there's no door, just a partition, and the water was constantly running.

Jane becomes Jean.

JEAN: Barbed wire. Barbed wire, they were all, oh yeah, it was all barbed wire.

And then there was the mess hall—and another thing was, we were in a horse stall, right? But a family is just closed in with blankets. I mean, how much privacy can you get, like, you know?

The men couldn't stay in our building. The men had the men's building: the older folks, and then my brother. Y'know, at thirteen. My dad was gone. They sent them to road camp. So there'd be kids from thirteen to seventeen that would have to stay in the men's building.

Teiko becomes Harold.

HAROLD: We're still kids—we wanna go see our mother, but you just can't walk into the building, you have to get a pass to go into the building. So, to get a pass, you have to go to an office, and you go to the office and they say, you know, we wanna go see our mother, "Yeah, okay, so, how long?" They give us an hour usually so . . . you get a pass, you take that pass, and you go see . . . and as you walk in the building there's a matron, she whispered to me "you GOTTA PASS? Okay." So we show the pass. So, then we go see our mother, get some money or whatever, and you come out. So anyways, you know it's a hassle, you know, to go through all that. So one day *(chuckles)* I went to get a . . . pass and the girl . . . now, it's not her fault, she's one of us, but she had a job there, you know, giving our pass, so she's got a whole stack of pass on the desk and she called away. I was just sitting by myself there, looking at all those pass, eh, so, my hand some- how (something) a whole bunch of the pass, took it to here, got a stack of pass. Somehow when I got back to my dorm, "Look at all the pass I got," so then I said, "Hey you guys wanna go see your mother?" "Yeah," "Five cents, five cents, five cents" "How long do you wanna be there, two hours? Three hours?" You can put your own time down, eh? Sell 'em for five cents. Make all kinds of money.

You know, I'll tell you something, I would never think of doing those things if I wasn't in Hastings Park, but the fact that you're there and you've got nothing else to do . . . So you start thinking that way and you do it! So I think sometimes, those things are good to be there.

Fairground sounds melts into "Auld Lang Syne."
Jean becomes Pat and Harold becomes Tad.

PAT: The strangest thing is, we were going to go somewhere else. We were sup- posed to go to Bay Farm. We were walking into this building and these children were playing with the ouija boards, and my mom says, "Ask them where we were going," because you know our suitcases, everything had Bay Farm written into it. We were supposed to leave within the week and they just all this: "You're going to . . . Tashme. Oh ho ho ho." "That's nonsense," she said, you know. A few days later we get this telegram from Dad saying, "You've got to go to Tashme."

The sound of the roar and jostle of a diesel truck is heard.

TAD: All I remember is that truck and I think they were playing "Aul' Lang Syne" as the truck pulled away *(laughs)* from anytime there was people leaving, eh, from Hastings Park to anywhere else they had that "Aul' Lang Syne" playing. Yeah!

PAT: We're all just standing, jammed packed, you know, like cattle. It wasn't in a car; it was in the back of a truck. I remember that . . . it was very scary. They just had these little railings on the side— We were all just standing. And that's how we went into Tashme!

Chapter Four / Tashme

*Shift. Fourteen miles out of Hope, BC, lies Tashme, the largest Japanese
Canadian internment camp. Shacks are being built, too close to each other, on
a vast piece of beautiful land surrounded by mountains. Fast Creek rushes by
on one side of the camp and Slow Creek on the other.*
Tad becomes Harold. Pat becomes Molly.

HAROLD: So, I went early to Tashme to help build it—me and this other guy,
Wally. We were the only boys there; all the rest were men. We had to make dinner
for everybody. Well not just me, but there's about three or four cooks and you
know, my dad, was one of them. So he's telling me, there's so many men that
they used to make hamburger in the tub. Washtub, you know that thing. So they
got whole bunch of meat in there and break all the eggs in there. Then he says,
"Okay, you going to help me mix it." So I said okay. I'm watching—he goes like
this, *(makes a spit sound)*. I said, whoa this taste, make it taste good. I'm going
(spit, smacking sound). Yeah, I still remember that. And it really tasted good!

MOLLY: Tashme was beautiful place. All surrounded by mountains and two rivers,
one on either side—one a fast, fast-flowing river and the other a quiet stream. It
was a very picturesque place, actually. It was wonderful! We never seen so many
Japanese, we made friends with oodles, eh, wasn't it? That's the way it was, I think,
for you, too! You know you saw all these Japanese people and you made friends.

Harold becomes Kunio and Molly becomes Teiko.

KUNIO: When we first got there, the place was so muddy, like, eh, it was all
field—no road or anything, it was all just ground and they had built a wooden
sidewalk, all the way down the street, so when people went to the bathtub, they
used to have the geta—

TEIKO: Wooden shoe.

KUNIO: And you could hear the clip clop all the way down the street, ya.

TEIKO: They had a bathhouse, didn't they?

KUNIO: Ya, the bathhouse was at the end. I think they had about four, four or
five altogether, bathhouses at the end of each avenue. Each avenue had about
twenty to / twenty-five houses.

TEIKO: Ya, ya, ya.

KUNIO: It's a community, community, / community bath. It's a long, long building—one side was for men and the other side was for women—it was a Japanese
bath and, uh, you wash yourself and you go in the tub after.

TEIKO: Ya, I remember going, they burn a fire underneath, uh, to boil water,
make it hot, and then you have to just wash yourself out on—outside the tub, you
know. They had little stools and little wooden buckets, and you wash yourself
and you go inside the tub.

Teiko becomes Pat.

PAT: Do you know what the buildings are like in Tashme? On the inside? It was
central door, central and then there would be . . . two bedrooms on each side,
and it's just all . . . tarpaper, you know. It's just shacks, so it was very, very cold.
And you would have the pot-bellied stove all, and then it was a dry sink. It was
filled with water, and when we woke up in the morning, it was ICE. I remember
that, in the winter time. And would have a sink outside with, initially they didn't
have taps, so that every two houses had sort of a tap in the middle outside. So
you'd have to take buckets and bring it inside. That's why if you spilled any on
your floor . . . ICE RINK—it was that cold, that cold, I remember that.

Kunio becomes May.

MAY: I-I-I was a tomboy, I was really a tomboy, but, ah, we used to throw a ball,
over a barn. Over the barn, and there's another guy on the other side. And you
have to catch it when it comes over, so you don't know where it's coming from,
right? From the right, or, or the left. So, you know, like, uh, it's coming and it's
just dribbling, dribbling, so we have to run. And there's a team. We have a team,
three on each side, you know. It was a tall barn. Well maybe, I was small, I was
very—I'm still short. But it was a barn, I still remember a barn. Did you play that?

Pat becomes Molly.

MOLLY: We used to play marbles. We got them from Woolworth, WOOLworth,
WOOLworth! woolworth, F.W. Woolworth! You have what they call keepers,
eh? Then you can win all kinds of marbles, so if you're really good you got a BAG
full of marbles, but then in some cases, some guy's got no more marbles. And
my sister, Toyo, was good at marbles and she had little hands. And she was good
with those steelies and all. She played with the boys! And she would get bags of
marbles. And when you win it, it's yours to keep!

And then, to be in high heels we would crush a can, put a heel in, you know, crush a can and then *clunk clunk clunk*—you know that was our high heels, wasn't it? That was fun! Wasn't it fun? Crushing that thing and *clunk clunk clunk*. Yeah, yeah, yeah, yeah, yeah, yeah. That was fun, yeah! It's good, those games, neh, you don't see them no more.

MAY: You're having fun. Just play and play and play. You know you just follow your parents, right? You just TAG along!

Molly becomes Jean and May becomes Kunio.

JEAN: My sister got married in Tashme. The wedding was just in the kitchen and my mom shoved us all in the bedrooms. We were kinda sneaky and watched. And it's Reverend McWilliams came to the house, and it was just the groom, my sister, and my mom and dad and the groom's mom, because, I mean, the father was already gone, so they just got married in the kitchen.

She just had a suit with a little flower on it . . . I got a picture. A wedding picture.

KUNIO: Did you have a party?

JEAN: No party! I mean, there's nothing to—it's just a ceremony and— Oh, maybe they had something—I don't know, Mom musta made something, but we didn't eat it! I don't recall— Maybe we did eat. I don't know—
All I remember is looking out from the bedroom . . .

Sounds of "Tanko Bushi." Jean sees the wedding party through the bedroom door. As she watches, she starts to follow the footsteps, and soon starts to dance. Kunio joins in.*
Jean is soon distracted by the sudden sight and sound of a dark, rushing river.

And so, they had this river, quite a big river—Fast Creek, going through Tashme—and I think there's one or two children that died, ya. You know, they got drowned in the river? Cuz the river that was running in Tashme was very fast, really, y'know, and if they were playing . . . One was, there was one girl for sure, and I think—there was one boy for sure—got drowned.

KUNIO: The girl lived on Fifth Avenue and the boy, I think, lived on Second Avenue, if I'm not mistaken.

JEAN: How old were they?

---

* *Tanko Bushi*: Traditional group folk dance performed at celebrations.

KUNIO: Three. Four. I'm not sure, but quite young.

JEAN: It was a tragedy. Really. Two kids. At separate times.

Shift. A pyre by the river.

KUNIO: When people died, they had no, no . . . funeral home, uh, they had a service, I guess most of them do, in, uh, Buddhism, and they had to, uh, burn the body, cremate the body. They used to take it out in the field and build a pyre with, uh, logs and put the casket on top, the wooden casket, it was all made there. I remember the kids weren't allowed to go there, but I remember going. Used to be across the river. We used to watch the fire from this side of the creek. Yeah. I remember Pop, Pop telling us that that sometimes, when the pile of logs when they start to burn, uh . . . The bottom part started to burn and would just topple over. The box—the burning box would fall down with the body in it, and the body came out and they would have to poke the body back in the fire. *(laughs)* Boy, what a terrible thing to be doing. I'm sure they were pretty squeamish about it, too. I guess they had to do it. They had no funeral home, eh?

Shift. Present.
Kunio becomes Matt and Jean becomes Julie.

JULIE: My mother was born there. Tashme. I always thought that Tashme was a Japanese name. Like my mom's name. Tamiko. It's actually the two first letters of the names of three officers from the BC Security Commission who dealt with the internees and their property. TAylor, SHirras, and MEad: Tashme. It's called Sunshine Valley now. It's a resort for RVs.

MATT: I thought it was Japanese, too. I went to visit. My grandparents actually took us all out to BC together; our first family trip. I was a teenager. There was just a barn, which they said is where some of the families were housed. While my family went in, my brother and I swung on this big zipline out in front. Maybe not too respectful but they didn't force us to pay attention and I wasn't super interested at the time. They later told us how they could see us zipping by through the windows as they were looking around.

JULIE: I visited, too. With my ex. I dragged him with me, retracing the steps of my family's dispersal from Port Alberni to Hastings Park and then Tashme. So, we're driving down the highway, east from Vancouver, and all of a sudden, we find ourselves surrounded by mountains. Out the front window, in the rear-view mirror—they just grew out of everywhere and nowhere. It was a really beautiful clear day, but I couldn't help but feeling claustrophobic. All those mountains. So when we got there, no one was at the visitor's centre, so I said, "Who cares, let's just go in." There was no fence or anything, but I still felt like I was trespassing. There were no more shacks, no more people, there wasn't even a sign to explain what Tashme used to be. But there was that barn and there was that zipline.

You know Fast Creek? The river Jean was talking about? I brought along some mandarins as offerings, you know, for those whose lives remain unmarked. I wanted to offer them into the water and hoped that it would be all . . . ceremonial and meaningful, but I didn't really know what to do and I was embarrassed my ex would see and then ask me what I was doing so I just . . . chucked them into the water when he wasn't looking. I watched them for as long as I could, floating away on the current, bobbing up and down. Just these stupid orange dots. Back then I didn't know kids had died in there.

The river takes over.
Shift. The quiet rising of a henotama.
Matt becomes May.

MAY: Have you ever heard of a henotama!? The old ones—the older people used to talk about henotama, like a fireball type of thing. Whenever there's a burial, or somebody dies at the hospital, that's near the butcher shop, well, you could see like, ah, the people's soul, body's soul rises up—on top of the hospital and on top of the butcher shop, they used to say stories like that—they used to SEE it!!! I'm not scared, no not really, I'm fearless. Really, I am fearless! You heard about it, eh? The soul.

May brings her hand to her chest. She touches her life spirit.

Or something deep in the body or something.

She lets it fly away.

That's what they say.

Julie echoes May's movements.
The henotama becomes the faint shadow of the nuclear bomb exploding in far-away Japan.
Julie and Matt witness the explosion.
End of war.

Chapter Five / Dispersal

Shift. Dispersal.
Matt becomes Kunio and Julie becomes Teiko.

KUNIO: Toward the end, when they started to move people around like, you had to make a decision as to where—repatriate to Japan or to stay—go east—and one of my friends, his parents went back to Japan and he stayed back because he didn't want to go back. He was about fifteen, I guess—

TEIKO: He studied and he's a Ph.D. now.

KUNIO: But he had to go through school and all that all by himself. He's a Ph.D. now, ya. He got a Ph.D.

TEIKO: He lived with some family and I don't know what he did for to earn some money, but he went to university and all that.

KUNIO: I know that when his parents were leaving on the bus that he was running after the bus.

TEIKO: Crying. Can you imagine?

KUNIO: I guess he just wanted to stay in Canada—get an education. He didn't want to go back to Japan.

TEIKO: That must've been hard, eh? To leave your child behind?

KUNIO: I remember Pop, he signed up to go back to Japan, and we were all supposed to go back and I didn't—I didn't care for the idea too much. But, uh, I guess they'd heard stories that Japan was having a hard time—and that we shouldn't go there, and so they changed their mind and decided to stay here.

Shift. A Nikkei seniors' home in Toronto.
Teiko becomes Jean and Kunio becomes Matt.

MATT: So, Jean, you guys were deported to Japan? Your family didn't stay in Canada?

JEAN: I had no choice because it was my dad's choice. We wouldn't say, "Dad, we want to stay here and you can go to Japan." We couldn't do that cuz we were underage. My sister got married in Tashme so she didn't have to go to Japan. But he didn't know what was gonna happen in Canada with—what's he gonna do with ten kids and how's he gonna feed them? Cuz at least in Tashme we were able to manage somehow, but he didn't know what was going to happen when we left, uh, Tashme. I guess that's what he musta thought. So he says, "Oh well, we'll go to Japan," cuz he had his sister there and, uh, he figured maybe they'll help out, which was a big mistake, but uh, anyways, ya. When we got to Japan, we went to their place and uh, right away, I mean, what are they gonna do with all OUR kids, you know, us kids, too? They were in the war and they lost the war, and they were hard up.

MATT: Did you feel welcome in Japan?

JEAN: No. Definitely no. We were discriminated. Discriminated here—but I mean, that I didn't see that much because we were put in camps, right? So how can you be discriminated when you're all together, you know, isolated from the . . .

MATT: Discriminators?

JEAN: Ya. Discriminators. But when we went to Japan, yes. They said we weren't Jap'nese—we didn't dress like them, you know, we didn't know the language, right? And especially us, our first language was English anyways—so when we went to Japan we didn't even know how to say "chair" in Jap'nese. Jap'nese would say, "taberu," as table, they would say "taberu," like the first generation? And chair was "cheya," you know? We thought that was Jap'nese when we were small—whenever the first generation talked. And then the cellar, the cellar they used to call it the "down below." And they said it "danburo." I thought, "Well, that's Jap'nese. Danburo!" But when we went to Japan, we found out that it's not Jap'nese. That's English! Down below is what they mean but they said "danburo." We went to Japan and we said "danburo" and they didn't know what we were talking about!

Shift. A boarding house in 1950s Hamilton.
Matt becomes Harold and Jean becomes Julie.

HAROLD: Now at that time, we're still enemy, as you know.

So, wherever you went to you had to report to the Mountie's office, so he can keep track of us, saying that, "Here I am, in Hamilton. I'm here from Tashme." So, when I went into the office, he took all that down, and my height and my weight, you know, and everything else; description. And after we finished all that, one of the Mounties said to ME, "What are you gonna do now?" I said, "I gotta go look for a job." "What kind a job are you looking for?" I said, "Anything I could get!"

So anyways, the Mountie says to me, "Would you like to be a Mountie?" I thought the guy was kidding. I said, "I don't think I could be a Mountie." He says, "Why not?" I said, "I don't know how to ride a horse!" Those guys kill themselves laughing. I was serious because I thought that all Mounties had to be able to ride a horse, right? That's why they're called mounted police.

But he said "No no no no, you don't have to ride a horse, okay? Now if you become a Mountie, wouldn't it be NICE," he said, "if the older Japanese people that come out East," if they come and see a Mountie who's also Japanese like them, they'll feel more comfortable to talk to them than to talk to a white Mountie." So he said, "Now you think about that!"

And he was serious now, now I gotta get serious, too. So I ask, "Can I have a few days to think it over?" He says, "Take your time." So I think, that's a pretty good deal, I don't have to worry about looking for a job.

So I went back to the boarding house and there's a whole bunch a Japanese guys there, and I asked these people, especially the older folks, how would they feel if they see a Nisei in Mountie uniform? You know what a Nisei is, right?"

JULIE: Yeah, second generation.

HAROLD: Some of them said "Well, there's whoooole thousands of Japanese people in Tashme that will be coming out this way. They'll say 'that guy—he's the enemy.'" Cuz I'm a Mountie, right? So they may be hard on your parents. They just come through, these people, from four years behind bars, I'm gonna call it that, if you see a Mountie, you hate them, you know. So he said, "think about THAT!"

So I thought it over and over, and I could just see people saying something bad to my parents, because I was a Mountie now, all of a sudden . . .

So I thank them very much and I didn't go back. So I, so I'm not a MOUNTIE.

After that it was not a very good time. It was hard time gettin' job because, you know, you're a JAP.

Shift. A sugar beet farm in the Prairies.

Julie becomes Molly and Harold becomes Matt.

MOLLY: We went to sugar beets. We went to a place called Barnwall, Alberta, which is close to Taber. And in our family, there was only Mama, Papa, Toyo, Shin, and I. Was a small family—and we would always get a farmer with twenty-five acres, and it was VERY hard work, very hard work. And at that time, Mama was our captain, you know. My father was not a farmer, he was not—good. *(laughs)* And then so maybe about one year after a friend told Papa that there's work at the sugar beet cannery, so Papa would ride the bike, and sometime he's on night shift and he's only got a flashlight on the bike and it's a speedy—TransCanada! Here he is on a bike and they go *swish swish swish* past him. Yeah! But the thing was, when we were working on the sugar beets, he would buy us a whole brick of ice cream and he would *pump pump pump*, bring it all the way and so it was quite mushy! *Hoohoo,* you could almost straw it up you know, but here we thank him, because it's his treat that he would, you know *pedal pedal* and it was himself in the hot sun, bringing us, you know those, what's you call, pint. Like a butter. Like a pound of butter, little bit longer, neh. Yeah that's my father, poor man, to treat us he would *pedal pedal* and all so melted! But he would do it about once a week.

Shift. In the middle of nowhere. A night train running over winter tracks. Matt becomes Teiko and Molly becomes Julie.

TEIKO: We went to that horrible camp in Ontario, after we left, on the way to Farnham. We stopped in a place called, way, way out in the sticks somewhere and, you know, coming from BC, we didn't have any boots or anything. It was called Angler, Ontario. They sent us there on a train. And we got there, I dunno, it was pitch black, during the night, I guess it was, and they stopped at this little station, like a little shack that we couldn't even all get in, and it was freezing cold and it was snow up to here. They just dumped us all off there in the deep snow. And nobody was there to greet us so we just shivered and stood there in the snow. And then in the wee hours of the morning we saw a light come on in one of the big buildings, which was the mess hall, the people coming in to cook and make breakfast in that place, and they open the door for us and we were frozen, we had no boots, nothing, and they gave us, uh, they made us a hot breakfast.

JULIE: So who dropped you off?

TEIKO: The train people.

JULIE: And then the train left?

TEIKO: Mhmm.

JULIE: And who was it? You and . . .

TEIKO: A whole bunch of us—it was a long train.

JULIE: A hundred people?

TEIKO: Oh ya. More. No one there to meet us so we didn't even know where it was. It was in the mountain, it was pitch black. No one there to greet us. Nothing. But they let us off.

JULIE: I guess they didn't really care.

TEIKO: No, they didn't care.

Chapter Six / Rebuilding / Buried / Post-War Years

Shift. Present.
Teiko becomes Matt.

MATT: Baachan Downstairs was in the hospital, so they said we had to visit her.

Baachan Downstairs: Grandpa's mom.

I always liked her, but I didn't see her very often because she was always living her life, walking errands on Kennedy Street in Scarborough; taking the bus to the racetrack. She was in her late nineties, and she lived in a retirement home, not a *nursing* home. Grandpa said she was so healthy because she was always walking around, and just as he said that she had gotten up and walked away from the table and he said, "See!"

So we were at her bedside in the hospital room, nothing seemed distressing, she was just lying there with us . . . I do remember I responded to my instinct to go up beside her. When I did, she reached over and took my hand like this *(demonstrates hand clasp)*, strong and healthy as I have always known her. And then she said, "Baachan die now." And that made me smile and think "all right!" My family around me were immediately shocked and protested, and I thought, "stop bugging us, she's just telling me something." But the moment was over then and I had to withdraw.

She actually didn't die then. She got better and died a few years later.

Baachan Downstairs—because she used to live downstairs in my grandparents' home. She was 102.

Shift. A living room.
Julie becomes Kazie.

KAZIE: Your grandmother was a lot of trouble!

MATT: Yeah?

KAZIE: She was the bad one. She had a curfew, and if she didn't come home at the right time, boy did she get it! We used to stick up for her. Oh, she never made it for twelve o'clock! She was terrible!

MATT: What are you talking about, what did she used to do?

KAZIE: Oh, I don't, I can't say, I'm on tape! Oh my God, she was in trouble all the time. She didn't care!

MATT: With boys?

KAZIE: No, no, because she came home, she was supposed to be home before eleven or twelve and she never made it. She was out with your, your grandpa or whatever. We used to stick up for her all the time. Etsie and I. My father was strict! He waaas strict!

MATT: You needed to sneak her in?

KAZIE: Yeah. Cuz she used to come home—she would vomit in the toilet, since she was drinking. But she didn't do that too often—she knew better. So Mom and I would stick between her so my father wouldn't get her. But she never learnt! She smoked, too, and our mom, your baachan, NEVER EVER knew. I remember Razie's Black Cat or whatever on the package, whatever she used to smoke. "Is Mother coming, is Mother coming?" she's going. Cuz she'd go downstairs, right. She'd watch Mother trying to come down the stairs. My father didn't know, nobody knew . . . them were the days.

MATT: Well what about you then, who'd you go with?

KAZIE: I hung around with Hakujin kids, eh. The white kids. We never bothered with Japanese kids there, in Toronto. It was always Hakujin kids or the Black kids.

MATT: Oh yeah?

KAZIE: Oh yeah, that's how we all went to the dance. There's couple dances. One on the Danforth and one in Thornhill we used to go, every week, Friday and Saturday. They used to come to the house you know. When we lived on Sullivan Street. But I told my mother before somebody else told her, you know, "I'm going out with Black kids."

MATT: What'd she say?

KAZIE: Nothing. I just told her because you know they talk, people talk; neighbours and things would say, to Baachan right: "There's a Black guy." They used to come to the door, you know, and the landlord used to answer the door— Oh my God!

Shift. A Nikkei home in rural Québec.
Matt becomes Richard and Kazie becomes Sumire.

RICHARD: In Farnham, there were no other Japanese people . . . The Japanese don't have a community. We were all, by the government, spread out into different areas, we were spread out—

SUMIRE: Not that we wanted to or our parents wanted to, but they were forced to go into different areas.

RICHARD: The Japanese parents wanted their children to be integrated into the white society, but I think they would have preferred us to marry Japanese. Don't you think that the parents, like Mom and Pop's age, wanted their children to marry Japanese?

SUMIRE: Oh ya, definitely.

RICHARD: So why did they give up after, uh—

SUMIRE: They figured there's not much point, eh? What are you gonna do?

RICHARD: Why fight it?

SUMIRE: Ya, you can't fight it.

RICHARD: Look at Betty, remember Betty?

SUMIRE: She wanted to marry a Hakujin.

RICHARD: Her father ruled her life.

SUMIRE: Ya, he did. She wanted to marry a, a Hakujin, and she was even gonna run away with him. She even asked me to go, you know, be her, stand up for her. Her father was so against it that she just gave up. She married a Japanese and she had a daughter. Daughter committed suicide—she died a few years later.

RICHARD: That was really a sad, sad thing. She was nice.

SUMIRE: She just gave up, I guess.

Shift. Light piercing the dark.
Matt becomes Terry. Sumire becomes Julie.

TERRY: In most Japanese families, I think, the eldest son is supposed to be the main breadwinner, or look after the family, so I think they're more pressured to go to university. In that sense, it sort of worked like that in our family. Although, when I was going to school in Montréal, I was a very self-conscious kind of person, or personality, so I wasn't really ah, aggressive. So it affected me in a negative way, like the pressure, you know . . . so. Actually, I was quite sick and after, ah, the second-year university, I think for one year, I never left the house. I was afraid to go out.

I came to the point where, there's a mental hospital, the Allan Memorial Institute . . . was there for I don't know how many weeks, but they couldn't find anything so, they said, we'll jot it down "anxiety," and then there was just, ah, tranquilizers and things like that.

My sister had come from Toronto and said, "You know there's a new book out, so why don't you just read it?" It was, ah, *The Power of Positive Thinking*. So one day, later on, decided, I started to read it.

I guess my thinking changed, and also I said, "If I continue like this, I'm going to deteriorate and also become dependent on my family, my elder sisters." I don't want it to happen like that. So from that point on, I guess, I sort of mentally changed my thinking and, ah, sort of forced myself to go out. So, ah . . . yeah there were bad times around that time, until, ah, 1954 until, ah, 1960, there was a very slow process.

Shift. A wall.

Julie becomes Sumire. Terry becomes Matt.

SUMIRE: My biggest source of frustration was not being able to communicate, like when my husband and I separated. I had to explain to the neighbour, and she had to interpret to my mother. The communication in Japanese is very hard when you're talking about, you know, separation and things like that. And it's hard when you don't speak Jap'nese, it's hard to explain that kinda thing. So that's how it happened that the neighbour translated to my mother. I just wanted my mother to understand.

Shift. Present.
Sumire becomes Julie.

MATT: Baachan Upstairs, because she lived upstairs, barely spoke English, but I saw her on a regular basis. She was our matriarch, and when she died, we knew the old world would begin to fall away.

I was searching for my baachan during her burial, and then ever since.

As my family was walking through the cemetery to bury her, the grass was long and no one spoke, but we were all brushing the grass as we passed along. The sound of the brushing was beautiful and a good way of talking to each other that day.

. . . Since then, we have not managed to speak any louder than that . . . to each other.

Shift. A family restaurant.
Julie becomes Teiko. Matt becomes Kunio.

TEIKO: When we went back to visit, uh, what was that, Lemon Creek or Slocan or whatever, people there were calling us, like, Japs, but not in a derogatory way, it was just normal to them. We stopped at a restaurant to have lunch, a small restaurant, and I started to talk to this lady that was working in the restaurant and she came out with this HUGE HUGE album and they had all the pictures of all of the Japanese people that used to live around that area—and they referred to the Japanese people as Japs.

KUNIO: Just a short-short form, I guess.

TEIKO: And she was pointing out to the outside, she said, "See that beautiful tree there? See that tree there? All the Japs planted that when they were living here."

Nobody there but the trees were still growing.

And I was talking to some people who were working in a garden and they were telling me, they were telling me, she says, "See my home there?" She says, "I bought that from the Japs," she says. She says, "I got it for—I got it for next to nothing. Beautiful home and a lotta nice work inside, she said. "The Japs did all that," she said.

KUNIO: They were all friendly.

TEIKO: Ya, they were all friendly.

KUNIO: I don't know what it would have been like if we hadn't gone through it.

TEIKO: We never knew what else existed—

KUNIO: So / we can't compare.

TEIKO: So we can't compare.

KUNIO: Can't be bitter.

Shift. Leaning on the hood of a car.
Teiko becomes Sed and Kunio becomes Matt.

SED: My dad said he will never go back there. BC. He said, "They kicked me out of this country, they kicked me out of here," he says, "I don't go back." I used to fight. Take on the whole school. When I first came here, they tried to push me around, callin' me Jap. I used to fight back. I never let nobody push me around. Once they knew I wasn't going to back down, they were all right. To this day, ahno, the older generation—my boss, he said, "I had to beat the white people." He had to be better than the white people. He kept pounding that into me, boy. Even in Toronto, I worked for the Japanese guys: "You gotta be better than them." they says.

Shift. In a high school classroom.
Matt becomes Dave and Sed becomes Julie.

DAVE: When I went to high school in Toronto, there was two Japanese, you know me and a little, my little friend, all this is at Central Tech! I mean back in the '50s, right. And this history teacher, teaching history, "Those Japs there," you know, and the two of us, he's sitting up here, I'm sitting back there and, "See those Japs." Yeah, pointing fingers yet! I mean in those days, you didn't know any better, so you just kept your mouth shut and right. I mean if it was now, you'd get out there and beat the hell out of the guy, but forty, fifty, sixty years ago, you had no choice but to take it and you know, crawl down. But A HISTORY teacher, saying "those Japs," I mean, you know and, when you think of it, it's really painful, right? I mean if it's some guys that you're playing hockey or baseball or something, they can call you names, it's a little bit . . . but not like when a teacher says a thing like that, you know. I mean how can you forget? I mean even if it's after sixty years, how can you forget? Right?

Dave throws down a crane onto the floor.

Chapter Seven / Redress

Shift. Present.
Dave becomes Matt. Julie picks up the crane and unfolds it.

JULIE: *(reading)* "Minister of State Multiculturalism and Citizenship. March 09, 1990. File # 2569.

Dear Mr. Sakamoto: I am pleased to inform you that your application for individual redress has been reviewed and that you are eligible to receive payment according to the terms of the Japanese Canadian Redress Agreement.

You will find enclosed a cheque in the amount of $21,000, as well as the acknowledgement signed by the Prime Minister. The acknowledgement summarizes my feelings and those of many millions of Canadians.

Thank you for your patience and cooperation."

Shift. A phone call.
Matt becomes Harold.

Harold.

HAROLD: Umhmm?

JULIE: Uh, you know redress?

HAROLD: Redress?

JULIE: Ya.

HAROLD: Yes.

JULIE: Now did your mom and dad, did they, did they have problems with redress? Or they were, they wanted, they were fine?

HAROLD: Ah, they were okay. I mean, if there was a problem it won't be just Baachan, Jiichan, it be all the people that age, eh. It would be for all that age group, which is, they're the Isseis. You know what that means, right?

JULIE: Ya, first generation.

HAROLD: If there was a problem it was not just the personal, it was a group thing. If my father had a problem, so did the guy down the street would have a problem, cuz it's the same problem. They must have some problem, but, ah, Japanese people got a word, they say "shikata ga nai," means "It can't be helped." That's what they live under—the saying. If something happens, it can't be helped, because that's how it is— Y'know what I mean?

So that word, "shikata ga nai," is very important word. So that's how they survived. It can't be helped. If the government say you gotta go to Tashme, even if you say no, you gotta go to Tashme. So, it can't be helped, right?

Shift. A wall.
Julie becomes Sumire. Harold becomes Richard.

SUMIRE: By the time each of us received the twenty-one thousand-dollar cheque, *we* got the money, right? I mean us, we were kids. Grandma and Grandpa, it affected them more. It meant nothing to us.

RICHARD: I remember thinking at one point that, being a little concerned, "What are my white friends gonna think about me receiving all their money from their tax-paying parents or friend or whatever?"

SUMIRE: I always felt that it should have been Mom and Pop, you know the parents . . . It was too late.

RICHARD: But then finding out I wasn't eligible. How did they come up with this cut-off date . . . 1949 or something? I mean like, how do you decide on a sibling who was born pre-April '49 and one that was born not even a year after?

SUMIRE: That money should have been done earlier and let THEM have it. Rather than the children.

RICHARD: I went through the same experience. Why would one deserve to get it and me not?

SUMIRE: Because as children, we didn't really suffer, you know.

Sumire becomes Julie and looks at Richard.
Richard becomes Terry.

TERRY: A lot of people say that it's a good thing that this evacuation happened, because otherwise, all the Japanese would still be in the Vancouver area in a ghetto type of thing and would have stayed in their own communities. Whereas now they were forced to disperse into all different cities and everywhere, instead of spending their whole lives together and not going outside their communities. You know, they're more accepted, I think, by the outside community cuz they're more exposed . . . everybody's more exposed to the Japanese. So, in one sense it was a good thing, but I'm sure for the parents it was not a good thing, cuz they lost everything. Start from scratch again.

Chapter Eight / Present

Shift. A Nikkei seniors' home in Burnaby.
Julie becomes Jane. Terry becomes Shoji.

JANE: Gee we're not much of a help, eh? I mean I'm not much of a help. Because I forget. I forgot so much. I think we might learn from each another. I find one thing—the Japanese, we're very conservative and we're not very open. Our English friends are more open. They talk more. Whereas we sorta sit there and be quiet. We gotta learn that. I'm a little too old to learn; young people will learn that. To be open.

SHOJI: Do you ever talk to your grandkids about your experience?

JANE: I find if they're interested, I'd talk about it. "Oh, that happened to Grandma?" But, uh, I think they'd take it as part of life. But they'd soon forget. It doesn't matter. It's in the past now, I feel.

SHOJI: Well I haven't spoken one-on-one with any of our kids about our past, but my oldest comes with his daughter to the Cultural Centre I tell him there's something going on and you should come and have a look anyway. This is why I am trying to keep my family history going. I started and I gotta pick it up again. But all I have is this family album.

JANE: It's difficult because when we came here, we were trying very hard to assimilate, which is pretty much what our kids have done.

SHOJI: Yeah, our kids, they assimilate so well that they disappear.

Stop. Present.
Shoji becomes Matt and Jane becomes Julie.
Beat.
Dejected, Julie begins to pack away the table's contents: photo albums, teacups, teapot, and jubako into the briefcase. Matt notices one more crane tucked away in the briefcase and retrieves it before Julie can pack it. He unfolds it and reads it aloud just as Julie moves to leave.

MATT: "Remember, you will one day be as old as I, and a hundred years and more will separate us then, and across such time you will not follow me as I do not follow you. Such a bridge would be too vast to build, wasteful, and besides, no foundation could anchor it. As I have invested my care properly, so you should do the same. Go forth, proceed, 'chan-tō, chan-tō,' properly, properly."

Beat.
Julie begins to unpack everything from the briefcase. She places the objects back on the table mindfully, building a shrine—a hotokesan—with the briefcase as the base, the photo album opened to photos of family on top, and a bowl of rice from inside of the jubako in front of the briefcase. She pours tea into the cups and places them on either side of the rice. Matt refolds the crane and places it in the centre of the hotokesan. They set out mandarins from the jubako as offerings. Julie and Matt honour the shrine.
Black.

A Dialogue Between Matthew Chin, Matt Miwa, Julie Tamiko Manning, and Izumi Sakamoto

The Tashme Project: The Living Archives explores the themes of Japanese Canadian identity, history, community, and intergenerational connection and disconnection through the lens of Japanese Canadian internment. While going through substantial changes over time, this play was initially written in 2015 by Julie Tamiko Manning, a Montréal actor and theatre creator, and by Matt Miwa, an Ottawa-based actor and performance artist. This verbatim theatre piece draws from over twenty interviews conducted between 2009 and 2014, both in person and over the telephone with Japanese Canadian men and women between the ages of sixty-five and ninety in Burnaby, British Columbia; Hamilton, Ontario; Toronto, Ontario; Belleville, Ontario; Montréal, Québec; and Farnham, Québec. These individuals were children who were wrongly interned as "enemy aliens" during World War II, along with 22,000 Japanese Canadians (JC) who had originally resided on the West Coast. After the war, many JC families chose not to discuss their experiences of internment and simply wanted to move on so as not to be singled out again. While remarkably successful as a community some seventy years later, the memories of internment are largely kept silent within JC communities to this day. This silence serves as the starting point for *The Tashme Project*. As descendants of JC internment survivors, Manning and Miwa occupy a special connection to the stories told by JC elders who were children in the internment camps in the 1940s.

Between 2011 and 2016, staged readings and workshop productions of the play have been held in various cultural and theatre-based venues in Vancouver, Montréal, Ottawa, and Toronto. In 2015, the first full production of the play was held at the MAI (Montréal, arts interculturels) and produced by Tashme Productions in association with Playwrights' Workshop Montréal.

The following text consists of selections of excerpts from the transcript of a conversation between Manning and Miwa and Izumi Sakamoto and Matthew Chin that transpired on October 9, 2017. Izumi Sakamoto is currently an associate professor at the Factor-Inwentash Faculty of Social Work at the University of Toronto, and Matthew Chin is an assistant professor at the Graduate School of Social Service at Fordham University. Together they are part of the research study, Many Faces of Japanese Canadians: Remembering Historical Trauma and Renewing Cultural Identity Through Activism, Art and Community-Building. This project attempts to understand the relationship between Japanese Canadian identity and internment through an analysis of Japanese Canadian art, activism, and community building. The selection of excerpts from the transcript below is meant to give a sense of the process by which Manning and Miwa brought *The Tashme Project* into being, how it has changed over time, and Manning and Miwa's reading of the social and cultural significance of the piece for Japanese Canadians.

The Tashme Project Origins

In this initial phase of the interview, Manning and Miwa discuss the impetus for *The Tashme Project* as a quest for personal, family, and community history. They touch on the challenges of bringing these histories forward when the violence in which these histories were forged often works against transparent and direct means of knowledge transfer. As Manning and Miwa illustrate, these challenges lie not only in eliciting information from those with experiences of internment, but also in addressing how to provide audiences with access to these experiences through their own personal relationship to internment.

MATTHEW CHIN: Maybe it would be helpful if we talked about the motivation for the start of the piece and how it changed over time.

IZUMI SAKAMOTO: And drawing from your [previous] use of the word "self," could you talk about how you changed over time as well?

JULIE TAMIKO MANNING: When we [Miwa and Manning] first met and discovered that we were both half-Japanese Canadian and that both of our families had gone through the same internment camp, we wanted to create something together, but neither of us had an idea of what we wanted to create. We hadn't even thought of verbatim theatre initially, but we figured that interviewing people would be a great way to start. So, we began by interviewing members of our family, and then graduated laterally to friends of family and then beyond that to strangers. The stories and voices of the people we spoke with were so powerful and their language was so beautiful that at a certain point we realized the best and most authentic way to tell their story was with their own words. We saw this as archiving their existence because once this generation passes away, we will no longer have a direct connection to the internment experience. We also wanted to make a living archive of the ways that the older generation speaks: the accent we thought was unique to our own families was, in fact, shared by Nisei and Sansei* across the country. This accent is different from the Japanese from Japan and more like the accents of Indigenous elders. Perhaps it has something to do with growing up on the West Coast, or perhaps it has something to do with their mother tongue being erased from their mouths to make room for English, the language of assimilation. The English language was all that remained post-war, and yet as babies and children, their mouths were formed with Japanese vowels and consonants. We don't actually know why their accents are so unique but we know that with the passing of these generations, their accents, comforting and familiar, will be lost to us. So that was part of our motivation. Correct me if I'm wrong, Matt, but we wanted to embody that rather than just . . .

MATT MIWA: Create or invent . . .

MANNING: . . . create or change their stories with our words. And then we had a really hard time putting ourselves into the story and really fought the dramaturg for . . . um . . .

MIWA: Years, I think.

MANNING: It took a really long time, and she kept saying, "We need you in the story," and "The audience needs to access these stories of the Nisei through you," but we fought and fought. We would say, "The stories are not about us; they are about our elders, about the internment experience."

---

* *Sansei*: Third-generation Japanese.

MIWA: We also just didn't know what to say as well.

MANNING: Absolutely. So, I think that's been a huge struggle. Our immediate struggle is, "What do we say as Matt and Julie in the play?" I think, Izumi, that is why you see our characters becoming more reflective in this version.*

SAKAMOTO: That was really powerful, Julie. Your reflection really touched me. Also, I didn't realize how the dispossession affects people a few generations later. At the same time, the juxtaposition to Matt's reflection [in the play] also gave alternative narratives. Someone might hear your [Julie's] story and say, "Oh it's like that for many JCs," but Matt's experience is so different and it was great to have the heterogeneity of experiences presented. It was great. You didn't have those reflections three years ago [in your play].

MIWA: I think that what we are discovering, or what we are more at ease with, is that we are different. Julie is a generation older than me and our voices are very different, and our perspectives and our prerogatives for what we both want for this play . . . It is a ritual, some kind of remembering, and embodied reverence. It's so satisfying to do the play. It's so satisfying to have the voices and the stories, and to just tell them because . . . we didn't really know how to define JC-ness then as much as we do today. Because it's such a tenuous identity. We're both half, as are many or most of my generation at least, and these stories were not talked about growing up. So, the quest of making the play was going to find the stories. And you know, many are lighthearted, many are funny, good stories, but still, nothing we had heard growing up. So, it was a very formal, anxiety-filled process to go to people's homes, sit down, say "We're going to record this, and we just want you to talk about these stories," or "What happened to you during internment?" It was anxiety-filled because they were anxious as well. They were like, "No, no, no. I don't remember anything," or "I was too young," or "Our parents would know more." But then they would say, "Okay well, we'll talk for a little bit," for half an hour or whatever. And then once everyone got comfortable, it always extended to longer sessions. So, the play, I guess, is a kind of quest for the JC community, changing the community dynamic, changing a sense of identity, deepening a sense of identity. However, I would say that through this

---

* In the current version of the play, Manning reflects on her visit to Port Alberni on Vancouver Island, where her ancestors lived before they were evacuated and incarcerated at Tashme. The play illustrates Manning's strong emotional reaction to the town, which appears to have no remaining signs of Japanese heritage.

play, I don't feel anxious about being JC anymore. I feel quite happy about it. That's not something I could have said six years ago.

MANNING: That's why we continue changing it as well.

Manning laughs.

The things that we wrote six years ago are not how we feel today. I think it's important to create when you're in the middle of things, of feelings and questions, but it doesn't always work dramaturgically. So, I think the further we get away from that time, the better we are able to see whether things work dramaturgically or not and still keep the characters of Matt and Julie in that questioning place.

On Community Input and the Incorporation of Redress

In this section of the interview, Manning and Miwa discuss the role of community input in the ongoing formation of *The Tashme Project*. While they were initially only focused on internment, conversations with their family members revealed the significance of redress* and how the differential relationships to redress in JC communities invoke the legacies of internment in complex ways. In addition to creating The Tashme Project using verbatim theatre, Miwa and Manning honour their communities by incorporating their constructive feedback in the piece.

---

*   In September 1988, then Prime Minister Brian Mulroney officially apologized to Japanese Canadians for the wartime internment and offered the redress settlement, which included:

> an acknowledgment of the injustice of the wartime events; individual payments of $21,000 to eligible Canadians; establishment of a community fund of $12 million; clearing of criminal records for those charged under the War Measures Act; restoration of Canadian citizenship to those exiled to Japan; and the creation of the Canadian Race Relations Foundation. ("Redress")

The redress settlement was the result of years of grassroots activism led mainly by the National Association of Japanese Canadians (NAJC). At the same time, there were disagreements within the JC community over whether to pursue redress or not and the terms of the redress itself.

MANNING: Can I tell a little anecdote about the redress section? Initially we hadn't set out with any questions about redress. I think that was partially because we weren't actually interested in hearing about redress. We wanted to hear about the internment experience. It's also a very difficult thing to talk about, even more so than the internment experience, I mean the redress experience and what families went through around that. So, we'd actually created the play, and I can't remember which version it was but it was before we got it to full production and one day, someone who had seen earlier readings of the play had asked me how it was going, because of course, we were still working on it. I said, "Fine," and then he just started talking, unsolicited, about his experience around redress. He wasn't given the money because he was born after the war, after the cut-off date. I asked him if I could come back to interview him because he was so [pause] . . . I'd never heard him speak like that. So detailed and so angry. His speaking out was surprising to me. So, I went back and interviewed him. And a lot of the text about redress is from him. And I think, Matt, we interviewed your grandpa after that, eh? About the redress?

MIWA: Mhmm.

MANNING: There were so many stories that we weren't able to include in the play, stories that are important to who we, as a community, are today, but we found that redress was one of those things that we had to at least touch upon. The feelings around redress are so complex: it created trauma in families and the community, but at the same time we, as descendants of the internment, are the beneficiaries of it.

MIWA: Yeah, and even if it was a political achievement and success, there is certainly not always a celebratory view of it. In families and individuals there is lots of shame attached to it still.

SAKAMOTO: Wow. I didn't realize that . . .

MIWA: Mhmmm. It wasn't like a "woohoo!" you know? For some people, it was. It was certainly a great achievement. But when we interviewed my grandpa, he didn't really want to talk about it in detail or with the usual candor that he usually talked about everything else.

SAKAMOTO: Oh wow. What is at the heart of that?

MIWA: I don't know. Who knows? But it's bringing it all back up again. The wound of internment happened and then thirty years pass and it's stretched open again and someone puts a number value on it. But it's not equivalent. You can't possibly make amends you know?

MANNING: I think that many of the Issei, uh, were worried about standing out again. You had to apply to get that money. Nobody wanted to stand out again in case something was going to happen again. In case they were to be labelled as enemy aliens again. To put themselves forward like that, it's also an admission that there was hardship. Your [Matt's] grandpa talks about shikataganai,* right? There's a shamefulness or weakness around the admission that you're stuck in victimhood and that you need to be reimbursed for something instead of letting it live in the past. There's a desire to get over things and not dwell on it.

Theatre as Living Legacy: *The Tashme Project* Co-Evolving with Personal and Community Growth

While this part of the interview began as a discussion about the consequences of the play, Manning and Miwa's explanation of the iterative nature of the play soon revealed how its effects are folded back into itself in ways that not only transform the play but also result in personal and community change. Miwa and Manning thus explain how their own process of personal transformation in relationship to JC identity has shifted the play. And as a result of input from community members as mentioned in the section earlier, JC individuals and families are engaging in JC history, identity, and community in different ways. As a practice of legacy-making, *The Tashme Project* is a co-evolving process occurring in an interrelated way with personal and community growth.

---

* *Shikataganai*: "It cannot be helped."

CHIN: Can you talk about what you see as the effects or consequences of the play?

MIWA: I think there's not one answer for that. Julie and I will not even give the same answers. There are so many prerogatives going into making it a public event—I will contribute something and I'm sure that Julie might contribute something else.

Manning laughs.

Legacy is one of the big themes that has always been with us. What is the JC legacy that we carry with us, even though we don't know how or why? Redress and internment were such huge public legacies, but this play is all about the private and personal, and it's about transforming or adding context or adding a voice or face to that public legacy that's not really there, and people don't know that. JCs are just a fact. Internment and redress are just bare facts. They are in the past and have been forgotten.

Pause. Miwa chuckles.

Anyways, that's all I have to say about that.

MANNING: Something that Matt had written, that we use in all of our grant applications, is that this play was created for our community to speak to itself and to foster conversation within that community. We set out to give value to voices, those personal voices of internment experiences. The documented narrative is that the community lost all kinds of things: they lost money, they lost property, they lost their freedom. We wanted to look at how to uncover and reinvigorate the pride within the community, to give value to the experiences of the Nisei and Sansei who were young during the internment camps, those who actually had a very different experience of it because they were young. Young children will find amusement wherever they are. When my mother first saw us doing a reading of it, she was quite emotional and said that it actually gave context to her childhood, because growing up, she only knew maybe one or two stories. But by watching the play and hearing the experiences, even though they're twenty different personal experiences, she was finally able to understand her own story.

SAKAMOTO: This is so helpful. Could you tell me a little more about the effects of the play on both of you? You've sort of grown with the play, as a JC person, and there is a reiterative process of your identity growing and evolving with the play. And then the play also changes with you. There's this sort of codependent process of the play and you yourselves changing in this evolving process. I do feel that you, Matt, when I met you three years later, you felt a bit different.

MIWA: Mhmm.

SAKAMOTO: Maybe it was just the location, but I talked to both of you briefly at the Groundswell Festival [in 2014] and I didn't feel the same kind of impression as I had of you [Miwa] three years later at Powell Street [in 2017]. You were trying on a kimono at the Powell Street Festival, so it was a totally different setting.

Miwa laughs.

SAKAMOTO: You somehow felt more squarely JC three years later. I wonder about the effects of the project on the different stakeholders involved: you, your families, audience members, and the people you interviewed. Julie, you spoke about the effects of the performance on your mother, but I also wonder what was the response for instance, when you staged this piece at the seniors' home in Burnaby. Did the performance create conversation? What was the conversation like? When you performed at the Powell Street Festival, what did that feel like? Did the audience members speak back to you? Of the people who shared their stories with you, what did they think of the piece? I know these are a lot of questions, but I'm trying to understand the diversity of the effects of the piece.

CHIN: To add on to that question, how do those effects later change the play, if at all?

MIWA: Sure. Well, for me this play was sort of a launching point to getting involved with the community. I had nothing to do with any JC communities or any JCs, aside from my family, before the play and now I've joined the board of the Ottawa Japanese Canadian Community Association, and I know so many more JCs across the country. Because the play is like a touchstone, you know? I can talk about it and what it is, and . . . ugh, it isn't "rally"—what's the word? I just have something to offer to JCs to say, "This is what we're doing," and it's always met with excitement or pride or, I don't know what the word is, Julie, but it's met positively.

Manning and Miwa laugh.

Even last weekend, Reika, a woman who's a supporter in Ottawa, a Nisei woman who's about eighty-five or something, invited me to her house for dinner—just because she knows me from the play. We ran into each other at an event and she said, "I've been meaning to talk to you about this for a long time, so let's connect," and it's nice to have a context around which to connect with other JCs or with that generation and converse meaningfully with people. Before, we didn't know how to do that. We didn't know how to initiate these conversations, sustain these conversations.

Miwa chuckles.

And how to, I don't know, for me to be part of the community. I feel much more calm, Izumi, than I did when you met me. And that confidence stems from performing the play; it's really comforting performing the play. To get deeper and deeper into the stories and more familiar with them is something that I hope we will have for a long time. Because it's just really joyful to perform those stories. And I think I draw a lot of emotional maturity from them, and learn a lot of emotional maturity from stories and how they manage their emotions. The Nisei teach me how to do the same. I automatically ride life easier because of that.

MANNING: It's interesting how putting ourselves in the play has affected how we perform the Nisei, how we embody the Nisei, and then us embodying the Nisei informs how we perform ourselves.

All laugh.

MANNING: I wanted to talk a bit about reverberations in the community. One of the things that lifts my spirits the most is seeing different generations from the same family who come to see the play, and the conversations that this play stimulates between the generations afterward. For example, my cousin's daughter, who just graduated from high school last year, was doing a history paper on the internment. She called me to ask questions, because she knew I had created this play, and I said, "Why don't you talk to your grandparents about it, they actually went through it." Then she actually came to see the play when we did it in Toronto. And since then, the conversation within their family and our extended family has become . . . much easier. So, the door has sort of been opened to be able to talk about that within families. There are also Sansei and Yonsei* who have seen the play and they say, "I actually don't know any other JC people, and now I want to know more JC people." So, it's a doorway into the community itself. They discover a desire to belong to their community.

SAKAMOTO: Hmm.

MIWA: And also, because it has been formally recognized in our national Japanese community that there's a huge concern whether the community will continue into the future, because there's such a huge disconnect between the generations. As I said before, stories are being lost or not transferred. Language is being lost, so I think what drew Julie and I to, to the Nisei and Issei, is that they knew how to be a community, you know? It was so dynamic. They knew how to be together, they knew how to celebrate together—it was so rich—and our generation does not. Julie was one of the few JCs that I met before [*The Tashme Project*]. We don't always know how to connect to each other, how to form lasting kinds of community bonds, but we are learning, and one of the things that we always say in the grants is that we offer *The Tashme Project* as a resource for the community, and younger generations of JCs, like ourselves, to be sources of vitality for the future. So, young people are just learning now how to mobilize. People who want to identify as JCs are learning how to mobilize, and how to make better connections. Because you know, internment worked. The community was dispersed after the war, and our huge, wonderful community dynamic was lost. And there's a real threat that in a generation or two, you know, it will not be here anymore. The legacy of the community would just be gone.

Works Cited

"Redress Movement." *Sedai: The Japanese Canadian Legacy Project*, http://www.sedai.ca/for-students/history-of-japanese-canadians/redress-movement/.

---

*   *Yonsei*: Fourth-generation Japanese.

Foreign Tongue: The Musical

Book and Lyrics by Lola Xenos

Music by Justin Hiscox and Daniel Abrahamson

Acknowledgements

This has been a labour of love. I immigrated to Canada thirty years ago, and that moment marked the time that I became "the girl with an accent." The correct way of labelling accents is "non-standard speech," but I just can't bring myself to do that because it doesn't roll off the tongue (pardon the pun) the same way. The accent has merged and shifted during this time, and with it my identity. Nowadays I can pass, or perhaps my accent is faint and doesn't bear the "where are you from" question anymore. Not sure which. But the story has to be told because there are new immigrants arriving all the time, and with them new strong accents. I can't sign this book and lyrics as Cynthia Ashperger, nor as Cintija Asperger. One is my anglicized name and the other is my name at birth, and somehow I feel like neither of those people when I write. So, I chose a new name—Lola Xenos. It simply frees me and allows me to love my accent and my immigrant experiences.

A huge thank you to my great friend Janet Burke for her constant, thoughtful help, and to my daughter, Sybil, for her genuine love and laughter. Sybil is the only person who says she has never heard my accent! She was the little girl who said, "It's not like you are an alien!"

A giant thank you to Ryerson University and the Ryerson School of Performance, who supported three workshops of *Foreign Tongue* in May 2013, June 2017, and May 2018, and without which I could not have completed three rewrites. I am indebted to Derrick Chua for his pro bono work in co-producing the initial workshop in May 2013, and to Justin Hiscox who wrote a wonderful original set of tunes. A great big thank you to the indomitable musical theatre duo Daniel Abrahamson (musical direction) and Kayla James (choreography/co-direction) for their work during the June 2017 workshop, and Dmitry Zhukovsky for his direction during the same time. Our creative team meetings were full of synergy and imaginative juice. Daniel extended the score with the "Prologue Song," "Stranger Song," and "Sexy Song" (our veritable hit!) during this collaboration.

Thank you to Deanne Taylor and VideoCabaret for offering us a three-day dramaturgy workshop in December 2016. Thank you to Franco Boni and the Theatre Centre for the Recommender Grant to develop the score further.

Deepest gratitude for the talent and hard work of all who contributed to the first full production of *Foreign Tongue* at the Next Stage Theatre Festival, with special thanks to Stefan Dzeparoski who directed this production.

I would like to acknowledge the spark and creativity of *all the actors* who participated to date. Special thanks for the insights of Munire Armstrong, Jasmine Chen, Tamara Bernier Evans, Lee Filipovski, Martin Julien, Sheldon Rosen, and Baṇuta Rubess. Finally, thank you to Yana Meerzon for editing this collection and for including *Foreign Tongue*.

In May 2013, *Foreign Tongue*, then known as *Foreign Accent Syndrome Play*, had a five-day workshop and two readings at the Ryerson School of Performance with the following creative team:

Kathy Woodrough: Tamara Bernier Evans
Višnja: Cynthia Ashperger
Nurse Cannon/Zaina: Jennifer Waiser
ESL Instructor: Randi Helmers
Madeline/Jan: Catherine Thomas
Fatima/Angela/Sara: Vicki Houser
Dr. Brooke: Nicholas Rice
Pele/Producer: Ryan Allen
Paul Lee: Sean Baek
David/Fatima: David Leyshon
Yura: Owen Stahn
Mr. Tan/Casting Director: Anthony Malarky

Director: Stefan Dzeparoski

In June 2017, *Foreign Tongue* had a workshop presentation at the Ryerson School of Performance with the following creative team:

Kathy Woodrough: Kaleigh Gorka
Višnja Anic: Cynthia Ashperger
Nurse Cannon/Zainab/Director: Jenna Daley
ESL Instructor/Ms. Givens: Mattie Driscoll
Madeline/Jan (Mommy One): Elyne Quan
Dr. Brooke: Sam Malkin
Pele/Producer: Ngabo Nabea
Paul Lee/Casting Director: Julius Cho
David/Fatima: Hugh Ritchie
Yura: Dmitry Zhukovsky

Director: Dmitry Zhukovsky
Musical Director: Daniel Abrahamson
Choreographer and Co-director: Kayla James

In May 2018, *Foreign Tongue* had a workshop presentation at the Ryerson School of Performance with the following creative team:

Kathy Woodrough: Georgia Bennett
Višnja: Cynthia Ashperger
Nurse Cannon/Zainab: Jenna Daley
ESL Instructor/Ms. Givens: Victoria Houser
Madeline/Jan (Mommy One): Rachelle Bradley
Dr. Brooke/OkCupid Date/Yura: Kevin Morris
Pele/Director: Ryan Allen
Paul Lee/Casting Director: Julius Cho
David: Allie MacDonald

Director: Dean Gabourie

In January 2019, *Foreign Tongue* was presented at the Next Stage Theatre Festival at Factory Theatre in Toronto in a ninety-minute one-act version with the following creative team:

Kathy Woodrough: Victoria Houser
Višnja: Cynthia Ashperger
Nurse Cannon/Pele: Jenna Daley
ESL Instructor/Ms. Givens: Kailea Banka
Madeline: Phoebe Hu
Yura/Farrokh: Mladen Obradović
Paul Lee/Director/Chinese Engineeer: Julius Cho
David/OkCupid Date: Allie MacDonald
Dr. Brooke/Casting Director/Dry Cleaner: Nicholas Rice

Director: Stefan Dzeparoski
Musical Director: Tim Monis
Choreographer: Colleen Snell
Projection Designer: Michael F. Bergmann
Set Designers: Joe Pagnan and Konstantin Roth
Costume Designer: Katrina Fletcher
Lighting Designer: Noah Feaver

Characters

Women

Kathy Woodrough: From Peterborough, Ontario, Canada. Eastern European (Russian, Polish, Ukrainian, Slovakian, Slovenian, etc.) and Standard Canadian pronunciation. Caucasian. Thirties–forties.

Višnja: From Sarajevo. Bosnian accent. Caucasian. Forties–fifties.

Nurse Cannon: English language dialect. She is a visible minority from a country colonized by the British. Nurse's dialect and race may challenge our typical expectations (i.e., a Jamaican of Asian background or an Australian of East Indian background). Visible minority. Twenties–fifties.

Zainab: From Saudi Arabia. Saudi accent. Any race. Twenties–fifties.

Fatima: From Saudi Arabia. Saudi accent. Any race. Twenties–sixties.

ESL Instructor: Standard Canadian pronunciation. Any race. Twenties–fifties.

Ms. Givens: Standard Canadian pronunciation. Any race. Twenties–fifties.

Madeline: Non-standard pronunciation. Possible: Vietnamese accent, Chinese accent, Punjabi accent. Details/specifics may be adjusted to suit the background of the actor. Asian, East Asian. Thirties–fifties.

Men

Dr. Brooke: Eastern European Jewish background. Standard Canadian pronunciation. Caucasian. Forties–sixties.

Farrokh: Any race. Non-standard speech. Possible Iranian accent, South African accent. Details/specifics may be adjusted to suit the background of the actor. Thirties–forties.

Dry Cleaner: Non-standard Canadian pronunciation. Any race. Twenties–fifties.

Director: Standard Canadian pronunciation. Any race. Twenties–fifties.

Paul Lee: From Korea. Korean accent. Asian. Thirties–forties.

Chinese Engineer: Chinese accent. Asian. Thirties–forties.

Casting Director for *Human Traffic*: Standard Canadian pronunciation. Asian. Thirties–forties.

David: Standard Canadian pronunciation. Caucasian. Thirties–fifties.

Yura: Russian accent. Caucasian. Thirties–forties.

OkCupid Date: As cast. Australian, British, Irish, Scottish, or Welsh accent. Twenties–thirties.

Cross Gender

Pele: From Brazil. Brazilian accent. Black. Twenties–forties.
(See Casting Note.)

Casting Note

Dr. Brooke and Yura can be played by the same actor. David and Yura can also be played by the same actor. Yura is then cut out of the final scene.

Female roles may be doubled in several ways: Ms. Givens/ESL Instructor, Nurse Cannon/Madeline, Nurse Cannon/Zainab.

Pele can be played by the actor who plays Nurse Cannon. In that case, this is a female role (she/her). Pele can be played by the actor who plays Dry Cleaner and Director. In that case, this is a male role (he/him). The context will be adjusted by L. Xenos.

Pronunciation and Transcription Note

This play contains a multitude of accented voices. The transcription of the pronunciation is only *an indication* of the different accents and is moderated for ease of reading. Accented speech is *italicized* together with songs, stage directions, and non-Enlgish words and phrases.

The songs are sung with the appropriate accents as well.

The Songs

"Prologue": Choral/Company
"My Head Hurts!": Solo/Kathy
"Vere Is Everyone?": Solo/Kathy
"Britons Who Sound Chinese": Solo/Dr. Brooke
"Sink Song (Rid of It!)": Solo/Kathy
"Where Are You From Song": Duet/Kathy and David
"Tongue Tango or Belong Song": Choral/Company
"We Left Our Mama Song": Choral/ESL Quartet
"The Long Winter Waltz": Choral/Company
"No One Came to See Me": Duet/Kathy and David
"Somebody's Song": Duet/Kathy and Višnja
"Sorry Song": Solo/Choral/Duet
"Stranger": Solo/Kathy
"Sexy Song": Duet/Kathy and David
"Proverb Song": Choral/Company
"Tongue Tango Reprise": Duet/Kathy and Višnja
"Where Are You From Reprise": Duet/Kathy and David
"I Know Who I Am (Foreign to Me)": Solo/Kathy
"Thank You, Canada": Choral/Company

Act I

Prologue

VIŠNJA: *Finally, it's been diagnosed and made known*

PAUL LEE: *Original research by experts has shown*

PELE: *An unusual condition, which follows a stroke*

DAVID: *Whereby an eloquent person who once beautifully spoke*

MADELINE: *Becomes an alien, a foreigner, a species strange*

COMPANY: *When the neurons in their brain rearrange*

ESL INSTRUCTOR: *Some may thrive in this condition, others find it horrid*

YURA: *By family and friends, they find themselves ignored*

KATHY: *They're speaking English but they don't belong*

ESL INSTRUCTOR: *And with New Canadians, they find themselves among*

COMPANY: *Try as they may, their conditions here to stay*

KATHY: *Never will they produce familiar sound*

VIŠNJA: *Desired lilt, soft dees and tees, o's perfectly round*

DOCTOR BROOKE: *Their r's become*

YURA: *Rolled*

DOCTOR BROOKE: *Their w turns to*

YURA: *Vee*

COMPANY: *Only their grammar comes out perfectly*
So now begins our little tale, based on stories true

VIŠNJA: *One accent is a birthright*

KATHY: *The other's new*

KATHY & VIŠNJA: *Both however happen to be true*

COMPANY: *And both are sounding Russian, to most of you*

DAVID: *Kindly give them now your eye and your heart*

COMPANY: *And your ear plays its part*

> *Kathy Woodrough is in her home office, working on the computer. We see a pro-jection of her screen. She is re-reading her messages on the dating site OkCupid. The last message shows that she has agreed on the first date that night at the Drake Hotel. She dials her cellphone.*

KATHY: Hi, I'm going on a first date with a guy from OkCupid. He's looking for a soulmate . . . I don't really know what that means, yeah . . . whatever . . . It's just a drink. I'll text you after. First I have my last client of the year . . . both at the Drake . . . I have to pick up my car before that—it's at the shop . . . No, I won't be coming to Jack's Christmas party. I really am not in touch with that crowd anymore and I am too tired. And I . . .

My Head Hurts!

KATHY: *I have a sharp pain in my head*
Christmastime fills me with dread
Are you ready for Christmas? If I hear it once more!
I'll swear. I need a drugstore. Not Christmas!
My head hurts! My head hurts! My head hurts!

It's the fourth Christmas that I'll spend alone
Since Dad died and Mom went to a home
Fifth Christmas since I talked to my sister, Eve
Five years later she still won't forgive

That I saw her stupid ex and that we had sex
It's just sex, Eve, and you broke it up, what the fuck!

Are you ready for Christmas? If I hear it once more?
I'll scream. I need a drugstore. Not Christmas!
My head hurts! My head hurts! My head hurts!

> *In another playing area, the "Punjabi Dry Cleaner" sign appears. Kathy, dressed*
> *stylishly, enters the dry cleaner's. A Punjabi Sikh man is at the counter. He wears*
> *a beautifully folded Dastar turban.*

DRY CLEANER: Hello, ma'am, can I have you *ree-st (receipt)?*

KATHY: My wrist?

DRY CLEANER: Your *ree-st?*

> *Indicates a rectangle with his fingers.*

KATHY: Oh . . . that. You know I never know where it is. Can't I just give you my phone number? Oh, I have a headache.

DRY CLEANER: Sorry about that, ma'am. I recommend you apply some sandalwood powder mixed with rose water for relief. Or you get your boyfriend to gently massage your neck and put five drops of lukewarm sesame oil in each nostril. Works every time for me. That will be thirty-six dollars. Hope you are ready for Christmas.

KATHY: *It's seven years since I broke up with Drew*
I didn't want kids at twenty-two
With my high school boyfriend of many years
There were no tears just a relief and he now works
As a chief executive officer and has two kids and a wife, he has a life
It's just an ex, Kathy, and you broke it up, what the fuck!

Are you ready for Christmas? If I hear it once more . . .
I'll swear!

> *In another playing area. A Farrokh Auto Body Repair sign is projected. Farrokh*
> *is a good-looking guy in his forties. He wears blue coveralls with "Farrokh"*
> *stitched on them. He speaks with a Persian accent.**

---

*   This accent can be adjusted to suit the actor.

FARROKH: I know I am just your mechanic, but I would love to take you out for dinner.

KATHY: Farrokh. NO. Please. I told you already . . . You are making my headache worse. I swear.

FARROKH: Okay, don't worry so much! That's what I always said to my ex-wife in Iran.

KATHY: I'm sorry—your what?

FARROKH: My ex-wife!

KATHY: *I have a sharp pain in my head*
Being alone for Christmas fills me with dread
I wanted somebody to ask me on a date offline!
Not the divorced immigrant mechanic of mine
The nerve! Asking me out to dine!
At least he didn't offer to rub oil into my spine
I need a glass of wine

> *In another playing area The Drake Hotel appears on a neon sign, projected. Kathy enters and scans the area. She sees her date from a distance. She pulls out her phone and texts.*

OKCUPID DATE: You must be Kathy. I got you a glass of wine.

KATHY: *He is too short, I'll abort, it's a waste of time*
No need to worry about it anymore, I'm sure he's fine
He's about to pay, he won't stay
Anyway, I can imagine what he'd say
Do you like baseball?
How tall are you, asshole?!?
Once again, I said, five-foot-ten
But again, can't blame the guy, it is Christmas and he wants to mingle
This time of year is not for big city singles
Get used to that fact and get your contract!

> *In another playing area well-dressed customers surround Kathy and a Chinese Engineer. Kathy is holding a glass of wine in one hand and massaging her head with the other. A plate of poutine is in front of them. The Chinese Engineer explains in a very thick Chinese accent:*

CHINESE ENGINEER: I specialize in solar energy. Not panels but solar thermal. But my English is a problem.

KATHY: Well you're a little hard to understand, but I've been in this business ten years and I can make your resume work . . . Ahhh . . . Sorry, I have a bit of a headache . . .

CHINESE ENGINEER: I understand . . . It's that time of the year. Say, are you ready for Christmas?

KATHY: *My head hurts, my head hurts, my head . . .*

Kathy topples the wine glass and wine spills all over her clothes. She looks at the spill and then faints headfirst into the poutine. This is followed by the sound of a siren.

Kathy is put on a stretcher and taken off the stage.

In another playing area, a door with a mail slot appears. A pile of mail is in front of it. A few letters come in through the slot and land on the pile.

Waking Up

Projection: Toronto Western Hospital sign. An Intensive Care Unit hospital bed appears. Kathy is asleep in the bed, hooked to all the various monitors. Višnja (pronounced Veesh-nya) is cleaning the floor. Kathy stirs slowly and then wakes up, looks around, and sifts through the things on her bedside table.

KATHY: *(in a Russian accent) Vhere* is my *New Yorker?*

VIŠNJA: Ah, you *voke* up!

KATHY: *Vhere* am I? *Vat* is *dis* place?

VIŠNJA: Ukraina! . . . No . . . Polska? . . . No . . . Wait . . . I know . . . Mother Russia?

(in Russian) Matyushka Russia!

KATHY: *Vould* you tell me *vhere ze fak* I am! Who . . . *ze fak* . . . are you?

Notices she is hooked up to a monitor.

And *vhere ze fak* is my *New Yorker*!?

VIŠNJA: I knew it . . . Serbia . . .

No reaction.

You guys really know how to swear hard. Hard! *De so bre u pičku materinu?*[*] NO?

KATHY: *VHERE IS MY NEW YORKER*!!!!

VIŠNJA: Okay. Okay . . . You are in a hospital. I am janitor. I haven't seen your *New Yorker*, but . . . good magazine!

KATHY: Could you pass me my purse please? My cell.

VIŠNJA: Your *mobi*[†] *(winks)* could be out of juice. You been in coma for at least five weeks, / maybe six.

Višnja hands her the phone.

KATHY: Five weeks . . .

VIŠNJA: Not sure how long. Long time. No one came to see you.

KATHY: No one?

VIŠNJA: Not that I *heard*. But they don't tell staff everything.

Silence.

I'm from Bosnia. My name is VIŠNJA. V-I-S-N-J-A.

Points to name tag.

J is silent . . . *Echtually* not quite silent. J is pronounced as a y . . . it is Veeshnya.

Silence.

KATHY: *Vat's* the time?

VIŠNJA: *It's that witching time of night! Now might I do it pat, now's a praying! And now I'll do't . . .*

---

[*] May loosely be translated as a phrase sometimes used in Serbia for a hearty greeting: "Hey man, how the fuck are you?"

[†] Slang word for mobile phone commonly used in many countries in Europe.

He can't do it. *Hamlet.*

KATHY: Are you *echtually* quoting *Hamlet* to me?

VIŠNJA: *Vhy* not? I only look like janitor, but I am actually an actress. I want to entertain you. You mind?

KATHY: No, it's okay.

VIŠNJA: So, where you from?

KATHY: I am from Peterborough, Ontario.

VIŠNJA: Yes and my grandma, too, is from Peterborough . . . not. That's a good one.

   Kathy speaks to Siri.

KATHY: *Ezy Leevink* Seniors' Residence.

SIRI'S VOICE: Sorry, I couldn't find any matching hotels.

KATHY: *Ezy Leevink* Seniors' Residence.

SIRI'S VOICE: Okay, I found this on the web for: is Livingston is residence.

KATHY: Fuck you!

SIRI'S VOICE: I'd never speak to you that way.

   Kathy types in the search.

KATHY: Okay I'll type it in *den.* Here *ve* go!

Hi, Mom, it's *Kedi* . . . *Kedi* . . . IT's ME, Mom. *Kedi* . . . MOM! . . . Mom, I am in a hospital . . . Mom. Dad has been gone for three years . . . Mom. It's me . . . You are at the Easy Living Seniors' Residence . . . Dad is not *dehre.* Dad is . . . She hung up on me!

NURSE CANNON: *VISHNU!* What is going on here?

VIŠNJA: Patient *voke* up.

NURSE CANNON: Why wasn't I called?

VIŠNJA: We started talking. She *vas* looking for *New Yorker.* I *vas* gonna get you.

NURSE CANNON: We have protocols in the ICU with those who've woken up from a coma, and making a phone call is not one of them.

Takes phone out of Kathy's hand and checks her pulse.

Ms. Woodrough. Good morning. How are you feeling?

KATHY: *Fahkink* awful.

NURSE CANNON: You just woke up from a coma. It's normal. Can you tell me your birthday?

KATHY: June 21, 1986.

Nurse Cannon checks her chart.

NURSE CANNON: WELL DONE!

(to Višnja) Do you mind?

KATHY: She *vaz* just *tryink* to help.

NURSE CANNON: I *was* talking to Vishnu. Do you mind leaving, Vishnu? *Tanks.*

I'll be right back, Ms. Woodrough.

Cannon follows Višnja into the hallway.

Vishnu, I want to talk to you. I told you before and I tell you again about using the phone, and now you give it to a patient! She just woke up from a coma. Curry chicken and rice and peas.

Kathy is left alone in the room. She reaches for the purse. The wires she is hooked to are holding her back, but she manages. Sound of a computer turning on. A pop-up appears:

"Meeting with Ms. Givens at 12:00."

KATHY: Shit . . . Shit . . . I can still make it!

Her next two speeches are also seen on a projection.

"Dear Ms. Givens. Confirming our meeting today. I am sorry but I will have to change our location. Can ve meet at the coffee shop at *zeh*?"

Kathy looks at her chart. Continues to type.

"At *zeh* coffee shop at Toronto Western Hospital at noon? Looking very much forward. Kathy."

Sound of an email being sent, followed by the sound of a knock on the door. Dr. Brooke and Nurse Cannon enter.

DR. BROOKE: Hello, I am Dr. Brooke. Oh my God, you are using a computer already. Nurse Cannon?

KATHY: I *fill* perfectly fine!

DR. BROOKE: That's good to hear.

Pulls a pencil from his front pocket and moves it side to side in front of Kathy's face.

Follow the tip of the pencil with your gaze.

She does.

Excellent. Well done.

Dr. Brooke pulls out the angiogram of Kathy's brain out of the folder. We see it on a projection.

You see this is where the embolism occurred. You were very lucky really. You could have been dead or paralyzed / but . . .

KATHY: *Vhat* are the chances of me *gettink* a *strok* again?

DR. BROOKE: There is always a chance of a repeat attack. Oh, by the way, why pick Woodrough? When my grandparents came here from Russia, the name was Bruk B-R-U-K. You know. *(winks)* Then at the border it became Brooke. B-R-O-O-K-E. The border guard just changed it. My grandfather had been Alexandr Bruk and became Alex Brooke. Spelled it with an "e" . . . And I recognize that *Ashkenazi punim!**

Dr. Brooke looks at her file. Shuffles papers.

KATHY: *Ve* didn't change our name. *Ve* are from Peterborough. I *vas* born *dere.*

---

*   Ashkenazi physiognomy.

Projection: Kathy's medical form, which shows that her place of birth is Peterborough, Ontario.

DR. BROOKE: *(looking at the form)* . . . Oh dear. According to the paperwork you WERE born in Peterborough . . .

KATHY: *Zat's vat* I'm *tryink* to tell you!

DR. BROOKE: You realize you are speaking with a thick Eastern European accent?

KATHY: I'm speaking in *vat?*

DR. BROOKE: Your speech . . . has changed . . . with the stroke. You sound like a foreigner.

Oh I just had a thought . . .

Exits hurriedly. During the next speech, Kathy records herself on the iPhone.

KATHY: Eastern European accent . . .

Starts recording.

Hi, I am Kedi Voodrough. Verry nice to *mit you . . . I try to be* as specific *vid zeh* message *as I kehn. I rreally trry to stay on duh* message.

She listens. Drinks a bit of water. Stretches her mouth every which way. Records again.

Vooo. Vooo. Vooo. Voodroguh. I am *Kedi Voodrough.* I *vas* just in a coma for five *veeks.* No one came to see me . . . No one came to see me. *Can't say dat.*

Listens. Stops.

Fak. Oh *Fak. Spik. Spik. I spik* English. *Fak. Red leder yelov leder. Oh* NO . . .

Vere Is Everyone?

KATHY: *Ze last ting I remember*
Is a plate of poutine
And a foreign client
Vorking for the climate
I needed to get hired

Who am I, vat now?
Vere is everyone, anyhow?

Nobody came to see me
Musn't think about zat
Have to stay on the message
To be aggressive, to get zat percentage
Make resume impressive

Who am I, vat now?
Vere is everyone, anyhow?

I know how to do zis
Don't be late miss
Have to keep going
Need to get results
Measurables

(aside) Vhat were those again?

Who am I, vhat now?
Vhere is everyone, anyhow?

Kathy overturns the contents of her purse onto the bed. She fishes makeup articles from the pile and then starts applying makeup quickly. Višnja enters carrying a džezva and two tiny cups.*

VIŠNJA: I noticed that you didn't drink your Canadian coffee this *mornink* so I brought you a proper Turkish coffee in a *džezva*. TURSKA KAFA. *Sad ćemo da kafenišemo.*†

---

* A pot designed to make Turkish coffee. Prounounced geh-zvah.

† Pronounced sadh che-moh dah kah-feh-nee-she-moh. "We will 'do coffee' now."

KATHY: Is *dat* what you drink in Bosnia? Turkish coffee?

VIŠNJA: The same *ting* on Danforth is called Greek coffee.

KATHY: I drink English breakfast tea.

VIŠNJA: In Bosnia *ve* call that Russian tea.

KATHY: I have a business meeting downstairs in an hour.

VIŠNJA: You don't *veyst* time.

KATHY: I have to get something to *vear*. They sell clothes downstairs, right?

VIŠNJA: Hey, you in luck. I have audition later. I brought extra clothes.

Višnja returns with a big bag full of clothes.

KATHY: You just saved my bacon.

VIŠNJA: We immigrants gotta stick together. Russian mafia part. Another Ludmila. Help yourself. Try *dis*—it is stretchy.

Hands her a sexy glittery black dress.

Or *dis*?

Pulls out another shiny piece of clothing.

And I have *duh* shoes in *dis bag.*

Kathy digs through the bag and holds up a couple of different items of clothing in front of a mirror.

KATHY: *Veeshnya,* do I really sound very foreign?

VIŠNJA: So you still won't tell me where you're from?

KATHY: Okay, let's change the subject!

VIŠNJA: Sure. Let's pretend to be English.

KATHY: *Vehl* I *vouldn't* really be pretending. *Zat* is my heritage. I AM CANADIAN! You really *dohn't* believe me?

VIŠNJA: No . . .

Kathy looks through purse for her driver's licence and slaps it in front of Višnja.

KATHY: Now do you believe me?

VIŠNJA: Peterborough, Ontario . . . Driver's licence . . . So . . . Are you illegal? O-M-G . . . you are . . . how come? Looks totally real. Good job. How did you come up with Peterborough? *Dat's* a good one!

KATHY: You *echtually* don't believe me?

VIŠNJA: *Kedi,* I von't tell anyone. I am not a snitch. How did you get in?

KATHY: Oh, forget it. I *vas* born here—it says so *heer* on my licence.

VIŠNJA: I guess is better I don't know. In case they torture me I *von't* sing. Listen, I think your accent is Russian and that's okay with me. But if you are Serbian then *vee* need to talk . . . about the *vohr* years.

KATHY: About the *vohr* years . . . what the fuck? Just forget it!

Silence.

VIŠNJA: Okay. Whatever. I don't need to know. It's okay if your cousin killed my cousin.

KATHY: *Voila!*

Kathy's new outfit is very flattering, albeit not appropriate for her meeting.

VIŠNJA: Wow!!! *Dis* looks great on you. Much better than on me.

KATHY: It'll have to do.

Višnja's cell rings.

VIŠNJA: Just pretend you don't hear it. I am not supposed to use cell here. Hello . . . hi . . . oh, great! . . . Yes, vow, shoots . . . in Bosnia . . . sure, I know Tuzla . . . vow, right down my alley!

Nurse Cannon enters.

Human Traffic. BIG PART. / Central Casting. Wednesday, 4:25 pm. I know where it is. *Tenks.*

Hangs up.

NURSE CANNON: *(to Višnja)* Vishnu, hang up the phone. Why are you on the phone?

VIŠNJA: Sorry. *Vehl*, I just . . .

NURSE CANNON: Vishnu, Mr. Baldwin threw up, his floor needs cleaning immediately!

VIŠNJA: Right away, Nurse Cannon.

Višnja exits.

NURSE CANNON: What in the Lord's name is going on in here? A fashion show?

KATHY: She just lent me some *clodes*. I *hef* a business meeting downstairs.

Nurse Cannon looks her up and down.

NURSE CANNON: I'm sure you do . . . Dr. Brooke is on his way to speak to you.

Nurse Cannon's speedy exit is followed by a knock. Dr. Brooke enters.

DR. BROOKE: Oh my God, what a transformation! What is the occasion?

KATHY: I have a visitor and I'm meeting her downstairs . . .

DR. BROOKE: Don't you look great, Kathy Woodrough!

(with gravitas) Kathy, I researched your case further and my hunch was right. I am able to diagnose your very rare condition . . . You have foreign accent syndrome!

(reads) "It was first diagnosed by a neurologist in the closing days of WWII, when a Norwegian woman injured by shrapnel fell into a coma and woke up speaking with a German accent. Fellow Norwegians ostracized her as a result. There are . . .

Britons Who Sound Chinese

DR. BROOKE: *Britons who sound Chinese*
Koreans who sound Japanese
Spanish who sound Hungarian
But you are the first Canadian

Fewer than a hundred cases worldwide
Your brain needs to learn some new tricks
Chess, paint by numbers, learn how to ride
Guitar and piano up to grade six

Britons who sound Chinese
Spanish who sound Hungarian
Koreans who sound Japanese
But you are the first Canadian

We'll feed your brain protein, amino acids
Enzymes, omegas, selenium
Electrical impulses so it's not placid
I'll do anything for your cranium

Britons who sound Chinese
Spanish who sound Hungarian
Koreans who sound Japanese
But you are the first Canadian

Human subjects sign ethics release
So their brain can be my child
It's just a formality, right here please
Your grey matter drives me wild

Your grey matter drives me wild!

   Kathy signs the release.

KATHY: I *vant* to get rid of it. *Duh ehksent.*

DR. BROOKE: The bad news is we don't yet really know how you could do that. The good news is—you will be going home tomorrow. For now, I'll put you on beta blockers and blood thinners.

Dr. Brooke gives her a prescription.

You can fill this downstairs.

He exits.

Business Meeting

Projection: Coffee Shop.

Kathy rushes toward Ms. Givens, a polished-looking woman dressed upscale and conservatively. David has finished lunch and is reading the paper at a table nearby.

KATHY: *(extending a hand)* I am so sorry I am late.

Ms. Givens clutches her purse.

MS. GIVENS: I think you have the wrong person.

KATHY: Ms. Givens. Twelve o'clock?

MS. GIVENS: IT'S 12:20!

Kathy slides Mrs. Given's file folder over to her side, while Ms. Givens clutches her purse.

KATHY: So, you are looking to move from your current position, yes?

MS. GIVENS: Right . . .

KATHY: You see, in my ten years in *ze* business I have learned *zat* recruitment is science, but it is also an art. Your motivation, *ehttitude*, and presentation are "*duh art.*" Just based on your clothes, the *vey* you carry yourself, or the *vey* you speak, a headhunter such as myself might decide NOT to put you in front of a client. But impress me and I'll put you in front of a client.

David looks over the paper. He overhears the entire conversation.

MS. GIVENS: Right . . . based on my clothes.

KATHY: *Zis vas* no reflection on what you are *vehring,* Ms. Givens. You are an elegant *voman.* I *vas* telling you some *truts zat* most headhunters *dohn't* share, but honesty has *vorked* for me in *ze* past.

MS. GIVENS: Your fashion sense might differ from mine.

KATHY: *(looking over the resume) Vehl,* I'm not going to be interviewed, you are . . . As for your resume . . . Avoid *heh-knid* vords* like "dynamic."

MS. GIVENS: What kind of words?

KATHY: *(trying to pronounce it better) Heh-kneed.*

MS. GIVENS: Hackneyed?

KATHY: Exactly.

MS. GIVENS: I mean it is no reflection on your accent—I'm sure you understand the word—but hackneyed seems a bit over the top . . . the word "dynamic" is not hackneyed.

KATHY: I *sink* it is, as are "proven track record" and "team player."

  Ms. Givens takes her resume out of Kathy's hands. She is fuming.

MS. GIVENS: I don't "sink" this is going to work . . . I don't know who you are . . . or if you are who you say you are. Thank you for your time . . . *(as she is walking out)* Good day!

KATHY: Ms. Givens . . . ! Fak, fak. Fak, fak.

  Kathy is horrified.

---

*   Hackneyed.

Sink Song (Rid of It!)

KATHY: *I don't want to sound like an immigrant*
I want to get rid of it. This predicament
I am a leper, a sicko, an alien
I will not submit. I want to get rid of it

> *Tries to pronounce . . .*

Hackneyed. Hackneyed. Hackneyed.

> *A bar of the "Stranger" intro music plays . . .*

A stranger . . .

Norwegian woman shunned by her community
Presumably because of her linguistic impurity
I don't want to sound like an immigrant
I want to get rid of it. I'm not inarticulate

> *Tries to pronounce . . .*

Ekh-sent, ekh-sent

> *Another bar of "Stranger" plays.*

> *A stranger . . . I am just a stranger*

I don't want to sound like an immigrant
I want to get rid of it. This predicament
A freak of nature, a cripple, I'm innocent

> *Tries to pronounce the word "think."*

I sssink, I sssink, I sssssink!
It's a consonant. A dissonant sibilant
I vant to get rid of it!

> *Another bar of "Stranger" plays.*

Kedi Kedi . . . Kedi Vudro

David has witnessed the entire scene from a nearby table.

DAVID: Excuse me . . .

KATHY: *(startled) Vat!* . . . Oh, hi!

DAVID: Hi . . . me again . . . Sorry, but I couldn't help but overhear . . . yes . . . hackneyed is the word to describe putting "team player" on a resume.

KATHY: Didn't *vant* to *verk vith* her anyway.

DAVID: BTW, your English is excellent! And your accent is delightful.

KATHY: Am I supposed to say *"senk* you" now? *Ehctually* I don't have an accent . . .

DAVID: Oh . . . no, no, no. You see. I beg to differ. We all have one . . . at least that's the theory.

KATHY: Lucky me . . . in *seeory!*

DAVID: I, too, have an accent. Standard Canadian accent. My family goes back TEN generations in this country. We fought for the British in the war of independence. We were United Empire Loyalists. Grew up in Picton. Canadian through and through, and I think your accent is really charming.

KATHY: *(trying hard to pronounce "th" correctly) Tenks* . . .

DAVID: So where are you from?

KATHY: I'm from . . . nowhere.

DAVID: Oh! So . . . you are a refugee? So sorry to hear that. You now my family thinks that just because UEL goes back 200 to 250 years in this country that this is ancient history. But I've been doing some research and I've come to learn that your history . . .

KATHY: My history?

DAVID: The history . . . of the refugee in this country . . . the complexity . . . and the grudges that are held for hundreds of years . . . the displacement . . . Thank you for not answering my dumb question, "where are you from?"

KATHY: I suppose you have *ze* right to ask . . . Sort of.

DAVID: And you have the right not to answer. Sort of.

KATHY: Yes, or not . . .

They share a laugh.

DAVID: I just love accents. They are so mysterious and juicy, and the history.

You know. It is so beautiful to have that sense of history and struggle and conflict. I hear your accent and I can see the Russian tundra . . . or maybe the Caucasian Mountains?

KATHY: Yes . . . and also the Hungarian plains.

Where Are You From Song

KATHY: *Belgium, Botswana, Burundi, Bulgaria?*
Take a wild guess

DAVID: *I know that it isn't Australian*
Outback and Wilderness

KATHY: *I'm at home in a hotel*
I like a bagatelle
I'm not an infidel
I'm still a mademoiselle
So guess where I'm from?

Estonia, Finland, France, Island
So picturesque?

DAVID: *Your eyes are so blue, hair is so blond*
you dress so . . . statuesque!

KATHY: *I'm at home in a hotel*
I like a bagatelle
I'm not an infidel
I am a mademoiselle
So guess where I'm from

Czech Republic, Kingdom of Norway
On the flag is there a crest?

DAVID: *Warsaw, Oslo, Reykjavik*
Budapest or Bucharest

KATHY: *(simultaneously) I'm at home in a hotel*
I like a bagatelle
I'm not an infidel
And still a mademoiselle
So guess where I'm from

DAVID: *(simultaneously) She's at home in a hotel*
She likes a bagatelle
She's not an infidel
And still a mademoiselle
Can't guess where she's from

I'm David, nice to meet you.

KATHY: ... *LUDMILA* ... *from* ... *BOSNIA*

DAVID: Wanna have a cup of coffee? Or perhaps a cup of tea? My treat! What do they drink in Bosnia? Coffee or tea?

KATHY: *Ve* prefer Turkish coffee. *Turska kafa.* Same *sing* in Greektown, it's called Greek coffee.

DAVID: Funny.

KATHY: But I drink English breakfast tea. Can't stand Canadian coffee. And *ve* can have a tea under one condition . . .

DAVID: Sure, anything.

KATHY: As long as I *dohn't* have to tell you my life story.

DAVID: Okay. As long as I can tell you mine.

Leaving the Hospital

Višnja is alone in the hospital room. She mops the floors.

VIŠNJA: "Vat an adorable child.

Makes a gun with her hand and points it at an imaginary child.

My name is LUDMILA. And dis is my .45."

Kathy enters.

I *hef* to clean your room, general *cleanink*. Means you are leaving.

Vat did Doctor Brooke tell you?

KATHY: I have an incurable disease.

Višnja gasps.

It is called the "foreign *eksent syndrohm*."

Višnja cracks up.

VIŠNJA: I mean you don't have to tell me what you have. Even I know that is private. But to tell me that you have "foreign *ehk-sent syndrohm*."

KATHY: It's true! I am Canadian—I started to sound like *zis* after *ze* coma!

VIŠNJA: *Vow . . . bed* luck! *Dat* sucks. You mean you were speaking like a real Canadian and now you sound like *dis?*

KATHY: YES! YES! DAT'*s what I am trying to tell you!*

VIŠNJA: Now *dat* is like *vining* the worst LOTTERY! . . . *Dat* REALLY sucks.

Silence. Višnja points at the dress Kathy is wearing.

I need *dat* back.

They are both changing their clothes through the next few lines. Višnja pulls out a pair of jeans from her bag of clothes and gives them to Kathy. Kathy in turn gives her back the dress.

KATHY: I met a guy.

VIŠNJA: Really. *Vow. Vhen?*

KATHY: I met him just now *ven* I was filling my prescription.

VIŠNJA: You REALLY don't *veyst* time!

KATHY: *Vee* just started talking. He asked me about the *eksent.* He said it *vas* charming.

I don't know *vhy* I did it. Kinda just slipped out . . . I told him I *vas* from Bosnia.

VIŠNJA: *Vow!* Vay?

KATHY: I didn't *vant* him to be disappointed. He *vanted* me to be a refugee.

I am Bosnian now. And I need help.

Višnja hands Kathy a sweater.

VIŠNJA: *Vehl, dat's* typical!

KATHY: Very funny.

Silence.

VIŠNJA: Now you can never again say, "I never quite understood *vat happent* in Yugoslavia."

KATHY: Told him my name is Ludmila. He *vants* to get together for coffee. Can you help me . . . be authentic?

VIŠNJA: *Kedi!* Oh my God! . . . Ludmila is not a Bosnian name. *Kedi! Kedi!* Ludmila is Russian name. Bosnian name is normal-sounding name, like Vesna, or if you Serbian, Dragana or Zorana, and if you Muslim it's Emina or Alma or Amira. And best is a simple Ana. And you need to know if you are Serb, Croat, or Muslim, and how you feel about *duh* other ones *dat* you are not. You need to know your mother and father—who *dey vehre, vhere* from? Ha? Maybe you could change? Tell him you Russian. *Den* you could be Ludmila.

They have both changed. Višnja into "Ludmila" and Kathy into street clothes.

KATHY: I could say I didn't *vant* him to know my real name. Because I am . . . help . . .

VIŠNJA: *Vat . . . vanted* for war crimes? Vat? Oh, *Kedi . . .* makes no sense. Why Bosnia anyway?

KATHY: I *vanted* a good story . . . like yours . . .

VIŠNJA: *Ve* are so passe . . . You should have been Ukranian or Syrian . . .

KATHY: Okay, I am going on a date with David. Can you please help me? Tell me *vha*t to do? V*hat* do I say? Please . . .

VIŠNJA: . . . Sniper Alley . . . just say Sniper Alley.

KATHY: Sniper Alley???

VIŠNJA: . . . Sniper Alley . . . you hauled water under fire through the Sniper Alley and you were just a child . . .

KATHY: I don't *sink* I *ken* tell *zat* story. I couldn't do it justice.

VIŠNJA: It's true. Are you sure you *vant* to tell him stories at all?

KATHY: Well I kinda *hef* to now, if I *vanna* see him again . . . And I do.

VIŠNJA: Okay you a big girl. You know best. *(suddenly)* OH! I tell you *vat.* Come to my ESL CLASS *vid* me. *Vinter* session starts tonight. You will get lots of inspiration . . . and *den* you can make up your own stories.

KATHY: *(horrified)* ESL?

VIŠNJA: Okay, *Kedi,* you are not in a position to be picky. Everyone *vill* be always *eskink* you were you from. *Dis* means you can never be Canadian. But you can be a New Canadian. It's not so bad. We can go together after my audition tonight! I come get you after my shift.

Intro music starts.

Tongue Tango or Belong Song

KATHY: *What . . . if my tongue is wrong?*
What if I sound foreign?
What if you don't belong?

COMPANY: *Where were you born?*

KATHY: *Where there is a will there is a way*

COMPANY: *TAKE SOME LESSONS*

KATHY: *Okay*

COMPANY: *You gotta be good*
Lotsa personality but not too much
Must be understood
Make sure you don't use the accent as a crutch
Have to find an angle
Perhaps you come from a war-torn place
It takes two to tango
You gotta join the rat race

> *During the second verse, the actors start to make the transition into the ESL class setting and Kathy is joined by the company.*

ESL INSTRUCTOR: *So what if your tongue is wrong?*
So what if you sound foreign?
So what if you don't belong?

COMPANY: *Where were you born?*
Where there is a will there is a way!

ESL INSTRUCTOR: *FOR PETE'S SAKE WILL YOU BEHAVE?*

COMPANY: *You mustn't be trite*

WOMEN: *Learn the right things to say*

MEN: *And always stay polite*

PELE & ESL INSTRUCTOR: *Hello, how are you, have nice day*

COMPANY: *Remember anger is the greatest sin*
This you must never feel
Just say, Happy Halloween
That's how you'll keep it real

So what if your tongue is wrong?
So what if you sound foreign?
So what if your tongue doesn't belong?
Where were you born?
Where there's a will there's a way
Take some lessons

ESL Conversation and Accent Reduction Class—Introductions

ESL Instructor, Pele from Brazil, Madeline from China, Yura from Russia, and Paul Lee from Korea are present.

ESL INSTRUCTOR: Okay . . . Welcome, all, to our Conversation and Accent Reduction Class. This means that we will be talking and learning about both grammar and pronunciation. Each class we will choose a topic for discussion and then we will discuss.

Paul Lee's hand goes up.

PAUL LEE: Sorry, I don't *undehstand-uh* "discuss."

ESL INSTRUCTOR: Thank you for asking! It means the same thing as to talk. It is a synonym, and as we will find out in our class English has many synonyms.

PAUL LEE: I *undehstand-uh*! "Talk" and "discuss" same meaning.

ESL INSTRUCTOR: Today's topic is "me."

Points at herself.

PAUL LEE: We will *discuss-uh* teacher?

ESL INSTRUCTOR: When I said "me" I meant each person will discuss themselves. Why don't we start with . . . sorry, what is your name?

PAUL LEE: Paul Lee. I am from Busan, Korea.

ESL INSTRUCTOR: Paul Lee who is from Busan, Korea. Paul Lee, how did you come to Canada?

PAUL LEE: Eeeeh, I came here on airplane.

Class laughs.

ESL INSTRUCTOR: How long have you been here?

PAUL LEE: Eeeeeh. Three year. 2015.

ESL INSTRUCTOR: You arrived not a long time ago.

PAUL LEE: Eeeeeh. *Feel* like LONG time.

Class laughs.

ESL INSTRUCTOR: Paul Lee, please tell us a bit about yourself. Do you have any children?

PAUL LEE: I have one children. I have car rental store. We specialize in Hyundai. My wife and I. You come here you . . . work *haad-uh* and live a good life.

ESL INSTRUCTOR: So, you are happy here in Canada?

PAUL LEE: Eeee . . . Yes . . . very happy.

ESL INSTRUCTOR: Would you like to share with the class something that in your opinion is not good in Canada?

Paul Lee looks puzzled.

It is a standard question.

Paul Lee looks even more puzzled.

PAUL LEE: I don't understand "standard."

ESL INSTRUCTOR: I ask every student this same question. Same question is a "standard" question.

PAUL LEE: Eeeeh . . . I *understand-uh*. I will answer "standard" answer then. I like Canada . . . but sometime people lu . . . rude but most of time . . . I like Canada but . . . sometimes . . . come in store they say . . . gimme . . . gimme . . . gimme . . .

ESL INSTRUCTOR: But in Korea they are well brought up.

PAUL LEE: Yes . . . very *please-uh* . . . *please-uh* . . . give me . . . *please-uh*.

ESL INSTRUCTOR: Very good. How do your children like Canada?

PAUL LEE: My one children has many friend . . . Canadian . . . I like. Good but, sometimes . . . very . . . very . . .

Covers ears.

ra . . . ra . . .

CLASS: Loud.

PAUL LEE: But when they are *raoud* I say to them like this, sᴛᴏᴘ-*uh!*

Paul Lee is quite intense whenever he does this.

You are ᴠᴇʀʏ ʀᴜᴅᴇ-*uh*. ᴠᴇʀʏ ʀᴜᴅᴇ-*uh*. And then they all *stop-uh*. Every time. They are good kids. Good kids.

Višnja rushes into the classroom late.

ᴠɪšɴᴊᴀ: Hello, sorry, Ms. Barber, I am late. I had audition again.

ESL INSTRUCTOR: That would be ᴀɴ audition. We must remember the article. Class, this is Veeshnya, our returning student!

ᴠɪšɴᴊᴀ: Hi, guys. I am Veeshnya from Bosnia. I am also an actress. And *dis* is my friend who would like to join *duh* class. Is it okay?

ESL INSTRUCTOR: Sure, we are just doing the introductions. Take a seat.

What was your audition for?

ᴠɪšɴᴊᴀ: I *vas bed* Russian Mafia lady. *Vid* Big Gun! And at home I did Shakespeare. And at home I played Helena, Ophelia, and Lady Anne! In big productions! *Vid* good directors! I really was *kinda* famous.

Madeline examines her portfolio. Says the following line in her language first then translated into English.

MADELINE: You were a star!

VIŠNJA: But then the war started. Bad luck . . . And where I lived in Sarajevo, we were surrounded! We were under siege for one thousand days and shelled, and we didn't have any water, food, or electricity; we just had the Sniper Alley. It was really tough.

We Left Our Mama Song

VIŠNJA: *There was a road to our airport*
And it became the no man's land
We called it Sniper Alley
Ruled by the quick of hand

You had to cross the Sniper Alley
That's where you learned to run
Down the alley there was drinking water
Guarded by the bastard's gun

You filled up all your canisters
Of sizes small and large
You carried them and ran for life
You ran while they recharged

We knew the guys who shot at us
We used to play hide and seek
Now they were Sniper Alley lords
Hunting all the meek

MADELINE: *In China it was very hard*
With Mao and his wife
Our parents were re-educated
And you could lose your life

My uncle and his family
Could sponsor me alone
So I left my mom and dad
And came here on my own

COMPANY: *We were looking for the grass that's greener*
And we crossed to the other side
We left our home, we left our mama
Oh, the tears we cried

YURA: *And when we got democracy*
We felt a lot pride
But the people, they stayed poor
Their rights again denied

Zeh safest is to shut your mouth
Is what Father said to me
And zat is why I wanted out
I wished for speaking free

PELE: *We had racial segregation*
Until 1888
There was much oppression
And a lot of hate

Latin America has racism
But it is underground
They don't say it to your face
But it is still around

COMPANY: *We were looking for the grass that's greener*
And we crossed to the other side
We left our home, we left our mama
Oh, the tears we cried

ESL INSTRUCTOR: Thank you so much for sharing. Your stories are very reflective of our Canadian experience, and well I am sure glad that you are here and that you are safe.

And now would be a good time to introduce our end-of-semester presentation. We share our talents, our cultures, and we always end with a skit about being Canadian. Do you all know what a skit is? . . . It is a short comic performance. It'll be fun!

Class nods yes, reacts enthusiastically.

So who else would like to join us and talk about themselves? And we have . . .

ESL Instructor addresses Pele, who speaks with a Portuguese accent.

PELE: Pele.

ESL INSTRUCTOR: From . . .

PELE: Brazil.

ESL INSTRUCTOR: Pele, you have a famous name.

PELE: My family likes *soccah.*

ESL INSTRUCTOR: What is your background?

PELE: I . . . Afro-Brazilian.

ESL INSTRUCTOR: I am Afro-Brazilian. You are Afro-Brazilian. Tell us a bit about yourself, Pele.

PELE: *(smiles)* I am Pele. I am Afro-Brazilian. I run *eh* capoeira studio. I teach capoeira.

ESL INSTRUCTOR: Can you explain to us what capoeira is?

PELE: Capoeira is *eh, eh* type of martial arts. But it no fighting, it is more using *reethm* where you move, like *eh* dance as opposed to *eh* actual fighting. It is deep in our culture and rich in *deh* music—it has become a celebration.

I enjoy being single.

PAUL LEE: Aaa . . . playboy-uh?

Class laughs.

ESL INSTRUCTOR: Why are you here, taking this class?

PELE: I am here long time. My expression is not good enough. I want to have *eh* better expression in English.

ESL INSTRUCTOR: We can help you with that in this class. Who would like to introduce themselves next?

Checks list.

YURA: Can you show us some of your moves, Pele?

Pele looks to the ESL Instructor for permission.

ESL INSTRUCTOR: Sure, go ahead.

PELE: Is three basic moves. It goes to the *reethm*.

Pele starts the rhythm and the class claps during his demonstration.

Whatever the *reethm* is to the drum. The berimbau is a stick. With a string. You start off like this.

Demonstrates.

If somebody comes to kick you like this, you go down and they kick over your head. But it is also a lot of acrobatics. People who do breakdance, they do lots of capoeira because it is more of a dance *den* it is a fight and it is low to *deh* ground.

Demonstrates some more.

Nobody get hurt.

Class claps.

You come to my place and seventeen dollars is two hours.

YURA: I'll be there, man. I love it.

PELE: Yes, and you see there are girls there who need partners. We get more women in *deh* studio. And all you use is language between bodies.

YURA: Like, I'll be there, Pele! In your studio you don't need to talk, only need your body language.

PELE: You can talk if you want to.

YURA: But you don't have to!

ESL INSTRUCTOR: Okay, so we might as well continue with you, Yura. Why did you come to Canada?

Yura answers in a thick Russian accent. He doesn't have the sunniest of dispositions.

YURA: I came simply because . . .

ESL INSTRUCTOR: Can you tell us where you came from?

YURA: Russia. I thought you wanted me to say *vhy* I came to Canada. *Vhy* you interrupt?

(attempting a joke) Typical *voman.*

ESL INSTRUCTOR: I am sorry to have interrupted you. Can you tell us your full name?

YURA: Is okay. Yura Shikolenko. I am 3D animation and *veb design.* I have university degree from Russia and now I have to take ESL courses here.

Yura rolls his eyes.

Like, it sucks for me and for many people. Because *zey* come here and *zey,* like, have good education and, like, *zey* don't get jobs they deserve. *Zey* have to step down because *zey* don't have Canadian experience.

MADELINE: Transfer. It is not the same thing over there as here.

Yura rolls his eyes.

YURA: But, like, it should be.

ESL INSTRUCTOR: I heard students say that it almost feels like when you cross the border you become a second-class citizen.

MADELINE: Yes, it is very stupid!

Class agrees.

YURA: *Vehl,* like, anyway, looking for a job in *veb design* is full-time job. I will not stay in *veb design.* I have plans. I will invest in Canadian oil patch. You know, like oil sands.

ESL INSTRUCTOR: Oil sands. Interesting topic. I have to admit I have quite a strong opinion on that.

YURA: Yes, many people do. But guys . . . This is FACT . . . : Only five percent of greenhouse gas emissions come from oil patch and it is responsible for twenty-five percent of wealth in Canada / . . . and *vhen* you take such percentages . . .

ESL INSTRUCTOR: Yura, I have to jump in here. This is NOT a fact. The oil industry is responsible for fifty to sixty million tons of carbon dioxide. You cannot put the oil patch in those percentage terms. Sorry!

YURA: You interrupted me again and you are not sorry!

PELE: My friend who is studying at U of T says people are afraid to publish their research in Canada! *Dey* are branded a traitor if *dey* suggest that we don't want this oil patch.

YURA: But they are a TRAITOR! Oil patch is the only thing that can save Canada!

ESL INSTRUCTOR: Yura, this is not appropriate!

YURA: *Vhat*, saving Canada?

ESL INSTRUCTOR: No, you can't brand someone a traitor because they have an opinion. Have you seen a picture of birds landing on tailing ponds, Yura?

YURA: OIL SAND IT IS NOT PHOTOGENIC? That is problem?

ESL INSTRUCTOR: It's not photogenic for a reason, Yura. It pollutes! Pipes break all the time. Let's not try to hide the real facts, Yura!

YURA: FACT, Ms. Barber, is *zat* oil sands are good for economy, and *zat* I am excited to go to Alberta in Canada because I like shooting and hunting and in Alberta this is good. I *vas* junior champion in my country. I *vas* on team.

ESL INSTRUCTOR: Thank you, Yura. Shooting and oil sands. Very good.

And please think about what you could do for our presentation. In the past students have shared lovely Russian poetry. I learned about your wonderful poet, Yevtushenko.

YURA: *Ve* need some vodka if we read Yevtushenko.

ESL INSTRUCTOR: Sorry, this is an alcohol-free campus. But we could pretend to drink it!

YURA: Okay, I *vill tink* about it.

ESL Instructor focuses next on Madeline.

ESL INSTRUCTOR: Madeline, you are next.

It's Madeline's turn to introduce herself. She speaks quickly and in an incredibly difficult-to-understand accent. It is not transcribed for ease of reading.

MADELINE: I am Madeline, from China. I have been here fifteen years and I have two daughters and a husband.

ESL INSTRUCTOR: Do you work?

MADELINE: Yes, I always work. I work in a company. Called GE. Means General Electric. Big company.

PAUL LEE: Samsung is bigger!

ESL INSTRUCTOR: What is your dream?

MADELINE: You know . . . to see my daughters . . . happy.

ESL INSTRUCTOR: Are they married?

MADELINE: No, both very young. Twenty and seventeen. Older one maybe marry twenty-seven.

She has a boyfriend in China. Met when she visit her grandma. I don't like him.

ESL INSTRUCTOR: Why is that?

MADELINE: She is very stupid. He very lazy.

Class laughs.

He works in restaurant but he needs to go back to school to get education.

Madeline looks at Pele.

You are perfect for her. You can be my son-in-law. You look like Obama!

Class laughs.

Hello. And what is your name?

KATHY: Ludmila Voodrough.

ESL INSTRUCTOR: Woodrough. Well . . . this is unusual. You must have one English-speaking parent?

KATHY: *Vehl,* my father died in . . . he . . . *vas* a British . . . *vehl* he died . . . and . . . and my mother who *vas* from Eastern Europe . . . from . . . and she . . . raised me alone and *zat* is how . . .

ESL INSTRUCTOR: I am so sorry. Where was your mother from?

KATHY: She *vas* . . .

Kathy takes her head in her hands.

. . . I can't do this . . .

VIŠNJA: Excuse me . . . *Ludmila* . . . do you mind . . . if I tell your story . . . very traumatic story . . . difficult . . .

I know *Mila* from back home, and you see her father was British but he died *vhen* she vas young. Her mother was Bosnian, from Sarajevo . . . and *Mila* and mama returned home to Sarajevo from London . . . and then the *vohr* started . . . *bed* luck. BAD LUCK!

Right, Mila?

KATHY: Yeah, right . . . BAD LUCK!

ESL INSTRUCTOR: That story is reflective of our diverse Canadian experience.

And what do you expect from this class, Mila?

KATHY: I *vould* like to *verk* on the pronunciation of my name. I *vould* like to be able to pronounce it correctly. I *vould* like to sound *neytif.*

ESL INSTRUCTOR: We aim to sound "like native" and I am sure this class will be helpful.

And our next question goes to the whole class. The question is: How do you like living in Toronto and Canada?

MADELINE: Too many culture in Toronto. I find other culture very strange. I don't like when I say something and I know they don't understand me and they pretend they do. I really don't like that. And winter . . . very cold and I don't like.

ESL INSTRUCTOR: Anyone else?

PAUL LEE: I like the *winter-uh.* In my country is too, too hot in the summer and too, too, how do you say? Many people, many, many people.

ESL INSTRUCTOR: Crowded. When there are many, many people we call it crowded.

PAUL LEE: YES! MANY, MANY PEOPLE. Busan beach very, very uncomfortable. Canada has space. In Busan beach very, very crowded. Body, body, body, body everywhere.

YURA: *Vehl,* I can't say I like winter, but like I deal with it. Like if I have *voman.* Like it's no problem *zen.* Another problem I have, here if I *vant* to see a friend of mine I have to call him *vay, vay* in advance, because if you show up at someone's door they *vould* think I am crazy.

Class laughs. Intro music starts.

VIŠNJA: Canadian *vinter* is too long.

MADELINE: Yes, the weather here is stupid!

PELE: Yes, I can't wear my Speedo!

Class laughs.

The Long Winter Waltz

VIŠNJA: *In Sarayevo we drink kefir*
And weather is nicer than here

MADELINE: *In Shenzhen can't make a snowman*
Have summer six months of the year

PELE: *In Brazil we can really feel*
Heat that never ends

YURA: *In Mother Russia when we feel the cold*

COMPANY: *We drink lotsa vodka with friends*

In Canada, oh Canada we have challenges thermostatic
Too cold in the basement and too hot in the attic
In Canada, our Canada, the weather is problematic

PAUL LEE: *In Korea we love to hear*
Warm evening breeze every night-uh

KATHY: *We hate the cold and the heat distain*
The northern wind drives us insane

COMPANY: *In Canada, oh Canada, we pray down on our knees*
Oh God, please don't let me freeze

In Canada, our Canada, we pray down on our knees
Oh God, please don't let me freeze

Oh God, oh God, oh please
Oh God, oh God, oh please
Oh God, don't make me freeze

> *Class ends up kneeling at the end of the song, teeth chattering, huddling together.*

The Date

> *David and Kathy on a park bench.*

DAVID: What a beautiful day . . .

KATHY: Yes . . .

DAVID: So what was your favourite television show as a child?

KATHY: I don't want to talk about the past, David.

DAVID: Not even about television?

KATHY: No!

DAVID: What kind a food do you like to eat? Do you like *chevapchichi*?

KATHY: What?

DAVID: I looked it up on the Internet . . . maybe I'm mispronouncing . . . *Chevapchichi* . . . your national dish . . . kind of little hamburger sausage thingies in a bun . . . I think.

KATHY: Yeah, they are all right . . . but I like Western food. I like regular-size hamburgers . . . I like Italian . . . I like French . . . Pizza . . . Thai food . . . I like all food.

DAVID: Me too. What about the music? What kind of music do you like? Do you like *Sevdah*, the Bosnian blues . . . I listened to it on YouTube . . . It's haunting . . .

KATHY: Yes, I LOVE DAT . . . but it is too sad . . . I prefer Lady Gaga.

DAVID: I love her, too.

He sings a bit of "Nebraska" by Lady Gaga. Kathy joins in. They inch closer.

Beautiful! What about your family? Did you lose someone?

KATHY: I will tell you one thing . . . I was in hospital for six weeks and no one came to see me . . .

DAVID: I would've come to see you . . .

No One Came to See Me

KATHY: *Six weeks in a coma*
I heard of a girl in England
She was dead a year in her apartment
Before they found her
She had a mail slot
On the front door . . .
No one came to see her
For a year

DAVID: *No one came to see her*

BOTH: *No one, not one, none*

KATHY: *A mountain of junk mail*
At the front door
A year's worth of mail at the door
And not one friend from Facebook
And not one friend from work
And not one friend from book club
And not one friend at all
No one came to see me, too

DAVID: *I would come to see you*

KATHY: *No one came to see me*

BOTH: *No one, not one, none*

KATHY: *No one came to see me*
Not my mother, she is in a home
Not my father, he is gone
Not my sister, we don't talk anymore
Nobody came, not one, none

DAVID: *None came to see you*
None, not one none
Not even your best friend?
Maybe she is married?
Went home for Christmas?
Not even your best friend?

KATHY: *I don't have a best friend*

DAVID: *Six weeks in a coma*
I would have come to see you
I would have brought you flowers
I would have whispered softly
Wake up, wake up, darling
I would have come to see you
I would have come to see you
I would have, this guy, I

I . . . is it okay . . . hug?

By the end of the song they are tightly snuggled with one another.

KATHY: Jeez, I'm hugging some random hospital guy.

DAVID: And if anything ever happens again, Ludmila, random hospital guy will come to see you. And he will bring you some *chevapchici* in a bun.

KATHY: *Zat* makes me so happy, David . . .

DAVID: . . . You can call me Dave.

KATHY: Dave. This feels so nice. I haven't snuggled in so long.

They kiss.

Preparing the Audition

Višnja is preparing her audition and Kathy is helping her. Višnja is wearing a very unflattering outfit and a babushka. Her hair is messy. She looks distraught. Kathy is holding the script while filming the audition on her phone.

VIŠNJA: No . . . no . . . no . . . you killed my son. You killed my son . . .

She collapses and cries. Shakes it off.

How *vas* it?

KATHY: *Zat* was your best one!

VIŠNJA: Good. I am exhausted . . . Let's have the wine . . . FINALLY!

She fetches a bottle and opens it.

You know I *vas* auditioning one time for something. I don't know what it vas, but I do know that I practiced my diphthongs for a week. D-O-N-apostrophe-T is not pronounced "*dohn't,*" it is pronounced "*douhn't.*" There is an O and a U in that letter O. *Dat* is a diphthong in case you didn't know. I hate *dem*! Stupid *diphthongs.* Anyway, *dey* asked me to do it Canadian accent.

KATHY: Canadian *eksent.* What is *zat* anyway?

VIŠNJA: Good question . . . but *den* . . . after *dat* audition, I was baby-sitting my blond angel neighbour, Ana. She caught me crying. "Why are you crying?" I said it's because I have an *eksent* so nobody will play with me. "Don't cry," she said. "I *vill* play with you. It's not like you are an alien!" True story!

KATHY: Dat's so nice . . .

VIŠNJA: You know my name is Višnja, not *Vishnu.* I might as well be Shiva or Krishnu.

Music starts.

Somebody's Song

This song is sung with the accents.

VIŠNJA: *I used to be somebody*
Dat somebody was me
Now I am somebody
I don't know how to be

Forget about her
Don't fret about her
Hold on to now, dat somebody's gone
Hold on to now

I used to be no one's fool
I thought I was pretty cool
Got back my innocence
But lost all self-confidence

KATHY: *Forget about zat*
Don't fret about zat
Hold on to now, and let her be
You're no longer she

VIŠNJA & KATHY: *I used to hang with the in-crowd*
Mom and Dad were very proud
Of that girl, who was me
Zeh girl that I was, used to be

Regret about dat
Forget about zat
Hold on to now, just learn to be somebody
You don't know how to be
You don't know how to be
You don't know how to be
You don't know how to be

Višnja pours wine.

VIŠNJA: You know "Veeshnya" means "sour cherry" in my language. Cheers!

KATHY: That's unfortunate. Cheers!

They drink.

VIŠNJA: *Vehl* it's not unfortunate in my language. *Vhat* about callink your kid Apple? *Dat vould* sound so stupid in my language. Yabuka. Come here. Everyone *vould* laugh at you.

I talked to this Polish girl once. She said her boyfriend proposed, and she asked herself if she should marry him in English and the answer *vas* yes. *Den* she asked herself in Polish and the answer *vas* NO.

KATHY: Did she marry him?

VIŠNJA: She still *stallink*! Okay, I gotta kick you out now. Tomorrow's my big day.

KATHY: You'll do great! I just know it!

The Movie Audition

"Tongue Tango" vamp plays and the set changes during this scene.

ARABIC ACCENT: No, no, my son. You killed my son. Nooo!

CASTING DIRECTOR: That was great. *Human Traffic* in Lebanon!

DIRECTOR: I'm not sure . . .

"Tongue Tango" vamp continues.

COMPANY: *What if you sound foreign?*

VIETNAMESE ACCENT: No, no, my son. You killed my son. Nooo!

DIRECTOR: I love the idea of *Human Traffic* in Vietnam. Gives me the chills!

CASTING DIRECTOR: There is one more.

"Tongue Tango" vamp continues.

VIŠNJA: No, no, my son. You killed my son. Noooo!

CASTING DIRECTOR & DIRECTOR: Great. *Human Traffic* in Bosnia. That's the one!

"Tongue Tango" vamp continues.

COMPANY: *Where there's a will there's a way*

ESL INSTRUCTOR: *Take some lessons.*

COMPANY: *Okay!*
Where there's a will there's a way.
Take some lessons.

So Sorry!

ESL INSTRUCTOR: Okay . . .

Zainab is new. She wears a full burka. She is behind the rest of the class in her English—pretty much a total English language beginner.

Now repeat after me. I am from Saudi Arabia.

ZAINAB: I am from Saudi Arabia.

ESL INSTRUCTOR: Can you tell us a bit about yourself, Zainab?

ZAINAB: I am Zainab. In Canada four weeks. Husband and Zainab new life in Toronto. I want learn English. I lost me when come first class. Sorry.

Zainab bows.

ESL INSTRUCTOR: No problem, Zainab.

Everyone please go to chapter five in your textbook.

Zainab, can you come here please?

ESL Instructor speaks to Zainab privately.

Zainab, I think that you should take the Friday evening class. Or the Tuesday class. You still need to learn some basics. This class is much more advanced.

Zainab shakes her head "No."

ZAINAB: I want study with teacher. Best teacher.

ESL INSTRUCTOR: But this is the first class you have attended. How do you know I am the best teacher? It will be hard for you to understand. This is an advanced class . . . we mainly focus on conversation.

ZAINAB: Friend Fatima said you best teacher. Friday not good, holiday. Tuesday not good for Zainab. Wednesday I learn English.

ESL INSTRUCTOR: But we will not cover grammar and vocabulary and basic comprehension.

ZAINAB: Okay. We will not cover. I like class. I like teacher. Best teacher.

ESL Instructor is at a loss.

ESL INSTRUCTOR: Okay, you can stay for now. We will see how you do. We will decide in a few weeks.

Zainab returns to her seat.

Zainab will join our class. Welcome!

Now let's warm up with a diphthong sound, "OH." "OH" is what you say when you are surprised by something or, in a slightly different intonation, when you are intrigued by something. Repeat after me: *(acting surprised)* "OH!"

CLASS: *(surprised)* "OH!"

ESL INSTRUCTOR: Now try a slightly different intonation: *(acting intrigued)* "OH!"

CLASS: *(intrigued)* "OH!"

ESL INSTRUCTOR: Excellent! It's spelling nearly always includes an "o," such as "go," "show," and "loan," but it also can include other spellings like "sew," with an "e." Now repeat after me: "Oh no, don't go, cowboy. I'll sew your chapeau for the rodeo!"

CLASS: "Oh no, don't go, cowboy. I'll sew your chapeau for the rodeo!"

ESL INSTRUCTOR: Excellent . . . the sound starts in the centre of the mouth, "ah," and moves to the back of the mouth rounded in "ou." And remember your "oh" when you're surprised and intrigued. That can be very helpful. Who would like to try alone?

Paul Lee's hand goes up.

PAUL LEE: *(using "surprise")* Oh no, don't go, cowboy! I'll sew your chapeau for the rodeo!

ESL INSTRUCTOR: Very good!

MADELINE: *(trying to top Paul Lee's pronunciation)* I will use intrigue: "Oh no, don't go, cowboy. I'll sew your chapeau for the rodeo."

PELE: I will try combination surprise and intrigue.

He does so while doing capoeira moves.

"Oh no, don't go, cowboy. I'll sew your chapeau for the rodeo."

ESL INSTRUCTOR: Bravo, Pele! And in English we pronounce "bravo" using the same diphthong as well! Brav-OH! This is unlike in the original Italian word! Bravo!

And now let's refresh our irregular verbs.

There are almost two hundred irregular verbs in English, and if you memorize those you are going to be fine. I promise!

Fatima, could you please give us an example of an irregular verb?

FATIMA: Have, had, had.

ESL INSTRUCTOR: Excellent choice, Fatima. Excellent! A very important verb in the English tongue because it uses three different tenses. Who can tell me what they are?

MADELINE: Present perfect tense, past perfect tense, and future perfect tense.

ESL INSTRUCTOR: Impressive! Can we have an example of each?

Paul Lee puts his hand up.

PAUL LEE: Yes, we can . . . have had, had had, will have had . . .

Višnja arrives late to class.

VIŠNJA: Sorry, Ms. Barber, I had audition.

ESL INSTRUCTOR: You must not be late all the time, Višnja.

VIŠNJA: Sorry, Ms. Barber. I have to go to audition *vhen* I have it. *Dis* was my second audition in two days!

ESL INSTRUCTOR: You are again forgetting the article. An audition or the audition?

VIŠNJA: Yes, an audition for *A Prolific Fancy*. It's about a lesbian couple having a baby. *Dey* get a sperm donor and *dey* have a baby. And then they decide not to raise the baby as a boy or a girl but to keep baby genderfluid.

ESL INSTRUCTOR: Oh, I see. That sounds very interesting. And where will it be playing?

VIŠNJA: At the Workman's Space.

PELE: Sounds like fun.

MADELINE: *Veeshnya,* you are too old to have baby. How old you?

PELE: How can you ask her that? You are embarrassing her.

MADELINE: It is true.

VIŠNJA: I auditioned for lesbian mommy number two! I would not be pregnant.

MADELINE: That is stupid. Parents don't know if she is a boy or girl?

PAUL LEE: That is not very nice thing to say.

MADELINE: It is hard to be grow up if you have mother and father, and now you have mother one and mother two AND baby is genderfluid? Double whammy!

ZAINAB: What means "lesbian"?

ESL INSTRUCTOR: That is when two women are married. No man.

ZAINAB: No man? Sounds good to me.

Class laughs.

YURA: Genderfluid! This is gay propaganda.

VIŠNJA: It's not propaganda, Yura. It is art!

YURA: Genderfluid? Gender neutral? Like boy and girl *dohn't* exists!

višnja: *Vhy dohn't* you go live back home, Yura? To Mother Russia where there is no propaganda.

yura: It is democracy here, and I have the right to say *vhat* I *vant*. And if I *sink* it is propaganda to say *zat zere* is no man and no woman and everything is NEUTRAL, *zen* I have the right to have opinion at least.

kathy: In Canada, we don't discriminate because of someone's sexual orientation or race or gender or nationality or . . .

yura: How would you know about Canada, Mila? You're just off the boat. Bosnian from England and *vhatever* else. You are a refugee! I can at least call myself an immigrant. I came here to *vork,* not to get free apartment and free ESL, and then you refugees go back if you feel like it. I am here to stay and to BUILD *ZIS* COUNTRY!

kathy: YURA, I am not going back!

višnja: Yes, there is NOWHERE for Mila to go!

zainab: Yes, not many refugees go back.

kathy: I AM NOT A REFUGEE!

paul lee: *(with authority)* Everyone, please *STOP-uh*! Sorry, Mila, but if you came because of war you are a refugee.

esl instructor: And Yura, making such a comparison between immigrants and refugees is NOT appropriate!

yura: But we are here for different reasons. And if you are telling me *vhat* I CAN and CAN NOT SAY, how can you call it democracy? It is bullshit opinion.

višnja: I cannot believe you! This is so Russian.

yura: Why do you bring Russia into it? Is that appropriate?

esl instructor: No, it is not! We are going to end this conversation. Those who want to know more about this show can speak to Veesnya individually and she will fill you in on the details.

madeline: I rather watch TV.

pele: *(to Yura)* I think there is too much racist stuff in Russia, Yura.

YURA: Are you talking about me?

ESL INSTRUCTOR: Class, please—this is not an appropriate subject!

PELE: This is an appropriate subject.

YURA: That is such bullshit!

ESL INSTRUCTOR: Excuse me!

YURA: Like you heard me. Why you say excuse me?

PAUL LEE: *Yula*, please *stop-uh*!

YURA: Yes, just because you say is inappropriate or appropriate it doesn't mean it is! And by the way, you are EXCUSED!

ESL INSTRUCTOR: EXCUSE ME!

PAUL LEE: Teacher, I think *Yula* said you *ale* excused. It's okay.

ESL INSTRUCTOR: Paul Lee, I didn't mean it as an apology.

PAUL LEE: BUT YOU SAID EXCUSE ME! I DON'T *UNDEH-STAND-UH*!

ESL INSTRUCTOR: Never mind, Paul Lee.

PAUL LEE: OKAY NEVER *MIND-UH*!

PELE: I read in paper that Russians are racist.

PAUL LEE: Everyone, please, NEVER *MIND-UH*!

Yura is starting to roll up his sleeves. Pele is up on his feet, ready with a few capoeira moves. They are about to come to blows.

PELE: I heard that I can't go to Russia. Not safe for me.

YURA: I AM NOT A RACIST! ARE YOU SAYING THAT I AM A RACIST?

Yura and Pele are about to come to blows. Paul Lee and the ESL Instructor speak over each other.

PAUL LEE: / You are all so *rude-uh*. *STOP-UH! STOP-UH! STOP-UH!*

ESL INSTRUCTOR: Class, please. Please, let's change the subject.

ESL Instructor starts to cry.

MADELINE: You can come to China. No one will have a problem that you black. We like Obama!

PAUL LEE: *STOP-UH*!

I want to apologize to teacher. Everyone please apologize to teacher.

(very upset) You are all so *RUHD-uh*. And I apologize I had to be *roud*! *Solly*! Say NEVER *MIND-UH*!

ZAINAB: *(in solidarity with Paul Lee)* Say never *mind-uh*!

Zainab bursts into tears. Random apologies from the students.

PAUL LEE: Teacher, how can we make you stop crying? Please *stop-uh*!

Pele stops crying.

PELE: Ms. Barber, I am very sorry. Please accept my handkerchief.

ESL INSTRUCTOR: Thank you, Pele. My brother Robert is gay . . . He and his partner Jake will adopt a girl from Romania . . . and as I was saying there are almost two hundred irregular verbs in English and if you memorize those you are going to be fine. Could everyone please give us an example of an irregular verb.

YURA: CUT, CUT, CUT.

PELE: HIT, HIT, HIT.

YURA: HURT, HURT, HURT.

PELE: BEAT, BEAT, BEAT.

PAUL LEE: GO, WENT, WENT.

ESL Instructor bursts into tears again.

CLASS: NO! GO, WENT, GONE!

Intro music for "Sorry Song" begins and continues until Višnja's phone rings.

Sorry Song

ESL INSTRUCTOR: *Sorry, excuse me, I'm so sorry*
My apologies and I really mean it
And in this we are in agreement
To be Canadian is to be sorry

Sorry

CLASS: *Sorry*

ESL INSTRUCTOR & CLASS: *I'm so sorry*
There is no excuse
I take it all back
Too much information
Not enough tact

CLASS: *We are Canadian and we're sorry*

ESL INSTRUCTOR: *You're Canadian and you're sorry*

Once again I'm very sorry. Class is over.

CLASS: *We are Canadian and we're sorry*

COMPANY: *Sorry, sorry, sorry*

The class has dispersed. The ESL Instructor is packing up and leaving.

ESL INSTRUCTOR: And I must apologize to you, Pele. You didn't get a word in edgewise.

PELE: It's okay, Ms. Barber! And Ms. Barber, by the way, I agree with everything you say.

Ms. Barber, can I help you carry your books to the car?

Pele is clearly smitten by the ESL Instructor, who is not indifferent either.

ESL INSTRUCTOR: Oh, Pele, thank you so much. You are a true gentleman. I am on my bike though.

Exits.

PELE: You are welcome. Really. Anytime. It's my pleasure.

Sorry, excuse me, very sorry
Pardon me, darling, I didn't mean to
I never meant to get so personal
I am Canadian and I am sorry

COMPANY: *(offstage) Sorry*
Sorry
Sorry

Višnja enters while speaking on the phone.

VIŠNJA: Sorry . . . *(excited)* yes, *dis* is her. It is *ehctually* Višhna. J is silent. Yes . . . you got my number from the production office . . . I auditioned for *Human Traffic* . . . yes, for the part of Sonya . . . Sorry . . . I see . . . to teach you my accent . . . Oh, low budget . . . I see, aha . . . no budget for coaching . . . I see . . . so you can sound just like me . . . you go to Tuzla and Sarajevo, right . . . and play me and then you *vill* do it so good that maybe you *vill* get an *ahword* for your accent it was authentic and consistent . . . how about I teach you *dis* . . . *Idi u guzicu.*˙

Hangs up.

KATHY: Višnja, what was that?

Višnja weeps.

VIŠNJA: *Dat vas "Idi u guzicu."*

KATHY: Meaning?

VIŠNJA: It's something about that audition and about someone's asshole.

KATHY: Don't cry.

VIŠNJA: I am just a *faking* immigrant!

KATHY: It *vill* get better.

VIŠNJA: No it *von't.* My tongue muscles are fully formed! That can never be changed. I *vill* never be an actress again. I *vill* never be an actress again.

Višnja exits. Alone, Kathy sings.

---

*   "Up yours!" in Bosnian.

Stranger

KATHY: *A stranger*
Of course it isn't how you see me
You see me all right, if I don't open my mouth

You talk first, they don't know . . . yet
They see one thing and den I say: Kedi Vooodro
And then they see another

A stranger
They feel a bit betrayed by dis
They are a little curious
They feel a bit superior
And it is quite obvious
That to them I am just a
Stranger

A stranger
Sometimes you are indifferent
(Indifference is superiority plus contempt)
Sorry can you repeat it
What did you say?
Say it really slow, Kedi Voudro?
Ke-di, that's an interesting name
Does it have a meaning? I don't know

A stranger
you feel a bit betrayed by dis
you are a little curious
you feel a bit superior
and it is obvious
That to them I am just a
A stranger. A stranger. A STRANGER.

Act II

Sexy Accents

Kathy and David are on the either side of the stage. Intro music to "Sexy Song" underscores the dialogue.

DAVID: Talk to me, talk to me. Tell me how you like it. I love it when you talk to me.

KATHY: So you like me to talk to you, Dave?

DAVID: Yes . . . You're the first accent I've had . . . I can't help it, but when I hear the accent it invokes so much mystery . . . female mystery . . . please talk to me . . . Your accent turns me on . . .

KATHY: David, oh Dave. Touch me *dehre*. Yes, touch me *dehre* and *dehre* and *dhere*. I *vant* you, Dave. Yes, kiss me. Oh my *darlink*. You smell soooo nice. Oh *vant* you, Dave . . .

DAVID: More, more talk to me more. I need you to talk to me into my ear . . . in your language.

KATHY: I *ken't*.

DAVID: Why not? I love it. I love it. That's what I need!

KATHY: I like it in English better. I love it in English. I have to practice my English.

DAVID: Don't deny this little pleasure . . . please . . . please . . . practice your language.

Sexy Song

DAVID: *What do you say for kissing?*

KATHY: *When we kiss we say . . . piki and when we kiss as lot we say piki, piki*

DAVID: *What do you say for petting?*

KATHY: *We say . . . shorash, yes shorash and when we pet a lot we say Shorashshashashasha*

DAVID: *Sounds yummy. Sounds yummy!*

DAVID & KATHY: *Oh yeah, aha. Oh yeah, aha. Shi, shi. Shi, shi. Oh yeah, aha Oh yeah, aha. Oh yeah, aha. Oh yeah, aha. Shi, shi. Shi, shi. Shi, shi*

KATHY: *But I need to practice my English. I'm so turned on by English*

DAVID: *Shorashzhezhe, piki, piki, shorash, shorash oh zha zha*

What do you say for necking?

KATHY: *We cay we say . . . karishiki, yes, karishki means necking, baby!*

DAVID: *What do you say for manhood?*

KATHY: *You mean your . . . ?*

DAVID: *I mean mine . . . ?*

KATHY: *We say barikchee*

DAVID: *Sounds yummy. Sounds yummy. SOUNDS YUMMY!*

Karishiki my barikchee, karishiki my barikchee, karishiki my barikchee, baby

BOTH: *Oh, zha zha. Oh, zha zha. Oh, zha zha. OH!*

DAVID: *What do you say for nooky?*

KATHY: *Dat one is kind of similar, ve call it yookey!*

DAVID: *Sounds yummy!*

DAVID & KATHY: *Oh yeah, aha. Oh yeah, aha. Shi, shi. Shi, shi. Oh yeah, aha*
Oh yeah, aha. Oh yeah, aha. Oh yeah, aha. Shi, shi. Shi, shi. Shi, shi
Oh, oh!
Nooky yookey nooky yookey oh zha zha
Nooky yookey nooky yookey oh zha zha
Nooky yookey nooky yookey oh zha zha
Baby. Baby.

KATHY: *But I need to practice my English. I am so turned on by English*

DAVID: *How do you say it's jiggy jiggy sexy time, jiggy jiggy sexy time?*

KATHY: *We say karishiki my barikchee it's jiggy jiggy sexy time*

DAVID & KATHY: *Sexy time*
When you say jiggy jiggy sexy time I karishiki you barikchee oh baby baby
Oh yeah, aha. Oh yeah, aha. Shi, shi. Shi, shi. Oh yeah, aha
Oh yeah, aha. Oh yeah, aha. Shi, shi. Shi, shi. Shi, shi
Oh, oh, karishiki my barikchee, karishiki my barikchee
Piki, piki, piki, piki. Shorasha, shorasha
Nooky yookey nooky yookey oh zha, zha
Oh yeah, aha. Oh yeah, aha. Oh yeah, aha
Shi, shi. Shi, shi. Shi, shi. Oh, OHHH!

DAVID: *OHHH, ZHA, ZHA!*

Bosnian Language Lesson

Kathy and Višnja are hanging out.

KATHY: I need help.

VIŠNJA: Sure, what's up?

Kathy still holding her head.

KATHY: It's about Dave . . . When we . . . how should I put it . . . *vhen vee* . . . Oh my God. I'm getting a headache.

VIŠNJA: Spit it out.

KATHY: Here it goes . . . *Vhen vee* are making love he *vants* me to speak to him in my language. That really turns him on.

VIŠNJA: Hmmm . . . *Eksent* is not enough of a turn on?

KATHY: It was at first but now it isn't *vorking* anymore. I need some sexy talk. I am gibberishing *vhen vee* make love.

VIŠNJA: Okay . . . *vehl den* . . . you can say something like . . . *Oh, lyubavee, day meh* . . . It means "my love, give it to me."

KATHY: *Oh lyubavee, day meh* . . . it really hurts.

VIŠNJA: What? He hurt you?

KATHY: No my head really hurts.

VIŠNJA: . . . You can say *day mee, day mee, malo jace, malo lijevo, malo desno* . . . *day mee malo josh, day mee josh malo, day mee, day mee*˙ . . . barikchee . . .

Višnja cracks up.

KATHY: Višnja, this is serious.

VIŠNJA: Okay, let's have a sexy language class. I *vill* teach you, *Kedi*. But you know you *vill* have to fess up sooner or later if you care for *dis* guy.

KATHY: Yes, but I *ken't* right now.

VIŠNJA: Okay. I'm not your mama. You a big girl. Okay assume position!

She reclines back in the chair and spreads her legs, and Kathy does the same.

KATHY: Position assumed.

Višnja puts hand on her breast.

VIŠNJA: *Dis* is *seesah, tzitza,* or *doodah.* To suck on it is *seesah-tee, tzeetza-tee, doodah-tee.* But the verb in the grammatical form of an order is *see-say, tzitz-ay, doo-day* . . . The suffix is *ay.*

KATHY: Dave, *lyubavee moya day mee doo-day!*

˙ Give it to me. Give it to me a little left. A little right. Give it to me a little more, a little more. Give it to me. Give it to me. Give it to me.

VIŠNJA: YES! That's it.

She points to her bum.

Guza, guzica, dupe . . .

Cracks up again.

I can't do this.

KATHY: Don't be such a prude, Veehnya. *Sisa, David, daj me malo,* auch, auch *guza,* auch . . .

VIŠNJA: *Vay* you saying auch? Now really, is he also into S and M?

KATHY: Auch, auch, ahhhhh . . .

Kathy's headache is getting worse so she holds her head in her hands, pressing against her temples and breathing hard.

VIŠNJA: *Vow! Kedi . . .* I get it . . . he's really something . . . and by the way if you want to sound *neytif* we don't say auch. *Dat* sounds to me like you are saying couch. We say *"yoy, yoy, yoy"* when it hurts.

KATHY: *Yoy, yoy, yoy,* auuuuuu . . .

As Višnja is talking, Kathy's eyes roll up and she faints. Višnja runs over to Kathy and shakes her.

VIŠNJA: *Kedi. Kedi . . .* oh my God, *Kedi!*

Manhood

Hospital room. Kathy is again hooked up to machines. Višnja comes in and removes Kathy's hospital bracelet with her name on it. She also removes her paperwork at the foot of the bed.

David enters holding a big bouquet of flowers.

VIŠNJA: You must be David. I am Višnja.

DAVID: I heard soooo much about you! Thank you so much for calling me. I was worried sick. I felt so helpless. I called all the hospitals, including this one, but no one had a Ludmila Vudrich.

David sits by the bed and is overcome by emotion.

VIŠNJA: Don't you *vorry*, David. I know our people. She *vill vake* up. I just know it!

Takes Kathy's hand.

DAVID: And the strange thing is, I feel like I've known her all my life. We are just so similar in so many ways. We think the same . . . we have the same sense of humour. She makes me laugh. And she is so smart. And you Bosnians are so kind.

VIŠNJA: *Vell,* love knows no borders.

Pause.

Did she tell you . . . we are taking the accent reduction class together.

DAVID: You don't need an accent reduction class. Your accents are lovely.

VIŠNJA: Yes, *Kedi* mentioned you like *eksents.*

DAVID: Who's Kitty?

VIŠNJA: Oh . . . er . . . Ludmila. I don't call her that. Ludmila is Russian name. Reminds me of the communist oppression so I don't like it so I call her Kitty.

DAVID: Like a kitty cat?

VIŠNJA: Yes, Kitty. We love diminutives. We often say *matza moya* which means "my little kitty."

So I just translated it to KITTY!

DAVID: You know, I could use that. I heard that if you whisper in the ear of someone in a coma this might speed their recovery. Don't mind me . . . Don't listen . . . This is just lover's talk that she taught me . . .

Takes Kathy's hand and kisses it. He leans in and whispers into her ear.

Matza moya piki, piki karishiki bikchi-chi-chi-tza. Shorashzhezhe, shorash shorash piki, piki-chi-chi-tza.

Dear God, please let her wake up. I swear, dear God, if she wakes up I'm gonna learn Bosnian. Please, God, do you hear me?

Whispering tenderly in Kathy's ear.

Piki, piki-chi-chi-tza. Matza moya. Matza moya.

VIŠNJA: Wow, David. That's hot!

DAVID: It really is only for her ears . . .

Piki, piki, shorashzhe, barrrikatchee, barrrikatchee . . .

Can you correct my pronunciation?

VIŠNJA: It's perfect . . . there is nothing to correct . . .

Višnja's phone rings.

Excuse me. . . . Hello . . . Oh hi . . . Aha . . . *A Prolific Fancy* at the Workman's Theatre . . . aha . . . *Vhat? Dey* REALLY WANT TO SEE ME? . . . BECAUSE I have an *eksent*! . . . Lesbian . . . Sure I can be a lesbian . . . I am available . . . okay . . . *tenk* you.

David . . . I can be a lesbian . . . I can be a lesbian!!!

DAVID: Sure . . . Can I watch?

VIŠNJA: David, you can and you *vill. Dat's* a PROMISE!

ESL Conversation and Accent Reduction Class—Proverbs

ESL Instructor, Zainab, and Fatima from Saudi Arabia, Pele from Brazil, Madeline from Vietnam, Yura from Russia, and Paul Lee from Korea.

COMPANY: "I WISH TO WISH THE WISH YOU WISH TO WISH, BUT IF YOU WISH THE WISH THE WITCH WISHES, I WON'T WISH THE WISH YOU WISH TO WISH."

ESL INSTRUCTOR: Excellent with voiceless fricative "w." Next week we will look at the voiceless labialized fricatives—so continue working through your fricative chapters.

And remember: fricatives don't need to freak you out!

Višnja is late for class.

ESL INSTRUCTOR: Višnja, you missed the labialized fricative W!

VIŠNJA: But Ms. Barber, I kinda didn't. I had a rehearsal! I got that job. I am going to be Mommy Number Two in *A Prolific Fancy*!

ESL INSTRUCTOR: You know that this topic is off limits!

VIŠNJA: Yes, love *dat* dare not speak its name. I just had to tell someone!

ESL INSTRUCTOR: Okay, but now CIRCLE TIME, CIRCLE TIME.

Class sits in a semicircle.

Our topic is "proverbs." A proverb is a saying. Something everyone in your country knows and understands but often it is a poetic way of understanding / a situation.

Višnja's hand goes up.

VIŠNJA: *Ima više dana nego kobasica.*

ESL INSTRUCTOR: Translation first and then the English equivalent?

VIŠNJA: "*Dehre* are more days *den* sausages."

ESL INSTRUCTOR: Yes, that sounds like a proverb . . . Let's see. And what does that mean? Can anyone think of an equivalent in the English language?

VIŠNJA: "*Dehre* are more days *den* sausages." Come on guys. It's obvious.

Class laughs.

PELE: Sort of like "putting all your eggs in one basket."

VIŠNJA: Perfect!

ESL INSTRUCTOR: Yes! I think that works very well. Bravo, Pele. That was quick! Someone else?

YURA: "Love and eggs are best when *zey* are fresh."

PELE: "Love, smoke, and cough are hard to hide."

Class laughs.

ESL INSTRUCTOR: Anyone else?

FATIMA: I have one "Insult . . . you must writing in . . . sand . . . nice words you must . . . writing in . . . stone." Must . . . writing . . . No not writing but when . . .

She mimes carving with a chisel.

What is this?

Mimes some more.

ESL INSTRUCTOR: Carving?

FATIMA: Yes . . . "Insult you writing in sand . . . nice words you must carving in stone."

ESL INSTRUCTOR: "Insults should be written in sand and compliments should be carved in stone."

Can anybody give us an equivalent in their own language? In English we say . . . anybody?

MADELINE: "Sticks and stones will break your bones but words will never hurt me."

ESL INSTRUCTOR: Excellent!

Class is impressed.

MADELINE: I like this stick-and-stone proverb. I like this because I learn it from my daughter. Sometime I say things to her and she get angry and she say that. She can get very angry.

ZAINAB: "Still water runs deep."

MADELINE: "Blood is *ticker* than water."

PAUL LEE: We say, "The deeper the waters are, the more still they run."

YURA: We too. We say quiet water wears down mountains. Blood isn't water.

Repeats the two proverbs in Russian.

Кровь—не водица тихая вода берега подмывает.

VIŠNJA: *"Tiha voda brege dere."* *"Krv nije voda."*[†] We say the same!

But listen to this one! *Nit luk jeo, nit luk mirisao.* "I didn't eat the onions, I didn't even smell the onions!"

Class is silent, lost in translation.

"I didn't eat the onions," because when you eat the onions you smell funny . . . You get it . . . ?

A few chuckles from the class.

That is when you are accused of something but you had nothing to do with the situation.

MADELINE: Like a policeman comes and says you stole that car, and you say, "I didn't eat the onions . . ."

COMPANY: . . . "I didn't EVEN SMELL THE ONIONS!" You got it!!!

Intro vamp for "Proverb Song" starts.

Proverb Song

MADELINE: *Ask no question you'll be told no lies*

PAUL LEE: Okay I will translate slowly: "If there is a rich man in the area three villages are ruined!"

ZAINAB: *Crows don't peck each other's eyes*

YURA: "Under capitalism man exploits man, under socialism the reverse is true."

Class laughs.

PELE: *Beauty is only skin deep*

PAUL LEE: "If *glandma* had balls she'd be *glandpa!*"

VIŠNJA: *As you sow so you shall reap*

---

[*] Quiet water wears down mountains.

[†] Blood isn't water.

ESL INSTRUCTOR: What about: "You can't have your cake and eat it, too."

YURA: "You can't hold it and fart!"

ESL TEACHER: *Fair without foul within*

PAUL LEE: *Faults are thick where love is thin*

YURA: *Choose an author as you choose a friend*

PELE: *A friend's counsel is no command*

COMPANY: *Live and let live*
Sink or swim
Slow but sure
As snug as a bug in a rug

PELE: God is big but the forest is bigger!

ZAINAB: *He who would crack the nut*
Must first crack the shell

PELE: He lives long who lives well

VIŠNJA: *Who laughs last laughs best*

PAUL LEE: *He that never climbed never fell*

ZAINAB: *You will please none if you try to please all*
It is a poor mouse that has only one hole
It is an ill bird that fouls its own nest
Many a true word is spoken in jest

COMPANY: *Live and let live*
Sink or swim
Slow but sure
As snug as a bug in a rug

ESL INSTRUCTOR: Okay. Okay. Class, let's . . . translate them.

COMPANY: *Better unborn than untaught*
Better untaught than ill-taught
Soon ripe, soon forgotten
Soon ripe, soon rotten

The early bird gets the worm
The quiet just before the storm
Scratch my back and I'll scratch yours
Sweep before your own doors

When pigs fly
Who breaks pays
Sink of swim
As snug as a bug in a rug

Live and let live
Slow but sure
Sink or swim
As snug in as a bug

Vamping out.

As snug as a bug in a rug
As snug as a bug in a rug

Déjà-Vu but Not Déjà-Hear

Hospital room a little later. Kathy wakes up again. Višnja sits next to her, reading from a New Yorker *out loud.*

KATHY: *(with perfect standard Canadian pronunciation)* Where is my *New Yorker*? What happened? How long have I been out?

Sees the New Yorker.

Oh, here it is. Wow, I am having déjà vu.

VIŠNJA: Yes, but I'm not having déjà hear.

KATHY: What happened?

VIŠNJA: You had another coma. You had a migraine. You fainted *durink* our sexy language lesson.

You sound . . . like native speaker!

KATHY: I am a native speaker. Remember?

VIŠNJA: Who are you?

KATHY: I am Kathy Woodrough from Peterborough.

VIŠNJA: *Vow.* Okay, *Kedi Vuhdroh* from Peterborough. Say it.

KATHY: I am Kathy Woodrough from Peterborough.

VIŠNJA: Say it five times fast.

KATHY: I am Kathy Woodrough from Peterborough. I am Kathy Woodrough from Peterborough. I am Kathy Woodrough from Peterborough . . . What am I doing?

Višnja claps.

VIŠNJA: Bravo. Bravo. You should go to accent reduction class and get A+++!

Nurse Cannon enters.

NURSE CANNON: *VISHNU!*

VIŠNJA: Nurse Cannon, you gotta hear this. Say it!

KATHY: I am Kathy Woodrough from Peterborough. I am Kathy Woodrough from / Peterborough . . .

NURSE CANNON: Vishnu, what on earth are you doing?

This patient just woke up from a coma and you are having her do tongue twisters.

KATHY: It isn't a tongue twister; it's my name and place of birth.

NURSE CANNON: VISHNU*!*

VIŠNJA: *Vishnu* is a Hindu God . . . I am Veeshnya!

NURSE CANNON: You are going to have to leave this room immediately, and you are going to have to report to me in the morning. This was the final straw. What you did goes against all the policies and procedures. *Me ah* make sure you get terminated!

VIŠNJA: Terminated!

NURSE CANNON: *(to Kathy)* My apologies, Ms. Woodrough. The staff aren't invited to deal with your medical condition.

KATHY: Veeshnya isn't the staff. She is my friend. Plus, she might have saved my life.

NURSE CANNON: The staff isn't invited to fraternize with patients. Only your next of kin is allowed to be present. It's the rule.

KATHY: She IS my next of kin. She is all I have. Satisfied?

NURSE CANNON: We'll see about that! I am going straight to Dr. Brooke.

Nurse Cannon storms out.

KATHY: Hey . . . does David know where I am?

VIŠNJA: Yes, I called him and he came right away.

He is having a bite downstairs. *Vill* be back any minute.

KATHY: I'm going to have to tell him.

VIŠNJA: Had to *heppen* sooner or later, *Kedi.*

Dr. Brooke's voice is heard in the hallway: "Now we have scientific proof!" Višnja flies out. Dr. Brooke enters.

DR. BROOKE: Hello, Kathy. Can I please hear you speak? Nurse Cannon says we've had an exciting development with your speech.

KATHY: Hello, Doctor. Yes, I don't have an accent anymore. I can pronounce my name. I can pronounce anything else. I can say "red leather, yellow leather, red leather, yellow leather," and not trip my tongue.

DR. BROOKE: YOU ARE THE MOST INTERESTING CASE I'VE EVER HAD!

You had a lesion on the left hemisphere of the brain. See here . . .

Dr. Brooke pulls the angiogram of Kathy's brain out of the folder. We see it as a projection.

. . . That is the side that's responsible for speech. Sometimes a sudden onset of a migraine like yours can trigger a type of brain damage, which is what yours did, but also during the second coma your brain was working overtime to repair itself. This is what started to take place while you were in the coma. Your brain repaired itself approximately ninety-five percent. Which is even more rare. A small lesion here—see?

KATHY: Yes.

DR. BROOKE: Right here. The lesion is now just a small spot. Which, by the way, is RAREST of the RARE. Kathy, you got your wish! Very, very lucky.

KATHY: Yes. Rare.

DR. BROOKE: You seem stunned.

KATHY: Yeah, I AM stunned. So lucky . . .

DR. BROOKE: I think my paper will likely become a seminal work on foreign accent syndrome. I'm thrilled.

Just a few days of observation and you will be out of here. Welcome back, Kathy.

   Exits. Kathy is alone for a moment.

   David enters.

DAVID: They called me and told me you were awake. That's great news!

   Kathy offers a hug. David accepts.

You had me so worried. I thought I had lost you. I even . . . you will laugh at me now . . . but I even went to church after so many years . . . and I prayed that you would wake up.

I think I have some part in this. I whispered "karishiki my barikchee" in your ear over and over again.

And I made a vow that if you woke up . . . that I would learn how to speak your language. Yes, I did. So, you will have to teach me now. Will you?

   Kathy's eyes are wide open. She nods no.

No? Why not?

KATHY: I can't. Please.

DAVID: I didn't mean this very second.

They kiss.

How are you feeling?

Višnja enters. She gestures behind his back, trying to find out if Kathy has told him.

How are you feeling?

Kathy gives two thumbs up. She is feeling okay.

VIŠNJA: She says she is GREAT! Right, KITTY?

DAVID: You're very quiet.

Kathy is silent.

VIŠNJA: . . . This is common for her condition.

DAVID: Oh, I see . . .

He moves closer to Kathy and speaks a bit more loudly.

HEY!

VIŠNJA: She can hear you.

DAVID: Oh, sorry. *(softer)* Hey.

KATHY: Hey, my *darlink*.

VIŠNJA: You know, David, it is really hard for her to speak English. Tires her out. Makes her head hurt.

DAVID: So sorry. Of course . . . then let's hear it!

VIŠNJA: Hear *vhat*?

DAVID: Let's hear you two rap in your own lingo. I swore to God I was going to learn it. So might as well start now.

Kathy speaks in a fake accent as if trying to overcome her temporary-blocked-speech condition. Her accent sounds different than the original foreign accent syndrome.

KATHY: Bosnian . . . brings up . . . too many things. I really don't like speaking it.

I can speak English.

DAVID: I thought English made you tired. I thought that Bosnian would relax you.

VIŠNJA: *Vee* Bosnians don't believe in multiculturalism. We *vant* to integrate!

KATHY: Yes, *vee* really like to belong.

Tongue Tango Reprise

KATHY: *So what if your tongue is wrong?*
So what if you sound foreign?
So what if you don't belong?
Was your homeland war-torn?

KATHY & VIŠNJA: *If you were born where they shoot*
If you were an army recruit
Attacked by the neighbour or Pentagon
If you were under the boot
You can grow a new root
The past is over and done

VIŠNJA: Ole!

DAVID: Sorry!

KATHY: It's okay, *darlink*. You are off the hook! You don't have to learn Bosnian.

DAVID: You sound different, Kathy.

VIŠNJA: David, I am really sorry to ask *dis* but *ken* you *vait* outside a moment? One minute.

DAVID: Oh? . . . Sure . . . no problem. *(whispers) Matza moya . . .*

    David exits.

KATHY: What's "*matza moya*"? Why is he calling me Kitty?

VIŠNJA: We had language lessons while you were in coma. Means "my little pussy cat."

I thought you were gonna tell him!!!

KATHY: I wanted to. I couldn't . . . I don't know how!

VIŠNJA: Just tell him you had foreign *eksent* syndrome and now you don't have it anymore. It's kinda true. Your fake accent is shit. You MUST tell him . . . NOW!

KATHY: But I lied. Not just once. I lied a lot! About many things.

VIŠNJA: Repeat this to yourself: I'm *Kedi Vudro* from Peterborough. I'm *Kedi Vudro* from Peterborough. I am a WASP. White Anglo-Saxon Protestant. Just say: David, I'm a White Anglo-Saxon Protestant.

KATHY: David, I'm a White Anglo-Saxon Protestant. Veeshnya, I can't do that to David! I simply can't. He won't love me if . . . He was into my centuries and centuries of history . . .

I want my accent back!

VIŠNJA: If I could give you my *eksent* I would.

Seriously, *Kedi*, no use . . . you have to tell him now. It is for the best. He loves you. He will forgive you.

I am going to call him in and you are *tellink* him. You just keep *repeatink*, "I am a White Anglo-Saxon Protestant."

KATHY: Okay.

VIŠNJA: You can do it! Just be brave, like you were in the Sniper Alley.

Exits. Kathy repeats "I'm a WASP" silently to herself.

David re-enters.

DAVID: All better? . . .

He sits by the side of the bed and kisses her.

KATHY: David.

Drops the accent.

Oh God. Here we go. There is no easy or nice way of doing this.

DAVID: You voice . . . You sound . . . funny.

KATHY: YES, David, I sound . . . like I am NOT Ludmila from Bosnia. My name is Kathy. I was born and raised in Peterborough. My last name is Woodrough and David . . . I'm a White Angle-Saxon Protestant. Two months ago, I had a heavy onset of migraine and ended up in a six-week coma. I woke up speaking with an accent and I was— /

DAVID: WOODROUGH.

KATHY: / Yes. I was diagnosed with foreign accent—

DAVID: Kathy? / From Peterborough?!?

KATHY: Yes!

Intro music starts.

DAVID: Don't you mean "da"?

KATHY: Dave . . .

DAVID: I have to pinch myself . . . is this really happening . . .

Where Are You From Reprise

DAVID: *Accent, language, refugee, history*
Thousands of years!
I wish I had never extended my sympathy
To your crocodile tears!
How do you do?
Do I know you?
Don't take kindly to
PRETENDERS *like you*
Guess this is it!

Give it I'm a boob, a fool, a chump, an idiot
Now you confess
Faker, bogus, counterfeit, phoney
Give it a rest!
How do you do?
Do I know you?
Don't take kindly to
Liars like you.
I guess this is it!

KATHY: David, please let me to explain . . .

DAVID: THERE IS NOTHING TO EXPLAIN. IT IS ALL PERFECTLY CLEAR. Goodbye!

KATHY: David, please don't go. I love you!

DAVID!

Storms out. Višnja rushes in.

It's OVER!

VIŠNJA: It *vas* big shock.

KATHY: Oh, why did I tell him?

VIŠNJA: He *vould* have found out sooner or later. It was the right *tink* to do.

KATHY: *I WASN'T READY*! I didn't think it through. Oh my God, my heart is pounding . . .

I'm gonna have another stroke!

VIŠNJA: Maybe if you do, you'll get your accent back!

Višnja laughs.

KATHY: EXCUSE ME!

VIŠNJA: YOU ARE EXCUSED!

KATHY: CAN'T YOU JUST GIVE IT A REST! You know what? YOU ARE EXCUSED . . . I'VE HAD IT WITH YOUR STUPID Bosnian humor! Just get out, GET OUT! GET OUT!

VIŠNJA: Okay, I am excused . . . you are excused . . . he she it is EXCUSED!

ESL Presentation Night

The students enter with platters and baskets of snacks. They arrange them on a side table while practicing. A Welcome To Our Presentation banner is set up.

COMPANY: We ARE, you ARE, they ARE. I AM, you ARE, he she it IS. We ARE, you ARE, they ARE.

The ESL Instructor is placing the programs for the evening's presentation on each chair.

MADELINE: A Russian proverb: You can't hold it and fart.

ZAINAB: The English equivalent: You can't have your cake and eat it too.

MADELINE: I didn't eat the onions, I didn't smell the onions.

PAUL LEE: A Bosnian proverb. Can anyone in the audience think of an English equivalent?

PELE: Actually YES. I didn't eat beans. I can't poop beans.

MADELINE: This proverb is used when you have nothing to do with the situation. Like a policeman comes and says you stole that car and you say . . .

VIŠNJA: I did not eat beans.

COMPANY: *(including the guys)* I CANNOT POOP BEANS.

Dr. Brooke enters.

DR. BROOKE: Hello.

ESL INSTRUCTOR: Hello, I'm the instructor.

DR. BROOKE: Oh, hi! Kathy invited me to this presentation. I am her doctor writing a paper about her journey. Dr. Brooke.

ESL INSTRUCTOR: Debra Barber. Welcome, Dr. Brooke. So glad you are here.

David enters.

Oh, perfect timing. You must be David.

DAVID: *(to both the ESL Instructor and Dr. Brooke)* Yes, hello. I'm David James.

ESL INSTRUCTOR: Please do come in! I will go get our "special guest"!

Exits.

VIŠNJA: David . . .

DAVID: Hello, Višnja . . . I have been wondering if your name is made up, too. Sure sounds like it.

VIŠNJA: It is not made up. It means "sour cherry."

Yura overhears from the other side of the space.

YURA: Yes. It mean *ze* same in Russian.

ZAINAB: Sour cherry?

The ESL Instructor returns with Kathy.

VIŠNJA & COMPANY: *(ad lib)* O.M.G., KATHY!!!

KATHY: Hi!

ESL INSTRUCTOR: EVERYONE, please, may I have a moment of your attention. I've been approached by Kathy here who wanted to join in our presentation today. Kathy's ESL journey has been very unique but still reflective of our Canadian experience. It is only fair that she, too, can share hers. So I included Kathy as a "special guest" on our program.

By now everyone has gathered and is listening.

DAVID: Special "guest star" is more like it.

ESL INSTRUCTOR: Unlike the rest of you, English was a foreign tongue for Kathy for only a short while. And Kathy felt like she owed you an explanation.

KATHY: Hi, everyone. Here it goes.

Pulls out a speech. Reads.

Dear ESL class . . . First of all, I want to say that I missed you all very much.

PELE: Excuse me, Ludmila . . . Mila . . . I mean Kathy . . . you have to use your own words. Isn't it right . . . teacher?

ESL INSTRUCTOR: Pele makes a good point. Kathy, you know what I say about reading and speaking . . .

KATHY: But I don't want to leave anything out.

ESL INSTRUCTOR: As long as it is true and it is from the heart it will be fine!

Kathy puts her speech away.

KATHY: Okay, here it goes. From the heart and true!

Hi . . . class.

Silence.

I wanted to say to you all how grateful I am about being allowed to apologize . . . because . . . what a lucky girl I was to have a chance walk in your shoes for short time. To become a New Canadian . . .

I Know Who I Am (Foreign to Me)

KATHY: *I was lonely and I was hard, numb and cynical*
So scared and critical, my life was pitiful
So predictable, unoriginal, alone, individual
Then a headache turned my life around
A change profound and my hometown became a different ground
From that new sound I found a friend
Sorry, Višnja, didn't mean to say that
You are funny, you're my very best friend
Sorry, Višnja, don't be angry please
I like how you tease
You are the one who showed compassion
You dressed me in your Russian fashion
You taught me all your sorrows through your jokes
Showed me the ropes. My friend!

I was lonely and I was hard, numb and cynical
So scared and critical, my life was pitiful
There was no love, it was unfixable, miserable
Then a headache turned my life around
A change profound and my hometown became a different ground
From that new sound I found my love

Sorry, David, didn't mean to lie
You loved me way more than I thought you ever would
Sorry, David, I didn't mean to pretend
Don't let it end
I got caught between a rock and a hard place
Because I imagined your face
After I confessed how distressed you'd be
But now I see, my true history
Shouldn't stop you from loving me

I know who I am, I am Kathy Woodrough
From Peterborough, and I'm not ashamed of that
Or that I changed my name
Or what I overcame
I only feel the shame of what I feel now
But not of feeling love and learning how

I love you, Višnja, you're not boring
And I love you, David, my heart is soaring
And love is now not foreign to me

MADELINE: What you did was very stupid.

PAUL LEE: I agree with you this *time-uh*!

ESL INSTRUCTOR: Everyone, let's not forget that Kathy DID have an accent just like all of you.

VIŠNJA: And NO ONE came to see her at the hospital and she was in a coma for five weeks!

COMPANY: NO ONE?!

KATHY: EXCEPT for David!

VIŠNJA: David came to see her every day during her second coma!

COMPANY: EVERY DAY!

Kathy stops . . . unable to continue.

David . . . My name is Kathy Woodrough, I am from Peterborough, Ontario. I am Canadian and I am deeply, truly, honestly sorry.

DAVID: HOW COULD I EVER TRUST YOU AGAIN?

Next six lines are overlapping.

DR. BROOKE: SHE HAD A STROKE! SHE HAD FOREIGN ACCENT SYNDROME.

PELE: SHE SAID SHE WAS SORRY!

MADELINE: AT LEAST THEY COME FROM SAME CULTURE.

ZAINAB: THEY ARE IN LOVE. LOVE IS THE MOST IMPORTANT THING IN THE WORLD.

ESL INSTRUCTOR: ONE IN FIVE CANADIANS SPEAKS WITH AN ACCENT. ONE IN FIVE!

VIŠNJA: DAVID, SHE LOVES YOU!

PAUL LEE: *STOP-UH!* EVERYONE *STOP-UH.* YOU ARE ALL SO *LOUD-UH, SO RUDE-UH! STOP-UH! YOU INTERRUPT. YOU ARE SO LOUD!*

The company stops and looks at Paul Lee.

EVERYONE WHO APOLOGIZES DESERVES A SECOND CHANCE. SHE SAID SORRY. MANY, MANY TIMES. AND ALSO EVERYONE, THIS IS A CANADA. AND IN A CANADA WE CAN BE WHO WE WANT TO BE!

VIŠNJA: Yes, *dis* is Canada and we can love whom *ve vant* to love!

KATHY: This is Canada. And everyone should know what it is like to be an immigrant!

YURA: *Echtually* you were a refugee! And *zis* is not the same.

ESL INSTRUCTOR: Making friendships across cultural divides is reflective of our Canadian experience!

KATHY: What is an accent? It is just about vowels and consonants. This is Canada! Sorry, David! I love you, David . . . Please forgive me! I did it all for love. AND YOU SAID YOURSELF THAT WE ALL HAVE AN ACCENT!

COMPANY: IN THEORY!

DAVID: OKAY I FORGIVE YOU! This is Canada and I can love this woman AND be turned on by her accent and her language you puritanical, prudish pricks.

Hugs Kathy.

COMPANY: YEAH!

YURA: Sure, and *zis* is Canada, where we don't care about colour of skin and hair quality!

COMPANY: YEAH!

ESL INSTRUCTOR: This is Canada, and you all have to use the proper articles.

COMPANY: THE YEAH!!!!!!!!!!

PELE: This is Canada and anything is possible. And that is why, teacher . . .

I would like take you on a date.

The ESL Instructor nods her acceptance.

I must strike while the iron is hot!

ESL INSTRUCTOR: Very good, and I accept.

MADELINE: Yes! This is Canada, where nice Black boy and white girl can make good-looking babies.

ESL INSTRUCTOR: I don't know about babies, but we can go on a date.

PAUL LEE: You are embarrassing her!

YURA: But! Wait a minute, you can't date him, you are teacher and you are in position of power.

PELE: I'll quit school!

COMPANY: Yeah!

PAUL LEE: Everyone that is much, much *bette-uh*. Now say THANK YOU, Canada!

COMPANY: Thank you, CANADA!

PAUL LEE: And now it is time for our end-of-semester presentation. Everyone, please, it is time to sing THANK YOU, CANADA!

Music intro for the grand finale.

Act II Grand Finale or Thank You, Canada

VIŠNJA: *Thank you, Canada, for putting up with us*
We are just off the boat, the plane, or a Greyhound bus

PAUL LEE & PELE: *We all love you in our special way*
And we are here to stay

PAUL LEE: *Here to stay*

COMPANY: *Hooray for Canada, God bless Canada and our hyphenated nationality*
Rationality and hospitality, that's Canada's reality

NON-IMMIGRANTS: *Thank you for giving a home to our first generations*
And for apologizing to our First Nations, in reservations
Fulfilling expectations

ZAINAB: *Accepting all religious denominations*
And that you didn't have any cotton plantations

YURA: But cotton can't grow this far north!

KATHY: *Hooray for Canada, long live Canada*
and our freedom of expression

COMPANY: *And that we are almost out of recession*
and for Canadian non-aggression

DR. BROOKE: You mean "passive aggression"?

COMPANY: *That too. Thank you.*

DAVID: *You're so sexy, Canada, in our bedroom you have no place*

COMPANY: *You have no place in our bedroom*

PELE: *Thank you, Canada, for not caring about gender or race*

COMPANY: *You're free to use any bathroom*

ESL INSTRUCTOR: *Thank you for ESL classes and accents galore*
All this we adore

COMPANY: *We can't thank you more*
Then one last HOORAY *for Canada in our final refrain*
Time for perogies from Ukraine and good old chow mein

KATHY: *With a nice tall glass of the Niagara Region champagne*

The company cheers!

YURA: That's not real champagne!

COMPANY: *Let's have some bubbly*

Kathy won't pour the bubbly yet. Before they drink, they have to sing the choral ode! Kathy gets everyone in a line and they sing.

(choral) Hooray for Canada, long live Canada
And our freedom of expression
And that we are almost out of recession
And for Canadian non-aggression

Kathy pours the bubbly.

(with accompaniment) Hooray for Canada, long live Canada
And our hyphenated nationality
Rationality and hospitality, that's Canada's reality

The company cheers, clink, and drink.

The end.

A Dialogue Between Cynthia Ashperger and Yana Meerzon

YANA MEERZON: Cynthia, we have known each for a long time. I think we collaborated for the first time in the early 2000s, on the production of Silvija Jestrović's play *Not My Story*, directed by Dragana Varagić for the Toronto Fringe Festival. You were playing one of the leading parts: a professor of visual arts from the former Yugoslavia who is now very successful as a performer in a peep show.

I know your real career as an actor-immigrant in Canada has been a little different—you've had lots of great moments of success, you teach acting at Ryerson University—but I also know that things have not been easy for you and that your accent was quite a significant obstacle in your professional journey here. I also know that you have been looking into the questions of "audible minority" and accent for a long time. You have spoken about these issues very openly, and have written about them as both an actor and an activist. I had a pleasure of publishing your statement on this topic in a special issue of the journal *Theatre Research in Canada /Recherches théâtrales au Canada*, in 2015. But here we are, in the summer of 2018, discussing your new and very exciting project, the musical *Foreign Tongue*, and it seems to me that all these issues remain pressing for you, as a theatre maker and as an immigrant from Croatia to Canada. Tell me, how did this project come to life, and what keeps you coming back to this very difficult issue of a foreign accent?

CYNTHIA ASHPERGER: Yes, indeed, how it all started! I read a newspaper article about this medical condition called foreign accent syndrome. It happens when someone has a stroke or other damage to their brain and wakes up speaking with a foreign accent—exactly what happens in my play to my major character, Kathy Woodrough from Peterborough, Ontario. And by the way, the correct way of referring to accented speech is non-standard speech. In sociolinguistics, the fact that we all speak with an accent is very much accepted and it is not thought of as a non-Canadian trait. In theatre, speaking differently than the mainstream majority is still referred to as "an accent," and it mostly signifies a foreigner or an immigrant. I still use it as well.

The first recorded case of this condition, of foreign accent syndrome, was in Norway. It happened during World War II, when a woman had shrapnel hit her in the head. After she recovered from her incident, she started speaking Norwegian with a German accent. As nobody could explain this phenomenon, she ended up ostracized by her fellow Norwegian citizens. I read about this medical condition and thought that it is a perfect metaphor for my life and the lives of many immigrants who arrive in Canada, learn a new language but speak it with an accent, and everybody asks where they are from for the rest of their lives. This was the starting premise for *Foreign Tongue*.

In an opening montage we meet Kathy Woodrough, who is a busy and lonely thirty-year-old living the life of a single young urban professional. She is doing her chores on her way to an OkCupid date and dreading the Christmastime ahead. Kathy gets a strong migraine followed by a stroke, which causes her to fall into a coma. Her life as an accented person begins with the scene in a hospital, when she wakes up and speaks with this perfect Eastern European accent, but of course she can't speak her "native" tongue and she cannot explain what happened to her. Upon waking she meets Višnja, from Bosnia, a former actor and now janitor who happens to be cleaning her room. Because of their shared accented speech, Kathy and Višnja become fast friends. *Foreign Tongue* follows Kathy's story as she tries to navigate this new situation, which results from her speaking like a foreigner, effectively making her a stranger in her own land. In the hospital, Kathy also meets David, who is Canadian like her and who becomes smitten with her because of her accent. During their chance encounter, David assumes that Kathy is a refugee, and Kathy plays along. But their relationship develops and she has to assume a new identity, one that matches her accent, and with it a new life that she never dreamt of. While her private life improves, she is immediately marginalized professionally because of the way she sounds. So essentially, Kathy's new circumstances put her in a situation of having to create a cultural identity that fits her accent. As she works out her new position, Kathy meets different people, mostly students in the accent reduction class—other immigrants from different countries who came to Canada either seeking protection or for economic well-being. They all need to learn English and figure out how to speak it so as to please the ears of native English speakers. But more than that, they need to reinvent their cultural identity and learn to navigate a multicultural society such as ours.

Here I draw on my thirty years in Canada as a new Canadian and a nonstandard speaker. Accent, of course, has coloured every aspect of my life as an actress-immigrant. In my personal life, it wasn't a hindrance. Even profession-ally, on occasion some parts came my way because of it, but mostly it was a problem, as an accent is very limiting to an actor. Most accented actors are cast only in some particular, culture-specific parts. I have been concerned about this for many years and have written and spoken about it. Still today the issue of audible minorities has not been properly recognized or dealt with in the least. And while everywhere I turn in Toronto there are accented people in all sorts or roles both professional and personal, on Canadian stages we are still very much "the other," and we are a very, very rare occurrence.

In the '90s, Canadian theatre began addressing the issues of visible minorities, but this was not true for the audible minority. We are the forgotten children. A while ago I met a Black woman from Germany who speaks English with a German accent, who has great difficulty finding work as an actor not because of the colour of her skin but because of her accented English. And even more so because her accent doesn't "match" her skin. Similarly, I have been in a situation where my hair colour was considered inauthentic for someone from Croatia which is my origin. So in *Foreign Tongue* I try to play with the notion of ste-reotyping through sound, but that also leads me to other ways of stereotyping (gender, religion, sexual orientation, and hair colour to name but a few). To a certain extent we stereotype each other all the time and yes, it is frustrating, but I also find it quite funny. I track the humorous side of stereotyping Kathy's life as an immigrant. It is ironic and at times completely absurd. I think of it as a "fish out of water" story, except this fish doesn't have to leave the water . . . and it speaks with an accent.

In 2013, I wrote the first draft of this script, including the lyrics, and we had a workshop at the Ryerson Theatre School; Justin Hiscox was the composer. The workshop was very successful, but I wasn't able to secure any funding for a full three years despite applying for many grants. In 2016, VideoCabaret offered me a three-day dramaturgy workshop. It was three days of reading and discussing the script with theatre artists who have been closely involved in the development of new Canadian plays and musical theatre, such as Baņuta Rubess, Martin Julien, Tamara Bernier Evans, Tatiana Cherny, and Jasmine Chen. Following this, I wrote the second draft of the play.

In 2017, I conducted a three-week workshop to work on the third draft. For this I received what is called a Small Development Grant from the Faculty of Communication and Design at Ryerson University. Apart from the creative team of a director, a new composer/musical director, and a choreographer, we had ten actors who played twenty roles. For Toronto independent theatre standards this was a very large cast. I needed this size of cast because it was vital for this show to capture the diversity of my city and the community at large, as well as to tell the intimate story of Kathy. During that workshop we sharpened the play's focus on Kathy Woodrough's throughline, to firm up the structure. In doing this, I closely collaborated with the musical director and composer, Daniel Abrahamson, who was writing new music while arranging the existing score.

And finally, in June 2018 we went to the last workshop, reflected in the final script published in this volume. For this workshop, I focused on the structure by editing and rewriting the dialogue, and also added lyrics for eight new songs.

MEERZON: So, let's talk about the relationship between words and music in this play. How would you define this play's genre? Why would you want to use the form of the musical to make a play about immigration and accents?

ASHPERGER: To begin with I just wanted this intuitively and I followed that impulse. In hindsight I recognize that Brecht's *The Threepenny Opera* was my main inspiration and my model for the structure of this work. The first thing I wrote was "Tongue Tango," and I wrote it in longhand, lying in bed at my cottage one lovely morning. "Tongue Tango" begins with: "What if your tongue is wrong? What if you sound foreign? What if you don't belong? Where were you born?" "Tongue Tango" is a satirical commentary on the situation and the action. In a Brechtian structure, this type of a song serves as a distancing mechanism. It uses humour to call attention to cultural differences: "You mustn't be trite. Remember anger is the greatest sin. This you must never feel. Just say Happy Halloween. That's how you keep it real." Most of my songs, sung by company members, aim to make audiences laugh but also encourage thinking about the issues that surround cultural norms. This type of humour, which uses irony and satire I think of as the Brechtian influence. I didn't write this play as a thesis, but it came from the heart. Only now I can analyze it in this way.

In North American musicals, the school of thought is that the songs and music must come at the highest moments of emotional tension for the character. All Kathy's solos and duets follow that rule. For example, Kathy sings "My Head Hurts" as things unravel at the top of the show, "Rid of It" at the moment she is rejected by her client because of her accent. Then, as she bemoans her fate to Višnja, they sing a duet called "Somebody's Song." The lyrics begin with "I used to be somebody. That somebody is me and now I am somebody I don't know how to be." This song is about acceptance of change. It concludes with "Just learn to be somebody you don't know how to be." The "Where are You From" duet with David in Act I and its reprise in Act II both come during emotional highs—their first meeting and their breakup. Kathy sings "Foreign to Me" when she is seeking forgiveness from David, Višnja, and the ESL class members for pretending to be someone else.

One of the things that I have done a lot as a Canadian actor-immigrant is that I've played lots of tragic roles of immigrants. I've cried on stage, I've suffered, I've played trauma and loss, lots of war plays and identity crisis, lost family members. I've played lots of sad immigrants. This was of course quite surprising and interesting for me at first, because in the past, in my country, I used to play many different parts and genres: comedy and farce, drama and tragedy, also Shakespeare. But here in Canada, I was asked to play mainly tragedy and sad immigrant roles. There were some stereotypical Eastern European mafia parts, such as a woman with a gun wearing stilettos, but for the most part it was only tragedy. So, for my own play, I wanted to explore the other side. I wanted to create a light and funny and uplifting story. I wanted a happy ending!

I also very much wanted to show the audiences (or better let them hear) the tapestry of accents in this country. Canada, and Toronto in particular, is so very rich in sounds—there are many languages spoken here, and we live with hearing accents (non-standard speech). I wanted to put this sonic abundance onto the stage. I wanted a native English speaker, a Canadian, to become a part of a truly amazing tapestry of languages from inside of their own accent. I celebrate accents, but I also know that accents are funny. The reaction to a different, "non-standard" pronunciation works on a subconscious level with audiences.

Similarly, I am interested in what happens to a person's psyche when she or he becomes a foreigner overnight, over an hour, and everybody starts asking them this very simple but difficult to deal with question: Where are you from? My aim was to take the frustration it causes and transform it through humour.

MEERZON: As an immigrant myself, and a person with an accent, I am quite grateful to you for bringing this issue on stage, and doing it in such lighthearted way. It is indeed true that in the literature and theatre of exile and immigration, the melancholia and sadness, the sense of rupture, and the themes of loss, nostalgia, and trauma are often used as leading if not the only emotional tones and experiences. But at the same time, I completely agree with you, to approach this topic artistically, like in the world of Brecht, we do need humour, we do need irony, we do need a sense of estrangement to be able to cope with this situation.

ASHPERGER: We do need humour for the audiences, both mainstream and immigrant. Because "mainstream" audiences can feel excluded from the immigrant's experience just as much as the immigrants feel excluded from the mainstream. The mainstream audiences might feel compassion for newcomers' struggles, but they might not want to witness another heavy immigrant story they cannot truly connect to. At the same time, immigrant audiences don't feel that their experience is valued on stage. So, you—as an artist who wants to tackle the immigrant theme—end up talking to the converted, to your own community or to the people in situations like your own, while Vietnamese people talk to other Vietnamese, Italians to other Italians, and so on, and at the same time you miss out on everyone else. I love the poetic justice of putting a mainstream character who sees us as "the other" in place of an immigrant as a way of looking at a shared "immigrant" experience.

MEERZON: In the script, you have characters, native speakers of English; and in the cast, I imagine, you also had actors who were native speakers of English. How did they navigate through this script, through this story?

ASHPERGER: One of the interesting moments during rehearsals for the actors, the native speakers of English, was to learn or rather encounter the rules of English grammar. As you know, children here are not taught the rules of English grammar at school, so my actors never had a chance to think about the difference between uses of grammatical constructions such as present perfect tense—"I have taken"—or present perfect progressive tense—"I have been taking"—or any such grammatical structures of the English language. They never learned the difference between regular and irregular verbs, which is the first thing that immigrants must study to function in English. So we had a couple of funny moments in rehearsal when I had to explain to them that a past tense of a regular verb has "ed" (i.e., laughed) at the end, and irregulars you had to memorize (i.e., be, was, been). So, the native English-speaking members of the cast got spellbound by this idea of English grammar, in particular the irregular verbs. They also never considered the difficulties with articles in the English language. The use of articles is something Višnja has a great deal of trouble with, and I must say it has taken me many years of study and I still get them wrong. Each time we workshopped the show, English-speaking cast members were fascinated with all the implications of living both in a foreign language and in an accent.

MEERZON: The scenes in the ESL class are very reflective of what Canadian experiences are for immigrants. People form long-lasting bonds in those ESL classes, or even marriages, as there is this atmosphere of comradeship and shared difficulties, and English becomes some sort of connector between them. But I do know that you had some second thoughts about the depth of those characters, because it is a musical and hence the characters cannot be too psychologically nuanced. Have you resolved these concerns?

ASHPERGER: I can say that the ESL scenes and characters are ones that audiences love the most! I wanted each ESL character to carry its own stereotype (a right-wing Russian, a very polite Korean, a Brazilian capoeira instructor, a tell-it-like-it-is Vietnamese mother, a humorous Bosnian, and a quiet Saudi woman in full burka). But at the same time, I wanted them to defy their stereotypes. The Russian character, Yura, is portrayed in these wide strokes of a typical Russian immigrant from the Bathurst Street of the Toronto's Russian diaspora. He can be quite annoying with his right-wing views on the economy, but at the same time he isn't a racist, he cherishes free speech, and he loves Canada. For me, he brings forth a very strong point, a very important value in Canada: his views remind us that this is a democracy and that people should have the right to express their opinions, because not every politically incorrect opinion is the statement of hatred. I think it is very important to remind people that immigrants come from very different cultures, they carry very different opinions on issues such as the oil sands or raising your child gender-neutral. These are very contentious topics for people who come from conservative communities and carry traditional values.

MEERZON: This is quite a well-known fact, indeed. There is this book, *The Big Shift: The Seismic Change in Canadian Politics, Business, and Culture and What It Means for Our Future,* published in 2013, in which the authors studied the strategies of success that kept Harper and the Conservative Party in power for almost a decade. One of their arguments was that the cultural values promoted by the Conservative Party very often appeal to traditional immigrant communities, including Chinese or South Asian communities (Bricker and Ibbitson). I would easily add the Eastern European folks and the Russians, because they want stability and economic prosperity—the qualities of life that they do not identify with the Liberal Party and what it stands for. Your play speaks to this argument very well.

ASHPERGER: They are or will become Canadian citizens and they must be given a chance to state their opinion, too. They must not be marginalized in a society that aspires to be deeply democratic. I play with this; I have very different characters, I have some who are very conservative and who are pro-liberal, I have some apolitical people, and I have those who do not have an opinion or cannot express it in English yet. There is Zainab, who is from Saudi Arabia and wears a full burka, and who speaks very little English. So, here you have another issue: not simply of non-standard speech but of a situation where you don't have the basic language skills to form your political opinion in English, let alone express it. But Zainab makes great progress in her English throughout the play, almost by magic. But then it is a musical after all.

MEERZON: My next question has to do with the process of creating these characters and the research that went into making them. I do realize that your play is not a documentary drama and that it is not really based on actual stories and real people, but it does have these pockets of truth, if you wish, because even though your immigrant characters are broad and a little stereotypical, they do come from Toronto's streets. So how did you work on making these characters?

ASHPERGER: At Ryerson, we have this acting class called the Donor Project,* where each student is asked to find a "donor" to donate his/her accent and story. The students are asked to interview these people and learn their stories—about their pasts, their families, their cultural customs, and eating habits. They learn people's movements and accents, and then they create new characters and stories based on what they learned in life. We do not restrict students by age or gender, so a male student can play a sixty-year-old grandmother and so on. The class ends with a final presentation, when the students present their characters and findings. Part of this exercise is to continue living in the body of a donor during the free-flowing discussion, as I could ask these "characters" all sorts of questions and the students could find ways to respond to these questions in their characters. I worked on the Donor Project in 2011, and it gave me the inspiration for this play and the basis for the immigrant characters. So, this technique resembles verbatim theatre but is also far from it, as it puts lots of emphasis on the actor's imagination, which was then included in my plot. I imagined these characters discussing themes such as the gender-free upbringing of a child. The characters might be based on someone real, but are never the same as that person.

MEERZON: How did Kathy come to life? In the end, she is the heart of the play.

ASHPERGER: My play is about the power structures and hierarchy attached to speaking English, which is the most powerful language in the world. It was essential for me to have Kathy in the centre, as it was important to make sure a native speaker of English undergoes the same experience as an

---

* The Donor Project at the Ryerson School of Performance was started and taught by Irene Pauzer and Philippa Domville.

immigrant character, when one is pushed onto the margins because of their language. I found several examples of people suffering from foreign accent syndrome on YouTube; there was this British woman who started speaking with a Chinese accent after she had a stroke, for example. And the story repeats itself—people get alienated, their friends laugh at them, and they constantly get asked "Where are you from?" The question is eye-opening and transformative for people born in that country. They experience depression and alienation, they lose jobs and respect, and they see the fabric of their life ripped to shreds, which is at times the true story of immigration, especially in the beginning. They also get laughed at and, as I already mentioned, accents are funny; I've been laughed at because of mispronouncing something, and I've been laughed at by fellow immigrants. These "funny" mistakes regarding the English language and mispronunciation tickles us on a subconscious and very intimate level.

MEERZON: I think what really makes Kathy's story relatable is the fact that she is truly alone. There is nobody who can vouch for her, who we can trust, and who could tell us the truth. Her mother is ill and in the seniors' home, her clients stop having faith in her and so she loses the job; and she has no husband or children who can recognize her. All this on top of the fact that she is speaking English with a foreign accent brings Kathy's experience very close to what immigrants go through in their new countries. For a new immigrant, one lives in a state of isolation and mistrust for a long time, as there is no institution, no close community or family—there are no friends or former superiors who can speak on your behalf. This state of isolation either forces people to work very hard and start achieving their goals, or it puts them in a state of misery. Some people cannot take this misery. They either get depressed or decide to go back home, if their home still exists and if return is possible. I think this is the major point you are trying to make: speaking with an accent brings isolation and mistrust, even if one is born in this country.

ASHPERGER: I actually play with this notion of isolation on both ends of the spectrum. Kathy is a very lonely young woman before she has the accent. She is a typical single young working woman who dates online and socializes through social media. At the outset, Kathy could lose her job, and with that who she is, and this is a very scary and identifiable moment not only for immigrants but also for any member of the mainstream Canadian audience. But as the play progresses, Kathy gains friendship, love, and community because of the way she speaks.

MEERZON: There is another important moment in the play that has to do with Višnja, from Sarajevo, who is the janitor but who used to be an actress in Bosnia. It is the scene when she is called to audition for a film about the war or refugees, and does not get the part despite her "right accent." I suspect it was somewhat based on your own experience, too.

ASHPERGER: I am a professional actor and there is of course a deep connection between what happens to Višnja in relation to acting and me. I did audition for such a Bosnian part, and then my agent was told that Bosnia is not Sweden and that a blond such as myself can't play the part of a Bosnian. For that project I also got hired as a language coach for the English-speaking actor who got the part and was a cultural consultant for the film. In another such instance, I auditioned for a former Yugoslav part, didn't get it, and was asked to coach the actress who got it, but this time for free. I refused. I have also been told to "lose the accent," as if that was a possibility.

MEERZON: And again, this story is very typical. I know lots of actors here, in Toronto or Montréal, who look differently or speak with an accent, and they are often called to play a certain ethnicity, always expected to produce a stereotype.

ASHPERGER: Yes, typecasting is a reality. But to expand on my previous point, on coaching someone else to play my ethnicity, it is possible to make a parallel of this with a visible minority actor being asked to coach someone to play them in blackface or being told to "lose their complexion." Sure, the actor who received the coaching might end up being terrific, but this becomes a question of appropriation and one I seriously grapple with on a daily basis. It is a very difficult question for me to answer. I don't want to play self-portraits only or to ask this of my colleagues. I find it a terrible proposition for a performing artist. My fundamental belief about acting and representation is that anyone should be allowed to play anything. I believe in imagination being inexhaustible, and in freedom of imagination and expression. As a result, I have to look at the question of appropriation in relation to the intention in which the appropriation takes place. There are no hard and fast rules. But my view about casting (anyone should be able to play anything) is a radical view and not one that is in vogue or that I put into practice in *Foreign Tongue*. The casting discussion is a longer one and will certainly continue as it is paramount in theatre.

Most importantly, I don't want to sound bitter as I'm truly grateful to this country and to the opportunities it has given to me. I also believe history can change. From what I have read I know that casting was very different in the '40s or '50s here; now people have become more tolerant, more understanding and open. This current model, which celebrates self-portraiture, might shift as well once we truly establish equity, diversity, and inclusion in casting. We are certainly not there on any level when it comes to actors with non-standard speech.

MEERZON: This brings me to my last question: musicals do have happy endings, most of the time, and yours is no exception. Earlier you said you were modelling your play on Brecht, and his finales are never happy. How can you reconcile this?

ASHPERGER: Just like how Mack the Knife in *The Threepenny Opera* gets his reprieve from the gallows, so too does Kathy get hers from the accented life. In Act II Kathy has another stroke and wakes up again, now speaking standard English and without any accent. This is actually medically possible and has been recorded, but it is very rare. Similarly, a reprieve from the gallows is very rare as well. Perhaps it can be seen as an exception that proves the rule.

I thought it was important to bring Kathy back to where she belongs, to create this theatrical miracle, and also I didn't want to reinvent the wheel. This is a comedy, and like most comedies it ends with a marriage or at least with happy couples. The play ends with them happily singing the "Thank You, Canada" song, but there is a little irony to it, and as much as it is an uplifting song the lyrics are meant to provoke. The immigrants are now reunited in their ESL class, they share the hope of integration, but there are shadows to this happy story; there is satire, there is still politics, like in this strophe:

NON-IMMIGRANTS: *Thank you for giving a home to our first generations*
And for apologizing to our First Nations, in reservations
Fulfilling expectations

ZAINAB: *Accepting all religious denominations*
And that you didn't have any cotton plantations

There could not have been any cotton plantations in Canada due to our climate, and it is very nice that the First Nations have been given an apology, but they still are in reservations.

So, there is a happy ending in this play, but it doesn't mean I believe all the problems have been solved, and it doesn't mean I can stop being critical or politically aware when it comes to the questions of multiculturalism, immigration, or accent.

Works Cited

Bricker, Darrell, and Ibbitson, John. *The Big Shift: The Seismic Change in Canadian Politics, Business, and Culture and What It Means For Our Future.* Harper Collins, 2013.

My Name Is Dakhel Faraj

اسمي داخل فرج

Based on Interviews with Dakhel Ali Faraj Al-Bahrani

by Nada Humsi
with print dramaturg Diana Manole

Acknowledgements

Supported by the Canada Council for the Arts, the Ontario Arts Council, the City of Kitchener, the Region of Waterloo Arts Fund, and MT Space, Kitchener.

Special thanks to Dakhel Faraj, Gary Kirkham, Varrick Grimes, Majdi Bou-Matar, and Diana Manole

My Name Is Dakhel Faraj first received a new play development workshop and presentation in 2014 at the Registry Theatre, Kitchener, with the following creative team:

ADF (Dakhel Faraj #1, a native Arabic speaker): Dakhel Faraj
EDF (Dakhel Faraj #2, a native English speaker): Varrick Grimes
ASL (Dakhel Faraj #3, communicates in American Sign Language/ASL): Corinna Den Dekker
Dumbuk Player, Singer, and Actor: Mohammed Mohammed Fakhri
Oud Player (Arabic lute): Ayad Mulki

Video Designer, Consultant, Directing Consultant, and Performer: Gary Kirkham
Lighting Designer: Jennifer Jimenez
Stage Manager: Nicholas Cumming

The play was first produced in 2015 at the Registry Theatre as part of IMPACT15 (International Multicultural Platform of Alternative Theatre) with the following creative team:

ADF (Dakhel Faraj #1, a native Arabic speaker): Addil Hussein
EDF (Dakhel Faraj #2, a native English speaker): Varrick Grimes
ASL (Dakhel Faraj #3, communicates in American Sign Language): Modela Kurzet
Dumbuk Player, Singer, and Actor: Mohammed Mohammed Fakhri

Video Designer, Dramaturgical Consultant, and Performer: Gary Kirkham
Lighting Designer: Jennifer Jimenez.
Stage Manager: Christopher Douglas

August 2017–May 2018: Nada Humsi prepared the production script for publication, working with Diana Manole as dramaturg and editor for the published version. The play's initial meaning was carefully preserved, with all changes aiming to facilitate the reader's clear understanding of the trilingual dialogues, as well as of the performance aspects. Special attention was given to marking the actors' transitions from one character to another, as well as to the detailed descriptions of their physical actions, given the extensive use of mime and imaginary objects in the show. The mime scenes are part of this play's narrative. For more information on the show, please see Diana Manole's essay, "Resignifying Multilingualism in Canadian Accented Theatre," in *Performing Exile: Foreign Bodies*, edited by Judith Rudakoff and published in 2017 by Intellect Books.

Staging Notes

Three actors perform the present-time Arabic, English, and ASL-speaking representations of Dakhel Faraj, ADF, EDF, and, ASL, respectively, in the Canadian Lawyer's office, as well as numerous other characters. The transitions from one character to another are indicated in the stage directions.

Each of the three performers of Dakhel wears an identical *keffiyeh*, the traditional Middle Eastern scarf. Depending on the scene and/or character, the cloth is worn as a shawl around the shoulders, neck, or waist, and/or as a head cover, but it may also be used as another type of object, such as a bag or a tablecloth.

The set should be minimal, consisting only of the backstage screen for video projections, the Lawyer's office desk and chair, plus two additional chairs: one for the Musician and one used by the actors in different scenes, such the market scene and/or the scenes when EDF is tortured.

Given the extensive use of mime, most props are imaginary with the following exceptions: a toy bus, symbolizing the bus owned by Dakhel's father; a pair of stilts used by the actors performing Dakhel; an orange; paper airplanes; a book version of *Hamlet*; a pencil; and the cloak of Uncle Salman. In addition, Dakhel gives some personal objects to the Lawyer, which the latter projects live onto the backstage screen when indicated in the stage directions: his passport; other documents and photographs of his family; and a small envelope full of debris, the only remnants from Dakhel's house in Baghdad. The main transitions between scenes, places, and/or time periods are marked in the text by video projections. In the 2015 production, Dakhel Faraj gave Humsi permission to use his authentic family photographs. In any future production, the director has the freedom to mark the transitions in the way that fits best the show's style.

The Arabic lines are in colloquial Iraqi Arabic, but written in a way that the Syrian playwright feels would be understood by other Arab-speaking people. Please note that English, Arabic, and American Sign Language should be the first language of the performers of EDF, ADF, and ASL respectively. In this way, it might be easier for the audience to relate to EDF, the English version of Dakhel Faraj, and to ASL for a victim of politics and human rights violations and not a foreigner with a family tragedy that might never happen to them.

Scene One: At the Canadian Lawyer's Office, Dakhel Introduces Himself

The Lawyer enters, sits at his desk, and rings a bell, calling for the next client.

LAWYER: *(loudly)* Next!

A children's toy bus rolls across the stage toward the Lawyer's desk. Three actors enter in a line, one behind the other; the last one, EDF, is on stilts. They are very enthusiastic to meet the Lawyer.

ADF: مرحبا سيدي المحامي . . . اسمي داخل فرج . . . داخل علي فرج البحراني.

ASL: *(signing)* Hello, Mr. Lawyer. My name is Dakhel Faraj. Dakhel Ali Faraj Al-Bahrani.

EDF: Hello, Mr. Lawyer. My name is Dakhel Faraj. Dakhel Ali Faraj Al-Bahrani.

LAWYER: How do you spell your name?

ADF: دال-ألف.

LAWYER: *(writing)* Yes.

ASL: *(signing)* K-H.

LAWYER: Yes.

EDF: E-L.

The Lawyer writes Dakhel's name. ADF, EDF, and ASL take one step toward his desk. They are close to each other, moving as a group.

EDF & ASL: I was born in Iraq, Baghdad, the Karradah neighbourhood, on 8 August 1963.

ADF: اني انولدت بالعراق، بغداد، منطقة الكرادة، بتاريخ ثمانية، ثمانية، ثلاثة وستين.

All Dakhels turn, facing the audience, still standing behind each other; they look like the god Shiva, a person with many arms, all holding documents in both hands.

جبت معي كل الوثائق من العراق. جواز السفر، بطاقة الهوية، بطاقة فنان، ملكية الباص.

EDF & ASL: I have all the documents with me: passport, artist ID, bus driver's licence, house title.

The three Dakhels turn to face the Lawyer. They hand the documents to each other, from back to front, and then to the Lawyer.

ADF: ممكن أجيب لك أي وثيقة تريد.

EDF & ASL: I can give you more things if you need.

ADF: *(handing the Lawyer the actual objects)* Passport . . . a little toy . . . my uncle's cloak . . . the book of *Hamlet* . . . and this is what's left of my home.

ADF hands the Lawyer an envelope that contains sand and small stones; he opens it to show its content to the Lawyer and lets the rubble fall on the desk; live projection onto the backstage screen of the debris on the Lawyer's desk. This projection will be repeated throughout the play.

دخلت كندا بتاريخ ثمانية، اتناعش، الفين وعشرة. كندا بلد عدالة، وقانون، وحقوق انسان. *(to the Lawyer)*

EDF & ASL: I am a father of five: three girls, Sarab, Sarah, Zaman; and two boys, Ehab and Karam.

ADF interrupts and starts arguing with the other two Dakhels.

ADF: ثلاث بنات وأربع اولاد ايهاب، كرم، محمد، أحمد . . . .

The three Dakhels argue; each of them counts how many boys Dakhel has, and each wants to prove his counting is right; the audience hear the names that are being uttered: Mohammad, Ahmad, and especially Ehab and Karam. The argument is about having two sons, Ehab and Karam, losing them in the tragic incident, and then having another two sons, Ahmad and Mohammad.

EDF & ASL: Three daughters and four sons: Ehab, Karam, and then Mohammad and Ahmad.

(ASL signs) I came to Canada in 2010.

A photo of Dakhel's Iraqi passport is projected onto the backstage screen.

Canada! Home of justice, law, and human rights.

They all sign the words "justice," "law," and "human rights" in American Sign Language. Then, slowly, each of them mimes holding a steering wheel as if each of them is driving a bus. This image of driving a bus is repeated several times throughout the play. It should foreshadow the bus, which Dakhel was driving when his family was attacked by US soldiers. The Lawyer quietly watches them until he notices EDF's stilts.

LAWYER: What happened to your legs?

All three Dakhels answer the question, overlapping each other; the audience will not understand their answer.

EDF & ASL: *(ASL signs)* Shot by American soldiers! At the hospital, doctors had to scrape them eleven times to remove the uranium left by the bullets.

ADF: الرصاص فيه يورانيوم. وبقت تنزف من اليورانيوم نظفوها مرمرة اداعش

ASL, EDF, and ADF continue to explain what happened, overlapping each other.

LAWYER: Stop, I am confused, please tell me the story from the beginning.

They all shout loudly.

EDF & ASL: *(ASL signs)* The market in Baghdad.

ADF & ASL: سوق بغداد قبل الحرب.

Scene Two: At the Market in Baghdad Before the American-led Invasion of Iraq

This is a scene at a nice, rich, and happy market in Baghdad before the American-led invasion of Iraq. Each production may create its own market, freely inserting Dakhel's memories. The actors abruptly transition from being silent into a chaotic, lively market atmosphere. ADF sells meat, calling out several kinds of meats, especially organs such as kidneys, livers, and hearts.

ADF: *(as a meat salesman)* قبل الحرب على العراق، سوق بغداد كان فيه كل شيء، قرب قرب قرب قرب . . . تعا
تفرج يا حباب . . . لحم، كلاوي، هبر، كبد، بيضات، مخ، كلاوي دجاج، كلاوي بقر، كلاوي خروف.. قرب قرب قرب

EDF, as a monkey owner, plays a small accordion. ASL, as his monkey, dances on the tunes. The Musician enters playing his dumbuk. He tries to sell it by proving to the audience how good the instrument is and how strong its sound is.

ALL: *(overlapping)* Before the invasion of Iraq in 2003. Everyone is here, everything is here. This is the rich Mesopotamia: music, poetry, dance, culture. People live in harmony.

EDF: *(as a fabric salesman)* The market in Baghdad. We have everything. Look at this fabric, it's soft. The colour suits you. Look at the price. It's cheap, cheap.

ASL: *(signing, as a vegetable salesman)* Eggplants, carrots, parsley, zucchini. All fresh from the fields. No chemicals. All natural, tasty, cheap.

The Musician asks an audience member to try playing the dumbuk. Then, he tries to convince the audience to buy the instrument by playing on it and making everyone at the market dance. The music makes the Dakhels start an Iraqi choby group dance. They stop; EDF reaches up to an imaginary shelf to get a stereo cassette player, which is for sale.

EDF: *(as a stereo cassette player salesman)* The stereo cassette player, yes! Good choice! I'll get it for you.

EDF, who is still on stilts, falls on top of ADF while trying to reach up to the shelf.

(while falling) No weapons.

ADF takes one of EDF's stilts and mimes as if it were a rifle.

Don't . . .

They all raise their hands under the threat of ADF's weapon.

(as a stereo cassette player salesman) . . . worry.

They laugh, the weapon turns into a musical instrument in ADF's hands. EDF becomes an old man. ADF goes back to selling meat. ASL sells vegetables again. EDF sits on a chair, points one of his stilts at ADF, and mimes shooting at him. The others come near him and all mime a torture scene: ASL stands behind EDF and holds his head; ADF pulls the stilt's belt; EDF screams as if he is being tortured, then breaks away from the screams of torture and into "Hello, Father" to ADF. They start selling the father's fish.

ADF: *(as Dakhel's father)* ابني داخل بيع هالسمكة انا رايح عالجامع.

ASL becomes the fish, moving as if dancing.

EDF: *(as young Dakhel, to the fish)* My father went to the mosque to pray and now I'm the one who must sell you.

(calling out for customers) Who wants to buy fresh fish? Dancing fish?

ASL, as the fish, and EDF, as young Dakhel, dance together to attract customers. EDF starts selling cakes. After a little while, actors change characters: ASL becomes Ehab, the fifteen-year-old handsome boy of Dakhel Faraj, and ADF becomes the younger Dakhel Faraj at the time.

ADF: *(as younger Dakhel, father of Ehab, to the pastry salesman, giving him instructions how to write the name of his son on the birthday cake)* ايهاب بحرف الهاء.

EDF: *(as the pastry salesman)* Yes, I got it; it's an H; here it is: E H A B.

The Musician becomes a fruit salesman; he calls out to sell strawberries at a high price. EDF calls to sell strawberries at a lower price. ASL becomes Dakhel, the father of Karam, a five-year-old boy played by ADF. Karam points at EDF's strawberries and begs ASL, his father, to buy some for him. ASL argues with the salesman.

(as a strawberry salesman) What's your son's name? Karam? I see. Karam, I can't open the box just for a few strawberries. I have to bag them all or they'll rot in the sun.

> *EDF stores his produce in a bag and closes the zipper with big gestures; in Dakhel's memory, his action resembles zipping a dead body inside a plastic bag. Next, the three Dakhels go toward the Lawyer; they stop in front of him and become serious. They go back to miming holding the steering wheel of a bus as if driving it; they look at the Lawyer as if silently telling him Dakhel's story.*

Scene Three: Dakhel Introduces his Mother, Brother, and Sisters

> *A photo of Dakhel's mother is projected onto the backstage screen.*

LAWYER: Then what? Who's that?

EDF & ASL: My mother, Tolba Nsaeif. She was a seamstress, but never wore a new dress. She was also skilled in traditional Arabic medicine. She could cure headaches with a needle.

ADF: أمي، طلبة نصيف، خياطة، بس عمرها ما لبست توب جديد.
تعالج الناس بالأعشاب، التهابات الأمعاء، الروماتيزم.
واللي عندا صداع، بالابرة تعالجا، تدق تدق تدق تدق تدق والدم يطلع الى أن يرتاح.

> *ADF and EDF mime pinching ASL's head with a needle, while the Musician drums in the rhythm of pinching in a merry way. ASL feels better and smiles. Suddenly, her expression changes and then the light changes as well. ASL falls onto the floor like a dead person. EDF and ADF become the US soldiers from Dakhel's memories; they stand still, looking at ASL's body as if in a photo. ADF mimes filming, while EDF speaks on his radio transmitter.*

EDF: *(as a US soldier, talking on his radio transmitter)* Affirmative, please advise.

> *Noise of the radio transmission breaking up.*

> *EDF and ADF break out of Dakhel's memory and come back to the present, helping ASL to get up from the floor.*

My parents had six daughters and two sons. My elder sister Badriyeh. She's like a mother to us: she bites.

A photo of Badriyeh, the eldest sister of Dakhel, is projected onto the backstage screen.

ADF: أبوي وأمي عندم ست بنات و ولدين.

ASL: *(signing to the audience, looking at the photo)* My elder sister, Badriyeh. She's like a mother to us: she bites. I hate number fifty-seven.

My elder brother Hussein was born in 1957. All those born in '57 were conscripted as young men. When they were released, they looked like they were fifty-seven years old.

ASL becomes Badriyeh, the eldest sister of Dakhel, teaching two children math. EDF and ADF become the children, Dakhel and his brother Hussein, both about seven to eight years old. ASL, as Badriyeh, stands between them, watching them doing their homework.

EDF & ADF: *(as Dakhel and his brother Hussein, both counting)* Fifty-three, fifty-four, fifty-five, fifty-six, fifty-seven . . .

EDF: *(as Dakhel, the child, looking at ASL, as his sister)* My elder sister, Badriyeh! She's like a mother to us: she bites. *(counting)* Fifty-three, fifty-four, fifty-five, fifty-six, fifty-seven . . . I hate number fifty-seven. My elder brother, Hussein, is born in 1957. All those born in '57 were conscripted as young men. When they were released, they looked like they were fifty-seven years old.

A photo of Hussein, the elder brother of Dakhel, is projected onto the backstage screen.

ADF: *(looking at EDF, as Hussein, the elder brother of Dakhel)* أخي الكبير حسين . . . مولود بالسبعة وخمسين . . . اني أكره هذا الرقم . . . كل مواليد السبعة وخمسين دخلوا الجيش بنص السبعينات واتسرحو، الواحد عبالك عمره ميت سنة.

EDF plays with a sheet of paper; he crumples it and throws it toward his sister. She bites him, he screams.

EDF: *(screaming)* Breakkkkkkfaaaaast!

ASL, as Badriyeh, uses her scarf as a tray of food. She puts it on the floor and calls out.

ASL: *(as Badriyeh, signing)* Breakfast.

They gather to eat breakfast; they sit on the floor around the scarf, which is now the food tray

(to the audience, signing, looking at EDF, as Hussein) My brother Hussein. He loves cheese.

ADF: *(as Dakhel, the child, looking at EDF as Hussein, sitting next to him; they mime looking at a dish in the middle of the scarf.)* أخي حسين يحب الجبن.

EDF: *(to the audience)* My brother Hussein loves cheese.

They mime eating cheese. First, ADF as the little Dakhel and ASL as Badriyeh stretch their hands toward the dish, pick up a piece of cheese, roll it up in pita bread, and eat. EDF, as Hussein who loves cheese, picks up a few pieces of cheese and throws them one after the other in his mouth. Then he picks up one more piece and puts it in his pita bread. Little Dakhel and Badriyeh stop chewing and look at him. EDF, as Hussein, slowly stretches his hand toward one more piece of cheese; ASL catches his arm and bites it. EDF screams. A photo of Masriyeh, Dakhel's other sister, is projected onto the backstage screen.

ADF: *(as Dakhel, the child)* بعدين أختي مصرية تحب النوم، ابوقمبل . تحب تلعب بالشخاط.

ASL: *(as Dakhel, the child, signing)* My sister Masriyeh. She's a sleepyhead and a naughty one. Loves to sleep and likes to play with matches.

ASL lies down on Dakhel's lap as Masriyeh, who likes to sleep.

EDF: *(as Hussein, the child)* My sister, Masriyeh, is a sleepyhead and likes to play with matches.

EDF switches from being Hussein to being Masriyeh. Then, she throws matches toward Badriyeh and Dakhel, who get scared. Masriyeh moves closer to the Musician and throws matches at him, too. A photo of Sooriyeh, the third sister, is projected onto the screen.

My sister Sooriyeh. We call her "Tamata"—tomato, the beautiful tomato.

ASL: *(as present-time Dakhel, signing)* My sister Sooriyeh. She's beautiful and she knows it, and she's very smart.

EDF: She's beautiful and smart and she . . . knows it!

EDF, who was Masriyeh, now becomes Sooriyeh. Both ASL and ADF become Sooriyeh. They make stereotypical feminine actions, like looking into the mirror or doing their nails. EDF, who is impersonating Masriyeh, starts walking in a sexy way.

ADF: *(as Sooriyeh)* بعدين اختي سورية. كانت ذكية و حلوة وتعرف انها حلوة. ونناديها طماطة.

Beautiful Sooriyeh walks in a sexy way, decently flirts with the others on the stage. The Musician is drumming in rhythm with her steps. A photo of Dakhel Faraj as a child is projected onto the backstage screen.

(as present-time Dakhel) بعدين آني داخل.

EDF & ASL: *(both as present-time Dakhel, ASL signing)* Me: Dakhel.

EDF: *(as present-time Dakhel)* My three younger sisters: Widad.

ADF: *(as present-time Dakhel, pointing to EDF, who is playing Widad, as she mimes sewing on an old-style mechanical sewing machine)* اختي وداد، خياطة.

ASL: *(as present-time Dakhel)* Widad, a seamstress.

EDF: My sister Nahida.

He becomes Nahida and mimes swimming.

ADF: *(as present-time Dakhel)* اختي ناهدة، سباحة.

ASL: *(as present-time Dakhel)* Nahida, likes to swim.

EDF: *(as present-time Dakhel)* My sister Fardous.

EDF becomes Fardous and mimes playing Ping-Pong.

ADF: *(as present-time Dakhel, looking at EDF/Fardous, the Ping-Pong player)* فردوس، بتلعب طاولة.

ASL: *(as present-time Dakhel, signing)* Fardous plays Ping-Pong.

A photo of Dakhel's three sisters sitting around a picnic table is projected onto the backstage screen. The three actors take the girls' positions in the photo; they remain still for a few seconds, to allow the audience to notice the similarity.

EDF: *(as present-time Dakhel)* My father named my sisters "Sooriyeh/Syria" and "Masriyeh/Egypt" because he dreamt of the unity of these Arab countries, Iraq, Syria, and Egypt.

ASL: *(as present-time Dakhel, signing)* My father named my sisters "Sooriyeh/ Syria" and "Masriyeh/Egypt" because he dreamt of the unity of these Arab countries, Iraq, Syria, and Egypt.

ADF: *(as present-time Dakhel)* ابوي سمى اخواتي سورية ومصرية لأنه كان يحلم بالوحدة بين العراق ومصر وسوريا

The actors and the Musician sing the national anthem of Iraq.

EDF slowly becomes Noosa, the cat.

وهاي نوسة، حمرة وبيضة، نشوي ونوكلها، تعظعظ بأصابيعي، بالليل تنام عالفراش *(as present-time Dakhel)* بَيني وبين مرتي، واثنينا نحبها

EDF, as Noosa, the cat, walks toward ADF and ASL, who sleep close to each other as Dakhel and his wife; Noosa lies down between them. They lovingly make room for her. Noosa suddenly falls down between them as if dead. ADF and ASL look at each other, scared.

ADF & ASL: *(as Dakhel and his wife, in the past)* Karam, my son!

ADF: *(as present-time Dakhel)* سميتها على اسم الاغنية: ياناعسة يا توسا يا مصر يامحروسة يا كل بنت. صبية في بيتها متخبيية

EDF: *(still as Noosa, the cat)* I am Noosa, red and white. If Dakhel sleeps in, I bite his toes. When they barbecue, I sit close and watch them. They all feed me because I am so cute. At night, I sleep between Dakhel and his wife. They both love me very much.

The Musician plays Noosa's song together with ADF and EDF. The song starts happily; ASL and the cat are playing, and ASL tries to make the cat look at a photo of Dakhel's father.

ASL: *(as Dakhel in the past, signing)* This is my cat, Noosa. Red and white. If I sleep in, she bites my toes. When we barbecue, she sits close and watches. Never steals. So we all feed her. At night, she sleeps between my wife and me. We both love her.

(to Noosa) Look, Noosa, this is my father's photo.

The cat snatches the photo from ASL's hand and tears it to pieces. The drumming becomes increasingly stronger and more aggressive while this scene takes place. The music stops when the cat rips the photo. Lights change. ASL takes the pieces of the photo to the Lawyer's desk to put it back together. EDF becomes a US soldier from Dakhel's memories; he talks on his radio.

EDF: *(as a US soldier, as if describing the bus and what he sees inside it)* Affirmative . . . two youth . . . and a boy . . . about eight years . . . old . . .

Noise of the radio transmission breaking up.

. . . affirmative . . . No, wait! There's a fourth . . .

Noise of the radio transmission breaking up.

. . . an old man on the bus . . .

Noise of the radio transmission breaking up.

Affirmative.

The image of the ripped photo of Dakhel's father is projected live onto the screen, including the Lawyer's hands trying to put it back together.

Scene Four: Dakhel Introduces His Father and Recalls His Two Jobs

ADF: *(as present-time Dakhel)* ابوي علي فرج البحراني، كان عندا شغلين . . . الشغل الأول حدقجي.. بيشتغل بالورد

He mimes watering plants with a hose.

ASL: *(as present-time Dakhel, looking at the photo and signing)* My father, Ali Faraj Al-Bahrani. He had two jobs: the first job was gardening, tending to roses.

EDF: *(as present-time Dakhel, pointing at the picture)* My father, Ali Faraj Al-Bahrani. He had two jobs: the first job was gardening, tending to roses.

A photo of a rose garden is projected onto the backstage screen. The three Dakhels mime doing gardening work while the Musician plays an Iraqi song and they sing its words. ADF slowly gathers a bunch of wood and throws it as if onto

a pile. ASL mimes using a mower. EDF explains to ASL, signing, that there is no mower and throws her a shovel. ASL mimes shovelling. Then ASL and EDF also mime gathering wood and throwing it as if onto the woodpile. They all sit around and look silently at the imaginary woodpile in the middle of the stage.

Lights change, EDF takes matches and slowly tries to start a fire. The Lawyer leaves his office desk with a real orange and a real paper airplane in his hands; he flies the airplane over the Dakhels's heads as they all look at it scared. The dumbuk music gets fast and loud. The Lawyer lets the orange fall onto them, as if it's a bomb; the bomb throws them backward, frightened; the music stops suddenly. They stay still for few seconds, then the mood and the lights change.

A photo of a boat on a river is projected onto the backstage screen. For some time, they enjoy sitting around the fire. EDF starts peeling the orange and giving some to everyone while ADF talks about his father's work as a fisherman. They mime being on a boat, which rocks on the river's waves. The lights change again. The three Dakhels mime eating bread, drinking tea, and stretching their hands toward the water.

ADF: الشغل الثاني لأبوي صياد سمك، وهاي المهنة توارثناها أبا عن جد. أبوي يروح للشغل بالحدايق الساعة سبعة. الصبح وينتهي الساعة تنتين. آني أروح للمدرسة الساعة سبعة الصبح وينتهي دوامي الساعة اتناعش الظهر

أرجع للبيت اوصل الساعة واحدة ألقى أمي محضرة الغدا، تقللي يلا يما داخل، اوخذ الغدا وروح لأبوك، أبوك هسة داينتظرك بالبلم ... يما عافية، اني جوعان، خلى اتغدى وأروح ... تقللي معقولة يما؟ تتغدى وأبوك جوعان؟ آخذ الغدا وأروح للبلم ... وألقى أبوي هسة واصل البلم

The Musician plays an Iraqi fishing song. When the music starts, ASL starts telling/signing the story about fishing with his father; the other two Dakhels are singing.

ASL: *(signing while the music is going on)* My father's second job was fishing on the Dajla river. At seven a.m., my father goes to the garden and I go to school. At one p.m., my mother makes lunch. I take the food and meet my father at the fishing boat. We eat and drink tea together. Then we start throwing the nets into the river until midnight. If hungry, we eat bread and drink tea. It's delicious. My mother baked the bread. Now my wife bakes the same bread. At midnight, we go to sleep on the boat. At four a.m., we get up to pull up the nets. My father reminds me of the old man and the sea. He's very patient; he can wait for twenty hours to catch one fish. When we catch a big fish, my father shouts: "Allahu Akbar!" One day, at four in the morning, I woke up hearing my father moaning. I panicked. He had his hand on his cheek. He said: "Don't worry, son! I will not die, I have a toothache. Go to school."

ADF: نقعد ناكل ونشرب استكانة شاي. ونبلش. نذب الشبك بالنهر، نهر دجلة. نذب سبع ثمان شباك للساعة اتناعش. بالليل. ما نجوع، أو ناكل شاي وخبز، لأنها طيبة، أمي كانت تخبز الخبز، وهسة مرتي تخبز نفس الخبز، أمي علمتها، وللساعة اتناعش بالليل يلا نخلص نصب الشباك، ننام بالبلم

ADF sleeps on EDF's lap, as if still on the boat rocking with the waves. A photo of Dakhel as a child on a boat is projected onto the backstage screen.

EDF: My father's second job was fishing on the Dajla river. At seven a.m., my father goes to the garden and I go to school. At one p.m., my mother makes lunch. I take the food and meet my father at the fishing boat. We eat and drink tea together. Then we start throwing the nets into the river until midnight. If hungry, we eat bread and drink tea. It's delicious. My mother baked the bread. Now my wife bakes the same bread. At midnight, we go to sleep on the boat. At four a.m., we get up to pull up the nets. My father reminds me of the old man and the sea. He's very patient; he can wait for twenty hours to catch one fish. When we catch a big fish, my father shouts: "Allahu Akbar!" One day at four in the morning, I woke up hearing my father moaning. I panicked. He had his hand on his cheek. He said: "Don't worry, son! I will not die, I have a toothache. Go to school."

They all sleep for a bit. Then ADF starts telling the toothache story in Arabic while the others are still asleep.

ADF: فد يوم الساعة اربعة الصبح، اسمع أبوي يون وشلون ونين يهد الحيل وايده على خده، ون ون ونن. قلتلا يابا شبيك.
قال: لا تخاف ابني لا تخاف أني ما موت، سنوني دا توجعني. انت روح للمدرسة.
أبوي كان يغني ويقول: الدنيا وياي زعلانة ووردها والهوى يزهي ووردها.

The projection of an out-of-focus photo of a burnt bus drifts over the previous photo. ADF sings while remembering. ASL slowly gets up and mimes driving the bus; spotlight on ASL, who is back to sleep for a moment then wakes up unhappy as if she has had a bad dream. She wakes everyone up. They are rocking on the boat with the waves. A video projection of a postcard of Iraq's Dajla river rocks as well. EDF washes his face with the river's water. They start pulling the fishing nets from the water.

الساعة اربعة الصبح نفيق ونجمع الشبك. آني أجذف وأبوي يجمع الشبك. ولما يكون في سمكة بالشبك ابوي يقول.
الله أكبر . . . صلي عالنبي . . . وهاي سمكة . . . صلي عالنبي . . . وهاي سمكة . . . صلي عالنبي.
الله اكبر . . . الله اكبر . . . الله اكبر . . . الله اكبر.

ALL: Allahu Akbar, Allahu Akbar!

They line up behind each other and mime fishing. ADF keeps repeating "Allahu Akbar, Allahu Akbar!" in a shocking way, as if seeing dead people. Sudden silence. ASL and EDF rock silently behind ADF, as if still on the boat.

ADF: الى ان سكت ابوي.

EDF: Suddenly, my father was silent.

ASL: *(signing)* Suddenly, my father was silent.

ADF: *(in a merry mood)* ولمن نصيد سمكة كبيرة نتعارك وياها.

EDF becomes the big fish, which fights for its life until it falls down dying.

EDF: *(as the dying fish)* His mother thinks he cannot breathe; she blows air into his mouth, but a fountain of blood comes out of his chest.

ASL, as Sabriyeh, Dakhel's wife, tries to save the life of the fish, as if the fish is now Karam, her son; she blows air into its mouth. ASL and ADF pull a red scarf from the fish's chest that looks like a fountain of blood.

ASL: *(signing)* She blows air into his mouth, thinking he has difficulty breathing. Blood shoots from his chest.

ADF: وتنفخ بحلقا عبالها مختنق، والدم ينفر من قلبه.

A photo of the burnt bus is projected onto the screen, quickly replaced by the live projection of the debris on the Lawyer's desk; harsh stage lights. ASL, as Sabriyeh, lifts EDF's head as the dying fish.

EDF: *(as the dying fish)* Don't worry son, it's just a toothache. I will not die, go to school.

Scene 5: Dakhel Goes to School as a Young Boy in Iraq

A photo of a school in Iraq is projected onto the backstage screen. The mood and the light change. ADF asks the students to stand up for the teacher's entrance.

ADF: قيام.

EDF and ASL hurry and take their seats in the classroom; they are sleepy because of the tiring fishing work. The Musician is right beside them, as if he is another student.

(as Dakhel's teacher) جلوس.

He starts the lesson. He mimes writing on an imaginary blackboard and says what he writes.

التاريخ: . . اروح للمدرسة ريحة الزفر مال السمك بي . . . يعني الطالب اللي يقعد يمي الله غاضب عليه، وحذائي البلاستيك. بيه رطوبة وما لابس جواريب، الحذاء كان يطلع صوت كل ما أمشي، بف بف بف، كل عمري أحلم ألبس حذاء رياضي، الطلاب كلهم كانوا فقراء، كانوا كلهم ينامون بالليل، بس آني ما كنت أنام بالليل، دائما نعسان

ADF, the teacher, turns his head slowly toward the students, as if he is remembering something. He sees EDF chewing gum and sticking his finger in ASL's ear, as if it's a rifle, just like when the US soldiers pointed their rifles to Dakhel's ears—a tense moment.

(as the teacher) Stop it.

The children stop playing.

صدت السمك من عمري ست سنوات حتى صار عمري ستاعش سباتعش سنة.

EDF and ASL are back to sleep through the lesson; ADF, the teacher, notices.

(calling EDF) داخل فرج.

EDF slowly goes to the blackboard, shuffling; his shoes make sound—a big, funny noise.

EDF: When I go to school, the fish smell of my clothes hits the other students with no mercy. My feet are always wet inside my cheap rubber sandals. I dream of one day wearing running shoes. Real running shoes! The other children could sleep at night. I fished every night until I was seventeen.

ADF, as the teacher, points at ASL, who looks at the blackboard and starts reading/signing the lesson.

ASL: *(signing)* When I go to school, the fish smell of my clothes hits the other students with no mercy. My feet are always wet inside my cheap rubber sandals. I dream of one day wearing running shoes. Real running shoes! The other children could sleep at night. I fished every night until I was seventeen.

Everyone is annoyed by ASL's fish smell; they whisper to each other nasty comments and cover their noses. ADF, as the teacher, also can't stand ASL's smell; he dismisses the class.

ADF: *(as the teacher)* انصراف.

The Musician plays the music of the next scene—the soldiers' game. They all leave the classroom, shuffling. ADF walks toward the Lawyer and takes a driver's position, as if he is telling the Lawyer about what happened. EDF and ASL wave a white scarf at the US soldiers to indicate that they are civilians and have no weapons. Next, they perform the scene when the US soldiers shoot Dakhel's legs. ASL mimes stealing a chocolate bar from EDF's pocket and eating it. The image of the burnt bus is projected onto the backstage screen for a moment. EDF and ASL argue like children over a game.

EDF: *(as a child)* Ready? I'm going to be the man, you're going to be the soldier.

ASL: *(as a child/signing)* No, you will be the soldier, I will be the man.   /

EDF: *(as a child)* All right. But you better do it well.

Using the stilts like weapons, EDF mimes shooting ASL's legs; ASL doesn't fall.

No, not like that, you become the soldier, I'll be the man.

Also using the stilts like weapons, ASL plays the soldier and mimes shooting aimlessly. EDF shows ASL how to do it. The game becomes more and more serious and real.

(as Dakhel, screaming at US soldiers and waving a scarf) We are civilians! We are civilians!

ASL, as a soldier, mimes shooting him with the stilt.

(as the child) Not yet. Don't shoot.

He waves.

Now.

ASL shoots; EDF screams and jumps on one leg.

We are civilians!

(to ASL) Good, shoot me here.

ASL shoots the other leg; EDF falls down.

(seriously, as present-time Dakhel) All this technology of yours, but you don't know this is a child, this is a woman!

(to ASL, as a child) See!

ASL keeps EDF pinned to the floor by stepping on his chest with one foot. ASL bends down to mime stealing the chocolate bar from EDF's pocket.

My chocolate!

End of the children's game, followed by the live projection onto the backstage screen of the debris on the Lawyer's desk. Lights change.

Scene Six: Dakhel Becomes a Student at the Fine Arts Institute in Baghdad

ASL and EDF, as young boys in Iraq, mime playing soccer with an imaginary ball. ADF starts telling the story of how he became interested in the arts.

ADF: أما كيف صرت فنان . . . كان بيتنا بجسر ديالى، كنا صغار، ماكو تلفزيونات بالبيوت . . . أخوي حسين ياخذني لقهوة.
سيد راضي الله يرحما، يوم الثلاثاء، القهوة تنملي ناس . . . نقعد ستة على القنفة حتى نشوف برنامج الرياضة في اسبوع . . .
كنت أكره هذا البرنامج . . . اللي خلاني أحبه هو موسيقى البرنامج . . . بعدين اعرفت انها حلاق اشبيليا . . . غووول

EDF & ASL: Goal!

EDF and ASL hug and high five. A family photo of Dakhel and his brother Hussein as young boys in Iraq in the 1970s is projected onto the backstage screen.

(saying the lines to each other, as if they are having a conversation; ASL is signing) My elder brother Hussein, the one who likes cheese, used to take me with him to watch the sports channel at a coffee shop in our neighbourhood.

The Musician starts playing the music from the TV sport shows.

I hated the sports program. But I loved the music.

A photo of an Iraqi musician playing music is projected onto the backstage screen.

EDF: Rossini!

EDF and ASL listen to the music. A photo of Iraqi children performing in a school play is projected onto the backstage screen; it looks like a historical and religious play.

EDF & ASL: *(preparing to perform a short play)* When I was eight, I started acting in a religious play. We did it once a year during the month of Muharram. We staged the story of Imam Hussain, the martyr.

Switching to the flashback scene.

If you're lucky, you get to play the martyr or a member of Hussain's family. If you are unlucky, you play one of those who tortured him and murdered his family.

ASL and EDF act out the religious play: ASL tortures EDF, who plays Imam Hussain. ASL mimes whipping EDF. He shows EDF a glass of water, but spills the water on floor without giving any to EDF, who is thirsty. EDF tries to lick the water from the floor, but ASL pulls EDF back by his hair to prevent him from doing it.

ADF: *(telling the story in Arabic)* من صار عمري 8 سنين أمي أخذتني سجلتني بالسبايا. والسبايا أو التشابيه هي قصة استشهاد سيدنا الحسين عليه السلام. اللي يمثلون شخصيات الل قتلوالحسين يضربونهم بالحجر، بالطوب، اللي يفلت يفلت واللي مايفلت يشعلون أبو أبوه. كل سنة يسووها يوم بعشرة محرم. أنا كنت أمثل مع أطفال الحسين، مربوطين ونصيح

ADF sings the traditional religious song from the play; the same play, which includes this song, is performed every year in Iraq during the month of Muharram.

فكنا من السجن بالله يا سجان.

احنا ولاد مسلم من أصل عدنان.

They all beat their chests in the traditional Shia Muslim religious ritual. ADF stops singing, but they continue the ceremonial chest-beating for a while.

(continues his story about how he became interested in the arts) عمي سلمان بيتا بصف

بيتنا . . . كان شيوعي

A photo of Salman, Dakhel's uncle, standing beside his bookshelves, is projected onto the backstage screen.

EDF and ASL look at the imaginary huge bookshelves and then mime taking some books from the shelves and looking at them.

EDF & ASL: Uncle Salman lived across the street. He was imprisoned because he was a communist. He had his own library full of banned books.

ADF: *(continues the same story)* . . . على الباكيت. كان يدخن سجائر الرومان، على الباكيت . . . أطب عليه ألقاه يقرا

فيه اسدين وعلم بريطانيا وعلم امريكا . . . عمي يباوع على الباكيت ويقول: ذولا رح يدمرون العالم . . . جابلي كتاب

. . . وقلبي اقرأ . . . اقرأ باسم ربك الذي خلق

خلق الانسان من علق . . . صدق الله العظيم.

EDF & ASL: *(ASL signs)* Every time I visited my uncle Salman, I found him reading. He was smoking Rothman cigarettes, and on the pack were two lions and two flags: Britain and America. My uncle used to look at the pictures and say: "These two will destroy the world." Once, he handed me a book and said, "Read. Read! Just like it's written in the Koran, in order: read."

EDF and ASL mime picking up books and looking at each of them. EDF shows a book by Iraqi poet Muzaffar Al-Nawab to ADF.

ADF: *(about the imaginary book in his hand)* مظفر النواب.. انحبس ويّا عمي سلمان وهرب..

مرينا بيكم حمد واحنا بقطار الليل

The Musician and ADF sing the poem "Marrena Beekom Hamad" by Muzaffar Al-Nawab, included in the imaginary book they hold.

مرينا بيكم حمد واحنا بقطار الليل

واسمعنا دق قهوة، وشمينا ريحة هيل

يا ريل صيح بقهر صيحة عشق يا ريل*

EDF & ASL: Muzaffar Al-Nawab, one of Iraq's most famous and influential poets. Imprisoned with my uncle Salman. Al-Nawab escaped, my uncle didn't.

ASL picks up another book and shows it to ADF; the book is by Salam Adil.

ADF: سلام عادل ... مفكر كبير. ذبوه بالثيزاب.

EDF & ASL: Salam Adil, a great thinker. A teacher and a member of the Iraqi Communist Party. Dissolved in Acid.

EDF picks up another book by Al Sadr Al Awwal. He shows it to ADF.

ADF: الصدر الاول، صاحب نظرية اقتصادنا. دقوا مسمار حديد براسا وحرقوه بالنار.

EDF & ASL: Al Sadr Al Awwal, the founder of modern Islamic banking, the author of *Our Economy*. Killed by having an iron nail hammered into his head and then being set on fire.

ASL picks up another book about Fahd, the founder of the communist party in Iraq, and shows it to ADF.

ADF: "الشيوعية أقوى من الموت وأعلى من أعواد المشانق"

فهد، مؤسس الحزب الشيوعي العراقي . شنقوه.

EDF & ASL: Fahd, the founder of the Iraqi Communist Party. Hanged.

ADF: *(as present-time Dakhel, talking to the Lawyer)* طبعا، دخلت معهد الفنون الجميلة.

Toby or no Toby.

بابا ايهاب يلا قول: توبي اورنو توبي.. بابا كرم قول توبي اور نو توبي.

Live projection onto the backstage screen of the debris on the Lawyer's desk.

EDF & ASL: *(as Ehab and Karam, repeating their father's line)* Toby or no Toby!

---

*   We passed by you, Hamad, on the night train.
We heard the pestle grinding coffee, we smelt the cardamom.
Oh train, shout in sorrow the shout of love, oh train! (Translated by Humsi and Manole, it could be included in the show with EDF singing in English to the Arabic tune.)

ADF shows how to act "Toby or no Toby" to EDF and ASL, who now play Ehab and Karam, his children. They imitate him. ADF then goes to the Lawyer's desk and gets the book of Shakespeare's Hamlet *and the uncle's cloak.*

EDF: *(reciting Hamlet's monologue)* To be, or not to be, that is the question:
Whether 'tis nobler in the mind to suffer
The slings and arrows of outrageous fortune,
Or to take arms against a sea of troubles
And by opposing end them. To die, to sleep.

ASL: *(signing Hamlet's lines)* To be, or not to be, that is the question:
Whether 'tis nobler in the mind to suffer
The slings and arrows of outrageous fortune,
Or to take arms against a sea of troubles
And by opposing end them. To die, to sleep.

ADF approaches ASL playing Karam, Dakhel's youngest son.

ADF: كرم، بابا، حبيبي، خلي معك هالكتاب، اقرأ ستانسلافسكي، بابا على طول اقرأ.

ADF as Dakhel, the boys' father, gives a small book, a copy of Hamlet, *to ASL as his son Karam. They hug goodbye. ADF then approaches EDF, who now impersonates Ehab, Dakhel's elder and handsome son. Dakhel gives Ehab Uncle Salman's cloak.*

بابا ايهاب، هاي عباية عمي سلمان، ما رضيت اعطيها لحدا، البسها.

ADF/Dakhel puts the cloak on the shoulders of EDF/Ehab; this is one of the few real props used in the 2015 production. They hug goodbye. Dakhel walks up stage slowly, as if disappearing.

EDF & ASL: *(return to impersonating present-time Dakhel; they comment on the previous scenes)* Of course, I became a student at the Institute of Fine Arts in Baghdad.

EDF, as the student at the Institute of Fine Arts in Baghdad. He takes various poses to suggest the theatrical style of each artist he mentions.

Qabbānī, Molière, Jibran, Shakespeare, tragedy, comedy.

The Musician drums after each name. The drumming continues. The three Dakhels start marching like soldiers to the rhythm of the drumming.

Scene Seven: Dakhel is Called to do His Mandatory Military Service During the Iraq-Iran War (September 1980–August 1988)

A photo of Dakhel during his first term of military service is projected onto the backstage screen.

EDF & ASL: *(staggering and lining up like soldiers)* In 1980, they put me in a military uniform and sent me to do my military service. I spent the eight years of the war between Iraq and Iran watching airplanes: Iranian airplanes, commercial airplanes, military airplanes, Israeli airplanes.

Sound of explosions, which EDF and ASL explain for the audience.

Israeli airplanes destroyed the Iraqi phosphate factory.

ADF: اباوع . . . من سنين ممّن إيران بحرب، الجوية، بالقوى خدمت . . . وأخدوني عسكري لبسوني . . . للجيش واستدعوني
وفاتت إيرانية، طيارات فاتت . . . خارج بطيء واطي مدني نقل واحد داخل، سريع عالي عسكري نقل واحد :الطيارات على
بعكاشات الفوسفات معمل قصفت وبووم اسرائيلية طيارة وفاتت عسكري، ونقل مدني نقل طيارات

ASL: *(signing)* Israeli airplanes destroyed the Iraqi phosphate factory.

A short intense pause. Then all three Dakhels mime holding a steering wheel and driving their family's bus full of fear.

Scene Eight: Dakhel Gets Married to Sabriyeh

EDF & ASL: After all my sisters got married, I had to fend for myself.

ADF: كل خواتي اتزوجن . . . بالجيش أغسل هدومي بإيدي وبالبيت أغسل هدومي بإيدي.

EDF: My father said:

ADF: ابني داخل، انت ليش ما تتزوج؟.

EDF: I said okay.

ADF: واتزوجت عام الف وتسعمية واربع وڠانين.

EDF: He found me a bride.

A photo of Sabriyeh, the bride, is projected onto the backstage screen. ASL becomes Sabriyeh, a shy bride.

ADF: *(looking at ASL/Sabriyeh, his bride)* كان عمري 21 سنة . . . صبرية .. كان عمرها 18 سنة.

Dakhel's wedding pictures are projected onto the backstage screen. The Musician and the actors suggest an Iraqi wedding atmosphere. The groom and bride walk on stage while the others follow them, singing.

ALL: *(singing a wedding song)* مبارك عرسك يا لهيبة.

EDF, as Dakhel the groom, and ASL, as Sabriyeh the bride, exchange wedding rings before going to their bedroom. EDF mimes shutting and locking the bedroom door. The bride and the groom look at each other, happy. She is shy. He lifts the wedding veil off her face; he's so happy. They giggle.

EDF: *(to the audience, as present-time Dakhel)* I got married in April 1984. I was twenty-one, Sabriyeh was eighteen. She was beautiful.

ASL: *(signing)* I was eighteen, Dakhel was twenty-one. He was beautiful.

EDF: *(to the Musician, in Arabic)* Shabab Shesawee! [What shall I do?]

EDF is nervous. The Musician encourages him. EDF and ASL play a child-like game with their hands, a courtship game. Suddenly, ASL gets shot in her back. She falls toward EDF, who doesn't catch her but lets her fall. Change of lights and mood. ASL lies dead on stage. EDF becomes an American soldier, he mimes zipping her body in an imaginary plastic bag while chewing gum. This moment foreshadows a later scene from Dakhel's memory, when Aliya, the girlfriend of his son Ehab, was shot in the back by the US soldiers and fell dead on the ground, and the soldiers put her in a black plastic bag and zipped her up. The mood changes again and the scene goes back to Dakhel and Sabriyeh on their wedding night. Dakhel lies beside her. He mimes writing on her back while singing for her.

(singing) Happy birthday to you!

Onto the backstage screen, a live projection of the Lawyer's hand, turning over Sabriyeh's photo; on the back we can see a few words, handwritten by Dakhel: "I'll love you forever." ADF stands with his back to the audience and writes in the air in Arabic: "I'll love you forever."

ADF: أحبك الى الأبد. داخل.

EDF: *(writes on Sabriyeh's back as they make love, and says what he writes)* "I'll love you forever, Dakhel!"

ASL: *(as Sabriyeh, the bride, signing)* All my love to you.

EDF becomes Noosa, the cat, slowly moving away from ASL/Sabriyeh as if pregnant. ADF takes EDF's place as Dakhel, the husband, beside his wife, Sabriyeh, who slowly becomes a pregnant woman.

ADF: *(looking at the cat)* نوسا شبعت أكل . . . طبعا عرس.

EDF: *(as the cat)* So much meat.

ADF: *(as Dakhel, the young husband)* بطنها انتفخت.

EDF: *(as the cat)* I had five kittens.

ADF as Dakhel, the young husband, puts his ear on the belly of ASL/Sabriyeh to hear the baby.

ADF: صار عدنا خمسة بعيون العدو.

EDF: *(as Dakhel, the young husband, and ASL as Sabriyeh, his young wife, signing)* We had five children.

All actors happily and loudly celebrate the children's birth.

ADF: *(as Dakhel, a young father, happy)* البنات: سراب، سارة، زمن.
الأولاد: ايهاب و كرم.

EDF & ASL: *(celebrating)* Look at this beautiful Iraqi family, with not one, not two, not three, not four, but five, five children!

The Musician and actors sing a children's song that starts with: أحمد ومحمد وحسين ... غاليين *A photo of Sarab, Dakhel's eldest daughter, is projected onto the backstage screen.*

ADF: *(as Dakhel, the young father, introducing their first daughter)* سراب: تحب الكتب
مثل عمي سلمان

EDF & ASL: *(respectively as Dakhel, the young father, and Sabriyeh, the young mother, signing)* Sarab. Loves books, like Uncle Salman.

A photo of Sarah, the second daughter, is projected onto the backstage screen.

ADF: *(as Dakhel, the young father, introducing their second daughter)* سارة: ترسم
وتنام هواي مثل عمتها مصرية

EDF & ASL: *(respectively as Dakhel, the young father, and Sabriyeh, the young mother, signing)* Sarah. Paints and sleeps a lot, like her aunt Masriyeh.

A photo of Zaman, the third daughter, is projected onto the backstage screen.

ADF: *(as Dakhel, the young father, introducing their third daughter)* زمن: ذكية مثل
عمتها سورية

EDF & ASL: *(respectively as Dakhel, the young father, and Sabriyeh, the young mother, signing)* Zaman. Clever like her aunt Sooriyeh.

Music starts and Zaman dances like her aunt Sooriyeh in the earlier scene.

ADF: *(as Dakhel, the young father)* الاولاد.

A photo of Ehab, their eldest son, is projected onto the backstage screen. EDF becomes Ehab, the handsome boy who likes to look good. He mimes looking in a mirror and grooming himself.

(as Dakhel, the young father, introducing their first son) ايهاب: كشاخ ، شعره اسود وعيونا
عسلي يشبه خاله وابتسامته تخبل

EDF & ASL: *(as Sabriyeh, the young mother, signing)* The boys: Ehab. Like Salman, his uncle, he has black hair, brown eyes, a beautiful smile, and always dresses well. And sings beautifully.

ADF: *(as Dakhel, the young father)* صوته يخبل.

ADF sings an Iraqi children's song. ASL and ADF dance.

أحمر اصفر ابيض ابيض اصفر احمر.
الوان الشمس تدور والارض تدور تدور.
وأنا وسمير وفائز والقطة والعصفور.

A photo of Aliya, Ehab's girlfriend, is projected onto the backstage screen.

ASL: *(as Aliya, signing)* I am Aliya, the most beautiful girl but also the best student at our school. I am Aliya! Clever, polite, and passionate! I love Ehab and Ehab loves me.

EDF: *(as Ehab, to ASL)* Oh, Aliya!

(to the audience as present-time Dakhel) When Ehab was seventeen, he fell in love with Aliya.

(to Aliya, as Ehab) Aliya, you're clever, polite, passionate, and the best student at your school!

ADF: *(as present-time Dakhel)* لما ايهاب صار عمره سبطعش سنة . . . قام قلبه ينبض بالحب . . . حب.
بنت خالته علياء، علياء بنت عاقلة ومؤدبة وحنينة، واشطر واحدة بمدرستها

A photo of Karam, their youngest son, standing in a theatrical pose, is projected onto the backstage screen.

(as present-time Dakhel, introducing Karam) كرم، اخر العنقود . . . اسمراني، وحرك، وبمثل.

All stand in exactly the same way Karam is posed in the photograph on the screen.

EDF & ASL: *(repectively as present-time Dakhel and present-time Dakhel signing)* Karam, the actor.

EDF: *(becomes Karam, who is acting in* Julius Caesar*)* You, too, Portia!

ADF: *(as Dakhel, the young father)* لا بابا ، شنو ديزدمونة.

EDF: *(as Karam)* I know it, I know it, don't tell me, Dad!

Toward the Lawyer, pointing his finger at him.

You too, Brutus!

EDF, as Karam, Dakhel's youngest son, starts miming that he stabs himself, as Caesar. At the beginning, he acts like in a child's game, fooling around. The stabbing becomes increasingly violent; the actors fall on their knees and bend forward as if praying. They all go down, with their foreheads on the floor, and they start praying. They greet the angel on their right shoulder, then the angel on their left shoulder, like in a Muslim's prayer.

ADF: *(as if praying to God)* يسألني كرم ابني الصغير: النجم يابا ليش ما يوقع . . . لا يا بابا النجم ابد ما يوقع . . . النجم ثابت . . . هون بقلبي ثابت . . . كرم يسأل ويسأل ويسأل . . . يابا ليش ليش ليش

EDF: *(as Karam, the child)* Yaba leish, why doesn't the star fall? Brutus, why Brutus why, Brutus, yaba leish? Leish? Leish? Leish? Leish? Leish? Why, why, why . . . Baba, leish.

ASL: *(as Dakhel, the young father)* Karam wants to know everything. He asks: "Does the star fall?" I tell him: "The star never falls, honey." He asks: "Why why why why why why!"

They all face the audience; the mood is serious, angry.

ADF: *(as present-time Dakhel)* ليش ليش ليش . . . كل هالتكنولوجيا اللي عندكم وما عرفتوا هادا طفل وهاي مرا

EDF & ASL: *(as present-time Dakhels; ASL signs)* All the technology you have! But you couldn't see there were children and women on that bus!

Live projection onto the backstage screen of the debris on the Lawyer's desk. The image of the burnt bus is projected onto the backstage screen for a moment. Harsh light. Actors look at the audience. Long pause.

Scene Nine: Dakhel is Called Again to Serve in the Army During the Iraqi Invasion of Kuwait (Started on 4 August 1990)

All actors break into the atmosphere of the scene: the story of Dakhel taking refuge in the Hore Region to escape being enlisted during Iraq's war on Kuwait. EDF and ASL toast a drink, both playing Dakhel in the Hore Region. Then, ASL runs to hide under the Lawyer's desk. EDF hides behind the Lawyer's chair.

ADF: *(as present-time Dakhel, to the Lawyer)* و بعدني ما شبعى من أولادي، استدعوني للخدمة مرة ثانية حتى يطب صدام الكويت... ولاجندي عراقي يعرف... امشي يمشي... اللي دخل هم الحرس الجمهوري والأمن الخاص... من عرف الجيش، نصا هرب وآني هم هربت... رحت للهور... الهور طبيعة وماي وقصب وبردي و مخابئ... بقيت أكثر من سنة، أصيد سمك وأشرب عرق. ولحيتي كانت لهنا... الناس تتبرك فيي ويصيحولي سيد داخل... إلى أن أمر بوش صدام بالعفو العام عن الهاربين... مو حبا بالعراقيين... حتى يضعف الجيش العراقي

A photo of Dakhel in the Hore Region is projected onto the backstage screen.

EDF: *(as present-time Dakhel, to the Lawyer)* Soon I was called to serve again in the army. Saddam was about to enter Kuwait. When the reserve and regular soldiers found out, all of them ran away. I ran away to Hore. I ran to the marshes, to the Hore Region. Only the Republican Guard entered Kuwait.

ASL: *(as Dakhel in the Hore Region; appears from under the table, signing to the audience)* Soon I was called to serve again in the army. Saddam was about to enter Kuwait. When the reserve and regular soldiers found out, all of them ran away. I ran to the marshes, to Hore. Only the Republican Guard entered Kuwait.

EDF & ASL: *(as Dakhel in the Hore Region)* In Hore, there was water, straw, papyrus, and shelters. Saddam destroyed the marshes to find us. I stayed there more than one year, fishing and drinking arak. I had a beard down to *(shows his belly button)* here. People were calling me Sayyed Dakhel. Thinking I was religious, they wanted my blessings.

ADF corrects EDF's impersonation of Sayyed Dakhel.

ADF: *(as present-time Dakhel to EDF, as Dakhel in the Hore Region)* مو هيك
هيك، هيك

EDF bows in front of ADF to get his blessings. ADF shows EDF how people behaved in front of Sayyed Dakhel: ADF takes EDF's hand and kisses it, then he touches him as if ADF is a sacred person who can bless him. EDF imitates him. Then, all three line up in front of the Lawyer as present-time Dakhel to continue telling him the story.

EDF & ASL: *(to the Lawyer)* Bush wanted to weaken the Iraqi army. He ordered Saddam to discharge a large number of soldiers and to allow those who escaped to return home for "humanitarian reasons." I returned home. I found Baghdad under UN sanctions. The once rich Mesopotamia was starving. I wasn't hanged, but I was transferred from the theatre where I worked before the war to the Ministry of Agriculture. I became a warehouse keeper. Every morning, I punched in . . .

A photo of Dakhel as a warehouse keeper is projected onto the backstage screen. ASL signs first his name in the air, unlocks the warehouse's door, checks that everything's fine by looking right and left, locks the warehouse's door, goes backstage, sits on the floor, feels bored, and smokes; EDF finishes his sentence, signing his name in the air.

EDF: *(signs his name in the air)* "Dakhel Faraj," and then I did nothing.

EDF unlocks the warehouse's door, checks it by looking right and left, locks the warehouse's door, stands up bored, picks his teeth, and spits. While EDF does those actions, ADF tells the same story to the Lawyer.

ADF: ارجعت من الهور لبغداد . . . وما انعدمت . . . ولقيت العراق تحت الحصار . . . ردت ارجع لشغلي بدائرة السينما والمسرح . . . قال احنا فيضناك لوزارة الزراعة . . . آني فنان مسرحي صرت مدير مخازن بوزارة الزراعة؟؟ سلموني مفتاح مخزن وزارة الزراعة . . . الوكيل المالي هو اللي يوقع ويؤمر وينهي . . . حجي ابراهيم، بعثي كبير، آني ما كنت اعمل شي
داخل فرج. *(signs his name in the air)*

ADF unlocks the warehouse's door, checks it by looking right and left, locks the warehouse's door, goes stage left to his chair. He is bored.

Scene Ten: The UN Sanctions on Iraq (Started on 6 August 1990)

ADF, EDF, and ASL as Dakhel, the warehouse keeper at the Ministry of Agriculture. They look bored and are silent until EDF starts talking about the UN sanctions.

EDF: *(as Dakhel, the warehouse keeper)* Baghdad under sanctions was . . . *(smokes and spits)*

ADF: *(as present-time Dakhel)* أبوي ترك الصيد، ما عاد مسموح بالصيد، وفتح محل صغير يبيع فيه.
جكاير وحامض حلو . . . وأخوي حسين عسكري وبعدين أبوي باع بيت الكرادة واشترى باص نشتغل عليه نقل داخلي..
أنا صرت فنان وسائق باص . . . وحصار كافر عالعراق

أبوي ترك الصيد.

EDF & ASL: *(as Dakhel, the warehouse keeper; ASL signs)* People were hungry.

ADF: *(as Dakhel, the warehouse keeper)* ماي ماكو.

EDF & ASL: Noosa was hungry, too.

ADF: الأكل غالي.

EDF & ASL: No water.

ADF: نفط، كهربا، ماكو.

EDF & ASL: No heating oil. No electricity.

ADF: دوا ماكو.

EDF & ASL: The only sweets were made with Iraqi dates.

ADF: الاستيراد والتصدير اتوقف.

EDF & ASL: No medicine, no books. No export, no import.

ADF: الحلويات الوطنية كلها بالتمر العراقي.

EDF & ASL: People started to sell their homes piece by piece.

ADF: الناس قام تبيع بيوتها قسم قسم عبين ما تمضي الازمة.

EDF & ASL: First the windows.

ADF: الشبابيك.

EDF & ASL: Then their doors, then the bricks from their walls. Women used bathrooms without doors to shut behind. The door was a blanket fixed with two nails.

ADF: البوب . . . الحياطين.
مرا تطب الحمام ما تلاقيلها باب. الباب بطانية ومسمارين.

EDF & ASL: Then they sold their kidneys to the rich people in the Gulf area.

ADF: حتى كلاويهم باعوها للخليج.

EDF & ASL: Under the UN's Oil-for-Food Programme (OIP), Havana cigars arrived regularly for Saddam. The sanctions were on us, on my children.

ADF: الجكاير الجروت تصل من هافانا لصدام . . . النفط مقابل الغذاء لصدام وحاشيتا . . . حصار امريكا كان علينا . . .
عليي وعلى أولادي

EDF & ASL: My father was forced to give up fishing and opened a small shop to sell cigarettes and junk. Then he sold our house in Karradah and bought a bus. All men in the family worked, driving people around. I became an artist and a bus driver.

Scene Eleven: Dakhel Misses Saddam Hussein's Birthday

ADF: *(as Dakhel, the warehouse keeper)* هيئة الاحتفالات بالدائرة حطت البيبسي والكيك كلا.
بالمخزن . . . يومها اسكرت ونمت

EDF & ASL: *(as Dakhel, the warehouse keeper)* The day before Saddam's birthday, they sent us a huge strawberry cake to have it for the celebration.

ASL and ADF, as casual workers, mime carrying a huge cake. EDF as Dakhel, the warehouse keeper, mimes taking a key from his pocket and opening the warehouse's door. ASL and EDF bring the cake inside the warehouse, then mime bringing boxes of Pepsi-Cola, juice, and Coca-Cola. EDF lists the supplies received.

EDF: (*as Dakhel, the warehouse keeper*) Pepsi-Cola, ten cartons.
Juice, ten cartons.
Coca-Cola, ten cartons.

They all stand, looking at the huge cake. ASL dares to take a strawberry; EDF snatches it from her hand and puts it back on the cake, trying to level the cream around it. ADF catches ASL's finger that has the cream on it and tries to lick the cream off, but the cream spills onto his cheek; ASL licks the cream off ADF's cheek and they look at the cake again. They all grab the keys from their pockets with synchronized movements, lock the warehouse door, and then put the keys back into their pockets. They are all now Dakhel, the impoverished storage keeper who craves a slice of cake. They all stand straight, salute the cake in a military fashion, and then sing "Happy Birthday." The Musician plays along.

ALL: (*singing*) Happy birthday to you, happy birthday, dear Saddam, happy birthday to you!

The song starts sounding like dogs barking. They bark; they mime having their tails between their legs, and then laugh and start partying. The Musician joins the party; they drink and dance the Iraqi choby dance. They all get drunk. A photo of Dakhel's party with his friends in Iraq is projected onto the backstage screen.

EDF: (*as Dakhel, the warehouse keeper, drunk, falling onto the floor*) Choby or no choby.

They lie drunk on the floor. EDF becomes Noosa, the cat, and slowly gets up. She bites ADF's toes. He wakes up.

ADF: (*as Dakhel, the warehouse keeper, still drunk, to the audience*) ورحت يوم تسعة
وعشرين . . . وشعلوا اهل اهلي . . . أول واحد الحجي إبراهيم . . . قللي المفتاح مال المخازن يمك. قلتلا اسكرت . . . قال
داخل شوفلك حل . . . ترى صوفتك حمرا: يعدموك: يعدموني؟

ADF falls back asleep.

EDF: (*as Noosa, biting ADF's toes*) The next morning, on Saddam Hussein's birthday, Dakhel didn't wake up. Even though I bit his toes, he kept on sleeping. Meanwhile, at the Ministry of Agriculture, his co-workers gathered in front of the locked warehouse. Even musicians gathered outside the locked door and waited. While the key was . . .

Noosa touches ADF's pocket, where the key is.

The Musician stands still, waiting; the Lawyer, as a singer, tests the microphone. After a long wait, they leave, telling each other that the key is with Dakhel, who didn't show up. ASL starts threatening Dakhel with many kinds of deaths, while Noosa translates neutrally.

ASL: *(signing)* Burn you, shoot you, chop off your head, bury you alive, boil you in oil. Oh, yes: they will kill you.

EDF: *(as Noosa)* They're going to burn you. They're going to shoot you. Chop off your head. Bury you alive. Boil you in oil. Oh, yes: they will kill you. You might as well do it yourself.

ASL tries to suggest to ADF a way to save himself, signing the word "Shakespeare." ADF struggles to understand her.

ADF: ش . . . شش . . . ششاك . . . شكب.. شيخ . . . شيخ.. شيخ اسبر؟ شيخ جابر؟ شيخ عبد الله؟ شيكس . . . شيكسب . . . شكسبير شكسبير

EDF becomes Dakhel's mother. He uses the keffiyeh around his shoulders as a head cover.

EDF: *(ironically)* Brilliant! Shakespeare! How is Shakespeare going to save you? Show me.

ADF and ASL, as Dakhel, show her how they will pretend to be "crazy."

(as Dakhel's mother) Okay, okay, good.

Scene Twelve: Dakhel Pretends to be Crazy and is Committed to a Mental Health Hospital

A photo of Dakhel pretending to be crazy is projected onto the backstage screen. EDF, as Dakhel's mother, walks toward the mental hospital with ASL and ADF as Dakhel pretending to be crazy. Once there, she pokes ASL and ADF to act crazy in a more convincing manner, and they put more effort into their performance.

EDF: *(as Dakhel's mother, talking to an imaginary clerk at the hospital)* Excuse me, this is my son, Dakhel Ali Faraj Al-Bahrani. He's hallucinating.

ADF and ASL start delivering lines from Hamlet, Act 4, Scene 3. *Dakhel's mother looks at them and translates the lines into English for the hospital clerk.*

ADF: *(whispering Hamlet's monologue in Arabic)* ليس انت الذي تأكل، انت الذي تؤكل . . . تؤكل تؤكل

الدود، يجتمع عليك الدود، تسمن نفسك، يأكلك الدود.

الصياد، الدودة أكلت الملك، السمكة أكلت الدودة . . . السمكة.

اكلنا السمكة، أكلنا الملك.

ASL: *(signing, as a crazy person)* Not where he's eating, but where he's being eaten. A certain conference of worms is chowing down on him. Worms are the emperors of all diets. We fatten up all creatures to feed ourselves, and we fatten ourselves for the fish. A man can fish with a worm that ate a king and then eat the fish he catches with that worm.

EDF: *(as Dakhel's mother)* "Not where he eats, but where he is eaten: a certain convocation of politic worms are e'en at him. Your worm is your only emperor for diet: we fat all creatures else to fat us, and we fat ourselves for maggots: your fat king and your lean beggar is but variable service, two dishes, but to one table: that's the end." Can you help him? Please?

ADF: *(as present-time Dakhel, to the Lawyer)* بقيت سنة بمستشفى الرشاد . . . طلعوني من . . . المستشفى وانطوني اجازة . . . عملت مسرحية حكت عن الوضع . . . كيف شواطي دجلة انترست قصور مسؤولين . . . كيف الصيادين تركوا الصيد . . . كيف اشترينا باص كوستر اتنين وعشرين راكب لنشتغل عليه . . . كنت ادز النص شكل للرقابة واشتغل شكل . . . اجو اخدوني من المسرح . . . بالامن العام حرقوا أهل أهلي

ASL: *(as present-time Dakhel, signing)* I got a leave of absence for one year. I went back to theatre. I wrote and directed a play about what was going on in Iraq. About how my father, Ali, and all the other fishermen were forced to give up fishing. It was called *The Two Brothers*.

EDF: *(as Dakhel's mother)* My son got a leave of absence from his job at the warehouse for one year. When he was discharged from the mental hospital, he went back to working in theatre, which is the same shi . . . He wrote and directed a play about what was going in Iraq. About how my husband, Ali, couldn't fish anymore because of those bands of . . . about how they have stolen away the shores of . . . Dakhel's play was called *The Two Brothers*.

Scene Thirteen: Dakhel is Imprisoned for Writing and Directing a Theatre Show That Criticizes Saddam Hussein's Regime

A photo of Dakhel acting in The Two Brothers *is projected onto the backstage screen. The photo shows a scene from the show: a man on his knees holds another man, forcing him onto the floor. ADF becomes the director of the play.*

ADF: *(as the theatre director, claps)* استعداد . يا شباب جاهزين نعيد، اتفضلوا.

The Musician drums an opening tune. EDF and ASL sit as if on a boat, rocking on the water, and become the two brothers from the play. ASL smokes on the boat.

EDF: *(as Brother 1, in Dakhel's play)* Brother, congratulate me! I have joined the army to protect our beautiful homeland. Will you join with me? You will stay a fisherman with our father?! Good luck, brother. I am off to serve with honour.

Brother 1 reports for duty, salutes, marches. Then he picks up one of the Lawyer's pencils.

(as Brother 1) With this bullet I swear to protect our beautiful land. With this bullet I swear to protect our president and his gang of toadies, cronies, and thieves. With this bullet I swear to shoot anyone who tries to fish in the Dijla River and their private . . . Hey, you! Yes, you, over there! Stop fishing! Put that fish back into the water or I'll shoot you with this bullet!

He shows the pen as if a bullet.

I'll shoot if you don't . . .

ASL looks at EDF. The brothers recognize each other.

Brother!?? No . . . Brother?! Please, don't . . . I will have to . . . if you take that fish . . . I will have to! Please, brother, I have sworn to protect—BANG! Noooooooo . . .

EDF carries the bullet/pen in his hand and walks with it all the way to ASL's head; he tries with his other hand to catch the bullet. The bullet hits his brother's forehead. EDF holds his falling brother with his arm, exactly like in the photo projected behind them.

Who has made brother kill brother? Who has made the Dajla run red with our blood? Whoooooo?

The Musician and EDF sing the Iraqi anthem, facing the audience. ADF, as the theatre director of The Two Brothers, *joins them in singing the anthem as if it is the finale of the show. They take their bows and applaud, encouraging the audience to do the same. ASL becomes a secret police officer and suddenly drags EDF backstage. ADF speaks to the audience. Live projection onto the backstage screen of the debris on Lawyer's desk. The stage lights change into a harsh green. ASL throws EDF onto a chair and starts beating and whipping him.*

ADF: *(as present-time Dakhel)* . . . شلون طلعت من السجن, طلعت وزني ثلاثين كيلو. اباوع عل المراية ايدي طولانة لهون . . . شكلي قرد

EDF & ASL: *(as present-time Dakhel)* By the time I got released from Saddam's prison I was thirty kilograms. My arms became longer, I looked like a monkey.

ADF, EDF, and ASL become monkeys. The Musician drums a cheerful, energetic tune; the actors dance like monkeys. EDF jumps on the Lawyer's desk and throws Dakhel's documents into the air.

Scene Fourteen: Dakhel Celebrates the Birthday of Karam, His Son, While the American-led Armed Forces Attack Baghdad

A photo of Karam's birthday party is projected onto the backstage screen. EDF starts baking a cake.

ADF: *(as present-time Dakhel)* بالألفين وتلاتة، كان عيد ميلاد ابني كرم . . . مْن سنين، الامريكان، الامريكان صاروا. يهددون يهددون ويتوعدون . . . القاعدة، اسامة بن لادن . . . اسلحة دمار شامل، سبتمبر اداعش صرنا نحنا العراقيين مسؤولين عليها

EDF & ASL: *(as present-time Dakhel)* In 2003, the Americans started to threaten Iraq. It was Karam's birthday, my youngest son.

EDF mime making the cake. ASL helps.

EDF: *(as Dakhel in 2003, reading the recipe, while ASL hands him the ingredients)*
Three eggs. Okay, one egg.
One cup of milk. Okay, water.
One cup sugar. Okay, dates!
One cup of dates. Yes, dates!

Actors make the sound of beating eggs.

ADF: *(as present-time Dakhel)* قام صدام يعلن انو عندا صواريخ كيماوية راح يفجرها ويسلم العراق تراب . . . تراب ولا بلاد ، شو بتفرق مع امريكا! وفعلا كانت صواريخ سكود مدفونة بالزعفرانية القريبة من بيتنا . . . والصواريخ اذا انفجرت تحرقنا . . . يوم خمسة اربعة اشتد الضرب على بغداد

ASL: *(signing, as present-time Dakhel, overlapping with ADF's line above)* Al-Qaeda, Osama bin Laden, weapons of mass destruction. Iraq became guilty for 9/11. My son Karam was waiting for his birthday cake. Saddam had Scud rockets hidden in the science centre in our neighbourhood. Saddam threatened to turn Iraq to dust before handing it to the Americans. Dust . . . dust! Why would Americans care? They said we were part of some "axis of evil."

EDF: *(as present-time Dakhel)* Al-Qaeda, Osama bin Laden, weapons of mass destruction. Iraq became guilty for 9/11. My son Karam was waiting for his birthday cake. Saddam had Scud rockets hidden in the science centre in our neighbourhood. Saddam threatened to turn Iraq to dust before handing it to the Americans. Dust . . . dust! Why would Americans care? They said we were part of some "axis of evil."

EDF brings the cake to ASL, who becomes Karam. They all sing "Happy Birthday." When ASL is about to blow out the candles, they all look at the right as Hussein, Dakhel's brother, comes in.

ADF: *(as present-time Dakhel, continuing the story for the Lawyer, in his office)*

طب أخوي حسين يركض، قال الامريكان دخلوا بغداد لا تطلعوا، الامريكان يستلقوك . . . قلت: والصواريخ؟؟

نروح لبستان أختي سورية . . . سألت أبوي: شو نسوي؟

EDF & ASL: *(as present-time Dakhel, continuing the story for the Lawyer, in his office)* On April 5, 2003, my brother Hussein came in running. He said: "Don't go out, the Americans entered Baghdad, they'll get you." The Scud rockets!!? "Shall we all go to my sister Sooriyeh's orchard?" I asked my father.

ADF: *(as present-time Dakhel, continuing the story for the Lawyer, in his office)*

قللي بكيفك.

EDF & ASL: *(as present-time Dakhel, continuing the story for the Lawyer, in his office)* He answered: "Do what you think is right."

ADF: جمعت العائلة كلها بالباص . . . آني بجيبتي ثمانمية دولار كل اللي املكا.

EDF & ASL: *(as present-time Dakhel, continuing the story for the Lawyer)* I gathered my entire family and asked them to get on the bus. I had only eight hundred dollars in my pocket.

ADF: *(as present-time Dakhel, continuing the story for the Lawyer)* أبوي شال مصلايتا وسبحتا وصعد الباص

EDF & ASL: *(as present-time Dakhel, continuing the story for the Lawyer)* My father took his prayer carpet and beads and got on the bus.

ADF: *(as present-time Dakhel, continuing the story for the Lawyer)* وكرم شال البوم صور العائلة وحاضنا على صدرا وصعد الباص

EDF & ASL: Karam got on the bus, holding the family photo albums to his chest.

ADF: وايهاب الكشاخ شال ملابسا الجديدة وقطع وردة حمرا من الحديقة كان يريد ينطيها لعلياء.

EDF & ASL: Ehab, the handsome, packed his new clothes, cut a red flower from the garden to give to Aliya, his girlfriend, and got on the bus.

ADF: نوسة ما قبلت تصعد بالباص . . . اتخبلت ونزلت وبقت تنتظر.

EDF: Noosa refused to get on the bus. She stood at the door, mewing.

ADF: وانملا الباص.. اتنين وعشرين مقعد.

EDF & ASL: The bus was full, all twenty-four seats.

They continue the story for the Lawyer, in his office. ADF recalls the names of the twenty-four people riding on the family's bus. EDF and ASL count everybody. A photo of each person is projected onto the backstage screen as their names are mentioned.

ADF: *(as present-time Dakhel)* محمد. Mohammad.

EDF & ASL: *(counting)* One.

ADF: بيداء. Bayda.

EDF & ASL: Two.

ADF: أحمد. Ahmad.

EDF & ASL: Three.

ADF: ماجد. Ma'jed.

EDF & ASL: Four.

ADF: أحمد. Ahmad.

EDF & ASL: Five.

ADF: ندى. Nada.

EDF & ASL: Six.

ADF: علي. Ali.

EDF & ASL: Seven.

ADF: ابراهيم. Ibrahim.

EDF & ASL: Eight.

ADF: أم ابراهيم. Ibrahim's mother.

EDF & ASL: Nine.

ADF: ماجد. Ma'jed.

EDF & ASL: Ten.

ADF: سامي. Sami.

EDF & ASL: Eleven.

ADF: سلمان. Salman.

EDF & ASL: Twelve.

ADF: ورقاء. Warka.

EDF & ASL: Thirteen.

ADF: نبيل. Nabeel.

EDF & ASL: Fourteen.

ADF: كوثر. Kawthar.

EDF & ASL: Fifteen.

ADF: وداد. Widad.

EDF & ASL: Sixteen.

ADF: سراب. Sarab.

EDF & ASL: Seventeen.

ADF: سارة. Sarah.

EDF & ASL: Eighteen.

ADF: زمن. Zaman.

EDF & ASL: Nineteen.

ADF: صبرية. Sabriyeh.

EDF & ASL: My wife. Twenty.

ADF: ايهاب. Ehab.

EDF & ASL: The handsome. Twenty-one.

ADF: علياء. Aliya.

EDF & ASL: His girlfriend. Twenty-two.

ADF: كرم. Karam.

EDF & ASL: The youngest. Twenty-three.

ADF: أبويا.

EDF & ASL: My father. Twenty-four.

ADF: أربع وعشرين راكب.

EDF & ASL: Twenty-four seats, Twenty-four people.

ADF: شغلت الباص ومشيت . . . ضرب وقصف والدنيا محترقة.

Lights change. We are back in 2003, when Dakhel and his family leave their home to take refuge at Sooriyeh's orchard.

EDF & ASL: *(as Dakhel in 2003)* I start the bus.

ADF: *(as Dakhel in 2003)* واحد ميت . . . طفل يبكي على جثة اما.. بزازين وشجر وطيور محترقة.

EDF & ASL: *(as Dakhel in 2003)* The American-led forces are attacking Baghdad. I am driving. Everybody is silent.

ADF: مرا تشاورلي لنوقف وتصرخ. وما نوقف. والكل ساكت.

EDF & ASL: We drive by a child crying over his mother's dead body. Burning cats, birds, and trees. A woman with a baby in her arms waves at us. We don't stop.

ADF: وما نحس إلا . . .

ALL: *(making the sound of the shootings)* Wrrrrrrrrr . . .

EDF & ASL: *(ASL signs)* The American soldiers are shooting our bus.

ADF: ررصاص عالباص مثل المطر . . . واسمعت . . .

EDF: *(crying)* Ahhhhhhh . . .

ADF: وقفت الباص وركضت باتجاه الضرب ألوح بالقميص الداخلي . . . مدنيين مدنيين ما عدنا سلاح.

EDF & ASL: I stop the bus and run toward the soldiers, shouting, "We're civilians, civilians with no weapons."

ADF: مدنيين مدنيين ما عدنا سلاح ما تفتهمون . . . انزلوا. انزلوا خلى يشوفوكم . . . أبوي يصرخ.

EDF & ASL: My father shouts:

ADF: الله اكبر.

(making the sound of the shootings) Wrrrrrrr . . .

EDF & ASL: *(to the people on the bus, ASL signs)* Get off the bus. Let the American soldiers see you.

I run toward the bus.

ADF: ضربوني بهاي الرجل.

EDF & ASL: They shoot me in my leg.

ADF: قمت اقمز.

EDF & ASL: I go toward them, jumping on the other leg. They shoot it, too.

ADF: ضربوني بالرجل الثانية.

EDF & ASL: I fall on the ground.

ADF: وقعت.

EDF & ASL: The soldiers surround me, laughing.

ADF: اتجمعوا علي الجنود يضحكون . . . حطوا البنادق بأذني.

EDF & ASL: Their rifles in my ears. Music in theirs.

ADF: واحد يعلك.

EDF & ASL: Dancing.

ADF: واحد يرقص.

EDF & ASL: Filming.

ADF: واحد يصور.

EDF & ASL: Chewing gum.

ADF: وواحد مد ايدا بجيبي وأخد الدولارات لجيبا.

EDF & ASL: One soldier stretches his hand and takes the dollars from my pocket and puts them into his pocket.

ADF: اني شفتهم.

EDF & ASL: I see his face and his hand.

ADF: اعرف وجوههم.

EDF & ASL: I see their faces, one by one.

ADF: باوعت قدامي . . . علياء نزلت تركض: عمو داخل، عمو داخل . . . ضربوها الامريكان . . . وقعت علياء عالقاع.

EDF & ASL: Aliya gets off the bus, shouting, "Uncle Dakhel, Uncle Dakhel!" The Americans shoot her. She falls.

ADF: احمد يقمز وحامل رجلا بايدا.

EDF & ASL: Ahmad, my cousin, jumps on one leg, holding the other leg in his hands.

ADF: الباص يحترق وابوي وابني ايهاب ببطن الباص.

EDF & ASL: The bus is burning with my father and my son inside it.

ADF: صبرية تنفخ بحلق كرم عبالها مختنق والدم ينفر من صدرا.

EDF & ASL: Sabriyeh blows air into Karam's mouth. A fountain of blood comes out of his mouth.

ADF: أغمي عليي.

EDF & ASL: I faint.

ADF: وصل الرتل الامريكي الثاني . . . حطوا علياء بكيس اسود وسحبو: تشيست.

EDF & ASL: *(imitating the sound)* Zip! More American soldiers arrive in haste. They put Aliya in a black plastic bag and zip it closed.

ADF: باوع الجندي على كرم بحضن اما ميت مدلها ايده بلوح شوكولاتة وقللا.

ESL & ASL: A soldier looks at Karam, dead in his mother's arms. He stretches out his hand with a chocolate bar for her and says:

ADF and EDF become US soldiers; they look at ASL, as the mother of Karam, and deliver the word "sorry" in English and in American Sign Language at the same time, with no special feeling in it.

EDF, ADF, & ASL: Sorry.

The three actors scream silently, suggesting Edvard Munch's famous painting The Scream. The silent scream starts growing in their mouths and bodies, followed by a sound effect similar to a high-pitched ringing.

Scene Fifteen: American Soldiers Have Fun Killing Iraqi Civilians

The three actors return to impersonating American soldiers. The Dakhels' silent scream is replaced by the loud, violent shouting of the US soldiers, having fun.

ALL: *(as US soldiers)* Let's kick some ass! Get the motherfucker down! Smash those cockroaches! Those fucking Iraqi terrorists!

The US soldiers sing "Bodies," the 2001 song from the rock band Drowning Pool, which was popular among American soldiers during the invasion of Iraq.

(singing) "Let the bodies hit the floor . . ."

Scene Sixteen: At the Canadian Lawyer's Office, in the Present

Lights change. We are back in the present, in the Lawyer's office. The three Dakhels line up, facing the Lawyer; they are all on crutches.

ADF: *(as present-time Dakhel).* وصرت لاجىء.

EDF & ASL: *(as present-time Dakhel)* I became a refugee.

ADF: دخلت كندا بالألفين وعشرة. كندا بلد العدالة والقانون وحقوق الانسان. رحت المحامي لارفع دعوى على الجنود الامريكان اللي قتلوا اولادي وابوي. وحرقوا بلدي. الأمريكان اللي قتلوا نوسا

الامريكان اللي زرعوا الطائفية والمحاصصة.

ASL: *(as present-time Dakhel, signing)* I entered Canada in 2010. Canada, the home of justice, law, and human rights. I came to you, Mr. Lawyer, to bring to justice those who murdered my father and my two sons.

Those who killed Noosa. The Americans who destroyed my country. The Americans who planted sectarianism and hatred in my country.

EDF: *(as present-time Dakhel)* I entered Canada in 2010. Canada, the home of justice, law, and human rights. I came to you, Mr. Lawyer, to bring to justice those who murdered my father and my two sons.

Those who killed Noosa. The Americans who destroyed my country. The Americans who planted sectarianism and hatred in my country.

The Lawyer looks at his papers and explains to them his official response. The Lawyer's words eventually start to sound like gibberish, as the other actors listen to him very carefully.

LAWYER: Huh. Huh. Well, hmm. A Canadian court cannot take jurisdiction over this matter because the murders were carried out in a foreign country and not within Canada's borders. The US is not a party of the Rome Statute, which established the International Criminal Court, and therefore the American soldiers . . .

The Musician starts singing a sad Iraqi song, "Izra' jamilan." His voice overlaps with the Lawyer's as he reads the official response.

MUSICIAN: *(singing.)* ازرع جميلا.

ازرع جميلا ولو في غير موضعه.

ما خاب قط جميل أينما زرعا.

ان الجميل وان طال الزمان به.

فليس يحصده إلا الذي زرعا.

يا ويلي يا ويلي يا معلم على الصدعات قلبي.

LAWYER: . . . cannot be prosecuted by the ICC. Theoretically, the US soldiers could be prosecuted in Canada under the Crimes Against Humanity and War Crimes Act. It is likely that the prosecutor would not pursue this matter because the perpetrators are not present in Canada, and the victims were not Canadian citizens. They had no connection to Canada at the time of their death.

The same text translated into Arabic is projected onto the screen.

ليس هنالك أية صلاحية لأي محكمة كندية في هذه المسألة لأن الجريمة وقعت في بلد أجنبي وليس في مقاطعة كندية لم توقع الولايات المتحدة على معاهدة روما التي أسست للمحكمة الجزائية الدولية ،لهذا، وبشكل عام لا يمكن محاكمة الجنود الأميركان في المحاكم الكندية ، نظريا يمكن رفع دعوى على الجنود الأميركان في كندا ليحاكموا استنادا الى قانون الجرائم ضد الانسانية او قانون جرائم الحرب ، ولكن من المرجح أن الادعاء العام لن يفعل هذا لأن المجرمين غير موجودين في كندا والضحايا لم يكونوا مواطنين كنديين ولم يكونوا مقيمين في كندا حين وقوع الجريمة، أي لم يكن للضحايا حيث قتلوا أي علاقة بكندا

Sorry.

The three Dakhels gather their documents from the Lawyer's desk, carefully handing them to each other, from the closest to the desk to the last in line. They take a few steps away from the Lawyer's desk, stop, turn and look at him one last time.

Sorry.

The three Dakhels leave the stage. The Lawyer rings the bell.

Next client, please.

The end.

A Dialogue Between
Nada Humsi and Diana Manole

DIANA MANOLE: In 2007, I wrote a play, *Me . . . here! Me . . . happy!*, which talked about the experiences of several newly arrived immigrants. Lebanese-bornMajdi Bou-Matar, the founder of the MT Space in Kitchener, Ontario, decided to pro-duce and direct it as part of the company's Theatre for Social Change Program. This is how we met, as you were one of the first- or second-generation Canadian actors performing in that show. In that context, your non-Canadian accent felt natural. Yet, my perception suddenly changed when you invited me to see *Black Spring*, written and directed by Hazim Kamaledin, an Arab-Belgian play-wright, and co-produced by the MT Space and TG Cactusbluem (Belgium), also in Kitchener, in 2013. In this show, you performed the only two speaking characters, the American journalist Hillary Ridders and the Iraqi writer Ishtar Kamaledin. As I was working on an academic article* about this production, I asked you what then I considered *the* crucial question: "How did you feel per-forming an American character with an accent?" Do you remember what your first response was?

NADA HUMSI: *(laughing)* Yep: "What accent?"

MANOLE: Indeed! Your subsequent response is a beautifully articulated plea for the actor's seemingly unlimited opportunities in the increasingly multicultural global theatre. You said:

> I'm an actress—I can play a tree, a bird, an old woman. I didn't care at all about my accent. Never wanted to learn the Canadian accent because I'm above that. I know that you can't make an American speak Arabic like

---

* "Accented Actors: From Stage to Stages via a Convenience Store."

an Arab; you can't make a Russian speak English like an Englishman; you can't ask a tulip to become a jasmine. Accent shouldn't matter. If the time comes to feel that accent matters, that means that I failed as an artist doing the kind of art I want to do and do what others want me to do. (Manole, "Accented" 270)

Has your attitude toward foreign accents on stage changed?

HUMSI: No, not really. Yet, it depends on what play you stage and in what way. If it's *Romeo and Juliet* and all actors are Canadian-born and speak standard Canadian English, except for Romeo and Juliet who have different accents, their accent is a red flag. It could be political, religious, or else. However, if the entire cast has different cultural backgrounds and accents—Asian, Middle Eastern, African, or else—the message is in the casting itself. This is part of the MT Space's mandate and it's meant to emphasize human similarities through difference.

MANOLE: In addition to performing numerous and very successful speaking roles, you also are the first female professional mime in Syria, your home country. You wrote and performed *The Option* (1988), a monodrama directed by Riad Ismat, which toured Syria, Egypt, Japan, and the United States. In this context, what do *words on stage* mean for you?

HUMSI: I wrote *The Option* when I was quite young and, just like the main character, I rebelled. Hana is a university student who writes poetry, truly bad poetry, but hopes to become a famous poet with thousands of people attending her readings. She plans to leave her parents' house because they pressure her to live as they have lived, get married, get a job, have kids, and so on. While she is packing, she wonders what will become of her if she follows the traditional way or if she goes on her own way. She samples all the options ahead of her, sharing them with the people around her and also learning about their fates. None of them seems a good option and she collapses, calling for her mother like a child. So, the show consisted of words, lots of mime, and dance. It used all skills I had at the time, even playing karate at one point.

By the way, this show was broadcast on TV in Syria. In 2005, during a short visit back home, I met a former political prisoner who was released after fourteen years. He told me that the prisoners saw *The Option* on TV and then created a song about me being stronger than the strongest of them. Did you know "Lili Marleen" was a popular song in the Nazi prisons?

MANOLE: Yes, of course!

HUMSI: Well, I was the "Lili Marleen" of Syrian prisons without knowing, haha-haha. Yes, *The Option* also has words, words that are an organic part of the whole. Humans and other creatures are both physical and aural; even trees make sounds when their branches are moved by the wind. On stage, I think the words are needed only when the physical action is not enough; in theatre, we need first *to see*, then *to hear* the story through music, sounds, and words. Still, a word can be as powerful as a gaze—they all, together, tell the story.

MANOLE: Since September 1999, you have lived in Canada—a multicultural country—worked with artists with various cultural backgrounds, and performed for multicultural audiences. Has this experience changed your view of theatre?

HUMSI: Yes! Since immigrating, I feel responsible for how I represent on stage my Syrian culture. Many immigrants succeed in their theatre careers here by portraying their birth countries as exotic and funny when compared to the West. They ignore the thin line between exposing their culture to be *laughed at* and presenting it authentically. This is a very sensitive area and I always try to be aware of its dangers. In addition, making theatre back home was like some kind of a prophecy, a self-sacrifice meant to entertain but also to increase awareness and provoke the audience to make changes for a better society. The mainstream theatre in Canada focuses more on entertainment and the subjects do not necessarily address the urgent issues of our time. The "prophecy" is rarely a priority. Or accepting the fact that Shakespeare, as well as Shaw and other classics, aren't relevant anymore "as is." The independent theatres do send their messages, but they might be very different from the ones needed in my home country. For instance, legalizing pot might have been a "hot" issue here in Canada, but the most important problems back in Syria are political. However, I think I've become more flexible in how I see theatre. At the very end, it's like cooking: we put the ingredients, spices, and effort together and who knows what comes out!

MANOLE: Theatre and cooking! What an original comparison: theatre as nour-ishment, as food for thought, but also for the heart! Has anything also changed in your acting style because you are now performing in English, your second language?

HUMSI: Somewhat. On one hand, when I feel the words, I feel them in Arabic. Then I say them in English. I've noticed that my pace has become slower because

I need more time to utter the English words clearly. I also need more time to make sure Canadian audiences are getting my point. On the other hand, human bodies preserve culture. There are certain physical and vocal codes that are familiar to people from the same culture. Back home, when I had to perform an old woman, for example, I searched for real people as inspiration who weren't necessarily common, although it would have been easy to adopt popular clichés. In Canada, however, I'd happily perform the Syrian older woman archetype, adding some nuances to make her authentic. Yes, I'd like to introduce her to the audiences here.

MANOLE: I hope this opportunity will arise soon! In 2015, you invited me to IMPACT, a festival produced by the MT Space, to see another show: *My Name Is Dakhel Faraj* (MNIDF), which you wrote and directed for the Kitchener-Waterloo Arab-Canadian Theatre (KW-ACT). This Docudrama, included in this collection, re-enacts the real-life story of Dakhel Faraj, a political refugee from Iraq. What triggered this project?

HUMSI: In 2011, I met Dakhel in Kitchener and became very passionate about telling his story and giving a voice to those who experienced similar tragedies: living through the horrors of two wars (the Iraq-Iran war between 1980 and 1988, and the American-led invasion of Iraq in 2003), losing his father and two sons, getting shot in the legs, and then fleeing Iraq to end up living on disability benefits in Kitchener, Ontario.

MANOLE: It must had been difficult for him to recall these events. How did you go about recording his story?

HUMSI: I asked him to give me the photos that he brought with him from Iraq. Then, we followed the same pattern: I invited him to my place, offered him a drink, handed him one photo at a time, and asked him to tell me about it. He was speaking, I was typing and typing. As he grew more intense, he told me more and more things. I wrote down most of them. After a few sessions, I had seventy-five pages to work on.

MANOLE: And then?

HUMSI: I worked on the play for almost one year. I put the events in chronological order and asked him further questions to clarify some details. It became a very, very long script. In 2014, I workshopped this draft with a group of actors and decided to keep only three plot lines: the story of Dakhel's extended family, the death of his sons and father, and the meetings with a Canadian lawyer in an attempt to have the US soldiers who killed them charged for war crimes.

MANOLE: After you finished writing the script, what determined that you would also direct it?

HUMSI: I felt from the beginning that it was *my* play and *my* message to tell the world. It came to me in one package, together with the idea of how to stage the show: including Dakhel's personal photos as video projections and having three actors portray him in three languages. But I wasn't totally alone. Gary Kirkham, a well-known Canadian playwright, made several suggestions regarding the script and answered some of my questions. He was very helpful. For example, Gary inspired me to insert short flashbacks of the disastrous incident during the previous happy times scenes, foreshadowing the tragedy in Dakhel's family. The audience was meant to understand them only toward the end of the show.

MANOLE: Did your rich and diverse acting experience influence your work on MNIDF as a director?

HUMSI: I guess, yes. Sometimes, while editing the script, I secretly had to "jump" into a scene and perform all characters to feel them in my body. Also, mime taught me the importance of isolating and completing an action, of big and small movements, and especially of pauses. In rehearsals, I also discovered that acting skills differ from one actor to another. Some couldn't organically hold a long pause or a long gaze for five seconds. I had to count for them. And once, when I asked an actor to be himself while saying a line, not the character, his reply was: "What do you mean?"

MANOLE: As an actress, has your relationship to spoken words on stage changed after writing and directing MNIDF?

HUMSI: It didn't change, but it has become clearer to me that the simplest, most common sentence, like "He didn't lock the door," can be important. As a director, I didn't want *unclear* scenes, even though I intended some of them to be ambiguous for a little while, until their meaning was revealed to the audience. Same with words, I didn't like *unclear* words. Now, I don't search for *good* lines, but for *clear* lines in a play.

MANOLE: Quite a change in perspective! Through its experimental style and *clear* message, MNIDF is proof of the artistic freedom and socio-political responsibility of multicultural and, in this case, multilingual theatre.* As you already mentioned, the main character, Dakhel Faraj, is played by three actors in three languages: Arabic, English, and ASL. This is one of the main features that gives this show its performative, semiotic, and cultural uniqueness. What informed this choice?

HUMSI: I wanted as many people as possible to understand how cruel it is to conduct a war on other people: to destroy their homeland, kill their children, and send them as disabled refugees around the world. I wanted this message to be heard but also seen across any physical barriers. I was inspired by one of Al-Mutanabbi's poems, who once described himself as:

"I, who the blind could read my literature
And I, who the deaf could hear my words."

MANOLE: Because you mentioned him, let me note that Al-Mutanabbi was an Iraqi poet from the tenth century. How did his lines come to your mind? Is his work still familiar to Arab people?

HUMSI: We learn about those old works in school, but their lines have become part of our popular culture. If you say, "You too, Brutus?" most people in the Western world would understand the meaning behind this phrase. Everywhere in the Arab world, one can find verses from the Kor'an, such as "إن احسنتم أحسنتم لأنفسكم وإن أسأتم فلها" [If you do good, you do it for yourself; if you do bad, it comes back to you], or citations from Prophet Muhammad's teachings, like "الجنة تحت أقدام الأمهات" [Paradise is under mothers' feet]. Some are often mentioned in daily life or written and framed on walls in stores, offices, houses. For example, another very well-known line by Al-Mutanabbi is: "ما كل ما يتمنى المرء يدركه، تجري الرياح بما لا تشتهي السفن" [Life doesn't fulfill people's every wish like the sea wind sometimes blows against a ship]. They enrich the mind, emphasize human values, and make the world more beautiful.

MANOLE: Let's go back to MNIDF's three languages. Why did you decide to use Arabic, a choice somewhat unusual in a show produced and performed in an English-language theatre environment?

---

* For more on this topic, please see Manole, "Resignifying Multilingualism in Canadian Accented Theatre."

HUMSI: Arabic is the language of the story itself. At the time of the tragic incident, Dakhel Faraj was an Arab man living in Iraq, an Arabic country. It is the language in which Dakhel told me, Nada, about this tragedy, the language of his memories, his pain, his words. Arabic is also the first language of many immigrants and refugees with similar stories and pain. As audiences, they needed to hear it in their tongue to feel its authenticity. They also share the history and the cultural codes of the same nation, codes that have been created over thousands of years. I added some details into the Arabic lines, one extra word here and there, or a sentence, or a quotation from a poem, to "poke" emotions and memories in the hearts and minds of the Arabic audience. In addition, Arabic is my mother tongue; I feel life in Arabic, and it was a given to "feel" the play first in Arabic and then let it spread into English and American Sign Language.

MANOLE: Please give me an example of additional details provided only in Arabic.

HUMSI: The poet Muzaffar Al-Nawab, among others, is very well known, loved, and respected by Arab readers. In English, the script only says:

EDF & ASL: Muzaffar Al-Nawab, one of Iraq's most famous and influential poets. Imprisoned with my uncle Salman. Al-Nawab escaped, my uncle didn't.

In Arabic, the untranslated line is longer; then, the Musician and ADF sing together a very well-known poem by Muzaffar Al-Nawab "Marrena Beekom Hamad." Again, no translation into English is included in the script.

EDF and ASL mime picking up books and looking at each of them. EDF shows a book by poet Muzaffar Al-Nawab to ADF.

ADF: *(about the imaginary book in his hand)* مظفر النواب. انحبس ويّا عمي سلمان.
وهرب. مرينا بيكم حمد واحنا بقطار الليل

[Muzaffar Al-Nawab was imprisoned together with my uncle Salman, then he escaped . . . The night train passed by you, Hamad.]

The Musician and ADF sing the poem "Marrena Beekom Hamad" by Iraqi poet Muzaffar Al-Nawab, included in the imaginary book they hold.

مرينا بيكم حمد واحنا بقطار الليل

واسمعنا دق قهوة، وشمينا ريحة هيل

يا ريل صيح بقهر صيحة عشق يا ريل

[We passed by you, Hamad, on the night train.
We heard the pestle grinding coffee, we smelt the cardamom.
Oh train, shout in sorrow the shout of love, oh train!]

The Arabic audience would understand that both Muzaffar Al-Nawab, the well-known poet, and Dakhel's uncle, a less famous intellectual, were imprisoned together because they were members of the same political party, the Communist Party. They were only two of the many people persecuted by Saddam Hussein's regime.

MANOLE: As an immigrant, I surely understand the differences between the emotional weight of first and, respectively, second languages. However, it is likely that some (or maybe most?) of your spectators in Kitchener didn't understand Arabic. In this context, why did you decide against translating the additional Arabic details and including them in the English lines spoken on stage?

HUMSI: Those small additions are based on common codes that Arabic-speaking audiences understand without any explanation needed. Translating them wouldn't have enriched the English text but rather confused the audience. It seemed neither a good practical solution nor an artistic one. A play has its own rhythm and mood. I chose to protect its integrity. Think of this: what is more artistic and challenging—to write a play in one language but insert the same lines in two other languages, one after each other? Or, to integrate the languages and the story? In MNIDF, three languages and three actors are telling one story! Moreover, the three actors are also playing all the other characters. How could it be possible to have simultaneous translation?!

MANOLE: Agreed! Yet, why did you decide to tell the same story also in English?

HUMSI: The show was produced for the audiences in Kitchener, born in Canada or elsewhere, all of whom supposedly understand English. It surely wasn't produced only for the Arab spectators! English is also part of the story. The US soldiers who killed Dakhel's family members spoke English. They also listened to songs in English, such as "Bodies" (often called "Let the Bodies Hit the Floor"), which was popular among the American troops at the time of the invasion of

Iraq. When Dakhel told me his story, he actually used some English words, although he doesn't speak English. For example, when one of the soldiers saw Karam, his eight-year-old son, dead in his mother's arms, he handed her a chocolate bar and said, "Sorry!" Dakhel said the word "sorry" to me in English, in the way the soldier said it to Sabriyeh, his wife.

MANOLE: Horrendous! And this became a very intense moment in the show. You included a third version of Dakhel who communicates in American Sign Language (ASL). How did you come to this choice?

HUMSI: Silence is also a part of the story, as millions of such stories haven't been heard in any language! The victims were silenced; they couldn't scream their pain, but they physically live it every day. Just like ASL, a silent language for silent people, to be told physically and with effort. It's the third language of this story, the language of the silent cries of the victims. Dakhel's real-life tragedy is so loud, although it had been silenced; it's so painful and so present, it's the story of millions who have only silence to express themselves.

MANOLE: Are there also differences between Dakhel's lines in English and in ASL?

HUMSI: ASL does not use the same grammar as English. For example, the sentence "The door is open" becomes "door open." The ASL actresses shortened the script, adapting it into ASL, both for the 2014 workshop and for the 2015 full production.

MANOLE: Is the opposite also true? Are some things only expressed in ASL, like in the Arabic version?

HUMSI: No. ASL goes to the basics—there was no chattering or adding details. But there were differences. For instance, the English- and ASL-speaking actors (EDF and ASL, respectively, as I identify them in the script) play together the gardening scene. When ASL mimes cutting the grass with a mower, EDF says/signs to her in ASL: "There is no mower," and mimes throwing her a shovel. This is a detail that only people who know ASL may notice. But it integrates ASL into the show and the audience can see the two actors communicating in ASL on stage.

MANOLE: Did you also think of potential deaf audiences and increasing the show's accessibility?

HUMSI: Accessibility is important in every theatre. We build wheelchair-accessible paths or describe what happens on stage for visually impaired spectators. Even on TV, we sometimes see a person translating the news into ASL. If I wanted to translate the play live into ASL, I had two choices: I could've had a person standing on the side of the stage (or on a screen) translating the lines; or I could've had that person acting in the show in ASL, just like in the other two languages. My choice was to have ASL, the language of silence, as an essential part of the play with the same weight as English and Arabic. I also didn't want to translate the exact sentences and have them being said one after the other. There are in fact three versions of the play—one in each language—for three kinds of audiences who can follow the same story, as it's being acted by three actors playing one character in three languages at the same time.

MANOLE: At my proposal, Yana has agreed to include MNIDF in this volume. Did you consider publishing it before this opportunity arose?

HUMSI: No. When I wrote this play, I didn't think beyond its production. When you asked me to publish it I was a bit uncertain. After you offered to work with me and guide me in making it ready, I trusted the play could be published.

MANOLE: Yes, we worked together on several drafts and focused on making everything clear for future readers, especially when it came to the stage directions. How do you feel about this rather long process and the new version of MNIDF?

HUMSI: I feel close, even closer to the text we prepared for publication. Working on it was a challenging playwriting experience but also an emotional one. It made me recall and in fact relive the performance to be able to clarify the stage directions. In the production script, I only made very short notes because I was deeply involved in the process and didn't need more than quick reminders. Now, I feel as if I've described the show like a movie, as it was "recorded" in my memory.

MANOLE: Why did you decide to leave the lines in Arabic untranslated in the print version?

HUMSI: The answer is simple: *My Name Is Dakhel Faraj* is a play in three languages and no language was translated into another language in the show. Each language must stay *as is* also in print.

MANOLE: However, publishing the script required you to make some decisions about the lines in Arabic. Can you please explain?

HUMSI: During the interviews, Dakhel spoke in colloquial Iraqi Arabic, and this is how I recorded his story. Afterwards, whenever I decided to add a sentence or more, I asked him to change it into colloquial Iraqi Arabic. I understand both Classical Arabic and colloquial Arabic, but my colloquial Arabic is Syrian, and we pronounce a bit differently.

I'll give you an example. The sentence "I talked about him" in Classical Arabic is "أنا حكيت عنه" with the pronunciation "Ana Ha'kaitu An'hu." In colloquial Iraqi, phonetic writing will make it somehow like "آني حتشيت عنا," with the pronunciation "A'nee ha'chet an'nah," In the type of transliteration I used, I wrote "اني حكيت عنا/A'nee Ha'ket An'na." All Iraqis will know they pronounce "k" as "ch. If I replace the "k" with "ch," to be linguistically accurate, other Arabs may not understand the word. I don't want to confuse you. My point is that I have written exactly what Dakhel said with Arabic letters in a way that every Arab person can read. Iraqi readers may approve my choices as they will understand everything, but other Arab readers might not have understood the Iraqi way of writing colloquial Arabic.

MANOLE: Very interesting and surely very useful for future readers. Would you agree to it if another director wanted to stage it? Would you have special requirements?

HUMSI: I would happily agree. No requirements.

MANOLE: What would you like to tell readers before they start reading MNIDF?

HUMSI: Many things—a whole book may not be enough! For example, do you remember when the war against Iraq happened? Do you remember a little dot moving toward the middle of the television screen, as if to its target, then a little splash, and then the report that a terrorist target was destroyed, a target that was dangerous for the safety of the US and the entire world?!! Do I have to explain this? That "target" could had been a village full of children, women, animals, birds, and plants. Of life!

Yes, I want to tell the future readers that this story may not be the most horrible story of all. I chose it because I had access to it. I was able to listen to it and then tell it. Whatever happens on the planet is our responsibility, all of us, but it seems that human nature is to ignore the harm being done as long as it's not yet *here*, in our front yard.

Works Cited

Manole, Diana. "Accented Actors: From Stage to Stages via a Convenience Store." *Theatre Research in Canada/Recherches théâtrales au Canada*, vol. 36, no. 2, 2015, pp. 255–73.

---. "Resignifying Multilingualism in Canadian Accented Theatre." *Performing Exile: Foreign Bodies*, edited by Judith Rudakoff, Intellect, 2017, pp. 233–50.

"In Sundry Languages"

Toronto Laboratory Theatre

"In Sundry Languages"[*] is a multilingual performance originally devised from personal stories, encounters, experiences, and ideas by Clayton Gray, Юрий Ружьёв/Yury Ruzhyev (Rouge), Felicia Nelson, Mark Dallas, Lyla Belsey, Sepideh Shariati/سپیده شریعتی, Amy Packwood, Мария Прозорова/Maria Prozorova, 손연지/Danielle Son, 高子莹/Ziying Gloria Gao, Mario Lourenço, 李明颖/Joy Lee-Ryan, and Արա Բաբայանց/Art Babayants, with dramaturgical support provided by Gabrielle Houle. Two workshop performances took place in May 2015 and March 2016 at the Centre for Drama, Theatre and Performance Studies, University of Toronto.

The production was redeveloped in 2017 for the Toronto Fringe Festival by a few members of the original cast as well as new cast members: Arfina, Ahmed Moneka/احمد مونیکا, Lavinia Salinas, and Angela Sun, along with dramaturg Shelley Liebembuk/שלי ליבמבוק, video dramaturg Montgomery Martin, assistant dramaturg Cristina Kindl, lighting designer Paul J. Stoesser, and production manager Giorelle Diokno. In September 2017, Deniz Başar took over the dramaturgy of the show to prepare it for presentation at Caminos, a festival organized by Toronto's Aluna Theatre. All presentations of *"In Sundry Languages"* were directed by Art Babayants.

---

[*] *"In Sundry Languages"* is a quote from Thomas Kyd's *Spanish Tragedy*.

Prologue: *"Zanoza v zadnits'e"* / *Pain in ahse*

House lights go down to fifty percent, lights up on the apron. A house door opens and Yury comes in carrying his headshot and resume. The casting director (Clayton) is invisible to the audience.

YURY/AUDITIONING: *(looking for the casting director)* Hello!

CLAYTON/CASTING DIRECTOR: *(from the house, hidden in the dark)* Hi!

YURY: How are you?

CLAYTON: Good. You?

YURY: Pretty good, too. Thanks.

Yury gives Clayton his headshot and resume.

CLAYTON: Good.

Looking at Yury's resume, squints.

Yury Ru . . . zi-yev?

YURY: *(pronounces his name correctly in Russian)* Юрий Ружьёв.

CLAYTON: Yury Ruchi-off?

YURY: Ружьёв.

CLAYTON: *(bastardizing the name even more)* Rouge-if.

YURY: Yep. This is perfect.

CLAYTON: What is it? German?

YURY: No, it's Russian. I'm Russian . . . and Canadian.

Raising his hand in an ironic gesture.

Proud!

CLAYTON: Okay, Mr. *(stumbles and produces by far the worst version of Yury's last name)* Ryouche-yov . . . Slate for the camera, please.

A projection of the live feed comes up on the screen. Live feed focus: zoom in on Yury's face.

YURY: *(looking into the camera)* I'm Yury Ruzhyev. Five-foot-nine. I'm reading for the part of Jeff.

Does a turn for the camera. Then turns to Clayton.

Excuse me, I'm wondering if you could tell me more about the character.

CLAYTON: *(annoyed)* Didn't you receive the breakdown?

YURY: I did. Thank you. But it just says he's thirty-five—there's only that much you can do with that.

CLAYTON: Hm . . . well . . . a Russian mobster, dumping his girlfriend. How about that?

YURY: Thank you very much.

Prepares. Looks at Clayton.

CLAYTON: *(slightly annoyed)* No-no-no! Don't look at me! Look at the camera.

YURY: Sure.

Prepares. Looks at the camera. Suddenly slaps himself hard.

CLAYTON: *(puzzled)* What? What is that?

YURY: Wha . . .? Ah . . . *(hastily)* This is the Grotowski method.

Looks at Clayton but gets no understanding or empathy.

He was a Polish theatre dir . . . It just helps . . . helps you get into a character . . . faster . . . I took a worksh . . .

No reaction from Clayton again.

Waste of money, anyway! If you don't want me to do it, I won't do it.

Clayton shrugs as if to say "whatever."

(prepares, looks at the camera, slaps himself) "That's what we do! We fight . . . "*

Yury recites his audition monologue. He is doing a great job showing range and commitment. Clayton slowly comes up on stage, looks into the camera. He is dissatisfied.

CLAYTON: *(interrupting)* Okay, okay . . . What's with the accent, man?

YURY: Sorry?

CLAYTON: What accent is that?

YURY: It's . . . mine.

CLAYTON: I need a Russian accent. You know what Russian people sound like?

YURY: *(ironically)* Yes, I think I have a pretty good idea.

CLAYTON: Good. So?

Yury is visibly uncomfortable. Prepares again. Slaps himself.

YURY: Zat is what we do.

CLAYTON: No!

He is on the edge.

You CAN do the Russian accent, Mr. Rouge-ief, can't you?

YURY: Yes, I am an actor. I can do anything.

Clayton, in indignation, gives Yury a gesture to start over.

(prepares and slaps himself) Zet is vot ve do . . .

---

* In this version, Yury used a monologue from the romantic drama *The Notebook* (New Line Cinema, 2004). Later in the scene, Clayton is trying to perform the same monologue but in heavily accented Russian. This monologue could be substituted by any other audition monologue.

CLAYTON: No! No!! No!!!!

Jumps up in fury. Approaches the stage.

Live feed: Clayton's profile enters the frame and moves close to Yury's face.

(in a horribly exaggerated but recognizably "Hollywoodish" Russian accent) Zyet . . . ees vot vyee do!

Pauses, looks at Yury, waiting for him to repeat.

YURY: *(visibly uncomfortable)* Zat . . .

CLAYTON: Zet . . . yees vot vyee do.

YURY: Zet . . . Ees vot vee doo!

CLAYTON: Vyee fight!

YURY: Vyee fight!

CLAYTON: Yoo coll me pain in ahse . . . Ant I coll yoo an arroguent sahn of beetch.

YURY: Yoo coll me pain in ahse . . . Ant I coll yoo an arrogent sahn of beetch.

Yury slaps himself. Simultaneously, Clayton slaps himself.

Sudden power switch: the self-slap turns Yury into the director and Clayton into the auditioning actor. Clayton is now auditioning in Russian, which he speaks with a thick anglophone accent. He remains in the shot. Yury moves toward the camera, assuming the position of director while correcting Clayton's pronunciation. Live feed: zoom in on Clayton's face.

CLAYTON: My tolko ee delayem, chto rugaemsya.

YURY: ругаемся!

CLAYTON: ruga . . . em . . . sya . . . Ty nazivaesh men'ya naglym kozlom.

YURY: КА-злом!

CLAYTON: КА . . . zlom . . . A ya nazyvayu tebya zanozoi v zadnitse.

Yury suddenly comes uncomfortably close to Clayton.

YURY: *(in perfect Russian, pretending to be a gangster)* Мы только и делаем, что ругаемся. Ты называешь меня наглым козлом, а называю тебя занозой в заднице.

Spits through his teeth, which completes his portrayal of a nouveau-riche mafioso.

Clayton is paralyzed.

Вот как надо играть русских мафиози! Слейт для камеры, пжалста.*

CLAYTON: *(turning around for the slate)* John White, reading for Jeff.

YURY: Спсиба, да свиданья!†

CLAYTON: Do svidaniya!

YURY: *(sarcastically)* Привет бойфренду!‡

Clayton leaves through the house.

(turns toward the house, yells) NEEEEEXT!

Abrupt blackout.

---

* This is how you play the Russian mafia. Slate for the camera, please!

† Thanks. Bye!

‡ Say hi to your boyfriend.

Scene One: Turn Off Your Cellphones!

It is pitch black. The audience is unaware of the actors seated in various locations in the house. Suddenly, one of the performers begins the following announcement in Hebrew (or any other language): "Dear friends, we're about to begin. Please, turn your cellphones off. And please, enjoy the show!" Another actor joins her by saying the same announcement in another language, then more actors join speaking all the other languages of the production with the exception of English. Some are speaking their first language, some their second/third, but all make an effort to transform the familiar sounds of the language into pseudo-ritualistic howling, which makes the words very difficult, almost impossible, to decipher. Eventually, the overlapping languages create a sort of terrifying Artaudian soundscape, which wraps around the audience and to which the pianist seated stage left starts adding a cacophony of high and low notes.

With the first notes of the piano, the ghost light located upstage centre turns on. The actors begin moving from the house toward the light, bending and contorting their bodies, and trying to reach the "ghost" light. Their voices grow louder and louder—the cacophony of sounds becomes almost unbearable. As one of them is about to touch the bulb, the light dies abruptly.

ACTOR 1: *(in Hebrew)* גבירותי ורבותי, ההצגה עומדת להתחיל. נא לכבות טלפונים סלולריים.

ACTOR 2: *(in French, overlapping with previous languages)* Chers amis! Nous allons commencer. Veuillez éteindre vos cellulaires. Bon spectacle!

ACTOR 3: *(in Russian)* Дорогие друзья! Спектакль начинается. Пожалуйста, отключите свои мобильные телефоны. Приятного просмотра!

ACTOR 4: *(in Spanish)* Señoras y señores, el espectáculo va a comenzar. Por favor apaguen sus teléfonos celulares. ¡Disfrútenlo!

ACTOR 5: *(in Portuguese)* Senhoras e senhores o espetáculo vai começar. Por favor desliguem os telemóveis e desfrutem do espetáculo!

ACTOR 6: *(in Armenian)* Հարգելի ընկերներ: Ներկայացումը շուտով կսկսվի: Խնդրում ենք անջատել ձեր բջջային հեռախոսները: Մաղթում ենք հաճելի դիտում:

ACTOR 7: *(in Cantonese)* 演出馬上就要開始啦， 請關閉你嘅手機， 請欣賞。

ACTOR 8: *(in Mandarin)* 演出马上就要开始了， 请关掉你的手机， 请欣赏。

As actors are about to touch the ghost light, it suddenly dies.

Scene Two: *"Where are you from?"* Interlude A

The piano accompaniment changes abruptly referencing the era of Modernism and silent film. One option would be playing Charlie Chaplin's "Je cherche après Titine" song, performed in French gibberish (from Modern Times*). An old film projection flickering light colours the following interlude. On the balcony above the stage there is Yury and Ahmed. Both are doing a pseudo soft-shoe routine, at the same time artificially stretching their smiles as much as they can.*

YURY: *(in an exaggerated Received Pronunciation accent)* Hello, neighbour! Your garden looks lovely!

AHMED: Thanks.

YURY: Say, neighbour, I've been meaning to ask you a question.

AHMED: Go for it.

YURY: Where are you from?

AHMED: I'm from here.

YURY: I mean, where are you *really* from?

AHMED: Toronto. T-dot. The Six.

YURY: No, where did you come from?

AHMED: Ah . . . North York.

YURY: No. Where are your *people* from?

Music breaks off.

AHMED: Africa!

YURY: Africa?

Pause for the punchline.

What a lovely country!

Scene Three: Home Country— The Sportscaster

Mario shows up dressed as a Portuguese football (soccer) fan. He is also wearing a red clown nose. Mario is reporting from the European football cup. It is the final match: Portugal vs. France. Mario speaks into a microphone. He starts speaking in a regular "reporter" voice, but as the scene progresses, he gets more and more engaged, eventually becomes aggressive, and starts spewing out nationalist pro-Portugal slogans, slowly turning into a fascist bully.

MARIO: *(to the camera)* Muito boa noite senhores telespectadores. Bem-vindos ao campeonato Europeu dois mil e dezasseis. Hoje, aqui no estádio parisiense a selecção Portuguesa defronta a selecção Francesa. A selecção Francesa e a selecção Portuguesa. Venham dai, somos milhares de ouvintes espalhados pelo mundo inteiro, os melhores ouvintes de futebol.

(to the audience, following the soccer match) Eu tenho indicação de que o jogo vai começar. Costinha vai dar o pontapé de saída, remata lá para frente, para a grande área . . . Ronaldo apanha a bola, perde para a selecção Francesa. O remate para frente . . . Ronaldo, corta a selecção Francesa. Franca a avançar lá para frente . . . Apanha Carvalho e corre lá para frente. Carvalho vai na luta com Pierre, a lutar, a lutar, a lutar, ressalto da bola, bola sobra para Pepe. Pepe toca na bola, esta a brincar, depois perde a bola para a selecção Francesa. A selecção Francesa, ali, a avançar, a entrar na grande área de Portugal, olha o cruzamento, olha o cruzamento, olha o cruzamento! Milagre! Oh Pepe, andas a brincar com a bola, pá!

(to the camera) Senhores telespectadores, momentos de aflição aqui no estádio parisiense. Podíamos ter sofrido o golo, o Pepe a brincar com a Bola. Mas vamos ver a resposta de Portugal. Eu só tenho uma coisa para dizer aos Franceses. Eles podem ser os campeões dos champignons, la baguete, café o'lei, mas nós vamos ser os campeões da Europa! Já o meu avô dizia, porque e que eles chamam aquilo fromage quando e só queijo.

(to the audience, following the game, getting more excited, rowdy) Senhores telespectadores, tenho indicação de que costinha já vai ali a meio campo, perde a bola para a selecção Francesa, bola colocada lá para a frente, para o intermédio, corta a defesa de Portugal, é o remate para fora da área . . . França de volta para o meio campo Português, e agora, ali vem a selecção Francesa, a tentar colocar lá na área, atenção é perigoso, é Pierre, vai cruzar pela área, é perigoso, vai cruzar, Pierre, já cruzou, olha o cabeceamento, tira, tira, tira tira . . . Bandeirola no ar! Senhores telespectadores é fora de jogo! *(in an exaggerated French accent)* J'aime Portugal. C'est per moi, c'est pour toi, c'est pour vous!

(to the camera) Momentos difíceis para Portugal, aqui no estadio Parisiense. Foi fora de jogo, e vamos aguardar com certeza a resposta de Portugal. Tenho indicação de que.

(to the audience, almost yelling, getting aggressive as Portugal scores the winning goal) A meio campo Ronaldo solta a bola para Eder, posse de bola para Eder. Eder lá na grande área francesa, pode chutar, vai chutar, chuta, chuta, chuta, chuta . . . chutou . . . golo, golooooo!!! Já lá mora, já lá mora, já lá mora! Campeões, campeões, nós somos campeões! Golo! Vamos para a festa, gritem Portugal, Portugal, Portugal, Portugal!*

---

* *(into the camera)* Good evening, gentlemen, viewers! Welcome to the European Championship 2016. Today, here at the Parisian stadium, the Portuguese team faces the French team. There are thousands of viewers scattered all over the world, the best football viewers!!! I am getting a sign that the game is about to start. *(Looks at the audience, following the game, leaves the camera frame.)* Costinha initiates the kick off—he kicks the ball forward, into the French big box. Ronaldo picks up the ball, but loses to the other team. They kick it forward . . . Ronaldo, blocks the French guys. France advancing forward . . . picks up Carvalho and he runs forward. Carvalho goes in the fight with the opponent—Pierre—fighting, fighting, fighting, bouncing of the ball, rebouncing of the ball to Pepe. Pepe plays the ball, is playing, then loses the ball to the French team. The French team, there, is advancing, entering the big area of Portugal, look at the cross, look at the cross, look at the cross! Miracle! Oh Pepe, you're playing with the ball, pa!

(back to the camera) Dear viewers, moments of affliction here in the Parisian stadium. We could have suffered the goal—Pepe was playing with the ball. But let's see the counterattack from Portugal. I only have one thing to say to the French. They can be the champions of *(adopt a ridiculous French accent)* champignons, la baguette, café au lait, *(drops the accent),* but we'll be the champions of Europe! My grandfather would say: "Ah, the French. Why do they call it 'fromage' when it is actually 'cheese'?"

(back to watching the game) TV viewers, I have an indication that Costinha is already advancing with the ball to the French midfield . . . loses the ball to the French team, places the ball forward, for the intermediate, blocked *(following the game, getting more excited, rowdy)* the defence of Portugal. And the free kick from outside the area . . . France is back

His chanting becomes more and more animalistic. He falls on the floor, dry humps the floor, gets up, rips his shirt off, yelling, "Já lá mora!!!!" Then he takes out an imaginary gun (folded fingers) and shoots in different directions.

Blackout.

Scene Four: Arrival—Taxi

Arfina is singing "Chamamaha," a Comorian song. She is dressed in a traditional Comorian dress. Yury and Mario bring out two black boxes representing taxi cab seats and place them downstage centre. They leave. Ahmed sits down on the left box—the driver's seat. Live feed: focus on the back of Arfina's head—once she sits down, she will occasionally turn to the camera to provide an acerbic aside in French.

ARFINA: Chamamha, chamamaye
Ni chichiye wagou moina na lime lima
Na voi ke djouwa na voike vouwa na voi ke ou pepo
Ni chichiye wagou moina na lime lima
Ou nou msside oyu limwe gouwe
Li tabouni li lime voumeno vola Mgou redo
Voi tsike mcoloni voi tsi ke mgou na djiye
Massiwa lende oussoni lidje ou fouzou˙

---

to the Portuguese field, and now, here comes the French team, trying to place it in the penalty area, attention! It is dangerous! It is Pierre, he can cross over to the Portuguese goal area, it is dangerous, he can cross, Pierre . . . he crossed!! Oh, the head . . . blocked it out, blocked it out, blocked it out . . . Flag in the air, gentlemen! It is an offside!

(mocking the French) Je t'aime, Portugal. C'est pour moi, c'est pour toi, c'est pour vous!

(to the camera) Difficult moments for Portugal, here in the Parisienne stadium. It was offside, and we are going to wait for Portugal's counterattack. I have an indication that . . . *(to the audience, almost yelling, getting aggressive as Portugal scores the winning goal)* Ronaldo passes the ball over for Eder, possession of the ball for Eder. Eder advancing, enters the French goal area, he can kick, kick, kick, kick, kick, kick . . . kicked . . . goal, goallllllll!!! Ha, ha, ha, ha, ha, ha! Champions, champions! We are champions! Goalllllll! Let's party, shout Portugal—Portugal, Portugal, Portugal!!!

* Patriots! Please hold my child for me to go protest. Rain or shine. The archipelago is going forward and flourishes. Troubles are gone, thanks to God! That there will be no more colonies. That no one will enter.

(notices Ahmed, raises her hand) Taxiii!

Ahmed gets out of the car. His character is struggling with English.

AHMED: Welcome . . . to Canada!

A blank stare from Arfina.

Er . . . Speak English?

ARFINA: Non . . . Français?

AHMED: *(disappointed)* Nooo . . .

ARFINA & AHMED: *(in sync, toward audience, sarcastically)* O Canada!

ARFINA: *(giving him her luggage)* Marahaba.

AHMED: *(very excited)* MARAHABA?!!!! Arabic!!!!

Ahmed gets more excited, switches to Arabic.

ARFINA: *(in horror, aside)* ARABE?!!! *(turns back to Ahmed)* Non!

AHMED: Ah! Okay. Welcome to Canada!

Takes her luggage, puts it into the trunk.

As Arfina sits down, she turns away from the audience, toward the camera, to share her private thoughts in French only.

ARFINA: A peine arrivée et la première personne sur qui je tombe—un couscous! Ils sont partout!*

AHMED: Address?

ARFINA: oh . . . ma daudeur . . .†

Arfina gives him paper with the address and starts humming again.

The one that fights through, please, hold my child for me to go protest.

* I've just arrived and the first person I bump into is . . . a towelhead! They are everywhere!

† "Daughter."

AHMED: ‏لماذا تتظاهر بأنها ليست عربية؟ هل هي تشعر بالخجل أم ماذا؟‏* Daughter . . .

Takes a long time to look at the address.

Please, I need my . . .

Ahmed moves his hand down to reach the glove compartment. He inadvertently brushes her knee.

ARFINA: *(yells)* What you do?! What you do?? *(aside to the camera)* Ces tajines toujours à essayer d'avoir plus d'une femme.†

AHMED: No . . . no not like that . . . please . . . please, me have wife. ‏يعتقدون دائمًا أنك تحاول تغاز لا انا لم اقصد ذلك ، اني متزوج‏‡ . . . this address . . . not good . . . see? This okay . . . but what is this?

ARFINA: *(aside to the camera)* Hm . . . c'est quoi ça encore? Il sait pas lire? Ben oui, c'est pas du taliban. Il comprend pas!§ *(turns back to Ahmed)* Donnes moi . . . hum. Je crois c'est un deux . . .

AHMED: ‏سأصاب بنوبة قلبية بسببها‏ ؟ꞋꞋ

Looks at Arfina's gesture.

Two?

ARFINA: Oui.

Switches to another language she can speak.

Ithnaan.

AHMED: Ithnaan??? No sure.

Enters the address into GPS.

GPS say no address . . . Call your daughter!

---

*   Why is she pretending not to be an Arab? Is she ashamed or something?

†   Those "tajines" always wanna have more than one woman.

‡   They always think you're trying to flirt with them.

§   What again? He can't even read? This is not Taliban. He doesn't get it.

Ɠ   I'll have heart attack because of her.

ARFINA: Non. No phone . . . donne-moi.

Takes Ahmed's glasses and puts them on.

. . . Oui, oui, deux . . .

Ahmed takes his glasses back.

AHMED: GPS not crazy! Please find address or . . .

ARFINA: Pourquoi tu cris?!*

AHMED: †ما!! هذه المرأة! انها ليست بخير. انه مصابه بشيء ما

ARFINA: Pourquoi??! Ah! Ah!!!

AHMED: Please, stop screaming! Not good here! People think I weird! What "alaam fi almoaakhra!"

ARFINA: *(mocking him)* Alaam fi almoaakhra!

AHMED: Ooooh, woman! Alaam fi almoaakhra!

ARFINA: Alaam fi almoaakhra! Toi même!!

BOTH: Alaam fi almoaakhra!!!!

AHMED: Get out from my car!

ARFINA: Oooh non je sors pas!!‡ No no! *(aside to the camera)* Il va pas me faire son terroriste la! J'ai pas peur de lui!§

Ahmed gets to her door.

Non!

She locks her door from the inside, right in front of his face. She turns to the camera.

---

* Why are you yelling?

† This woman! She's not okay. Something is wrong with her!

‡ Nope. I'm not getting out.

§ He is not going to make me a terrorist. I am not afraid of him.

Je savais qu'il allait me voler! Tous des escrocs ces wahidis!"*

AHMED: *(swears in Arabic)* Get out from my car . . .

ARFINA: Non, emmène-moi à ma fille . . .

Ahmed takes her luggage out of the trunk then walks back to his door, swearing in Arabic.

(aside to the camera) Ha, il commence à prier!† *(yells to Ahmed)* Calme-toi! Ne fais pas ton attaque kamikaze! T'as une bombe dans le cul ou quoi?‡

AHMED: *(gets into his seat)* Okay . . . This is the address for your daughter?

ARFINA: Oui!

He throws out the paper with the address.

AHMED: This? . . . look . . .

He throws the paper out of his window.

Arfina screams and runs out of car to fetch the piece of paper. Ahmed immediate drives away. Blackout.

Scene Five: *"Where are you from?"* Interlude B

YURY: Hello, neighbour. Your garden looks lovely!

LAVINIA: Thanks.

YURY: Say neighbour, I've been meaning to ask you a question.

LAVINIA: Go for it.

YURY: Where are you from?

---

*   I knew he wanted to kidnap me! Those Wahids are all scammers!

†   Hah, he is starting to pray!

‡   Calm down! No need for a suicide attack. Do have a bomb in your ass or something?

LAVINIA: I'm from here.

YURY: I mean, where are you *really* from?

LAVINIA: Toronto. T-dot. The Six.

YURY: No, where did you *come* from?

LAVINIA: North York?

YURY: Hm. I mean . . . You speak English real good.

Music breaks off.

LAVINIA: Thank you! I speak English *really well.*

Scene Six: A Newcomer

AHMED: *(voice in the dark)* Newcomer!

He opens the camera shutter. Close up on his tightly closed eye.

I've been touring the city, searching for eye contact.

At first I thought maybe it was because I was a stranger that people didn't look at me. Except Replay: he had that kind look in his eyes and that he gave me the energy to discover a lot of things around me.

Covers the camera with his hand. Then opens it as if documenting different periods of his life.

I came here because I was an actor in a movie that was being screened at TIFF. Cool? Not cool. Because I played a gay person in the movie, I can no longer return to my home country. I was forced to stay here, in the city, in order to save my life.

Covers the camera with his hand. Then opens it again as if it is a new shot.

I didn't speak a word of English. For three months I felt that I was living in a very dark space. I wanted to talk with girls, so body language was what I used to communicate. Some of them would just smile at me, and then leave. Others would invited me to their home, and then would also . . . leave!

Covers the camera with his hand. Then opens it again as if it is a new shot.

There's no energy exchange anywhere here. The one place in the whole city that felt different was Kensington Market. I met some musicians there: they were sitting in a circle and playing in a park in Kensington Market. I walked up to them and I wanted to say:

He moves farther away to allow for a wider shot, starts speaking Iraqi Arabic and gesticulating excitedly. He introduces himself to the musicians.

قادم جديد

منذ فترة طويلة وانا ابحث عن الاتصال بالعين , في البداية فكرت ربما بسبب كنت غريبا الناس لا تنظر الي , ما عدا ريبلي في عينيه تلك النظرة المليئة بالمودة وهذه النظرة اعطتني الكثير من الطاقة لاكتشاف الكثير من الأشياء حولي. على فكرة ريبلي كلب.

جئت الى هنا بسبب كنت ممثلا في فلم عرض في

TIFF

مهرجان تورنتو السينمائي الدولي جيد؟ ليس جيدا! بسبب لعبت دور مثلي الجنس في هذا الفلم، ليس من الحق على الرجوع إلى وطني الأم, لقد جبرت ان ابقى هنا لأحفظ على حياتي!

He passionately "kisses" his imaginary conversation partner on the right and then left cheek.

But I didn't know how to say it in English. So, I just took one of their drums and started jamming with them.

Covers the camera with his hand. Then opens it again.

When I went to the ESL school, for the first time I realized: my English was horrible. I felt sorry for all the people that I had talked with before I learned all the new things.

عندما ذهبت الى مدرسة اللغة ، لأول مرة أكتشف ان الغني الإنكليزية مزرية. شعرت بالأسف لكل الأصدقاء الذي تكلمت معهم، قبل لا أتعلم كل الكلمات والمعاني الجديدة.

Ahmed hears Arfina's singing. He shifts the camera position and then changes into his costume to become an immigrant taxi driver. Arfina enters.

Scene Seven: Comprehension— Blah-blah-blah!

GLORIA: *(as property manager)* Hello! . . . How can I help you?

AHMED: *(as potential renter)* Hello. Um, my name is Ahmed. I am looking for apartment, uh room, flat.

GLORIA: Great. We have, uh, one-bedroom blah September.

AHMED: Sorry?

GLORIA: We have a one-bedroom blah September.

AHMED: Oh, I need apartment next month.

GLORIA: Um, okay, we blah blah blah BUT UH SEPTEMBER blah blah blah blah blah blah . . .

AHMED: Sorry what?

GLORIA: Um . . . we blah blah blah blah September blah blah blah now blah blah, right?

AHMED: Um . . . what is the cheapest price?

GLORIA: Well um blah blah RECESSION blah blah blah blah blah blah blah 950 DOLLARS blah blah blah . . . ?

AHMED: Okay does it include electricity? Parking?

GLORIA: Blah blah blah blah blah blah blah blah blah blah blah blah blah blah blah blah blah blah blah blah blah blah blah blah blah blah blah blah blah blah blah blah blah OIL SPILLS blah blah blah WINTER TIRES blah blah blah blah blah blah blah blah blah blah blah 750 THOUSAND DOLLARS blah blah blah blah blah blah blah blah blah blah blah BIKES.

AHMED: Can I see that room . . . uh, I mean apartment?

GLORIA: Uh, sure, I just uh blah blah blah questions?

AHMED: Oh yes, of course.

GLORIA: What is your name again?

AHMED: Ahmed.

GLORIA: Eh-med, blah blah blah blah blah blah blah blah blah blah blah blah blah blah blah income?

AHMED: Oh, I am a newcomer and I don't have a job yet.

GLORIA: Okay so blah blah blah blah blah blah blah blah blah blah blah blah blah blah blah blah blah blah INCOME blah blah blah blah blah blah blah blah blah blah blah blah blah blah blah blah blah blah blah blah blah blah blah blah blah blah DONALD TRUMP blah blah blah blah blah blah blah blah blah blah blah blah blah blah blah blah blah.

AHMED: I'm very sorry . . . I don't understand. Can you explain in different words?

GLORIA: Sorry sorry . . . Um blah blah blah blah blah blah. Sorry. *(raises her voice significantly)* BLAH BLAH BLAH BLAH BLAH BLAH BLAH BLAH BLAH BLAH BLAH BLAH BLAH BLAH BLAH BLAH BLAH BLAH BLAH BLAH BLAH BLAH. Blah?

AHMED: I'm sorry . . . Could you repeat?

GLORIA: Uh. *(slows down and enunciates everything)* BLAH. BLAH. BLAH. BLAAAAAH.

Turn to camera/close up on tongue.

BLAaaaaah. BLAaaaaah. BLAaaaaah. BLAaaaaah. BLAaaaaah. BLAaaaaah. BLAaaaaah.

Lights out. "Je cherche après Titine" starts again.

Scene Eight: *"Where are you from?"* Interlude C

MARIO/WHITE MAN: Hello, neighbour. Your garden looks lovely!

ARFINA/BLACK WOMAN: Thanks.

MARIO: Say, neighbour, I've been meaning to ask you a question.

ARFINA: Go for it.

MARIO: Where are you from?

ARFINA: I'm from here.

MARIO: I mean, where are you really from?

ARFINA: Toronto. T-dot. The Six.

MARIO: No, where did you come from?

ARFINA: North York?

MARIO: No, where did you grow up?

ARFINA: Paris, France, Europe.

MARIO: Paris? Why do I hear an *African* accent?

Music breaks off. Arfina stares at the audience in silence and disbelief.

Scene Nine: The Accent—Interdental Fricatives

SEPIDEH: *(camera focuses on her face)* When I came to Canada seven years ago when I couldn't speak absolutely no word in English. First time, I went to McDonald's I had to point to the cheeseburger on the wall to order the food because I couldn't make one simple sentence in English. When they brought the burger, it was smaller than its picture, but I couldn't complain, I couldn't speak English.

> *There comes a sudden hissing sound from the back of the theatre that sounds like the voiceless "th" in English. It puzzles Sepideh. She pauses, then shrugs it off to continue.*

D/en, I signed up for ESL program. D/at was absolutely a bad idea.

The program was full of people who want to learn some English to use it for d/eir daily lives tasks. D/hey didn't want to go to university or get a professional job. D/hen I applied for a college.

VOICE: Then!*

SEPIDEH: Then I applied for college. That was absolutely another bad idea.

VOICE: That!

SEPIDEH: That was another bad idea. No one told me **th**ere are **th**ousands.

VOICE: Thousands!

SEPIDEH: . . . thousands of colleges in Canada with an infinite number of programs with certifications that no employer would care for. Then, I applied for university. To go to university, I had to pass TOEFL exam. They call it standard test, but it is absolutely not standard. They asked me to read **th**ree reading passages and answer to forty-two questions in one hour. I can't do **th**at even in my first language. After attending **TOEFL** for **th**ree times . . .

VOICE: Thththree!

---

* Letters in bold indicate potential "pronunciation mistakes" that could be corrected by the voice.

SEPIDEH: Three!

(to the voice) Tank you! I got to university.

VOICE: THTHTHTHANK you!

SEPIDEH: My research was to design an energy monitoring **system** to measure the energy **consumption** of the portable devices. **Even though** I was academically doing **wery vell** . . .

VOICE: Vvvvvery wwwwwell!

SEPIDEH: Wery well!

VOICE: Vvvvvery wwwell!

SEPIDEH: Very vell!

VOICE: Vvvery well!

SEPIDEH: I was doing good.

VOICE: *(no interruption)*

SEPIDEH: My accent sometimes embarrassed me. I had to defend my t/hesis in front of the whole faculty members. I graduated successfully. D/hen, I felt confident enough to apply for teachers' college. My dream was to become a math teacher. I did well there, too. I graduated. After graduating, getting my Ont/ah/rio

VOICE: Ontario!

Clayton, the teacher, gets on stage and starts pacing back and forth.

SEPIDEH: OntArio . . . OntArio certification was another dramatic story on its own. OCT people were insisting that I should contact my university via email; they couldn't understand email is not the way to communicate in all countries in the world. Basically, I had to send my dad to go there in person and bribe my university to get my transcripts.

Clayton starts correcting more and more pronunciation "errors" including those that have nothing to do with the / th / sounds.

Now here I am, an **Ontario** Certified Teacher who applied for over **fifty** jobs and got only two **interviews**. Of those two interviews, one of the employers rejected me; they commented on my language **skills**. And the other employer hired me with **big workload** and not **enough** money.

But now I am thinking, maybe it is time for me to **stop** listening to that voice. Maybe it is time for me to stop **pushing** myself. Maybe I had **enough**!

Sepideh turns to Clayton with the Iranian "fuck you" gesture, which looks like a fist with the thumb up. Clayton transforms it into the English "fuck you" gesture—the middle finger. Sepideh scolds Clayton in Persian while keeping the "fuck you" gesture up, then she leaves. Pianist plays a melody hinting at "O Canada," and then switches back to the fast-paced "Je cherche après Titine" again.

Scene Ten: Work—Phone Sex

Pitch black. Yury and Lavinia place themselves behind the back row without the audience knowing it. They perform the following scene in the dark.

YURY'S VOICE: Ring-ring!

LAVINIA'S VOICE: *(overdoing an Espanophone accent, very sexily)* Hello! Welcome to Hotcom.ca . . . For English, say one. Pour le français, dites deux. Para español, diga tres.

YURY: *(excitedly)* Tres, tres!

LAVINIA: ¡Hola! ¿Como estas?

YURY: Bien.

LAVINIA: Yo bien. Me llamo . . . Virginia. ¿Y tu?

YURY: *(making up a name)* Julio.

LAVINIA: Oh, Julio, papacito. Julio, acabo de salirme de la regadera de bañarme y tengo puesto un negligé . . . ¿me comerías?

YURY: Sí . . .

LAVINIA: Aha . . . ¿por donde empezarías . . . ?

YURY: *(begins to produce sounds of sexual pleasure)* Ah ha.

LAVINIA: ¿Te gustaría continuar en inglés?

YURY: No, no, español, por favor, español!!!

LAVINIA: Okay. Entonces, ¿empezarías a comerme desde los pies y irías subiendo poco a poco por todo mi cuerpo?

YURY: Poco a poco.

Moans.

LAVINIA: ¿Y que te gusta hacer, papacito?

YURY: *(getting more excited)* Papacito!!! Mamacita!!!

LAVINIA: Continuamos entonces. ¿Que quieres que te haga?

YURY: Aha, "ya-ga," "ya-ga."

Yury realizes he is fetishizing her Spanish accent.

LAVINIA: Would you like to continue in English?

YURY: No, no! Español!

Yury continues to intermittently produce sounds of sexual pleasure through this monologue.

LAVINIA: Estoy ahora muy excitada, puedo sentir tus manos recorriendo mis piernas, mis caderas, brazos, pechos *(groans)* . . . Ay tengo que ir al baño, pero realmente no puedo parar en este momento, porque me están pagando, unos dólares por minuto, y me da mucha lástima que tenga que hacer este tipo de trabajo pero es lo único que puedo conseguir en este país . . .

YURY: *(orgasming)* AAAAAAAAAAH!

Scene Eleven: *"Where are you from?"* Interlude D

WHITE GUY: Hello! I love your garden.

ASIAN GIRL: Thank you!

WHITE GUY: Can I ask you a question?

ASIAN GIRL: Sure.

WHITE GUY: Where are you from?

ASIAN GIRL: I am from Toronto.

WHITE GUY: Hm . . . no . . . Where are you really from?

ASIAN GIRL: The big TO. The Six.

WHITE GUY: Hm . . . No, but where are you from originally?

ASIAN GIRL: North York.

WHITE GUY: No-no-no, where are your *people* from?

ASIAN GIRL: China . . .

Music stops.

. . . town!

Lights die—pseudo Chinese music starts.

Scene Twelve: I Live Here

GLORIA: Thank you for your question! Um, I live here, and yet I exist in two separate worlds. One is called 中国, and the other is called 加拿大.*

In the world called 中国，I know the language and culture inside out, therefore I could *(notice the camera/pause/stare at the interviewer)* 做任何我想做的事情. In 中国，I have been 歌手、演员、舞者、模特。 However, I've always been seen as 傲慢 only because I am quiet. Well, you know, 少说话、多做事。

In the world called 加拿大，I have language and cultural barriers. My quietness is often perceived as 害羞。 In 加拿大，if you're not 大大咧咧， then you must be 害羞。 I am also broadly categorized as 亚洲人。 So in Canadian theatre, my 亚洲脸 has got me cast as 傻逼穷小子， or 跑龙套的， because I don't look like 主角！

Did you notice though, we 亚洲人 are not exactly the minority in 加拿大。 But we 中国人 often only hang out with *(gesture)*. Hanging out with 外国人 would make me seem 崇洋媚外 to the 中国人。 In fact, *(gesture)* and *(gesture)*. In your culture, *(gesture)* are always seen as 下等公民。

就在上个月，我在一间中国超市。一个白人女人走进來，突然就发火了！因为超市里的员工不会讲英文！你知道她说什么吗？她说："在加拿大法律规定你一定要讲英文才能在这里工作！" 她说："Go back to China!"

Gloria stands up in indignation. The camera focus slides down to her legs.

(to Yury) Excuse me?

She means "my eyes are here."

Yury moves the camera focus to her face.

Gloria suddenly decides to play along and speaks in a sexy voice, looking straight at the camera.

---

*   Each time Gloria inserts Chinese, she makes a large performative gesture that either hints at the meaning of the Chinese expression or subverts it.

你有种再说一遍？我是会讲英文啊，但又有个屁用啊！

Walks toward the camera.

我看这根本就不是因为英语的问题吧！

Slides her finger down her body.

大姐，你以为就你可以有意见啊？我也有意见啊！意见就像屁眼一样，人人都有！你以为就你有屁眼啊？我也有屁眼啊！

Spanks her butt.

Suddenly blocks the lens with her hand.

食屎啦你！

Scene Thirteen: Body

Set 1. One woman. Gloria, bathed in an abstract light, demonstrates "Chinese" cultural gestures of emotion. Pianist plays pseudo-Chinese music.

Order of gestures:
-Hello
-Come here
-Laughter
-Excitement
-Selfie (with hand-gesture over mouth)

Set 2: Two women. Lavinia takes the space occupied by Angela; Angela shifts stage left. Angela demonstrates English versions of the cultural gestures; Lavinia demonstrates Chinese version

Order of gestures:
-Hello
-Come here
-Laughter
-Excitement

Set 3: Two men and two women. Yury and Ahmed enter stage right; Lavinia joins Gloria stage left. Men demonstrate Chinese gestures; women the English/ North American gestures.

Order of gestures:
-Hello
-Come here
-Laughter

Actors slowly take out their cellphones and prepare for a selfie.

-Selfie: all four actors do "cute" Chinese selfie gesture—two fingers (the V-sign) placed on the mouth with the tongue sticking out.

Scene Fourteen: *"Where are you from?"* Interlude E

Spotlight stage left: Yury is doing the soft-shoe routine stage left. The spotlight stage right is empty. Yury begins to keep step to the music, glancing over stage right, waiting for his scene partner. No one appears. He looks again. He keeps dancing. Looks again. He is lost. Music breaks off.

YURY: Where am I *from*?!!!

All of a sudden, his right hand slaps his cheek hard against his will.

(in pain) Ouch!

Blackout.

Scene Fifteen: Letter Home

Lavinia is on the floor, looking up at the camera. Ahmed, in a separate light, is moving in response to the sonic quality of her speech without understanding the actual Spanish words.

LAVINIA: Querida amiga . . . ¿Cómo está la familia?

Han pasado muchos años sin vernos y siento que hemos perdido ese contacto que solíamos tener. Yo pienso . . . I think we are both afraid of revealing things that we had not told anyone. Look at me! I am using English, our secret language in high school, to keep your mamá out of the loop.

A veces nos escribimos un par de frases en Facebook . . . o le damos "Like" a nuestras fotos. No me gusta mucho publicar fotografías familiares, no es seguro, pero también porque no quiero que la gente piense que mi vida es perfecta y que somos una familia de sueño. Creo que somos más sinceros, capaces de explotar con gritos y sombrerazos, y se que no es lo ideal, pero a lo mejor no tan malo como esconderse detrás de una "happy face" y de pronto aparecer en las noticias como algún caso trágico de sociopatología.

No importa la distancia, solo sé que siempre seremos amigas, cómplices, porque compartimos muchas memorias. ¿Te acuerdas cuando descubrimos a los filósofos griegos y a Sor Juana Inés de la Cruz con?:

As she speaks, her words violently attack Ahmed's body.

Detente, sombra de mi bien esquivo,
imagen del hechizo que más quiero,
bella ilusión por quien alegre muero,
dulce ficción por quien penosa vivo.
Si al imán de tus gracias, atractivo,
sirve mi pecho de obediente acero,
¿porque me enamoras lisonjero
si has de burlarme luego fugitivo?
Mas blasonar no puedes, satisfecho,
de que triunfa de mí tu tiranía:
que aunque dejas burlado el lazo estrecho
que tu forma fantástica ceñía,
poco importa burlar brazos y pecho
si te labra prisión mi fantasía.

Lavinia collapses in a loud laugh. Ahmed kneels, exhausted.

(whisper) Recuerdo nuestros años en la preparatoria y la universidad, nuestro primer amor, yo, tratando de escapar de la delincuencia en la Ciudad de México, yendo a países lejanos. Sé que no te gustó mucho que fuera a Israel, *(While lying on her back. Switches to Hebrew)* ארץ ישראל, להתחבר לשורשים היהודיים שלי. It was hard for me to refuse the opportunity to remain in Israel, but I decided to go back to Mexico. Every time I went back to that country it was easier for me to leave than to stay . . . tan difícil, tan difícil . . .

Lavinia's body begins to writhe on the floor.

Desempleo, pobreza, delincuencia, secuestros, violencia, injusticia, impunidad . . .

On seeing her cry, Ahmed goes over to Lavinia and embraces her.

Believe me: I am happier in my new country, relieved to know that I can safely walk on the streets and that my kids can do so, too. *(suddenly switches to Hebrew again)* חזק ואומץ!

Scene Sixteen: Tim Hortons

This scene is fully improvised. It is set at Tim Hortons, the staple Canadian coffee and doughnut shop. As customers arrive, they order a cup of coffee to go. They place their orders in their first or second language (with the exception of English). The conversation—as well all kinds of misunderstandings that occur—always happens in two languages, with no English translation provided.

Order: All the cast is in a line, waiting, downstage left:
Lavinia and Ahmed—in Spanish and Arabic or Kurdish.
Angela—in Mandarin.
Arfina—in French.
Yury—in Russian (as manager).
Mario—in Portuguese.
Yury cutting the line.

Live feed: focus on the hands of the actors.

Scene Seventeen: Futebol

The scene begins with Mario placing the soccer ball on top of the Tim Hortons counter.

Yury hits the ball away with his hand, and Mario grabs it and takes it to the floor, beginning to play soccer. As Mario and Yury play soccer, the rest of the cast turns upstage and joins the game. Soon, Yury gets kicked out of the game; he is crawling off stage. The game becomes more and more violent, resembling Mario's monologue in Scene Three. The actors rip off their shirts, groaning and yelling in an animalistic manner.

Suddenly, Yury appears through the backdrop opening carrying his ghost light, which prompts the cast to quiet down and slowly disperse across the stage, hiding from the light. Yury slowly drags the light forward to the edge of the stage, to begin the next scene.

Scene Eighteen: "How Do You Say 'Kiss Me'?"

Yury stands up and drags the ghost light downstage centre—he lights the audience.

YURY: *(addressing the audience)* Sorry, can I just . . . ? Can I see if we have anyone here for whom English is their second (or third) language? Could you put your hand up if you can speak that other language fluently? If you speak Russian, could you put your hand down?

Finds a "victim" and makes a gesture inviting them on stage. For the rest of the scene he keeps speaking Russian mostly, using gestures that encourage the audience member to respond. If the response comes in English, Yury rejects it—he wants to hear the audience member speak their first language to him. The following scene is mostly improvised—Yury's questions depend on the audience member's responses and how much comprehension occurs in the process of chatting.

(introduces himself) Привет. Я Юра.

Waits to hear the audience member's name.

Очень приятно, [name]. *(says "Nice to meet you")* Очень приятно.

A handshake.

(says "Where are you from?") Я из Москвы. Я из России, я русский, а ты?

Audience member responds in their first language. Yury repeats to the best of his ability.

(says "Hello") Привет!

Audience member responds in their first language. Yury repeats to the best of his ability.

Thanks the audience member by drawing a heart shape in the air, then says "heart" in Russian.

Сердце! *(mimes "sky")* Небо. *(mimes "stars")* Звезды. *(mimes "moon")* Луна. The moon has two words in Russian: one is male and one is female. Луна и месяц. How many words for moon are there in [language]? Are they male or female?

Audience member responds in their first language. Yury repeats to the best of his ability.

I wrote something, do you mind if I read it to you?

Waits for the audience member to respond.

"If you were an umbrella, and he'd lost you, or forgot you in a cab, there is a good chance someone would pick you up, bring you home, and be happy to have you.

If you were a shirt—a fluffy, comfy shirt—he might possibly grow tired of you, or you would not fit him anymore. There is a good chance he would donate you and you'd be rediscovered and get a new chance to be needed and useful and be loved again.

If you were a book—smart, heavy, with a soothing leather cover—he might read you more than once, but at some point he will lend you to his friend, or sell you on a garage sale, and someone will pick you up and would get a great joy reading you.

If you are a human, there's a good chance that when he leaves you, you may never be found, needed, or loved again.

If you were an umbrella . . . "

(to the audience member) Have you dated anyone who didn't speak your language?

Living in the second language is like being a child again. When I was a child, мама . . . называла меня Юрашка.

Yury says his diminutive name—the way his mom used to call him.

Yurashka!

Asks the audience member to provide their diminutive name in their mother tongue, and then repeats it to the best of his ability.

A warmer handshake or hug follows.

I hope you are feeling comfortable . . . in my bed.

Beat.

Have you dated anyone who didn't speak your language?

Audience member responds.

You know I can't make love in my first language because it's my MOTHER's tongue. It's really weird for me. I can only do it in English. What about you? How do you flirt (or express love) in your first language?

Audience member responds.

How do you say "Kiss me, please" in [language]?

Audience member responds. Yury attempts to say, "Kiss me, please," and points to his cheek. They exchange kisses.

Now, how do you say "tongue"?

Yury turns off the ghost light. Blackout.

The end.

A Dialogue Between Art Babayants and Shelley Liebembuk

Devising *"In Sundry Languages"*: A Conversation about Process

This dialogue was conducted on January 10, 2018, in Toronto, between the Toronto Laboratory Theatre's artistic director Art Babayants and dramaturg Shelley Liebembuk. It discusses certain key elements of the process of creating *"In Sundry Languages"* (*ISL*), from the impetus for the work, to the multilingual and multicultural rehearsal process, video dramaturgy, and the positioning of being an étranger.

ISL is a multilingual theatre experiment conducted by the Toronto Laboratory Theatre with a diverse group of performers, including recent immigrants to Canada and refugees. The stories told on stage are of immigration, displacement, hybrid identities, constant learning, and unlearning. The performance's structure is a series of short scenes of three different types: personal stories that have been reworked in various styles; a comical vignette, which gets repeated with slight variations throughout the piece; and group improvisational games. The multilingual performers speak in various dialects of Mandarin, Arabic, Russian, English, French, Spanish, Portuguese, Persian, and Comorian, among many others. The actors never translate what they are saying, and there are no sub- or surtitles.

SHELLEY LIEBEMBUK: A key element of *ISL* is its multilinguality in the absence of sub- or surtitles. It employs ten or so different languages, and, as a result, for most members of the audience, there will be moments of incomprehension. In order to sustain audience engagement, the scenes are short and vary in style. Ideally, this structure allows an audience member to move through both the frustrations and joys of navigating comprehension and access. Significantly, our use of multilinguality without direct translation does not aim to reduce languages to sound. While the very first scene [Scene One: Turn Off Your Cellphones!] plays with the idea of a medley of languages as a sonic cacophony, many of the scenes are invested in relaying personal stories, wherein the actors are speaking their own truths in their own languages. Unlike a grammalot, this piece contends with the tension of attempting to convey something very specific to audience members who will not understand. The process of creating the piece included working multilingually in rehearsal and, dramaturgically, exploring the decentring of comprehension and the critical negotiation of an audience's expectation of access. Here, we are not invested in excluding anyone, but we are playing with and against the question of accessibility, specifically majoritarian access—in this case, that of the anglophone monolingual.

ART BABAYANTS: Yes, and I think doing this is also very dangerous. So, let's say, an anglophone, who speaks no other languages, comes to the show, and realizes that about 60 to 70 percent of the show will be incomprehensible for them, and so they will have to deduce meaning differently. And we've had really interesting reactions from people who love that process of being completely, let's say, alienated, and we've also had violent reactions from people who absolutely hated it; they said: "Why would you do that? Why would you alienate me? As an audience member, I find it counterproductive, you want the audience to like your show." And it *is* a difficult, potentially counterproductive, in terms of ticket sales, decision, sure, but aesthetically I think it is very interesting, because those who are privileged enough to constantly understand are suddenly put in the position of those who are not able to understand all the time, and have accepted it as the norm.

I think that if you want your audience to be multilingual and multicultural, and to offer multilingual and multicultural interpretations of your work, you need to make the process multicultural and multilingual, and you need to have at least two people in the room constantly looking at an actor and perceiving what's happening: one that understands the language, and one that doesn't. One of the most important lessons of this process is to always have a director and a dramaturg. You want to have someone who has access to the language, and to keep an eye on what's happening—what if you know the language, would you perceive the scene the same way or not? And you are often in the position of the audience. I speak three languages really well, and two more really badly, so it's five overall—but the show uses ten languages or more, so most of the time I can't follow, I might have snippets of knowledge, so I'm in the position of the audience, too. So I start listening to other things: the rhythm of the language . . . and so having someone else in the room who understands the language and gives you a different perspective on what's happening and how it can be read is tremendously important. I think you can also speak to that as a dramaturg: you said when you were listening to the Spanish poem you found it difficult to abstract your understanding, to be removed from your understanding.

LIEBEMBUK: Yes, as a Spanish speaker, when I was working with Lavinia [Scene Fifteen: Letter Home], I couldn't help but listen to the words, and that was distinctly different than when I was working on scenes where I only knew what the actors were saying through their translation of it in conversation. Here I was tasked with both attending to the text and resisting it becoming the centre of my focus. The challenge in the process is how to engage with text as, at once, more than language for direct comprehension, and yet not reduce it to gibberish.

I wonder if we can return to your provocation: we are asking the audience to deduce meaning differently from what they are used to. Can we go back to the beginning of this process, and to how this piece negotiates the different languages on stage, both verbally and non-verbally?

BABAYANTS: My first experience seeing a show where I couldn't understand a single word, except for some basic words, I was glued to the stage for maybe two and a half hours because of the multitude of theatrical languages used in the show, it was watching *For the Disconnected Child* by Falk Richter, which we saw in Berlin at the Schaubühne, where I think German and Czech were used. There was a live orchestra, excellent video dramaturgy, the physicality of the actors—it was interesting enough to watch the show without understanding the plot, or the language, because there was something that the actors were doing, and the director, and the *mise en scène*, that was so rich and diverse that you could still watch it as an opsis, as pure spectacle. When I started working on *ISL,* I was reading a lot of research about how body and language are inseparable, and on semioticians who follow Ferdinand de Saussure, who isolated language as a sign system. That isolation was important and relevant for that time, but now we know that body and language are intertwined on every level: physiological, syntactical, even grammar is embodied and there's more and more research on that. I really wanted the audience to reassess their understanding of language as something verbal, so we wanted to zoom in on different parts of the body. And the parts of the body inextricably connected to language would be our face and our hands (gestures). The research says that similar parts of the brain are activated for language and for hand gestures, which is not the case with our feet, for instance. We originally introduced the camera during the Tim Hortons scene [Scene Sixteen] to make the audience focus on the body, rather than on verbal language.

LIEBEMBUK: One element of the process has been the development of the video dramaturgy. When we introduced the camerawork into the Tim Hortons scene to focus on the hand gestures, that scene was the most cacophonous, with each of the different cast members entering in a different language, attempting to order a cup of coffee. This basic precept was coupled with the specification that each of these interactions would be quick, with different languages meeting at this interchange, and generating chaos—

BABAYANTS: No English—

LIEBEMBUK: Exactly. So by guiding attention to the performers' hands, that was a way for us to make a path through the linguistic chaos, and focus the audience member on the gestural vocabulary as well as the different cultural vocabularies. I want to take up, too, that question of perspective. In this work, the performers and creators of *ISL* are coming from the experience of having different socio-linguistic contexts, and that might be different from the mainstream audience member's perspective. For instance, when I watch the Tim Hortons scene, I'm seeing the different body languages coming into play; but perhaps, for someone who is coming from sociolinguistic contexts in which hands are not often used, the gestural vocabularies in this scene might be reduced to a cluster of "foreign languages"—the reductive stereotype that we often see in mainstream North American representation, wherein "others" use their hands in communica-tion but anglophones don't. Our aim is to decentre what constitutes normative communication, and emphasize that everyone uses their body when they com-municate, though differently, and to try and work against the assumption of a neutral gestural representation. But, depending on the audience member's perspective, this show might question that assumption or reify it.

BABAYANTS: I agree with that, and another judgment that people pass—which I know because the first time we did the show, I did 180 post-show surveys and analyzed how people try and deduce meaning especially in the scenes where there is no English, which is the only language that everyone understood in the audience—is that they do look at the body languages, facial expression, and gestures; that's their second means of understanding meaning. But a lot of people, when they analyze that process of perception, they also claim that body language is universal. Which, to me, is absolutely hilarious: we don't even do the same gestures for yes and no across all cultures—some people nod their heads, some people don't. For me, it is radically non-universal. But apparently for some people, the assumption was: I didn't understand the language, but, because body language is universal, I could still understand. So, as we worked on the show, and made new versions, I really made an effort to make it explicit that body language is also not universal, and that you might be completely misinterpreting the facial expressions and movements of the actor—especially symbolic gestures, the ones that carry meaning. "Thumbs up" is a symbolic gesture, but it is not universal.

Often, people are not aware of their own lens, and pass judgment on other languages and those speaking other languages because they think their own lens is normal. And once you start paying attention to who's doing the listening and the looking—which we made more explicit by using the video dramaturgy—it becomes a powerful aesthetic tool. For me, one of the findings that I really like is when, after a point in Gloria's monologue [Scene Twelve: I Live Here], the camera starts sliding down her body, from her face to other parts . . . more voluptuous parts of her body; and the man behind the camera, the cameraman is a man, and while she's talking about things that are very important to her—double identity—he is actually not listening. The audience might still be looking at her face, but on the screen, you can see how the cameraman is shifting his attention to her behind.

LIEBEMBUK: Indeed, this moment captures how the performing subject is speaking and yet can still be objectified—reduced to an object. In that scene, Gloria is ostensibly the subject, she is being interviewed, and our focus is supposed to be on listening to what she has to say, and yet the live feed reflected on the screen guides our focus to Gloria's body parts.

BABAYANTS: No matter how serious the conversation is, it's not just about power; it's also about how humans actually listen. For instance, if you see a person you are incredibly attracted to, it is hard to listen to the meaning in their words. We keep paying attention to people's looks, and the question is why do we constantly do that, and whether we are also casting some critical eye on that process or not. And I think that's what the video dramaturgy is allowing us to do.

LIEBEMBUK: And just to place this example in contradistinction with another scene and the use of video dramaturgy there, we have Ahmed's monologue [Scene Six: A Newcomer], where he is controlling his own camera, and so he is the one forcing the focus on different parts of his own body—zooming in on his eyes, his lips, and so on. In this scene, Ahmed is telling us his autobiographical story; it is a personal and very difficult story, and yet the camera—which he himself is controlling—is forcing us, as the audience, to recognize the mediation that is happening within the process of listening to his story. One of the reactions to that scene when he performed it at the Fringe, from Prof. Laura Levin, was to read it as a kind of denial of direct address. I love this reading, because it critically reconfigures the solo autobiographical narrative. We are so used to hearing the immigrant's story through these solo, autobiographical performances, where they are talking out to us directly. However, in this scene, we can't just assume that we can sit there and take in Ahmed's lived experience. We are forced to recognize the space between his embodied narrative and our ability, as auditors and spectators, to sympathize and empathize with it. It asks us as the audience to question our assumption that we can have an unmediated experience or direct communication.

BABAYANTS: This is a great point, because it takes us to the idea that in the show, there is not a single moment when we have an actor speaking directly to the audience: they are always talking to either another actor, or to the camera, or . . . There is always an "internal" listener, someone set up to perceive, even though it might not be a real listener—it might just be a camera, but it always sets up the communication as a two-way process, questioning the authenticity of any story and who is listening.

LIEBEMBUK: I think that the final scene plays with this as well [Scene Eighteen: "How Do You Say 'Kiss Me'?"]—where Yury invites a member of the audience to have an intimate, cozy conversation with him. I think it's notable that for many of the audience members this moment is quite moving as it lets one in, in a certain way. That scene is very comforting, after a show that has continued to play with questions of access and comprehension. I, as well, enjoy that final scene partly because it is a warm invitation, and a counterbalance to what some of the scenes have done prior. And yet, dramaturgically, I feel like the reason the scene works is because it continues to critically comment on its own mediation. This intimate moment is coupled with a framing that highlights the space of meeting: Yury sits on the edge of the stage, inviting an audience member to join him there. Notably, many audience members perceive that this scene is primarily in English, which it actually isn't, but I think that is the perception because the conversation is more intimate—people assume it is in English because they feel brought in.

BABAYANTS: And that was Yury's idea. He really wanted to have this genuine connection with an audience member: to talk about being human, about connecting despite not having a common language, trying to connect through each other's languages. And he always invites a person who speaks English as their second or third language—that is how he chooses the participant. But you are right in that it's a very constructed conversation. And the way it is lit with one old-fashioned bulb, without any other theatrical lighting, to emphasize the coziness . . .

LIEBEMBUK: And the presence of the other performers: they are a visible audience, sitting on the stage, watching Yury interact with the audience member.

BABAYANTS: And the audience is also very visible, with the light shining out onto them.

Also, Yury actually has a clear-cut plan for the scene. It's an improv, but Yury is going through a series of beats—which we've distilled through having him improvise the scene with about twenty or so people. He is "forcing" the audience member to perform a character. If they met in real life, they would probably speak in English as their shared language. But through this scene, Yury is forcing them to speak in their other languages, usually—in their first language, which is a performance one might or might not be willing to do.

LIEBEMBUK: And the resistances to that, which the scene shows so many times. For example, when the audience member doesn't remember a word in their other language, or is unsure, or is code-switching—the sense is still to try to speak to Yury in English—and then to switch . . .

BABAYANTS: Or it is uncomfortable to say the word; there are so many options there. And also, Yury is also constantly hinting to a sexual tension between them, and what if the person on stage is not attracted to Yury . . .

LIEBEMBUK: Exactly, so Yury is already imposing a certain dramatic relationality onto that scene.

BABAYANTS: Yes, so I really hope that the audience doesn't buy that scene as "aw, this is such a moment of human connection." Yes—but it is also deeply constructed, and there's a non-stop performance going on.

LIEBEMBUK: It promises to be the warm and fuzzy thing you are hoping to see in a multicultural interaction, where the immigrant meets a local—

BABAYANTS: Or immigrant meets another immigrant . . .

LIEBEMBUK: Now that we have discussed the rehearsal process, let's talk about translation and subtitles, and why we decided not to use subtitles. We were negotiating the endurance on the part of the audience—the ability to be in a space where you don't understand and are being faced with a certain performance style—across a structure that kept scenes shorter than five minutes, weaving scenes across different languages, and always returning to English, with the reiterated versions of the "where are you from?" scene. Dramaturgically, we are creating the work for an audience that will not have full access or may not fully understand it. From a performance perspective, we are challenging ourselves to figure out how to perform across this tension, how to create and sustain connection, and how to check in for that connection.

BABAYANTS: The observation I made after the Fringe run was that the scene that Lavinia did in Spanish, that was almost six minutes of Spanish—there was almost no English there, and a lot of people complained about that scene as incomprehensible and difficult if they didn't speak Spanish. Those who spoke Spanish of course didn't complain—[and yet] there was a lot of feedback from dancers who indicated that that was the most interesting scene for them, because suddenly there was this moving body (Ahmed's body responding to Lavinia's text), and they said they never cared about the meaning of the language; they were looking at the body and how it was responding to the language. To them, the conceit of the scene was absolutely clear, because their perception is different—they read the body first. And I was like, oh, that's a wonderful testament to what we tried, and maybe failed to do in many cases, but for them it worked. So that was really fascinating, and unexpected.

LIEBEMBUK: This highlights that our project is testing the conventions of an oratorical theatrical tradition. For me, this is what makes the piece interesting, because it isn't a dance piece or a sound piece; it isn't a piece about being past language. The piece resides in that moment of how we seek to understand each other through language—verbal and non-verbal. It invites and exacts that of its audience. Even as I'm listening to someone I cannot understand, as far as language comprehension, I feel it asking me to pay attention in a different, possibly new way; as much as I'm deducing the meaning from something else—as you've said—I'm beholden to listen—

BABAYANTS: Or zonk out, which some people did. I remember a comment from a dear friend, who is a theatre director. He called me after the show and told me, well, the Russian scenes really outshine all the others. And I said, what do you mean? There's very little Russian there. Well, he's a Russian speaker, and he's not mastered other languages really well, despite having lived in Canada for a very long time. He said the Russian scenes were excellent, and the other scenes lagged behind. Because he probably decided to zonk out on other scenes, he decided not to make an effort. But you constantly have to make an effort to understand, no matter what language is being spoken, so I think there's a personal attitude toward *otherness* that people have. And I think to me that is such a valuable experience through working on this show, because it constantly tests my own—not tolerance—my ability to perceive the Other, to work with the Other, to construct who the Other is in my mind. And it tests you the same when you are an audience member, and also when you are an actor. As a dramaturg, can you speak to that experience? Did you feel there were challenges for you, when you were faced with otherness?

LIEBEMBUK: Yes, if I'm working on texts that I don't understand, or I've only understood them through the actor's translation, I am giving feedback from a space of partial access. I think, again, it's a very fruitful space, because it sheds light on the fact that we are always in a space of partial access. So I think it forces a respect, a kind of creating together in a space where you have to recognize that you can give feedback, but you are speaking from a limited perspective. In this process, the way I work with each performer is different, and at times I can only provide very broad feedback, because I don't have access to work on certain details. For example, going back to Lavinia's scene, with the Spanish text, I had a lot of dramaturgical ideas for that scene, but I actually had to restrict myself not to impose those because I wanted to allow that same space in her exploration of that scene as I was inevitably giving to other scenes wherein I didn't have access to what the performer was emphasizing, what physical gestures they were connecting to what verbal gestures, and so forth.

BABAYANTS: Right, so you forced yourself to be *l'étranger* on purpose.

LIEBEMBUK: Exactly.

BABAYANTS: For me, it was a very strange experience, too, because I'm not used to it. I'm much more used to either being the insider or being the outsider. That's what a lot of theatre forces me to do, to make that choice, to place myself. And in this show, if you don't know the language, or the codes, or the references, you are like, oh, I'm an outsider, or I'm a little bit of an outsider, or I'm very much of an outsider. At the same time, even when you know the language, you are always in the space of *l'étranger*. And, I don't know how to explain it, but that's a very strange experience, and we want the audience to never feel that they are the insiders or the outsiders. Nobody is an insider or an outsider.

About the Contributors

Cynthia Ashperger/Lola Xenos is a theatre director, writer, actor, acting peda-
gogue, and producer. She teaches acting at the the Ryerson School of Performance
where she was also Director of the Acting Program from 2003 to 2018. In Toronto,
she has worked as an actor with many independent theatre companies as well as
in film and TV. In 2013, she was nominated for a Dora Award for outstanding
female performance in *Feral Child,* by Jordan Tannahill. In 2016, for her role in *The
Waiting Room,* by Igor Drljača, she was nominated for a Canadian Screen Award
(CSA) for Best Performance by an Actress in a Supporting Role in a Feature Film.

She co-wrote *Out of Spite: Tales of Survival from Sarajevo,* which had several
productions in Canada and the US. Her two feature film scripts, *YU-798* and
Veronica, both garnered interest from producers and were developed. *Foreign
Tongue* is her first full-length musical. Ashperger is a master teacher of Chekhov's
acting technique. She spends most of her time directing theatre productions
and teaching at Ryerson, as well as teaching Chekhov's acting technique all
over the world.

Art Babayants is a theatre artist, educator, and researcher who has worked in
Canada and abroad. His research looks at the phenomenology of multilingual
acting and spectating, as well as the concept of multilingual dramaturgy. Art
has published on the issues of stage multilingualism, diasporic theatre, queer
dramaturgy, applied theatre, and contemporary musical theatre. He also co-
edited *Theatre and Learning* (2015) and the special bilingual issue of *Theatre
Research in Canada/Recherches théâtrales au Canada* (Fall 2017), dedicated to
multilingual theatre in Canada. As a theatre practitioner, Art has presented
his work at various Toronto festivals such as the Fringe (2017), SummerWorks
(2016), Nuit Blanche (2015), and Caminos (2017). Since 1997, Art has also been
developing theatre projects integrating acting and second-language teaching—
his most recent ESL/drama creation, called *Embodied English,* is a sought-after
course for advanced ESL learners. Art holds a lecturer position at the Faculty
of Media, Art, and Performance at the University of Regina, Saskatchewan.

Fourth Poet Laureate of Toronto (2012–15) and the seventh Parliamentary/ Canadian Poet Laureate (2016–17), **George Elliott Clarke** was born in Windsor, Nova Scotia, in 1960. Educated at the University of Waterloo, Dalhousie University, and Queen's University, Clarke is also a pioneering scholar of African Canadian literature. A professor of English at the University of Toronto, Clarke has taught at Duke, McGill, the University of British Columbia, and Harvard. He holds eight honourary doctorates, plus appointments to the Order of Nova Scotia and the Order of Canada at the rank of Officer. He is also a Fellow of the Royal Canadian Geographical Society. His recognitions include the Pierre Elliott Trudeau Fellows Prize, the Governor General's Literary Award for Poetry, the National Magazine Gold Award for Poetry, the Premiul Poesis (Romania), the Dartmouth Book Award for Fiction, the Eric Hoffer Book Award for Poetry (US), and the Dr. Martin Luther King Jr. Achievement Award. Clarke's work is the subject of *Africadian Atlantic: Essays on George Elliott Clarke* (2012), edited by Joseph Pivato. Though Clarke is racialized "Black" and was socialized as an Africadian, he is a card-carrying member of the Eastern Woodland Métis Nation, Nova Scotia. He is, at last, a proud Afro-Métis Africadian.

Matthew Chin is an assistant professor at the Graduate School of Social Service at Fordham University. He received his Ph.D. in Social Work and Anthropology at the University of Michigan. He is currently conducting a historical ethnographic study on the transnational politics of same-sex desire in late twentieth-century Jamaica.

Nada Humsi is a graduate of Damascus University with a B.A. in English Studies, who also trained with pioneers of avant-garde and experimental Syrian the-atre in the 1970s and '80s, becoming the first professional woman mime in Syria. She played leading roles in dozens of plays and monodramas in numerous countries and was awarded Best Actress awards in India (1993), Japan (1992), Tunisia (1983), and Syria (1980). Humsi immigrated to Canada in 1999, and in 2008 joined the MT Space in Kitchener, where she co-created, acted in, and helped produce original productions such as *The Last 15 Seconds* (winner of Best Performance, Sharm El-Sheikh Youth Theatre Festival, Egypt, 2019), *Body 13*, and *Amal*, as well as several Theatre for Social Change projects, including *Me . . . Here. Me . . . Happy* by Diana Manole. In 2013, Humsi co-founded the Kitchener-Waterloo Arab-Canadian Theatre, for which she wrote, directed, and produced *My Name Is Dakhel Faraj*, her first published play among the few she wrote. In 2017, she received the Women Who Inspire Award for artistic accomplishments from the Coalition of Muslim Women of Kitchener-Waterloo. In 2018, she was awarded Best Actress at the International Festival of Liberal Theatre in Jordan and Outstanding Artist at the Awal International Theatre Festival in the Kingdom of Bahrain. She is passionate about doing theatre with the community and for the community, and she also paints and loves animals.

Playwright and director **Olivier Kemeid** has written, among other plays: *Five Kings: l'histoire de notre chute* (2015, Leméac), based on the historical saga of Shakepeare's kings, a five-hour play created at Théâtre Espace Go in Montréal and the National Arts Centre in Ottawa; *Women On Top* (2015), created at 7 Stages Theatre in Atlanta; *Icare* (2014), created at the Théâtre du Nouveau Monde in Montréal; *Œdipe* (2013), a personal take on Sophocles's play, created at the Théâtre Royal du Parc in Brussels; *Bacchanale* (2008), created at Théâtre d'Aujourd'hui in Montreal; and *The Aeneid* (2007), his personal adaptation of Virgil's epic poem, which he directed himself. *The Aeneid* is published in French by Lansman Editeur, and has been translated in English, German, Hungarian, and Italian. He is a three-time nominee for the Governor General's Literary Award for French-language drama: *L'Énéide* in 2009; *Moi, dans les ruines rouges du siècle* in 2013; and *Five kings: l'histoire de notre chute* in 2016. The production of *Red Ruins* toured all across Canada in 2013 and 2014, and won the award for best production in Montréal by the AQCT—Québec's Theatre Critics Association. *The Aeneid* has been produced or read in France, Belgium, Germany, Italy, Hungary, the United States, and the United Arab Emirates. In July 2008, the play was read at the celebrated Avignon Festival, and played at the Stratford Festival in 2016. Olivier Kemeid was also guest professor at the Université du Québec à Montréal (UQAM) from autumn 2014 to spring 2015, and the artistic director of Théâtre Espace Libre in Montréal from 2006 to 2010. Since October 2016, he has been the artistic director of Théâtre de Quat'Sous in Montréal.

Maureen Labonté is a translator, dramaturg, and teacher. She has translated over forty Québec plays into English. *And Slowly Beauty* (Talonbooks), her translation of *Lentement la beauté* by Québec City playwright Michel Nadeau, was a finalist for the 2014 Governor General's Literary Award in Translation. Maureen has worked as a dramaturg and coordinated play development programmes in theatres and play development centres across the country. She was Co-Director of the Playwrights' Colony at the Banff Centre for Arts and Creativity from 2006 to 2012, and has taught at the National Theatre School of Canada since the mid-'90s.

Shelley Liebembuk is a theatre scholar, dramaturg, and the Crake Teaching Fellow in Drama at Mount Allison University (2018–2020). Her research focus is on multilingual ensemble performance in Canada and Germany. As the recipient of the Canadian Consortium on Performance and Politics in the Americas's post-doctoral fellowship, Shelley conducted dramaturgical research on Canadian Latinx performance and its multiple fluencies. She received her doctorate from the University of Toronto's Graduate Centre for Drama, Theatre and Performance Studies, and her dissertation was on the intersectional body in performance. She teaches acting, dramaturgy, and theatre courses, and is a graduate of the Atlantic Theater Company's acting conservatory in New York City.

Keira Loughran has been pushing the boundaries of Canadian theatre for over twenty years as a producer, director, actor, dramaturg, and playwright with companies across the country. She was the inaugural associate producer for the Forum and the Laboratory at the Stratford Festival, spearheading organizational change through these initiatives. Directing credits include *The Comedy of Errors*, *The Komagata Maru Incident*, *The Aeneid* (Stratford Festival), *Deportation Cast* (York University), *Titus Andronicus* (Canadian Stage Company), and *Pu-Erh* (k'Now Theatre), for which she was nominated for a Dora Mavor Moore Award. She was Artistic Producer of the SummerWorks Performance Festival in Toronto from 2005–2007, founding Artistic Director of k'Now Theatre, and she spent over twelve years as an actor playing lead roles in theatres across the country including Theatre Passe Muraille, Nightwood Theatre, Alberta Theatre Projects, Persephone Theatre, and two seasons at the Stratford Festival. Keira is a third-degree black belt in aikido, which she teaches in Stratford.

Julie Tamiko Manning is a mixie of Japanese and British settler heritage, born and raised in the Eastern Townships of Québec, now living and working out of Montréal as an actor and theatre creator. She shares her first play, *Mixie and the Halfbreeds*, about mixed identity in multiple universes, with Adrienne Wong. She is currently writing her third play, *Mizushōbai (The Water Trade)*, about Kiyoko Tanaka-Goto, a Japanese picture bride turned "underground" business woman in 1930s British Columbia. Julie is the co-artistic director of Tashme Productions and is proud to be a mentor to emerging theatre artists in Black Theatre Workshop's Artist Mentorship Program.

She has received multiple META (Montreal English Theatre Award) nominations and awards including Best Text for *The Tashme Project*, which she shares with her creative partner, Matt Miwa and all of the Nisei who have allowed their stories to be used in the piece.

Diana Manole is a scholar, educator, writer, translator, and theatre artist who earned a doctorate from the Centre for Drama, Theatre and Performance Studies at the University of Toronto and an M.F.A. in Directing from the National University of Theatre and Film in Bucharest. Her scholarship focuses on post-colonial, postcommunist, and multicultural/exilic theatre. A collection of essays she co-edited, *Staging Postcommunism* (University of Iowa Press, 2019), examines alternative theatre in several European countries. In her native Romania, she scripted, directed, and/or produced over four hundred shows for TV Romania International (1996–2000) and directed several theatre productions, while also publishing nine books of poetry and drama. Recently Diana has been writing and publishing poems in English and has translated Mihaela Drăgan's *Tell them about me* (included in *Roma Heroes: Five European Monodramas*, 2019); her own play, *The Child Who Didn't Want to Be Born* (published in *Ecumenica*, Spring 2017); and several collections of poetry. Her work has earned her fourteen creative writing prizes in her native Romania and second prize in the 2017/18 John Dryden Translation Competition. Since November 2018, she has been on the board of the Toronto-based Modern Times Stage Company. Most of all, she enjoys teaching both academic and practical courses and is grateful to her students for sharing their thought-provoking insights and enthusiasm.

Professor **Yana Meerzon** teaches at the Department of Theatre, University of Ottawa. Her published books include *A Path of the Character: Michael Chekhov's Inspired Acting and Theatre Semiotics* (2005) and *Performing Exile, Performing Self: Drama, Theatre, Film* (2012). She also co-edited *Performance, Exile and "America"* (2009); *Adapting Chekhov: The Text and Its Mutations* (2012/2015); *History, Memory, Performance* (2014); and *The Routledge Companion to Michael Chekhov* (2015/2017). She edited a special issue of *Theatre Research in Canada/ Recherches théâtrales au Canada* on theatre and immigration in 2015 and a special issue of *Modern Drama* on the dramaturgy of multilingualism and migration in the fall of 2018. Her current book project is on performance and cosmopolitanism.

Matt Miwa is an Ottawa-based independent theatre, performance, and video artist, and with Julie Tamiko Manning, he is the proud co-creator of *The Tashme Project: The Living Archives*. Matt is happily committed to independent art-making, and enjoys balancing the roles of artist, producer, administrator, and community outreach coordinator that are necessary to independent art-making. Deeply committed to community vitalization, Matt works to build bridges across communities through the creative process and strives to interconnect their respective resources, artistic wisdom, and cultural practices. With strong ties to Ottawa-Gatineau's queer community, English theatre community, francophone art and theatre communities, as well as the local and national Japanese community, Matt has high hopes and plans for Ottawa-Gatineau's intersecting future. With projects all over the map, Matt's recent activities include producing a collaboration between Japanese drumming group Oto-Wa Taiko and Indigenous drumming group Bear Nation at Ottawa's 2017 Summer Solstice Pow Wow; releasing *Murder at the Circus,* a short, silent, and non-scary horror film co-created with Lesley Marshall and premiering at Ottawa's ByTowne Cinema in December 2017; and performing *Swallow,* a piece combining drag, singing, and tightrope walking at the opening night of Axenéo 7's performance art festival PERF in Gatineau, QC, in October 2017. Matt is excited to have launched *Tashme's* national tour in 2019, and was honoured to be part of the Ottawa Fringe's 2017/18 under development residency program for his new play *Bold Woman, Love!* where he directed for the first time.

Izumi Sakamoto is Associate Professor, Factor-Inwentash Faculty of Social Work, and an Academic Fellow of the Centre for Critical Qualitative Health Research at the University of Toronto. A former Fulbright Scholar, Dr. Sakamoto received her M.S.W., M.S. (Psychology), and Ph.D. (Social Work and Psychology) from the University of Michigan, and her B.A. and M.A. (both in Social Welfare) from Sophia University, Japan. With six grants from the Social Sciences and Humanities Research Council (SSHRC) as Principal Investigator, Dr. Sakamoto's research and writing have focused on immigration, anti-oppression, critical consciousness, and homelessness. Her current research project examines the intersections of artistic practice, community engagement, and activism within the contemporary Japanese Canadian community, which will draw upon the historical legacies, embodied knowledges, and emotional terrain generated by the mass incarceration of Japanese Canadians during the Second World War.

Toronto Laboratory Theatre was founded in 2012 in order to develop, support, and produce artistic work and education projects that explore the "new," the "unknown," and "the difficult" through practice-based artistic research. Each TLT project is a new adventure, a new challenge, and features a new team. TLT's participants and audiences are always diverse, the process is always non-linear, and the results are always unexpected.

First edition: June 2019.
Printed and bound in Canada by Imprimerie Gauvin, Gatineau.

Jacket photos of Rodrigo Beilfuss, Josue Laboucane, Mike Nadajewski, Tiffany Claire Martin, Monice Peter, Gareth Potter, Andrew Robinson, Lanise Antoine Shelley, E.B. Smith, Michael Spencer-Davis, Saamer Usmani, Bahareh Yaraghi, and Malakai Magassouba by David Hou from the 2016 Stratford Festival production of *The Aeneid* by Olivier Kemeid, with designs by Joanna Yu. Photos provided courtesy of the Stratford Festival.

Jacket design by Leon Aureus.

PLAYWRIGHTS CANADA PRESS
202-269 Richmond St. W.
Toronto, ON
M5V 1X1

416.703.0013
info@playwrightscanada.com
www.playwrightscanada.com
@playcanpress